A COURSE IN RUSSIAN HISTORY

The Seventeenth Century

The present volume deals with the story of the Russian people at a time when they had just acquired a new dynasty—the Romanovs, and a new upper class—the military land-owning gentry. After describing the major upheavals of the first half of the seventeenth century, the anarchy of the Times of Trouble, and the schism of the church, and having meticulously traced the growth of the Muscovite state power, Kliuchevsky interprets the second half of the century as the age of transition, preparatory to the reforms of Peter the Great. For Kliuchevsky the seventeenth century still retained a unity and a wholeness which was subsequently lost because of Peter's ruthless destruction of traditions and customs standing in the way of change.

—Dmitri von Mohdrenschildt

A COURSE IN RUSSIAN HISTORY

The Seventeenth Century

V. O. Kliuchevsky

TRANSLATED FROM THE RUSSIAN BY
Natalie Duddington

INTRODUCTION BY
Alfred J. Rieber

M.E. Sharpe
ARMONK, NEW YORK
LONDON, ENGLAND

Library of Congress Cataloging-in-Publication Data

Kliuchevskiĭ, V. O. (Vasilii Osipovich), 1841–1911.
  [Kurs russkoi istorii. Chast′ 3. English]
    A course in Russian history—the 17th century /
Vasili O. Kliuchevsky : editor, Alfred J. Rieber : translator, Natalie Duddington.
        p.   cm.
      Includes index
    ISBN 1-56324-316-4.—ISBN 1-56324-317-2 (pbk.)
      1. Russia—History—1613–1689.
    2. Russia—History—Time of Troubles, 1598–1613.
          I. Rieber, Alfred J.
        II. Duddington, Natalie.
              III. Title.
        DK114.K573   1993
          947′.04—dc20
            93-26721
              CIP

Printed in the United States of America

The paper used in this publication meets the minimum requirements of
American National Standard for Information Sciences—
Permanence of Paper for Printed Library Materials,
ANSI Z 39.48-1984.

∞

| BM (c) | 10 | 9 | 8 | 7 | 6 | 5 | 4 | 3 | 2 | 1 |
| BM (p) | 10 | 9 | 8 | 7 | 6 | 5 | 4 | 3 | 2 | 1 |

Vasili O. Kliuchevsky (1841-1911) was the most eminent Russian historian of his day—a pathbreaking scholar, a spellbinding lecturer, an engaging stylist, and a great synthesizer whose works have stood the test of time. *The Seventeenth Century* is the third volume of Kliuchevsky's five-volume masterpiece, *A Course in Russian History*, originally published in 1907. This unabridged translation is based on Volume 3 of the 1957 Soviet edition of Kliuchevsky's collected works.

Alfred J. Rieber, professor of history at the University of Pennsylvania, is a prolific author on Russian history and a recipient of the E. Henry Harbison Award of the Danforth Foundation for distinguished teaching.

Contents

Note on Transliteration

The question of transliterating Russian proper names has never been resolved in a way to suit everyone's taste. In order to standardize spelling in the translations in this series, I have adopted, sometimes to the despair of the translator, a uniform system based upon the Library of Congress model. The modifications include the use of a single *i* at the end of given names (Vasili) and a *y* at the end of family names (Kliuchevsky). By and large I have retained the Russian forms of given names (Vasili instead of Basil), but have given English equivalents to the less familiar ones, such as Metropolitan Job (instead of Iov).

Common usage and the absence of exact equivalents in English have also determined the choice of Russian terms such as *Zemsky Sobor* (Assembly of the Land) instead of translating them wherever they occur. An attempt has been made to keep these to a minimum, even at the cost of employing rather unsatisfactory translations, such as "gentry" for *dvoriane*.

The system used by W. E. D. Allen in *The Ukraine* has been borrowed for Ukrainian and Russo-Lithuanian (e.g., Orthodox as opposed to Roman Catholic) names in order to distinguish them from Great Russian and Polish.

A. J. R.

Introduction

In the annals of Russian historiography, Vasili Osipovich Kliuchevsky occupies a central and dominant position. Indeed, he deserves to be counted among the great historians of the world. Since his death more than fifty years ago his reputation and influence, although not always publicly acknowledged, have continued to grow both in his native land and abroad. His magnum opus, *A Course in Russian History*, is the only multivolume history of Russia that has been translated into English. The Russian original has been reprinted twice in the Soviet Union, and when, after Stalin's death, a project was begun to publish the collected works of prerevolutionary historians, it was only natural that Kliuchevsky was the first to be so honored. Until very recently some of his former students occupied important positions in the Soviet historical profession, and others, like Sir Bernard Pares at London and M. M. Karpovich at Harvard, imbued a generation of English and American undergraduates with the spirit of his work. What makes Kliuchevsky a figure of such enduring interest?

For more than three decades before the First World War, Kliuchevsky's brilliant lectures packed the main auditorium of Moscow University and inspired some of the best historical brains of the succeeding generation. The beauty of his language and the power of his ideas held his audience spellbound. In a flash, this unprepossessing little man, looking more like a deacon than a professor, with his high-pitched voice, his stutter, and his myopic stare, could be transformed into Peter the Great, all seven feet of him striding across the stage of Russian history. Kliuchevsky was a consummate actor. His wit was a formidable weapon, admired by his students and colleagues, feared by his hapless victims. He once characterized a historian who praised Catherine the Great excessively as "her posthumous lover." The poor fellow never lived it down. Moreover, Kliuchevsky gave what certainly must be considered the most learned introductory course in Russian history ever taught. Not only did every lecture resemble an elegant monograph, combining great erudition with superb writing, but the entire series was held together by several interconnected themes which, even as they unfolded, illuminated each part of the imposing structure. A happy marriage of formidable scholarship and stimulating teaching, these lectures, often reworked and rewritten over a period of twenty years, became the chapters of *A Course in Russian History*. Kliuchevsky first published it at the turn of the century, only after serious misgivings that the work was incomplete had been overcome by the constant pleading of his students. It remains, in the words of M. M. Karpovich, "the last great synthesis of Russian history." [1]

What enabled Kliuchevsky to sustain such a high and continuous level of interest among the students who crowded to hear him? In a word it was the sense of immediacy that permeated the entire course. "The value of any knowledge," he stated in his second lecture, "is defined by its connection with our needs, aspirations, and deeds." [2] His real subject was the identity of Russia, its place in the world, the limitations imposed and the opportunities presented by a thousand years of history. When Kliuchevsky was at the height of his career, the Russian intelligentsia still valued the discipline of history as a solid and practical basis for political action. Although Kliuchevsky himself did not take an active part in politics, he allowed his students to discuss the so-called burning questions of the day after his formal seminar in history, which was held in the com-

---

[1] M. Karpovich, "Kliuchevsky and Recent Trends in Russian Historiography," *Slavonic and East European Review*, 21 (1943): 31.
[2] V. O. Kliuchevsky, *Sochineniia* (Moscow, 1956) 1: 42.

fort and safety of his home. In his lectures he had already
encouraged them to search for the regularities of Russian history that might lead to a general law of the construction of
human society independent of local conditions.[3] Some of his
students seized upon the implications of these historical views
to help fashion their political programs. Several went on to
become leaders in Russia's first liberal party, the Constitutional
Democrats (known as Kadets).

Regardless of the activities of his students, Kliuchevsky deserves a prominent place in the intellectual history of Russia.
Among his many achievements were his efforts to reconcile
conflicting philosophical views, his awareness of the need for a
multidisciplinary approach, and his commitment to the idea of
multiple causality, all of which strike a remarkably "modern"
tone. Kliuchevsky was sensitive to the dilemma of the historian
caught between the shifting sands of relativism and the rigid
grip of determinism. In working out a solution within the context of the historical narrative itself, he sought to obviate the
terrible choice of "either-or."

It is a tribute to the originality and complexity of Kliuchevsky's historical outlook that continuing debate over his contribution has involved so many distinguished historians. From
the rich tapestry of his scholarship, representatives of widely
divergent views have pulled out threads to weave their own
historical interpretations. To each one Kliuchevsky stands for a
distinct phase in the development of the writing of Russian history. But the position they accord him both reflects their own
commitment and also justifies their criticism of him. For example,
Marxist historians have tried to separate Kliuchevsky's early
work, which they praise as part of the materialist tradition, from
his later work, which they condemn as infected with idealism.
The liberal historians extol Kliuchevsky's attachment to gradual
change but regret the absence of any guiding principle in his
work. The issue around which the controversy centers is the
precise location of Kliuchevsky in the mainstream of Russian
intellectual life at the end of the nineteenth century. Was he a

[3] *Ibid.*, 1: 19.

Slavophile or a Westerner, a materialist or an idealist, a historian or a sociologist, an innovator or an eclectic? To answer these questions it is not enough to analyze his work; we must first of all seek out the man himself.

During the long evening's discussion with students which followed his seminar, Kliuchevsky would often recall scenes from his childhood. He remembered most vividly how as an eight-year-old boy he stood crying over the body of his father, the local priest, which lay lifeless beside a deeply furrowed dirt road lined with sagging wooden houses in a remote village in the depths of Penza province. This memory was deeply symbolic of the formative influences in Kliuchevsky's life. Throughout his career the indelible mark of rural Russia upon his personality and outlook set him apart from colleagues and students. Compared with such elegant professors as B. N. Chicherin, Kliuchevsky seemed "too Russian," with his slight, bent figure and nondescript dress, his habit of avoiding his companion's eyes in conversation, his soft voice, the soundless laugh, and the unmistakable stutter. To be sure, Kliuchevsky was one of the most brilliant conversationalists and lecturers of his day, but these achievements cost him a great effort and a long struggle to overcome the stigma of provincial origin.

Born in 1841 as the only son of a poor priest, Kliuchevsky was raised in the village of Voskresensk until he was eight, when his father died and the family moved to the provincial capital of Penza. In the 1840's and 1850's the province was still isolated from the mainstream of Russian life and retained many of the aspects of a frontier area. Four to five months out of the year deep snows blanketed the heavily forested hills, and the swarms of streams that watered the narrow valleys froze solid. Timbering was the main industry, and frequently peasant woodsmen encountered bears and, more often, wolves. Other serfs scraped a scant living from the poor soil. Life for the village priest's family was hard.

When the widow Kliuchevskaia took her small family to Penza, the town's population could not have been much larger than 20,000. Originally a frontier fortress built to pacify the

Mordva and Meshcheriaki tribes, Penza boasted a violent history. It had fallen to Stenka Razin in 1670, and ten years later the Bashkirs were hammering at the gates. In 1774 Pugachev seized the town. Although primarily Russian in character, life in the provincial capital and even more in the surrounding countryside reflected the age-old conflict for the land between colonizers, Finns, and Tatar tribes. For the young Kliuchevsky, conquest of the forests and expansion to the east were more than historical memories; they were the vibrant themes of life around him.

As a boy Kliuchevsky listened avidly to the telling of Russian fairy tales, but he insisted with childish pedantry upon absolute accuracy of detail. No doubt his great sensitivity for the rhythm of the spoken word came from these long hours of exposure to the great oral tradition. Later an equal passion for reading took hold of him. "God knows when he slept," his sister later mused.[4] Yet in spite of his devotion to learning, school was an ordeal. A speech impediment held him back, but he strove to overcome it and succeeded in the most extraordinary way: by converting the stutter into a dramatic pause. Later, in his lectures, the result was nothing short of theatrical.[5]

An intelligent but impoverished boy who was the son of a priest had little choice in preparing for a career. The church schools were free, thanks to a scholarship, and in 1856 Kliuchevsky applied to enter Penza Seminary. His entrance examination produced "a stunning impression" upon the committee. At the seminary Kliuchevsky won the respect and affection of teachers and students alike. "Only a learned theologian can write like this!" one of his instructors exclaimed upon reading his essays. A quiet and modest young man, he possessed "a magnetic strength" of character which inspired his comrades. But the deadening routine and petty tyrannies of the seminary soon irritated and disgusted him. Although Kliuchevsky remained profoundly religious throughout his life, the years in the Penza

[4] S. A. Belokurov, *Vasili Osipovich Kliuchevsky. Materialy dlia ego biografii* (Moscow, 1914), p. 415.
[5] A. Kizevetter, *Istoricheskie otkliki* (Moscow, 1915), p. 364.

Seminary left a bitter residue which accounted for his frequent biting criticisms of men and institutions, including, at times, the church itself. His sharp tongue, together with a certain slyness more characteristic of a suspicious peasant than of an intellectual, were, in the eyes of his contemporaries, the least attractive qualities he acquired in this difficult period.

While contemptuous of the seminary's "stifling atmosphere," Kliuchevsky found compensation in the close intensive life of the seminarists' circle. In the evenings a small but surprisingly varied group of students, including believers, rationalists, and political activists, gathered in one of their number's room to read the more lively thick journals like *Sovremennik* and *Russkii vestnik*, which smuggled into their provincial world the fierce controversies raging in a press just recently freed from the "censorship terror" of Nicholas I's last years. Avidly digesting the latest historical works of S. M. Solovyev, N. I. Kostomarov, K. D. Kavelin, and B. N. Chicherin, Kliuchevsky and his comrades felt a fresh wind stirring in Russian historiography.[6]

That the intellectual ferment in post-Crimean Russia penetrated so easily the thick walls of the seminaries underlines the paradox of the state's educational policy. By intensifying the separate and corporate nature of student life and at the same time trying to exclude contemporary issues from the course of study, the government unwittingly created tightly knit groups bound together by the strongest personal loyalties and engaged in intellectual activity which it could only regard as subversive if not downright revolutionary. Yet Kliuchevsky resisted the drift toward illegal activities that swept other students and seminarists of his generation into open opposition to the state. More like M. N. Speransky than N. G. Chernyshevsky, he drew heavily on those elements of seminary training that stressed disciplined thinking and lucid expression, rather than those that emphasized abstract reasoning and messianic zeal. For all that, he struggled to break out of the confining limits of the seminary and, after overcoming the stubborn resistance of the administration, applied for and was accepted by Moscow

[6] Manuscript Division, Lenin Library, Fund 131, folder 14, p. 6.

University. His brilliant performance on the entrance examination prompted an astonished reaction from Patriarch Filaret: "Only I could have answered as well." [7]

In 1860 Kliuchevsky arrived in Moscow in the midst of great intellectual excitement on the eve of the emancipation. The relaxation of censorship and the drafting of new liberal rules for the university stirred long dormant passions. A small group of professors sought to play a more active political role, and many students responded so vigorously that they soon outstripped the demands of their teachers. But the young man from the provinces refused to be carried away. As revealed in his letters to an old friend in Penza, Kliuchevsky regarded the scene with detachment. The liberation of the serfs moved him profoundly, to be sure, but as for the rest, he alternated between witty and sarcastic comments on the folly of his fellow men. Although he disdained to take part in the student demonstrations of 1861, he reproached the police for their zealous brutality.[8] Yet, as his diary reveals, the public pose of aloofness masked a deeper private anguish. He found no cure for "the sickness of moral loneliness," but he set himself a demanding regime. "Most uneasily and persistently of all," he wrote, "I strive for a moral stability against fleeting impressions and an ability to maintain the position of an observer while revolving on the drum of life. . . ." [9] In general, he was appalled by the eagerness with which his fellow students "snatched at the latest conclusions of European science and [then], without succeeding in mastering them, squeamishly turning up their noses, they declare them outdated and old fashioned." [10] This is not to suggest that Kliuchevsky ignored Comte, Marx, and Spencer, but his reaction to them was different. Remarkably like his great contemporary Leo Tolstoy, Kliuchevsky had a corrosively skeptical intellect which in its relentless pursuit of truth gave him no

[7] Kizevetter, *Istoricheskie otkliki*, p. 367.
[8] *Trudy gosudarsvennogo rumiantsevskogo muzei* (Moscow, 1924), vol. 5, *Pisma V. O. Kliuchevskogo k P. P. Gvozdevu (1861–1870)*, p. 22.
[9] R. A. Kireeva, *V. O. Kliuchevsky kak istorik russkoi istoricheskoi nauki* (Moscow, 1966), p. 192.
[10] *Ibid.*

peace. Like Tolstoy, too, Kliuchevsky was a destroyer of systems, an enemy of abstract reasoning whose temper both matched and expressed the spirit of the times. He could easily have adopted as his own the motto of another great contemporary, the German historian Wilhelm Dilthey, whom he resembles in a number of ways: "Thought is fruitful only when it is based upon the special investigation of one aspect of the *real.*" [11] Already devoted to the precepts of realism when he entered the university, Kliuchevsky held more closely to them for the rest of his life than either Tolstoy or Dilthey, yet even his steady course could not save him from growing disillusionment.

Kliuchevsky's natural reluctance to attach himself to abstractions or fixed dogmas placed him in a unique position to take advantage of the realignment of intellectual forces after the Crimean War. As Herzen had predicted, the old quarrels between Westerners and Slavophiles then seemed irrelevant. The impending reforms from above challenged the intelligentsia to reformulate their antagonistic views or to reconcile them. Kliuchevsky was eminently suited to play the role of conciliator. The key to understanding his success in this quest lies in his relationship with two outstanding scholars who, while on the periphery of the Westerner-Slavophile debate, represented the universalist and particularist elements inherent in the two rival schools of thought. They were the great historian S. M. Solovyev and the eminent comparative philologist F. I. Buslaev.

When Kliuchevsky entered Moscow University in 1860, Hegelian philosophy dominated the teaching faculties, and nowhere was its influence more pronounced than in the field of history, where the towering figures of Chicherin and Solovyev held sway. In his second year Kliuchevsky slipped into the great auditorium to hear Solovyev lecture in Russian history to the third- and fourth-year students, only to be repelled by the Hegelian overtones, which, he confided to his provincial comrade, "smack of Muslim fatalism." "From this point of view, you must accept everything, justify everything and never take action against anything." It came as a shock to Kliuchevsky that

[11] Carlo Antoni, *From History to Sociology* (Detroit, 1959), p. 4.

under the influence of this scheme Solovyev "justifies and even defends the Muscovite centralization with its unpardonable despotism and arbitrariness." [12] To Kliuchevsky the state was a means of reconciling conflicting interests of different social groups rather than a logical development of the world spirit.[13]

On the other hand, there was much in Solovyev's work that Kliuchevsky admired: "his harmony of thought and word"; an ability to arrange the facts into a "mosaic of general historical ideas which [in turn] explain them"; and his "pragmatic moralism," which, like the figures of an antique bas-relief, seemed to grow organically out of the bedrock of facts.[14] By revealing the natural links between events, Solovyev had brought Russian history out of chaos into the realm of scientific analysis.[15] Kliuchevsky recognized Solovyev as the starting point for all future work in Russian history. "I am a student of Solovyev," he frequently said. "As a scholar that is all I can be proud of." [16] Yet Kliuchevsky could never reconcile himself to accept what he called Solovyev's one-sided application to political forms of the idea of regularity in history.[17] Characteristically, Kliuchevsky shrank from openly attacking his revered teacher, but privately he expressed strong reservations. In his eyes Solovyev lacked the suble and anatomical touch without which he "could not probe to the bare bones of life but only grasp its physiognomy." [18] Just as disturbing to Kliuchevsky was Solovyev's lack of discrimination. In an unpublished draft article he rebuked his teacher for taking "a fact from a source and [introducing] it

[12] *Trudy*, p. 84.
[13] *Ibid.*, p. 87.
[14] Kliuchevsky, "S. M. Solovyev kak prepodavatel" (1895), in *Ocherki i rechi* (Moscow, n.d.), pp. 30, 33, 34.
[15] Kireeva, *Kliuchevsky*, p. 205.
[16] A. E. Presniakov, "V. O. Kliuchevsky 1911–1921," *Russkii istoricheskii zhurnal*, 8 (1922): 206.
[17] Kliuchevsky, *Sochineniia*, 7: 464.
[18] Kireeva, *Kliuchevsky*, p. 208. Like other historians of his generation, Kliuchevsky expressed great admiration for Guizot as a guide to socio-historical analysis; a "master historian-anatomist," he called him. For a similar view on Guizot see G. P. Gooch, *History and Historians in the Nineteenth Century* (London, 1913), p. 181.

into a text of narrative history in its untouched state," thus revealing "an aversion to historical criticism." [19]

As a leading Soviet specialist has pointed out, Kliuchevsky's concept of society as an organism and his awareness of the critical approach owes far more to the influence of Buslaev than to that of Solovyev.[20] Buslaev taught him how to read and analyze ancient texts and monuments by demonstrating that language is a function of social structure. Buslaev's own studies had tapped a new source for the study of prehistorical and nonliterate cultures. In his work on the *Lives of the Saints*, Buslaev found in the language of ancient proverbs and riddles themes and forms of purely pagan origin.[21] This methodology had enormous significance for Kliuchevsky's work, especially his master's dissertation, "Ancient Lives of Saints as a Historical Source." Even more important, Buslaev reinforced Kliuchevsky's growing conviction that the material and spiritual aspirations of the people played a basic role in the historical process. As a comparative philologist, Buslaev was more interested in analyzing the terminology of family relations than idealizing old Russian social institutions. Thus he was "indifferent to Slavophile convictions and ideas." Yet, as he admitted in his memoirs, his love for Italy, antique Greco-Roman culture, and the theories of the German philologist Jacob Grimm did not make him a Westerner. His respect for the Russian epics (*byliny*) was as

[19] Kireeva, *Kliuchevsky*, p. 206. Curiously enough, a similar charge was leveled against Kliuchevsky by his most famous student, P. N. Miliukov, who remarked that Kliuchevsky's selection of dramatic incidents to illustrate his ideas provided "the clearest unifying thread of *A Course in Russian History* [but] was at the same time the most speculative part." P. N. Miliukov, "V. O. Kliuchevsky," in *Kharakteristiki i vospominaniia* (Moscow, 1912), p. 193. The link between fact and generalization is a tenuous one indeed.

[20] A. A. Zimin, "Formirovanie istoricheskikh vzgliadov V. O. Kliuchevskogo v 60-e godye XIX v.," *Istoricheskie zapiski*, 69 (1961): 185–87. See also Kireeva, *Kliuchevsky*, pp. 203–4, and L. V. Cherepnin, "V. O. Kliuchevsky," in *Ocherki istorii istoricheskoi nauki v SSSR* (Moscow, 1960), 2: 146–47.

[21] Kliuchevsky, "F. I. Buslaev kak prepodavatel i issledovatel," in *Sochineniia*, 8: 292–93.

great as for Homer.[22] Standing above rather than midway between the Westerners and Slavophiles, Buslaev served Kliuchevsky as a model of the objective social scientist. Like his teacher, Kliuchevsky saw attractive qualities in the outlooks of both camps. "The Westerners were noted for their clear thinking and love of exact knowledge and respect for scholarship; the Slavophiles displayed a fascinating breadth of ideas, a lively faith in the nation's potentialities and a streak of lyrical dialectic which covered over the slips in logic and gaps in erudition." [23] In the words of Miliukov, Kliuchevsky's mind belonged to the Westerners and his heart to the Slavophiles.[24]

For a brief period before and after the emancipation, Kliuchevsky's thinking seemed merely to run parallel to that of the rest of the informed public. In a burst of national enthusiasm the nihilist Pisarev praised the Slavophile Kireevsky, and Chernyshevsky extended his hand to Samarin.[25] Soon, however, disappointments over the implementation of the reforms and the outbreak of the Polish revolt in 1863 splintered this fragile and unreal unity. But Kliuchevsky resisted the pull of extremes. His great love of Russia's past never overwhelmed his rigorous scholarship. He remained too critical to tolerate utopias, and his social conscience saved him from despair.

In his years as an undergraduate (1860–65), Kliuchevsky laid the basis for his two most significant contributions to Russian historiography. He freed history from its subservience to philosophy and cleared the way for a multidisciplinary study of the past. With the help of sociology and comparative philology he then broadened the range of his investigations to accommodate contradictions that in the idealist scheme could have been resolved only by logical rather than historical necessity. At the same time he wove together into a brilliant new synthesis the

[22] F. I. Buslaev, *Moi vospominaniia* (Moscow, 1897), pp. 124–29, 289–300.

[23] See below, pp. 280–81.

[24] Miliukov, "Kliuchevsky," p. 200.

[25] A. A. Kornilov, *Obshchevstvennoe dvizhenie pri Aleksandr II* (Moscow, 1909), pp. 21–22.

two main interpretive themes of Russian history, the Westerner and the Slavophile, which up to that time appeared hopelessly irreconcilable. Thus, while preserving for Russia a place in the historical development of European civilization, he also explained the particular and peculiar character of Russia's situation within that general process.

For fifteen years following his graduation from Moscow University, Kliuchevsky worked out his ideas in such a way as to give the superficial appearance of a single directional attack upon the state school of Chicherin and Solovyev. But it would be misleading to equate a natural tendency to correct some imbalances in the views of the state school with a total rejection of the state as a powerful element in the historical process. Beginning tentatively in his thesis for the first graduate degree of *kandidat, Tales of Foreigners About the Muscovite State* (1866), he gave increasingly greater prominence to geography and the economic life of the people. By the time he wrote the first draft of his master's thesis (1872), he brought into sharp focus his differences with the state school. Concerning the colonization of north and central Russia he wrote: "The government did not summon and direct this movement of people . . . it was itself to a significant degree a result of this movement." [26] Appropriately enough, his Ph.D. dissertation, *The Boyar Duma*, was his real declaration of independence. In the introduction Kliuchevsky rejected as "self-deluding" the idea that a satisfactory history of the Russian state could exist without an understanding of the history of its people. Criticizing the idealist position (though not in name) for lavishing attention exclusively on the forms of the state, he set himself two goals in analyzing the growth and development of state institutions: to identify the foreign and domestic sources of the administrative structure, and to reveal its social basis. "In the history of political institutions," Kliuchevsky concluded, "the building material is frequently more important than the structure itself." [27]

Despite Kliuchevsky's emphasis on the social foundation of

[26] Zimin, "Formirovanie," p. 192.
[27] Kliuchevsky, *Boiarskaia Duma* (Moscow, 1881), pp. 13, 15.

politics, he did not fall into the mistake of other historians, like Kostomarov, who almost lost sight of the state altogether. He understood too well the powerful influence that the state institutions, once created, could exert upon the nature and functioning of social groups. In order to portray in all its changing complexities the relationship between the state and society, Kliuchevsky needed a broader canvas—the whole sweep of Russian history. In fact, it is only in that context that it is possible to grasp the full implications of his theoretical views and arrive at a balanced judgment of Kliuchevsky as historian. The opportunity for him at least to consider a general course in Russian history came under the most auspicious circumstance soon after he completed *The Boyar Duma*. He was invited to succeed Solovyev in the history chair at Moscow University, and although he had already been lecturing at the Moscow Theological Academy, the new post gave him an eager and more sophisticated audience from which would emerge some of Russia's outstanding historians in the next generation. Kliuchevsky responded to the challenge by preparing the lectures that, over the course of the next two and a half decades, were ultimately to be fused into *A Course in Russian History*.

In the two introductory lectures or chapters of *A Course*, Kliuchevsky came as close as he ever did to setting down in print a full account of his philosophy of history. But his conclusions have never been accepted universally as the definitive statement of his views. Writing logically and clearly but too concisely, Kliuchevsky simply failed to develop some of his more complex ideas. Consequently, sharp differences of opinion have divided historians over the real meaning behind his words; and some Soviet historians have questioned whether these lectures represent a viewpoint consistent with all of Kliuchevsky's writings.

To summarize even the most stimulating interpretations of Kliuchevsky's work would require an extensive essay, but at least the main ones deserve mention. Marxist historians from G. V. Plekhanov to the present day have argued that Kliuchevsky was one of the first "bourgeois historians" to reserve a crucial place in the historical scheme for the class concept. Plekhanov went so far as to imply that Kliuchevsky was a Marxist in spite of himself.[28] But the most famous Marxist historian of Russia and a former student of Kliuchevsky, M. N. Pokrovsky, saw in his teacher's work a formless eclecticism with elements of positivism, Hegelianism, and individualism, held together by nothing more concrete than the personality of its creator.[29] This very jumble of influences, thought Pokrovsky, testified to the "crisis of the bourgeois order." [30] More recently this interpretation has taken on a more subtle shading at the hands of A. A. Zimin and others. Relying primarily upon works written in the 1880's, they claim that Kliuchevsky's world view was firmly rooted in the materialism of the 1860's and reflected the democratic socialist aspirations of that tumultuous decade. But frightened by the rising tide of the revolutionary movement, Kliuchevsky returned to the precepts of the state school in a belated effort to defend the monarchy. By the end of his life he was drifting into neo-Kantian idealism as the last refuge of individualism.[31]

A respectful critic from the St. Petersburg school, A. E. Presniakov, offered a more personal analysis of the apparent contradictions in Kliuchevsky's views on history. He claimed that in *A Course in Russian History* political and economic facts occupied the central position not because of their relative significance in the historical process, but because they were the only objects suitable for the critical methods of historical scholarship. The order of research, he added, reversed the order of life, from effect to cause and from result to origin. This led him to conclude that Kliuchevsky was an idealist according to his

[28] G. V. Plekhanov, *Istoriia russkoi obshchestvennoi mysli* (Moscow, 1918), 1: 16, 24.
[29] M. N. Pokrovsky, "Kurs russkoi istorii prof. V. Kliuchevskogo," in *Istoricheskaia nauka i borba klassov* (Moscow-Leningrad, 1933), 2: 49–50.
[30] N. L. Rubinshtein, *Russkaia istoriografiia* (Moscow, 1941), pp. 445, 469.
[31] Zimin, "Formirovanie," pp. 179, 195; Kireeva, *Kliuchevsky*, pp. 219–20. The final point is not novel and owes much to the perceptive article by another of Kliuchevsky's famous students, A. S. Lappo-Danilevsky, "Pamiati V. O. Kliuchevskogo," *Vestnik evropy*, vol. 270, no. 8 (1911), especially p. 339.

theoretical views, a materialist in his methodology, and a sociologist in his presentation.[32] It is ironic but not surprising that
Miliukov's penetrating appreciation of his master resembled in
some ways that of his fellow student Pokrovsky. The great
Russian liberal's charming aphorism that Kliuchevsky "borrowed
everything, but it was all original," could not mask his disap-
pointment at failing to find in the great synthesis a "vital
nerve." What both men sought in vain from opposite vantage
points was a clear-cut guide to political action.[33] Lesser figures
have seized upon one or another aspect of Kliuchevsky's works
as ammunition for an anti-Marxist polemic. For example, the
émigré scholar S. I. Tkhorzhevsky emphasized Kliuchevsky's
treatment of those periods in Russian history when overriding
national and religious concerns "muffled class differences," as
in the seventeenth century, when Russia was a "single moral
entity."[34] Of all the interpretations, the one that most nearly
approaches the one expressed in this essay was written by the
editor of Kliuchevsky's letters, S. A. Golubtsov. Although not
an important historian, Golubtsov perceived from his study of
Kliuchevsky's early years that a balanced and consistent outlook permeated Kliuchevsky's work from his student days to
the writing of *A Course in Russian History*.[35] Clearly, Kliuchevsky, like all great historians, has left behind such a rich heritage
that it has become in itself an object of historical study, an
inexhaustible source of commentary, interpretation, and dispute.
From a different perspective, a reexamination of Kliuchevsky's
views on history is still bound to yield insights into the man and
his society.

[32] Presniakov, "Kliuchevsky," pp. 216–17.
[33] The personal relationship between Kliuchevsky and Miliukov was
complex and ambivalent. Miliukov never forgave his teacher for preventing
him from receiving the degree of doctor as a special tribute to the quality
of his master's dissertation, "The State Economy of Russia in the First
Quarter of the Eighteenth Century and the Reforms of Peter the Great."
See P. N. Miliukov, *Vospominaniia (1859–1917)* (New York, 1955), 1: 138–
42.
[34] S. I. Tkhorzhevsky, "V. O. Kliuchevsky kak sotsiolog i politicheskii
myslitel," in *Dela i dni* (1921), bk. 2, pp. 159–60.
[35] *Trudy*, pp. 16–24.

Kliuchevsky recognized that history meant both a movement over time and a cognition of that process, though he paid little attention to the latter problem. As a prelude to analyzing his methodology, it is important to identify the components of the historical process as he defined them.

As we have seen, Kliuchevsky accepted the premise of an underlying structure of human activity but resisted the temptation to express this in terms of an abstract philosophical scheme; that is, an *a priori* system borrowed from another discipline rather than hewn from the hard data of historical evidence. To be sure, Kliuchevsky admitted that "historical facts, by their very essence, are conclusions, generalizations of specific phenomena similar in character; they are what concepts are in the logical sphere; like the latter they can differ in their comprehensiveness by the amount of generalized material in them, but also like the latter they always retain logical relationships to their material." [36] To Kliuchevsky, then, the quality of the general in historical facts and the logical relationship between these facts constituted the methodological assumptions that permitted him to maintain that the essence of history as a separate and distinct science was the historical process; that is, "the life of mankind in its developments and results." Human life or society was, in Kliuchevsky's eyes, just as proper a subject for scientific study as nature. The form of human activity is most fully expressed in a variety of associations which Kliuchevsky likened, in the fashionable physiological metaphor of his generation, to the organic bodies of nature, which are born, develop, and die.[37] The form and function of these associations change in response to the biological and moral requirements of the individual, the collective interests of social groups, and the need to overcome natural obstacles to these expanding aspirations. In sum, the human personality, human society, and the natural environment are the three basic historical forces that determine the kinds of associations or ties—economic, social, cultural, political, etc.—

[36] Presniakov, "Kliuchevsky," p. 209.
[37] Kliuchevsky, *Sochineniia*, 1: 14.

men create, modify, and discard.[38] The relationship between these three forces is subtle, complex, and dynamic. For example, the human personality emerges from the individual's aspirations within a social environment, but many individuals acting in this way create a society that represents more than the sum of its parts because as a collective organization it formulates its own goals. The interplay between individual creativity and the demands of the group, tempered by geographical conditions, gives rise to a pattern of life that may be called the national temperament.[39] A society's level of achievement—that is, the acquisition of experience, knowledge, and physical comforts that contribute to the well-being of the group and the individual—Kliuchevsky called the history of culture or civilization. The organization of human associations, the structure of society that man evolved within the limitations imposed by the human condition and the natural environment, he defined as historical sociology.[40] In *A Course* Kliuchevsky probed deeply into the historical sociology of Russia, but he never claimed that even here he had reached the bedrock of the historical process. Rather he conveyed a sense of awe mingled with frustration in his quest for the elusive wellsprings of human motivation in history.

Shying away from the lure of first or ultimate causes, Kliuchevsky emphasized, nevertheless, the historian's duty to peel off successive layers of facts in order to get at the deepest sources of human behavior. In *The Boyar Duma* he had already discerned behind the imposing façade of institutional arrangements more fundamental social and economic relationships. Later, in an unpublished manuscript, "The Methodology of History," he clarified the distinction by separating the basic or natural

---

[38] *Ibid.*, 1: 21. This was a refinement of an earlier plan in which Kliuchevsky made a fourfold division of the historical forces into geography, the physical nature of the people, personality, and society. He considered the first two elements as "natural" and the second pair as "spiritual." A fifth factor, "the burden of the past," disappeared from his later writings. Tkhorzhevsky, "Kliuchevsky," p. 160.

[39] Kliuchevsky, *Sochineniia*, 1: 21.

[40] *Ibid.*, 1: 15.

human associations from the artificial or secondary. The six
natural associations proceeded in roughly historical progression
from primitive society, where he assumed no family existed,
through matriarchal and patriarchal family organizations to the
tribe. The inner dynamics of social change he attributed to deep-
seated, instinctive responses to moral and environmental stimuli.
In contrast, the secondary associations, the two principal ones
being the church and the state, reflected man's more conscious
efforts both to identify his aspirations and to create the institutional forms best suited to achieve them.[41]

More concretely, two themes dominated Kliuchevsky's view
of the sweep of Russian history: colonization or mastery of the
land, and unification or the creation of common identity and
purpose. Out of the struggles to realize these aspirations within
the shifting geographic boundaries of their society, the Russian
people evolved a peculiar set of social and political institutions.
The complex relationship between the physical setting, the
human aspirations, and the institutional response gave a pronounced character to the dynamics of change in four distinct
periods. Although these periods take their names from the predominant geographic and ethnic traits (Dnieper, Volga, Great
Russian, and All-Russian), Kliuchevsky viewed them as representing a totality of human experience, the class structure, the
political-legal framework, and the forms of spiritual life. Thus in
the fourth period (1613–1855), which this volume introduces,
the state reached out to encompass the entire Russian plain
while a new dynasty came to power based upon the supremacy
of a new class, the *dvorianstvo*. As the state power increased, so
did both the obligations of the people and the rigidity of the
class structure designed to meet those obligations.[42] Although

[41] Tkhorzhevsky, "Kliuchevsky," pp. 159–60. Tkhorzhevsky claimed that
the scheme was borrowed by Kliuchevsky from the French sociologist
Marc Giraud-Teulon, *Origines du mariage et de la famille* (Geneva, 1884).
There is a marked similarity of views; see especially the conclusion, pp.
471–83. But Kliuchevsky did not accept Giraud-Teulon's thesis that the
nuclear family is the most fruitful source of production and the repository
of the highest form of property rights (*ibid.*, p. 483).

[42] See below, pp. 4–5.

political thought failed to keep pace with these developments, the hereditary dynastic view of the state gradually yielded to "the conception of the nation as a political union." [43]

The discussion over whether or not Kliuchevsky was a materialist whose youthful rebellion yielded to some form of latter-day idealism must center on the place he accorded in his historical scheme to class struggle on the one hand and the human spirit or the moral factor on the other. As might be expected, Russian and Soviet historians have disagreed strongly over these questions. On both sides the polemics have suffered from a narrow or, to be more precise, linear treatment of Kliuchevsky's attitude toward class, and hardly suggest nuances in Kliuchevsky's analysis of the relationship between man's primary and secondary associations. In part this shortcoming arises from the failure to make clear the important distinction in Kliuchevsky's mind between class and estate. Yet in that distinction lies the key to his remarkable explanation of the different paths of historical development taken by Russia and western Europe.

Estate, as distinct from class, was a juridical entity that enjoyed advantages bestowed upon its members by law in the form of corporate rights. Faced by threats to its security, the state had given legal sanction to informal relationships that had evolved spontaneously within the society. In this way the state sought to regularize its relationship with different groups within the population on the basis of their ability to contribute to the maintenance and defense of society as a whole. The initial inequality of these estates (based upon wealth and military prowess) shifted or broke down more rapidly in western Europe, where, to begin with, the socio-economic differences had been smaller and society had been fragmented into a more complex hierarchy of social groups. Kliuchevsky argued that the distinction between the growth in western Europe of an economic elite whose control of capital assured its hegemony and the superior status of a military-warrior elite in Russia was responsible for an entirely different set of obligations to the state. Everywhere in Europe under an estate system obligations were

[43] See below, p. 52.

assigned to whole classes according to their political importance, but the commercial-industrial-professional groups, riding the tide of economic expansion, were able to increase national wealth to the point where their contribution to state power raised them to a position roughly equivalent to that of the administrative-warrior estate. As a result of this admittedly complex and uneven process, obligations were placed upon a new basis: "the state demands from everyone in relation to what it offers him in return." Thus the social order rested upon reciprocal rights and obligations. No longer assigned to a legal estate with corporate obligations, the individual found his own level, so to speak, where, by means of an elaborate set of economic and juridical transactions, he assumed obligations that guaranteed his own welfare. Kliuchevsky called this political freedom. Equality of civil rights and personal obligations was balanced by inequality of political rights and property obligations. As a result, man became "an eternal nomad," roaming from one political group to another according to his success or failure in economic and social competition.[44] The very "openness" of this society rested upon the need for capital to be active and to grow; the fewer institutional checks on people's activities, the more dynamic the social and economic change and the more responsive the political structure.

By contrast, in Russia the continued existence of the estate structure well into the nineteenth century reflected the need, in the absence of rapidly expanding economic relations, to guarantee by political means the hegemony of the administrative-warrior elite. To Kliuchevsky, then, the history of estates revealed two veiled but closely related historical processes: the increasing awareness by individuals of the general welfare, and the freeing of the individual from the bonds of the estate in the name of that general welfare.[45] In this analysis Kliuchevsky came as close as he ever did to enthroning economic activity as *the* motive force in history, but even here, as we shall see, he

[44] V. O. Kliuchevsky, *Istoriia soslovii v Rossii* (Petrograd, 1918), p. 27.
[45] *Ibid.*, pp. 27–28.

harbored a reservation, briefly stated but no less profoundly significant.

Like other European historians of his generation, Kliuchevsky perceived the difficulty of treating the human spirit in history without falling prey to metaphysics. "The soul is not the proper study of historians," he admitted in the introduction to *A Course*. Logical concepts and aesthetic forms reflect social consciousness in a refracted light, but historical criticism in Kliuchevsky's eyes "has not found the proper means by which to measure exactly this angle of refraction." [46] Kliuchevsky concluded that ideas as the products of the individual mind could have no impact outside a small circle of family and friends—that is, they could not become historical factors—unless they acquired power through acceptance by the masses or the owners of capital. Pokrovsky scored a telling point, however, when he complained that Kliuchevsky never explained just how this occurs.[47] But once "the fruits of individual consciousness" fell on fertile soil, they became, in Kliuchevsky's words, "the best builders of society, the most powerful movers of human development." [48] In fact, Kliuchevsky continued, "Society is already an idea because society begins to exist from the moment when people who make it up begin to realize that they are a society." In other words, political structures and economic relations are ideas that have been processed and take on a collective character in the form of social norms or law.[49] This is why for Kliuchevsky the study of law was the key to personality as a historical force, for law was the imposition of the individual's will upon society. His particular interest in the historical figures of the seventeenth century lies precisely in the conversion of their private thoughts and aspirations into legislative issues which were resolved in the creation of new state institutions.[50] In the

---

[46] *Ibid.*, p. 28.
[47] Pokrovsky, "Kurs," p. 50.
[48] Lappo-Danilevsky, "Pamiati," p. 339.
[49] Tkhorzhevsky, "Kliuchevsky," p. 161.
[50] S. A. Golubtsov, "Teoreticheskie vsgliady V. O. Kliuchevskogo," *Russkii istoricheskii zhurnal*, bk. 8 (1922), p. 188.

light of this reasoning it is clear that Kliuchevsky seemed to be striving to fight clear of the idealist-materialist polarity. "The facts of individual consciousness," he wrote, "this is also a part of a way of life (*byt*), no more or less real than the facts of the external world." [51] On the one hand, the interplay between man's quest for food as well as freedom gives birth to specific social relations and, on the other hand, external events bring forth new ideas or reveal the inadequacy of old forms. In this complex exchange Kliuchevsky refused to assign primacy to one aspect of human nature or of its historical expression. The sensitive reader can detect in Kliuchevsky a touch of regret that the nature of his task set limits upon his restless imagination.

Kliuchevsky's admiration for the precision of the scientist in search of natural law was balanced by his envy of the freedom of the artist. He remained convinced that it was possible to reveal man's "inner nature" by working out the regularities of social history, but he yielded more than once to the temptation of probing intuitively the spiritual depths of man through literary masterpieces. Stating the ideal goals of social history, Kliuchevsky insisted that "the triumph of history" would be to set down "a science of general laws of the construction of human society which [could be] applied independently of transitory social conditions." [52] In his *Istoriia sosloviia* (1886) he posed four basic hypotheses on the creation and transformation of estates which he hoped could serve as a basis for the study of other societies and gradually acquire the meaning of historical laws.[53] In this context a study of Russian history could serve as a possible model. Because of the relative simplicity of the historical processes in Russia, the historian could clearly observe them in action, and even though these processes did not have a direct effect upon the general movement of history outside the frontiers, or even achieve a similar state of activity, they might well reveal a great deal about "the mechanics of historical life." [54]

[51] Tkhorzhevsky, "Kliuchevsky," p. 168.
[52] Kliuchevsky, *Sochineniia*, 1: 19.
[53] Kliuchevsky, *Istoriia sosloviia*, p. 13.
[54] Kliuchevsky, *Sochineniia*, 1: 26.

Kliuchevsky's terminology may now seem a bit old-fashioned, but his ideas are not. Both Soviet and Western scholars now continue to seek in Russian history either a revolutionary or a developmental model to explain the problems of change in the non-Western world.

It may be argued that as a historian seeking to present his ideas in the most precise terminology for purposes of empirical verification, Kliuchevsky gave greater emphasis in his formal methodology to sociology than to intuitive insights. But a man's mind does not stop at the limits of his professional competence. As a human being Kliuchevsky could not be satisfied only with an historian's analysis of the world, even though he thought a total explanation could never withstand the rigorous test of a historian's critique: "research is still far from that moment when a full, strict, and pragmatic description of our intellectual history will become possible." [55]

In at least two essays Kliuchevsky overcame his scruples as a historian in order to treat an aspect of the Russian mind; these were "Eugene Onegin and His Predecessors," written in 1887, and "Melancholy," written in 1891. To Kliuchevsky the underlying mood of Lermontov's poetry was a complex state of mind that, "deprived of happiness, does not await it or seek it or grieve over it." [56] Although this feeling was always individual, it corresponded to the general mood of the Russian people, to their evaluation of life. Between the sluggish fatalism of the East and the vibrant self-confidence of the West, melancholy in Russia took on the peculiar hues of the national religious experience and became "a historical fact," expressed, for example, in the words of Tsar Alexei Mikhailovich as he comforted one of his boyars at a moment of personal grief: "You shouldn't grieve overmuch, my dear prince, but of course one can't help grieving and shedding tears, and indeed it is right to weep, but within reason so as not to offend God." [57]

[55] Presniakov, "Kliuchevsky," p. 216.
[56] Kliuchevsky, "Grust. Pamiati M. Iu. Lermontova," in *Ocherki i rechi*, p. 127.
[57] *Ibid.*, p. 133. This passage is also cited in the present volume; see below, p. 350.

Similarly, "Eugene Onegin and His Predecessors" was for Kliuchevsky the aesthetic expression of a historical fact, less universal than "Melancholy" but no less compelling. Pushkin's creation, as a "cultural-psychological curiosity . . . awaits the hand of the artist, but as the transmission point of ideas and tradition, as the mediator between 'two centuries' which are prepared to quarrel with one another, he occupies an important place in the history of our society." [58] Onegin was the personification of "total moral confusion" summed up in the principle "It is neither possible nor necessary to do anything." [59] In this classic portrayal of the superfluous man, the victim of the uneven cultural development of the *dvorianstvo* in the eighteenth century, Kliuchevsky revealed his contempt for the process of artificial Europeanization, which doomed an entire class of men who were fitted for neither intellectual nor practical work to a socially destructive role. The intensity of their isolation, however, drove them to speculate upon the future of Russia, and their reflections were suffused not with despair and even less with high hopes, but with melancholy.[60] Thus, despite powerful external influences and sharp class differences, a persistent moral outlook characterized Russian history.

Kliuchevsky's intellectual journey, like his concept of history, cannot be traced, it must be plumbed. For Kliuchevsky human activity took place on a number of distinct but interconnected planes. No metaphor, perhaps no language—which in itself is a set of symbols—can capture it, because no activity of nature is as complex as the human, and no abstract scheme can repro-

---

[58] Kliuchevsky, "Evgeni Onegin i ego predki," in *Ocherki i rechi*, p. 84.
[59] *Ibid.*, p. 88.
[60] These sentiments were an outgrowth of Kliuchevsky's early love for Russian folk songs and reflect his debt to Buslaev. On October 27, 1862, in a letter to his Penza friend, he extolled the "Igor Tale": "These words, though not from a pure folk song . . . express superbly the entire history of Russian poetry . . . in every song the Russian bemoans his fate." At that time Kliuchevsky shared the fashionable disdain of his generation for Pushkin and Lermontov, who offered, he wrote, "songs which are brilliant like fireworks, but, also like fireworks, empty" (*Trudy*, p. 72). Only later did he see the same expressive line in the entire development of Russian poetry.

duce it. The interplay of the factors is so great as to defy existing categories. Kliuchevsky appears to question whether there
is a real antithesis of spirit and matter. The natural environment
exists apart from human society, but human society cannot exist
outside that environment. Neither can human aspirations. They
can only adapt to it or transform it. To abandon it means to
die. Although Kliuchevsky found it difficult as a historian to
investigate the source of those aspirations, he had no doubt as to
their belonging to the reality of the world and resisted any
attempt to confine the definition of that reality to idealism or
materialism.

To suggest, as have Soviet historians, that Kliuchevsky deserted his original commitment to economic materialism in the
1880's and 1890's, returned to the assumptions of the state
school, and gradually drifted into neo-Kantian idealism by the
turn of the century obscures the consistency of Kliuchevsky's
outlook and ignores its complexity. He was simply capable of
viewing the multiple levels of history simultaneously, though
until the publication of *A Course* his monographs usually dealt
with only one aspect at a time. For example, in 1885 in his
classic work "The Origins of Serfdom in Russia," he sharply
attacked the prevailing view of the state school, arguing that
"legislation did not impose serfdom upon the landlords' peasants
either directly or indirectly." [61] The briefer analysis in *A Course*
published in 1906 remains essentially the same: "Legislation to
the end of the period under consideration [beginning of the
seventeenth century] did not establish serfdom." [62] In both cases
Kliuchevsky regarded legislation as the definition of an accomplished fact and in some sense a limitation upon the extent of

[61] Kliuchevsky, "Proiskhozhdenie krepostnogo prava v Rossii," in *Opyti
i issledovaniia* (Petrograd, 1918), p. 244. When Kliuchevsky was asked to
review I. E. Engelman's book *Die Leibeigenschaft in Russland* (Dorpat,
1884), he complied with characteristic thoroughness by writing this eighty-
three-page monograph. It was not enough to show where Engelman had
gone astray; Kliuchevsky felt obliged to present a full and scholarly alternative explanation.
[62] Kliuchevsky, *Sochineniia*, 3: 327. See below, chapter 9.

peasant dependence on the landlord in order to guarantee the fiscal and police purposes of the state. Where is the evidence of a return to the state school?

As for the drift to neo-Kantianism, a similar test can be devised. "Eugene Onegin and His Predecessors" was written only two years after "The Origin of Serfdom." In addition to its intuitive methodology, it reveals Kliuchevsky's conviction that an aesthetic experience has the power to generate human aspirations. Onegin represented Kliuchevsky's "first textbook on life." "Reading Onegin," Kliuchevsky reminisced about his student days, "we learned for the first time to observe and to comprehend living events, to formulate our own unclear feelings, to gain an understanding of our disorganized impulses and aspirations." [63]

If the different conditions of men were caused by varied experiences, then Kliuchevsky could explain their interconnection only by attacking a problem large enough to encompass the full range of human activity. That he regarded this task with trepidation can best be seen in his reluctance to publish his lectures on Russian history for twenty years after he began to deliver them at Moscow University. "My general course," he confessed, "is a bargain between my scholarly conscience and a recognition of my obligations as a teacher." [64] The seriousness, care, and thoroughness with which Kliuchevsky prepared a lecture were legendary. One of his former students, V. A. Maklakov, has related the now familiar story of how Kliuchevsky demurred when asked by a group of students to deliver a lecture on the fifteenth anniversary of Nekrasov's death because he would have had only a month to prepare it. He then proceeded to hold the students spellbound for an hour in his study while he talked impromptu about Nekrasov.[65] On the twenty-fifth anniversary of his professorship at the Theological Academy he reflected upon the need to master completely "a historical moment," implying at least that his standards for

[63] Kliuchevsky, "Onegin," p. 68.
[64] Presniakov, "Kliuchevsky," p. 210.
[65] V. A. Maklakov, *Iz vospominanii* (New York, 1954), p. 191.

writing history were so high that neither he nor anyone else could propound a wholly satisfactory synthesis of Russian history.[66]

Time alone mocked the historian. But even more challenging was the problem of fitting together those "historical moments" into a larger period of time. What was to hold together a thousand years of Russian history? Would the unifying themes emerge naturally from the analyses in depth of a few selected topics? Kliuchevsky acknowledged this difficulty when he admitted that he was not altogether satisfied that the fourth period represented anything more than "an unbroken chain of centuries."[67] One factor held constant throughout—serfdom, which, in Kliuchevsky's words, "profoundly lowered the level of our sense of citizenship [and] . . . gave a distorted and deformed tendency to all Russian culture."[68] Yet the extent of political and cultural change over these two and a half centuries seriously weakens the cohesion of the scheme. Despite Kliuchevsky's original and lasting interpretation of the seventeenth century as a time of preparation for the Petrine reforms, he himself could not deny the profound differences between the nature of political and social life before and after Peter. Perhaps, as Kliuchevsky suggested, the real link in the fourth period was autobiographical, "the study of my own spiritual essence in so far as it is linked with the past of our society."[69] The fourth period was a time of great schism. The seventeenth century still retained a wholeness, a unity that aroused Kliuchevsky's sympathy without involving him in the sentimental idealization of the Slavophiles. It was not Peter's reforms that Kliuchevsky opposed, but his brutality in destroying traditions and customs that did not really stand in the way of change. Therefore, the Petrine era belonged to that deplorable category of "antihistorical moments of public consciousness." Ravaged by arbitrary force, society then gave birth to a misshapen child in the form of the eight-

[66] Presniakov, "Kliuchevsky," p. 210.
[67] Miliukov, "Kliuchevsky," pp. 194–95.
[68] *Ibid.*, p. 209.
[69] *Ibid.*, p. 205.

eenth-century *dvorianstvo* culture. With the liberation of the serfs Kliuchevsky saw the first signs of a reverse movement that might draw Russians together again. In his university teaching and in *A Course* Kliuchevsky sought to become an instrument of this reconciliation.

At times he despaired of the outcome: "This dynasty will not live out its political life, will die earlier," he confided to his diary in 1901–02. "Russia is threatened again by anarchy, a Time of Troubles." [70] His fears seemed to be borne out by the revolution of 1905. But the establishment of a parliament revived his hopes, and he appeared to sympathize with the program of the Kadet party under the leadership of his most famous student, P. N. Miliukov. But behind Kliuchevsky's attachment to historical gradualism stood the shadow of peasant Russia. In his characteristically sarcastic fashion he would twit his liberal friends by saying that he was further to the left than the European-style Kadets. Always lurking in his mind was the doubt whether the cultural gap that separated the people and the educated elite was closing fast enough, whether the state mechanism could adapt rapidly enough to the new demands made upon it and respond to the shifting class structure. Symbolically, the reconciliation he sought in Russian society he could not find in his own soul. To the end of his life he remained the blend of the poor priest's son and the learned university professor, reflecting the profound dualism that characterized tsarist Russia on the eve of war and revolution.

[70] Kireeva, *Kliuchevsky*, p. 220.

A COURSE IN
RUSSIAN
HISTORY

The Seventeenth Century

Chapter

I

The Crisis at the End of the Sixteenth Century

The forms of Russian political life that arose before the end of the sixteenth century were largely determined by the geographical distribution of the population. The Muscovite state was created by people of the Great Russian stock who had settled at the very center of the eastern European plain, at the heart of the river system in the region of the upper Volga. Under the rule of Ivan Kalita's successors, these people became consolidated as a nation. The Tsar of Muscovy reigned over the united Great Russian territories with the help of the Moscow aristocracy, composed of old boyar families of the city and former appanage princes and their nobles. The state was being organized more and more closely on the principle of compulsory duties distributed among the various social classes by the state. Peasant labor, which was the main productive power of the country, still remained legally free, although in fact a considerable part of the peasantry was already entangled in debts to the landowners, and was thus menaced with the loss of its legal freedom.

Beginning with the second decade of the seventeenth century, a series of innovations sharply distinguishes this period of Russian history from the preceding one. First of all, a new dynasty acceded to the throne of Muscovy and steadily widened its field of activity. The territory of the Muscovite state had once coincided with the lands occupied by the Great Russian tribe that originally settled there. Now it spread far beyond those limits until eventually it came to include the whole of the Russian plain right up to its geographical limits, and extended to nearly all parts occupied by the Russian population. The Russian state gradually brought under its control the Ukraine, White Russia, and finally New Russia, a province created by the Russian colonization of the southern steppes. Stretching from the shores of the White Sea and the Baltic down to the Black Sea and the Caspian, to the Ural and the Caucasian mountains, the Russian state territory crossed the Caucasian ridge and reached far to the south of it; in the east it extended beyond the Ural Mountains and the Caspian Sea.

At the same time an important change was taking place in the inner structure of the state. Hand in hand with the new dynasty came a new ruling class. The old aristocracy was gradually fading out, growing scarcer in numbers and poorer economically, and with its disappearance went political relations that in the old days, by force of custom, restrained the power of the tsars. Its place at the head of society was taken by a new class, the landed gentry, consisting of men who had done government service in the capital or in the provinces. Its diverse, heterogeneous mass engulfed the dwindling numbers of the old nobility. Meanwhile, the former basis of the state's political structure, the distribution of duties among the different social groups, became more firmly established, giving new emphasis to the divisions between social classes. Gradually this system gained more ground, and an increasing number of special duties was imposed as a new burden upon the various classes. In the course of this continual strain on the nation, the peasants' freedom of labor was finally wiped out: the landowners' peasants were made serfs, and this bondage became their new class obligation to the state.

The peasants' labor, restricted politically, was given wider scope economically; traditional agricultural work was now supplemented by industrial activity. Agriculture still remained the chief productive element in the state, but manufacturing industries that exploited the hitherto untouched natural resources of the country increased in importance for the national economy.

Such are the main innovations that come to light in the seventeenth century: a new dynasty, new territorial boundaries, a new social structure with a new ruling class, and new developments in the national economy. The interrelationships among these things seem perplexing. At first glance it is easy to detect in them two parallel currents: (1) In this period the territorial expansion of the state was inversely proportional to the people's freedom within it. (2) The political rights of the working classes were inversely proportional to the economic productivity of their labor; that is, the more productive labor was, the less free it became.

This relation between the national economy and the people's social position conflicts with our usual idea that the more productive the people's labor is, the freer it is. We are used to thinking that slave labor cannot be as efficient as free labor, and that an increase in labor efficiency cannot worsen the social status of the working classes.

This economic contradiction is further sharpened by the political one. In considering the psychology of nations as well as of individuals, we have come to think that an increase in the intensity and the extent of collective and individual activity creates both in the individual and in the group a sense of power, and that this leads to a desire for political liberty. This surmise, however, is not borne out by the effect that territorial expansion had upon the relations between the government and the people in Russia. As its territory expanded and the nation's external might increased, the people's freedom was more and more curtailed. The strain upon the nation's resources sapped the strength of the people. The sweep of state authority grew mightier and mightier in its expanding territory, but the people's spirit of initiative and enterprise weakened. In its external successes and inner weakness the new Russia resembled a bird caught in a whirlwind and hurled aloft, regardless of the strength of its wings.

These two contradictions are closely connected with a third. We have just said that the old Moscow aristocracy was gradually absorbed by the gentry. The law of 1682, abolishing the law of hereditary precedence, sanctioned this absorption and formally equalized the position of the two classes with regard to government service. The hereditary aristocracy had been the ruling class. Abolition of the law of precedence was the first step toward a more democratic social order, and it might have been expected to lead to a democratic equalization of society. But while being thinned out numerically, the ruling class was fattening politically. The ennobled plebeians obtained personal and social rights that the old aristocracy had never had. Service estates became the gentry's property, and the peasants their serfs. Thus the democratization of the ruling class went hand in hand with increasing social inequality. Social inequality was intensified by the moral alienation of the ruling class from the masses.

Culture is said to bring people together, to level social distinctions, but in Russia it was not altogether so. The ever increasing contacts with western Europe brought us new ideas, customs, knowledge, a great deal of culture, but this influx glided along the upper layers of society and drifted sparsely to the bottom in the shape of partial reforms, for the most part cautious and sterile. Education became an upper-class monopoly, which common, unenlightened people could not share without endangering the state until they somehow became enlightened.

The three processes that have just been described are observable in all the main developments of the period. But although they are full of contradictions, they cannot be called anomalies, incompatible with the idea of historical laws. They were, rather, historical antinomies, exceptions to the usual course of history, results of peculiar local conditions. Having once arisen, they developed in accordance with the general laws of human existence, in the same way that an organism with a deranged nervous system functions in conformity with the general norms of organic life, although in consequence of its derangement, the results of its activity are abnormal.

The explanation of these antinomies of Russian history must be sought in the relationship that came to be established between the needs of the state and the nation's capacity to satisfy them. When a European state is faced with new and difficult problems, it tries to find among its people new means of dealing with the situation. It generally succeeds because people living and evolving normally, free to work and to think, can usually help the state without special strain by giving it some of the accumulated surplus of its work and thought, in the form of increased taxation and well-trained, skilled, and conscientious public workers. The whole point is that in such a nation, cultural work is carried on imperceptibly by the concerted efforts of individuals and groups independently of the state, and usually forestalls its needs. In Russia the reverse was the case. When, after the Time of Troubles, Michael Romanov became Tsar of devastated Russia, he appealed to the country through the Assembly of the Land (*Zemsky Sobor*) for help. But although the people's representatives who had elected him were his devoted and obedient subjects, they were neither fit to be good administrators nor rich enough to be of financial assistance to the state.

The necessity somehow to obtain both money and men who could manage it came to be recognized by thinking people, and they wondered how the countries of western Europe were able to find them in such abundance. Moscow merchants pointed out to the government that foreigners could be useful in providing a livelihood for poor Russians, by teaching them handicrafts and industries.

From that time onward the same thing happened over and over again. The state was constantly becoming involved in fresh difficulties. The government usually failed to foresee or forestall them, and sought in the community for men and ideas. Unable to find them, it reluctantly turned to the West, where it saw an old and complex cultural system that produced both men and ideas. It hastily imported craftsmen and scholars who could organize something similar to the Western model in Russia, and it hastily built factories and founded schools to which pupils and apprentices were forcibly driven. But the needs of the state could not wait for the conscripted pupils to master their textbooks. It had to be satisfied, so to speak, with raw material and compulsory sacrifices, which undermined natural prosperity and restricted the people's freedom. Demands of the state strained the nation's powers to the utmost and exhausted them instead of increasing them. Education introduced for government purposes, and not in response to a spontaneous desire for it, bore stunted, frost-bitten fruit. Sporadic efforts to implant enlightenment bred in the young generations merely boredom and the same aversion to learning as to conscription for the army. Popular education acquired the character of a government order for the supply of a requisite number of teen-agers to be taught according to a certain program. Expensive cadet schools for sons of gentry were established, along with engineering schools, "education societies" for young ladies and girls of humble origin, academies of arts, and gymnasiums on the German model. Tropical plants were grown in the gentry's hothouses, but in the course of two centuries not a single agricultural school or popular school for general education was founded.

For four or five generations the new Europeanized Russia was a Russia of the guards' barracks, government offices, and the gentry's country houses. Home-bred scions of the gentry, after a slight polishing up in a private school or an exotic *pension,* found their way from their country seats into the army or the civil service and came home as retired and uniformed brigadiers. Squeezing out of the population the requisite number of civil and military officials, the state instilled in the people's minds a crudely utilitarian view of learning as a means to promotion and to bribe taking; and at the same time it formed from the upper classes, especially from the gentry, a new caste of government servants severed from the people by hereditary and bureaucratic privileges and prejudices, and even more by their abuse of office.

The territorial expansion of Russia, overstraining and exhausting national resources, increased the power of the state without raising the intellectual level of the community. The government pushed new and lower-class elements into its administrative machine while making social inequalities and differences more acute. It complicated the nation's economic activities by introducing new industries that enriched not the people, but only individual employers and the Treasury, and at the same time it lowered the political status of the working classes. All these irregularities had one common source: the unnatural relation between the state's external policy and the internal development of the people. National energies did not increase fast enough to meet the challenges that the country's rapid expansion put before it. The people's spiritual growth did not keep pace with the material activities of the state. The state put on flesh and the people grew lean.

Probably in no other country was the influence of the state's international position upon its social and political structure so powerful as in Russia, and at no other time in Russian history was this so clear as during the seventeenth century.

Let us briefly survey the main tasks of Muscovy's foreign policy in the fifteenth and sixteenth centuries, their origin and connection with Russia's past.

In the first period of Russian history the scattered and heterogeneous elements of the population, under pressure from external foes, clung together in a certain kind of unity, and the Russian nation came into being.

In the second period this nation, subject to increasing blows from the Tatars and the Lithuanians, broke up into two branches, the Great Russian and the Ukrainian, each of which henceforth had its own special destiny. The Great Russian branch, in the forests of the upper Volga region, conserved and developed its powers in a patient struggle with inclement nature and external enemies. In time it succeeded in forming a fairly stable state well able to defend itself.

In the third period this state, having united the Great Russian people, set itself the task of reestablishing the political and national unity of the whole Russian land. To define that task and take the first steps toward achieving it was the main work of the old dynasty of the Muscovite tsars. In striving toward this aim the Muscovite state acquired an extraordinarily cumbersome political organization.

In the seventeenth century, after the territorial losses of the Time of Troubles, which we shall examine in a moment, the external struggle grew harder than ever, and so did the conditions of life within the country. Certain social ranks and small economic groups that had retained some freedom of labor and mobility were drafted into large social classes, in the interests of efficient service and of the Treasury, and burdened by the wars with Poland and Sweden. A large part of the village population became serfs.

This sequence of events and their interrelation are closely connected with the growth of political consciousness in Russian society; that is, with the development of ideas lying at the root of the events. By the end of the sixteenth century the Muscovite state was firmly established and had acquired the usual forms and means of political life. It had a supreme ruler, a legislature, central and local administration, a considerable and ever increasing number of officials, a division into classes, an army, and even a vague conception of popular representation. The only thing lacking was national debt. But institutions as such are mere forms; to be efficient they need content. Ideas are needed to help the officials to understand the purpose and meaning of the institutions. Finally, there must be certain norms and traditions to direct their work. All this cannot be had ready made; it is achieved by strenuous thought and by difficult, sometimes painful experience. By the time the old dynasty was coming to its end, Muscovite state institutions were in full working order, but the question is, were Muscovite statesmen ready to make them work in accordance with the aims of the state, for the good of the people?

Let us make a kind of estimate of the political consciousness of the nation, testing it by their interpretation of the idea of the state in its simplest form. That will enable us to see to what extent their conception of the necessary constituents of state order accorded with the true nature and purpose of the state. These essential constituents are: a supreme authority, the people, law, and public welfare. We know that rulers of the Muscovite state adopted in their titles and addresses several exalted definitions; these, however, were not political prerogatives, but rather, ceremonial ornaments or diplomatic exaggerations, such as "Tsar of All Russia." The everyday routine, the usual relations and interchange of ideas were still dominated by the old idea of appanage, which formed the real historical basis of the Muscovite rulers' power and implied that the state of Muscovy was the tsar's hereditary domain. New political ideas, forced upon the people by the course of events, were twisted by slow-moving minds to fit the old established pattern. The unification of Great Russia under Moscow gave rise to the idea of a national Russian state, but that idea, which meant the very opposite of hereditary possession, was expressed in the old way, and made people think of the Tsar of All Russia not as supreme ruler of the Russian people, but merely as the hereditary owner of the Russian land. "All Russian land from of old, from our ancestors' time, has been our domain," as Ivan III often said. Political thought did not keep pace with territorial acquisitions and dynastic claims, and thus allowed appanage-system prejudices to become political misconceptions. It ascribed to the sovereign two irreconcilable attributes: he was both ruler and owner of the country. This anomalous conception influenced the people's attitude to other aspects of state organization. The idea of the nation was not yet amalgamated in the popular mind with the idea of the state. The state was conceived of not as the people's union administered by sovereign

power, but as the tsar's property, which included, as a part
of its economic resources, the population settled within its
boundaries.

Accordingly, the idea of public welfare—the whole purpose
of the state—was subordinated to the dynastic interests of the
owner of the land, and even law had the character of administrative orders issued by the Kremlin estate office. Law regulated
the activities of the subordinate (mainly provincial) administrative organs and the manner in which various civic duties
were discharged by the inhabitants. Before the seventeenth
century we find in Muscovite legislation no enactments that
could be regarded as constitutional laws, defining the structure
and the rights of the sovereign power and the fundamental
rights and duties of the citizens. The meaning of the basic
elements of state order were therefore not as yet understood
by the people. Political forms molded in the course of history
by unconscious elemental laws of national life had not yet
been filled with appropriate content and were beyond the
political understanding of men who were acting within their
framework. The most interesting aspect of the period before
us is the way those forms come to life through ideas that
gradually develop in popular consciousness and constitute the
very soul of the political order, the way the skeleton of the
state, vivified and nourished by them, gradually becomes a
political organism. When we have seen these developments,
the antinomies that we noticed earlier will no longer appear
irrational, but will receive their historical explanation.

Such are the facts we have to investigate and the problems
we have to solve. We will observe the facts from the moment
the new dynasty ascends the throne of Muscovy. But before
that happened, the Muscovite state experienced a terrible upheaval that shook its very foundations. That upheaval gave the
first and very painful impetus to the formation of new ideas,
nonexistent in the political framework created by the old
dynasty.

The upheaval took place in the early years of the seventeenth century and is called by historians the Time of Troubles,

in Kotoshikhin's [1] words. Russians who had survived that trying period called it, especially the last years of it, "the great devastation of the Muscovite State." Signs of the Troubles appeared immediately after the death of the last tsar of the old dynasty, Feodor Ivanovich. They ended as soon as the people's representatives, assembled in Moscow at the beginning of 1613, elected to the throne the first tsar of the new dynasty, Michael Romanov. Accordingly, the name Time of Troubles may be applied to the fourteen to fifteen years between 1598 and 1613. A contemporary, Avraami Palitsyn, who was steward of the Troitsky Monastery and wrote the account of its siege by the Poles, also reckoned that the Troubles lasted fourteen years. Before starting on the study of the seventeenth century, we must consider the origins and the significance of that upheaval. How did these Troubles, or this "Moscow Tragedy," as foreigners called it, begin? Here is the plot of the tragedy.

Some two and a half years before his death in 1581 the "Terrible Tsar," Ivan Vasilievich, in one of his bad moments, which occurred rather frequently at that time, gave a beating to his pregnant daughter-in-law because when he came into her room he found her too scantily clad. The Jesuit Anthony Possevin, who arrived in Moscow three months after the event, when the memory of it was still fresh, said that she was *simplici veste induta*. Her husband, Tsarevich Ivan, heir to the throne, stood up for his insulted wife, and his father, in a fit of rage, struck him dead with an unfortunately effective blow of his iron staff. The Tsar went almost out of his mind with grief for his son. He would jump out of bed at night with a heartrending wail; he wanted to abdicate and become a monk. Anyway, owing to this unhappy accident, the Terrible Tsar was succeeded by his second son, Tsarevich Feodor.

An instructive case in the history of the old dynasty is presented by its last tsar, Feodor. Ivan Kalita and his descendants, the builders of the Muscovite state, were noted for their

[1] Grigori Kotoshikhin, who died in 1667, was a Russian diplomat who fled to Sweden and there wrote *On Russia in the Reign of Alexei Mikhailovich*, a sharp critique of Russia's backwardness. [Editor's note.]

remarkable ability to secure their own advantage. Too great a concern for earthly things was a family failing. But in approaching its end, Kalita's stock suddenly shone with the light of complete detachment from things of this earth, and flickered away with Tsar Feodor Ivanovich. His contemporaries said that all his life he avoided worldly cares and vanities, thinking of heavenly things alone. The Polish ambassador Sapiegha described Feodor this way: "The Tsar is of small stature, rather thin, with a gentle, almost ingratiating voice and a simplehearted expression; he has but little intelligence or, indeed, as I have heard from others and observed myself, none at all, for while seated on his throne receiving the ambassadors he never ceased to smile, admiring his scepter or his orb." Another contemporary, Petreins, a Swede, also remarked that Tsar Feodor was by nature almost bereft of reason, found pleasure in spiritual matters only, and would run from one church to another to ring the bells and hear the liturgy. His father bitterly reproached him for this and said he was more like a sexton's son than a tsar's.

No doubt these reports are exaggerated and to some extent a caricature. Contemporary Russian thought, pious and respectful to the throne, saw in Feodor the familiar and beloved image of a special kind of sanctity. We know that in ancient Russia "foolishness for Christ's sake" had great significance and was highly honored. A "fool in Christ," a "blessed one," renounced all earthly goods, both material and spiritual comforts and attractions, honors, glory, his neighbors' respect and affection. He was a living challenge to all these goods and attractions. A homeless beggar, he wandered about the streets barefoot and in rags, behaving like one bereft of reason, saying unseemly things and ignoring polite conventions. He strove to make himself a laughingstock for the thoughtless, and mocked at worldly goods and the people who valued them. Such humility to the point of self-abasement was regarded by ancient Russia as a practical fulfillment of the lofty precept "Blessed are the poor in spirit, for theirs is the kingdom of heaven." The spiritual poverty of the "fools in Christ" was, so to speak, an expression of popular conscience, a living, personified denunciation of men's passions and vices. The blessed fool had many social privileges and enjoyed complete freedom of speech. The mighty of this world, the nobles and tsars, Tsar Ivan the Terrible himself, patiently listened to the bold, ironic, or abusive speeches of a saintly tramp and dared not lay a finger on him.

Tsar Feodor's Russian contemporaries made him into the likeness of the loved and well-known figure of a sainted fool. In their eyes he was a blessed innocent, one of those "poor in spirit" destined for the heavenly and not the earthly kingdom, whom the church lovingly included among its saints as a reproach to the Russians' unclean thoughts and sinful propensities. One of Feodor's contemporaries closely connected with the court, Prince I. M. Katyrev-Rostovsky, wrote of him: "He was endowed from birth with saintly foolishness and cared for nothing except salvation." Another contemporary says that in Tsar Feodor monkhood was perfectly intertwined with tsardom, and one was an ornament to the other. He was called "a sanctified tsar, predestined from above to holiness and a heavenly crown." In short, to use Karamzin's [2] phrase, Tsar Feodor would have been more at home in a monk's cell or a hermit's cave than on the throne.

In our own day Feodor inspired a poet's imagination. Count Alexei Tolstoy [3] devoted to him the second part of his dramatic trilogy in verse. In it the image of Tsar Feodor is very close to its ancient Russian prototype. The poet obviously drew the portrait of the saintly tsar from the iconographic descriptions of him in the chronicles. But whereas Feodor's contemporaries were chiefly impressed by his touching piety, Alexei Tolstoy brings out his moral sensitiveness and shows him as an "inspired simpleton" who by the mysterious light of intuition could understand things incomprehensible to the cleverest minds. It grieved him to hear of factional dissensions, of the hostility between Boris Godunov's and Prince Shuisky's supporters. He wanted to see the day when all would be supporters

[2] Russian writer and historian (1766–1826). [Translator's note.]
[3] Poet and novelist (1817–75). [Translator's note.]

of Russia only; he wanted to reconcile the enemies. When
Godunov doubts the possibility of such universal reconciliation,
Feodor answers him with much feeling:

> . . . no, no!
> You do not understand these things, Boris!
> Look after state affairs as you think fit,
> You're good at it—but here my grasp is better,
> Here knowledge of men's hearts is required.

In another passage he says to Godunov:

> I am no tsar! In the affairs of state
> It's easy to deceive or to confuse me.
> But there's a thing I cannot be deceived in:
> If I must choose between white and black
> I'll choose aright—I will make no mistake.

One must not lose sight of the actual background of pious
or poetical presentations of historical figures given by their contemporaries or by later writers. Tsarevich Feodor grew up in
the Alexandrovskaia Sloboda, among the horrors of the vile
Oprichnina.[4] Early in the morning his father, abbot of the
burlesque Sloboda monastery, used to send him to the belfry
to ring for matins. The health of his mother, Anastasiia Ro-
manova, was failing by the time he was born, and, a weakling

[4] The word *oprichnina*, originally applied during the appanage period to
certain areas set apart for special purposes, was used by Ivan IV to designate
his private domain and government. The Oprichnina was both an institution
and a group of noncontiguous territories, a state within a state. By means
of the Oprichnina Ivan broke up the power of the old boyars and distributed their lands and positions among his tough, loyal followers, known
as Oprichniks. Eventually numbering 6,000, the Oprichniks had a free hand
to terrorize, torture, and kill wherever Ivan saw signs of treason—and he
saw them everywhere. They formed an elite corps with semimystical overtones, wore special black uniforms and rode black horses with black trap-
pings, and were responsible for monstrous outrages not only among the old
boyar families, but among the entire population. Ivan picked 300 of them
to play monks to his abbot at his palace near Alexandrov, which he turned
into a parody of a monastery, complete with compliant or terrorized "nuns"
and torture chambers. Here Ivan himself participated in the same kind of
orgies of sex and violence that the rest of the Oprichniks were enjoying in
the towns and countryside. It was the Oprichnina more than anything else
that caused Ivan to be called "the Terrible." [Editor's note.]

from birth, he grew up motherless in the hideous surroundings of the Oprichnina. A pale, undersized youth, inclined to dropsy, he walked with the slow, uneven tread of an old man because of a premature weakness of the legs. That was how the English ambassador Fletcher described him when Feodor was in his thirty-second year. In the person of Tsar Feodor the dynasty was visibly dying out. He perpetually smiled, but there was no life in that melancholy smile, which seemed to beg for mercy. It was his defense against his father's capricious anger. The deliberately pitiful expression became in time, through habit, and especially after his elder brother's terrible death, an automatic, involuntary grimace. Under his father's tyrannical rule he lost his own will and preserved forever the studied expression of servile obedience. When he became Tsar he looked for someone to guide him. His clever brother-in-law cautiously stepped into the place of his formidable father.

On his deathbed Tsar Ivan solemnly acknowledged that his "humility-laden" successor was not fit to reign and appointed as a help to him a special committee, a kind of regency, consisting of several noblemen closely connected with the court. For the first months after Ivan the Terrible's death Nikita Romanovich Iuriev, Feodor's maternal uncle, had most influence among the regents, but soon his illness and death opened the way to power to another regent, Boris Godunov, the Tsar's brother-in-law. Taking advantage of Feodor's temperament and the support of the Tsaritsa, his sister, he gradually pushed back the other regents and began to rule the state himself in Feodor's name. To say that he was the prime minister would not be accurate. He was more like a dictator. In Kotoshikhin's words, "The Tsar made him the ruler of the state in all things, devoting himself wholly to humility and prayer"; Boris' influence over Feodor was that great. According to Prince Katyrev-Rostovsky, he acquired such power "that the Tsar himself had to obey him in everything." He had regal honor paid to him, received foreign ambassadors in his rooms with the majesty and splendor of a real potentate, and was honored by the people no less than the Tsar. He ruled wisely and cautiously,

and the fourteen years of Feodor's reign were for the nation
a time of rest from the violence and horrors of the Oprichnina.
"The Lord had mercy on His people," writes the same contemporary, "granted them a propitious time, and allowed the
Tsar to reign undisturbed and in peace, and all Orthodox Christians were comforted and lived in peace and quiet." A successful war with Sweden did not disturb a happy general
mood.

But anxious rumors began to spread in Moscow. Tsar Ivan
was survived by his youngest son, Dimitri, to whom he had
given, in accordance with the ancient custom of the Moscow
rulers, the city and district of Uglich as a small appanage. At
the very beginning of Feodor's reign the young Tsarevich and
his maternal uncles were sent away from Moscow to prevent
court intrigues and upheavals. It was said in Moscow that this
seven-year-old Dimitri, son of Ivan's fifth wife (the unmarried
ones don't count) and therefore a tsarevich of doubtful canonical validity,[5] would grow up to be exactly like Tsar Ivan
at his worst. It was also said that he was in much danger
from men who were close to the throne and had designs on
it should Tsar Feodor die childless, as seemed very probable.

As though in confirmation of these rumors, in 1591 news
spread through Moscow that Tsarevich Dimitri had been
murdered in broad daylight at Uglich. The murderers were
killed on the spot by indignant townsmen, so there was no one
left to be questioned and give evidence at the inquest. A commission sent to Uglich, headed by Prince Vasili Shuisky,
Godunov's secret enemy and rival, conducted the inquiry in-
effectively or in bad faith. It asked many questions about
trifles and forgot to investigate the most important matter,
failed to clear up contradictory statements, and made a complete muddle of the whole thing. It tried in the first place
to persuade itself and others that the Tsarevich was not mur-

---

[5] The church allowed no more than three marriages, and Ivan's fourth
wife was still alive (though dead to the world) in a nunnery. [Editor's
note.]

dered, but had killed himself in a fit of epilepsy, falling on a knife with which he and some other boys had been playing. Uglich citizens were therefore severely punished for having dealt in their own way with the supposed murderers. After receiving this report from the commission, Patriarch Job, a friend of Godunov, who had helped to raise him to the rank of patriarch a couple of years previously, publicly declared that the Tsarevich's death was an act of God. And there the matter rested for the time being.

In January 1598 Tsar Feodor died. There was no one left of Kalita's dynasty to occupy the vacant throne. People swore allegiance to the Tsar's widow, but she became a nun. The dynasty did not die a natural death.

The Zemsky Sobor (the Assembly of the Land), presided over by Patriarch Job, elected Boris Godunov as tsar. Boris ruled as wisely and cautiously from the throne as he did while standing beside it in the reign of Tsar Feodor. By birth he belonged to the upper nobility, but not to its highest circles. The Godunovs were the junior branch of an old and important noble family descended from Mirza Chet, who came to Moscow under Kalita in flight from the Tatar horde. The senior branch of the family, the Saburovs, occupied a prominent place among the Moscow nobility, but the Godunovs came to the fore much later, under Ivan the Terrible, and the Oprichnina seems to have been a great help to them. Boris acted as proxy father at one of Tsar Ivan's numerous weddings. Later he became son-in-law to Maliuta Skuratov-Belsky, the chief of the Oprichniks, and Tsarevich Feodor's marriage to Boris' sister Irina made his position at the court more secure than ever. We find no Godunovs in the Boyars' Council before the Oprichnina was instituted. They appear in it only in 1573, but after Tsar Ivan's death they come into it in great numbers and hold high offices. Boris himself was not included in the lists of the Oprichniks, and thus did not lower himself in the eyes of the populace, which looked upon them as moral outcasts.

Boris began his reign very successfully, even brilliantly, and his first actions as tsar met with general approval. Contemporary rhetoricians wrote in high-flown style that in both his domestic and his foreign policy "he exemplified a most commendable, wise, and prudent way of ruling the people." His mind was "exceeding wise and highly reasonable in all things." He was said to be "wonderful courteous in his speech, full of beneficent thoughts, and greatly concerned for his people's welfare." They spoke with enthusiasm about the Tsar's personal appearance and character, and wrote that "no one among his councilors could be likened unto him in splendor of countenance and powers of reasoning." The chroniclers observed with surprise, however, that he was the first Russian ruler who could neither read nor write, "having never had any book learning or been accustomed even to simple letters."

But while admitting that no one could be compared to him in goodness and intelligence, that he did much that was praiseworthy, was clearheaded, merciful, and charitable to the poor (but unskilled in the arts of war), they found certain failings in him. "Although he was full of virtues and might have resembled one of the kings of antiquity, those virtues were marred by envy and malice." He was accused of insatiable love of power and of being inclined to trust slanderers and to persecute the slandered without proper inquiry, "for which he suffered just retribution."

Knowing that he was not proficient in the arts of war and distrusting his generals, Boris adopted an indecisive, ambiguous foreign policy. He did not take advantage of the bitter hostility between Poland and Sweden, which would have enabled him, through an alliance with the Swedish king, to wrest Livonia from Poland. "His chief concern was to put things in order at home, and set to rights everything that the state needed," in the words of Avraami Palitsyn. And he observes that during the first two years of Boris' reign "Russia flourished and enjoyed every kind of blessing." The Tsar took great care of the poor and the destitute and showered favors upon them, but dealt harshly with evildoers; in this way he gained great popularity and "was beloved of all." He showed bold initiative in his domestic policy.

The idea that Boris was responsible for serfdom is one of Russia's historical fairy tales. The very reverse was the case. He was ready to introduce a measure that would have secured the peasants' freedom and welfare. He was, it seems, preparing a decree that was to define the peasants' duties toward the landowners and the taxes they had to pay. That was a measure which the Russian government did not venture to take until the emancipation of the serfs.

That was how Boris began his reign. But in spite of his long experience as a ruler, in spite of the favors he showered on all classes on coming to the throne, in spite of his gifts as administrator, which all admired, his popularity did not last long. Boris was one of those unfortunate people who both attract and repel others—attract by obvious brilliance of talent and intelligence, and repel by invisible but inwardly perceptible moral failings. He could call forth admiration and gratitude, but he did not inspire confidence. People always suspected him of duplicity and treachery, and thought him capable of anything. There is no doubt that the terrible experience of Ivan IV's reign left an indelible mark on Godunov. While Tsar Feodor was still living, many came to regard Boris as a man of high intelligence and practical ability, but as one who would stop at nothing, be undeterred by any moral consideration. In writing about Boris, careful and unbiased observers, such as the clerk Ivan Timofeev, author of interesting notes on the Time of Troubles, passed from stern condemnation to enthusiastic praise. They wondered at the source of all his good works. Was his goodness a gift of nature or the result of a strong will, which enabled him artfully to wear any mask he chose to adopt? This plebeian Tsar seemed to them an enigmatic mixture of good and evil, a gambler whose conscience was always trembling in the balance.

Taking such a view of him, people did not hesitate to spread the wildest rumors and suspicions about him. He was said to

have brought the Crimean Tatars to attack Moscow, to have
caused the deaths of the good Tsar Feodor and his baby
daughter, Fedosia, Boris' niece, and even to have poisoned his
own sister, Irina, Feodor's consort. The half-forgotten proxy
tsar of half the country, Simeon Bekbulatovich, appointed for
the job by Ivan the Terrible and gone blind in his old age,
was, it appears, blinded by Godunov, who also, by the way,
had set fire to Moscow after the murder of Tsarevich Dimitri
so as to distract public attention from the Uglich crime.

Boris became the favorite victim of every kind of political
slander. Who except Boris could have murdered Tsarevich
Dimitri? Such was the popular verdict, and this time there
was some ground for it. This rumor, fatal for Boris, spread
from mouth to mouth throughout the country. He was said
to have had a share in the sinister business. He was supposed
to have sent the murderers to the Tsarevich so as to clear his
own path to the throne. Contemporary chroniclers' accounts
of Boris' part in the affair were of course entirely based on
rumors and surmises. There was, to be sure, no direct evidence,
and there could have been none. In such cases men in power
can hide their traces, and they know how to do it. But in
the chroniclers' accounts there are none of the self-contradic-
tions and confusion in which the report of the Uglich inquiry
committee abounds. The chroniclers rightly understood Boris'
difficult position during Tsar Feodor's reign. It would naturally
incite him and his partisans to give a blow so as not to receive
one. Had Tsarevich Dimitri come to the throne, his relatives the
Nagoys would have shown no mercy to the Godunovs. Boris
knew very well from his own experience that men crawling to
the steps of the throne do not like to be magnanimous and
are no good at it.

The only thing to cast doubt on the chroniclers' accounts
is the reckless frankness that they ascribe to Boris. They do
not merely accuse him of taking a direct and active part
in the plot; they suggest that he actually took the initiative.
They mention unsuccessful attempts to poison the Tsarevich,

consultations with friends and relatives about some other way to destroy Dimitri, bad choice of the first batch of assassins, Boris' grief at the failure, Kleshnin's comforting him by promising to carry out his wish. One would have thought that a person accustomed to intrigue would have avoided all this unnecessary talk. There was no need to be so frank with Kleshnin, the leader in the Uglich murder conspiracy. He was in every way indebted to Boris and a master of his craft. A good hint, an impressive gesture would have been enough to make him understand. But in any case, it is hard to believe that the deed was done without Boris' knowledge. It is unlikely to have been arranged by some overzealous friend who tried to guess his secret thoughts and wanted to please him as well as to make his partisans' position secure.

Seven years passed under Boris' rule, seven years of unruffled calm. Time was gradually removing from him the stain of Uglich. But after Tsar Feodor's death suspicious rumors began to spread again. It was whispered that Boris had been elected to the throne unfairly, that having poisoned Tsar Feodor he obtained the crown by means of police trickery specially organized for this purpose. Agents, including monks from various monasteries, were supposed to have been sent to every part of Moscow and to other towns to incite the people to beg Boris to reign over them. The widowed Tsaritsa was said to have assiduously helped her brother, secretly bribing the officers of the *streltsy* regiment [6] with alluring promises and gifts of money. It was reported that in Moscow the police drove the people, under threat of heavy fines, to the Novodevichy monastery to beg the Tsaritsa, now a nun, to let her brother be tsar. Numerous policemen saw to it that this communal petition was offered with "tears and great wailing," and many people who had no tears at their command smeared their eyes with saliva so as to escape blows from the police. When the

[6] The hereditary military force commanded by gentry, garrisoned in the suburbs of Moscow and other towns, where they lived with their families and engaged in crafts and trade. It was abolished by Peter I. [Editor's note.]

Tsaritsa appeared at her cell window to see for herself if the people had really come weeping to her, at a given signal they all had to bow down to the ground, and the slow or the reluctant were prodded in the neck by the police; and on getting up, they all howled like wolves. Men almost ruptured themselves with frantic wailing, and went blue in the face with the strain. The noise was earsplitting. This went on and on. At last the Tsaritsa, touched by the sight of such devotion, blessed her brother's acceptance of the crown.

However exaggerated these accounts may be, they reflect the bitterness that Godunov and his supporters had inspired in the population. At last, in 1604, came the most terrible rumor of all. For some three years previously there had been whispers in Moscow about some unknown man who called himself Tsarevich Dimitri. Now it was said aloud that Godunov's minions at Uglich had made a mistake and killed the wrong child. The true Tsarevich was alive, and was advancing from Poland to regain his ancestral throne. These rumors befogged the Russian people's minds, and the Troubles began. Tsar Boris died in the spring of 1605, overwhelmed by the news of the Pretender's success. The Pretender was enthroned in Moscow, but soon afterward was assassinated.

That was how the Troubles began. As we have seen, it was set going by two events: the violent and mysterious extinction of the old dynasty and its artificial return to life in the person of the first pretender. The violent and enigmatic end of the dynasty gave the first impetus to the Troubles. In a monarchy, the extinction of a dynasty is of course a serious matter, but in no other country has it been followed by such disastrous consequences as in Russia. A dynasty dies out, another one is chosen in its place, and life goes on. Usually no false claimants to the throne appear, or if they do, no one takes much notice of them and they fade into obscurity. But in Russia the first False Dimitri set the fashion, and pretendership became a chronic disease of the state. To the end of the eighteenth century there was a pretender in almost every reign, and for lack of one in Peter the Great's time, popular rumor declared the Tsar himself to be a pretender.

Neither the extinction of the dynasty nor the appearance of a pretender could in themselves have caused the Troubles. There must have been other circumstances that gave those two events such a destructive force. The real causes are to be sought behind the superficial ones that called it forth.

Chapter

II

The Time of Troubles

The hidden causes of the Time of Troubles come to light when we consider the interconnections of the period's events and their gradual development. It was a distinct characteristic of the Troubles that all classes of the population took part in them, one after another, in accordance with the places they occupied at the time in the structure of Russian society and with their relative importance in the social scale. The aristocracy was at the top of the scale, and these people started the Troubles.

Tsar Boris ascended the throne lawfully, having been unanimously elected by the Zemsky Sobor (Assembly of the Land), and he might have become the founder of a new dynasty, because of both his personal gifts and his political achievements. But the boyars, who had suffered greatly under Ivan the Terrible, were not prepared now, under an elected tsar who was one of themselves, to let their political influence rest on mere custom, as under the old dynasty. They expected Boris to provide a securer basis for that influence; they expected him to limit his power by a formal declaration, kissing the cross and swearing allegiance to the state, in accordance with a charter submitted to him beforehand. This is stated in a document dating back to the period in question and preserved among the papers of Tatishchev, the eighteenth-century historian.

Boris acted with his usual duplicity. He well understood the boyars' secret expectations, but he wanted neither to yield nor to refuse outright. The whole comedy of obstinately refusing the offer of tsardom was simply a trick to help him avoid the conditions on which the offer was made. The boyars said nothing, expecting that Boris would himself speak to them about those conditions, but he kept silent and went on refusing sovereignty in the hope that the Zemsky Sobor would elect him without any reservations. Boris' silence won the day and he was elected tsar unconditionally. But his policy was a mistake, and he and his family paid cruelly for it.

He put his sovereign power on a totally false basis from the first. He ought to have made the most of being the people's chosen ruler, but instead he tried to link himself with the old dynasty by bogus testamentary dispositions. The Sobor's declaration boldly asserts that on his deathbed Tsar Ivan IV entrusted his son Feodor to Boris, and that he further said, "After Feodor's death, I entrust the tsardom also to you." As though Ivan could have foreseen that Dimitri would be assassinated and Feodor die childless! It was also stated that Tsar Feodor, dying, "passed on his crown to Boris." All these inventions were the fruit of Patriarch Job's friendly zeal; it was he who edited the Sobor's declaration. Boris was not the hereditary owner of the Muscovite state, but the people's chosen ruler, the first in a new succession of tsars with a new political significance. To avoid being ridiculous or hated, he should not have parodied the old dynasty and the customs and prejudices of the appanage period.

The foremost boyars, with the princes Shuisky at their head, were against Boris' election, fearing, as the chronicler puts it, that "he might persecute them and the people." Boris had to dispel these fears, and for a time, apparently, the high aristocracy expected him to do so. One of the supporters of Tsar

Vasili Shuisky, writing at his instigation, remarks that the great boyars descended from Riurik,[1] related to the former tsars of Muscovy and worthy of being their successors, did not want to elect one of themselves as sovereign, for they had already obtained greatness and renown under the former dynasty, not only in Russia, but in distant countries as well; so they left the matter to the will of the people. But their greatness and renown had to be safeguarded against tyranny, which has no respect for either, and security could be gained only by limiting the power of the elected tsar.

That was what the nobles were hoping for. Boris ought to have taken the initiative in the matter, and at the same time to have transformed the Zemsky Sobor from a group that met occasionally for a special purpose into a regular representative body. That idea was in the Moscow people's minds as early as Ivan the Terrible's time, and Boris himself demanded that a sobor be called to ensure his being elected by the whole people. By limiting his power, Boris would have pacified the hostile boyars and perhaps averted the disasters that befell him, his family, and Russia. He might have become the founder of a new dynasty. But "the artful trickster" did not have enough political insight, and he overreached himself. When the nobles saw that their hopes were disappointed, that the new Tsar was determined to rule as autocratically as Ivan the Terrible, they decided to act secretly against him. Boris' Russian contemporaries definitely attributed his misfortunes to the anger of all the dignitaries of state, "who were responsible for the many evils that befell him."

Conscious of the boyars' subdued discontent, Boris took measures to protect himself from their intrigues. He wove a complicated net of secret police supervision, in which the chief part was played by house serfs who informed against their masters and by thieves released from prison who flitted about the Moscow streets listening to what was being said about the Tsar and grabbed anyone who dropped an uncautious word.

---

[1] The legendary founder of the Russian state. [Translator's note.]

Denunciation and slander soon became a great public evil. People of all classes, even the clergy, informed against one another. Members of a family were afraid to speak freely among themselves. It was dangerous to utter the Tsar's name; a spy might seize the speaker and take him to the torture chamber. Denunciations led to official disfavor, torture, executions, destruction of homes. According to a contemporary's remark, "Under no former tsar was there such misery." Boris attacked with special venom an aristocratic circle headed by the Romanovs, Tsar Feodor's cousins, whom he regarded as his rivals and ill-wishers. Five sons of Nikita Romanov, their friends and relatives, with wives, children, sisters, and nephews, were banished to remote parts of the country. The eldest, the future Patriarch Filaret, and his wife were forced to take monastic vows.

At last Boris lost all common sense. He wanted to know people's private thoughts, to read their hearts and rule over their consciences. He dispatched everywhere a special form of prayer that had to be recited in every house at dinner when the health of the Tsar and his family was drunk. Reading this hypocritical and boastful prayer, one is filled with pity at the thought that any man, even a tsar, can so completely lose his power of judgment.

By adopting these measures Boris made himself hated. The aristocrats with their age-long traditions were lying low, confined to their city residences, country estates, or far-off prisons. Their place was taken by Godunov's obscure relatives and their associates, who had crept out of every cranny; this greedy band surrounded the throne and filled the court. Instead of a dynasty, there was a crowd of kinsmen headed by the unanimously elected ruler of Russia, who had degenerated into a mean-spirited tyrant and coward. He shut himself up in the palace, seldom appeared before the people, and did not personally accept petitions, as former tsars did. Suspicious of everyone, tortured by memories and fears, he showed that he was afraid, like a thief who expects to be caught at any minute, as a foreigner living in Moscow at the time aptly expressed it.

The idea of a pretender was probably hatched in the nest of

the boyars chiefly persecuted by Boris and headed by the
Romanovs. The Poles were blamed for producing the Pretender,
but although he was baked in a Polish oven, the dough was
mixed in Moscow. It was not for nothing that when Boris heard
of the False Dimitri, he said at once that it was the boyars'
doing, that they had put forward the Pretender.

The mysterious stranger who ascended the throne of Muscovy after Boris presents an interesting problem to historians.
His identity still remains an enigma, in spite of all efforts to
solve it. It has long been the prevalent opinion that, as Boris
himself believed, the False Dimitri was Iuri Otrepiev, whose
monastic name was Grigori, the son of a poor Galician landowner. In Moscow he was a bondsman of the Romanovs and
afterward of Prince Cherkassky. Then he took monastic vows.
He was made the Patriarch's copyist as a reward for his book
learning and for composing a eulogy to the Moscow saints,
and all of a sudden he began saying that he might be a tsar
someday. He would have been sent to some distant monastery
for life in punishment for this, but some influential people
helped him and he escaped to Lithuania at the very time when
the Romanov circle came to grief. The man who in Poland
called himself Tsarevich Dimitri confessed that his protector
was V. Shchelkatov, an important officeholder who was also
persecuted by Godunov. It is hard to say whether the first
pretender was this Grigori or some other person, although
that is less likely. What is of greater interest than the Pretender's
identity, however, are his personality and the part he played in
history.

The throne of the Moscow tsars had never had such an
occupant. A young man of less than middle height, he was
awkward in movement, with reddish hair, plain features, and
a melancholy and thoughtful expression. His exterior belied
his inner nature. He was highly gifted and had a quick mind,
which easily solved the most difficult questions before the
Boyars' Council. He was of a lively and even ardent temperament;
at moments of danger he displayed courage that bordered

on rashness, and he was easily carried away by his feelings. He was a fine speaker and had a good deal of all-round knowledge. He completely changed the ceremonial routine observed by the former tsars in daily life, and simplified the cumbersome and oppressive court etiquette. He did not conform to the sacrosanct Moscow traditions, did not sleep after dinner, did not go to the bathhouse, addressed people simply and courteously, all quite unlike a tsar. He proved himself from the first to be an active administrator, avoided cruelty, saw to everything himself, was present every day at the Boyars' Council, and personally trained the soldiers.

All this made him widely popular and inspired genuine affection for him among the people, although in Moscow some suspected him of being an impostor and openly denounced him. The best and most faithful of his servants, P. F. Basmanov, secretly admitted to foreigners on occasion that the Tsar was not the son of Ivan the Terrible, but that the people were loyal to him because they had sworn allegiance to him, and besides, no one else could be a better tsar than he. But the False Dimitri took a different view of himself. He behaved like a legitimate hereditary sovereign, completely certain of his royal descent. No one of those who knew him intimately ever noticed in him a shadow of doubt on that score. And he was convinced that the whole country took the same view of him.

When the Shuiskys began spreading rumors that he was a pretender, he submitted the case to the judgment of the country and called the Zemsky Sobor into session. This was the first assembly of a representative type, with members elected from lower ranks as well as from the aristocracy. They passed a sentence of death on the Shuiskys, but Dimitri commuted it to banishment, and soon allowed the exiles to return and reinstated them in their rank of boyar. A tsar who knew in his heart that he was an impostor and had stolen royal power would scarcely have ventured on so risky and trustful a course of action. Boris Godunov in a similar case would have been sure to deal with the culprits secretly in the torture chamber and afterward do away with them in prison. But how Dimitri came to look upon himself in this way remains both a historical and a psychological riddle.

Be that as it may, he did not remain on the throne, because he disappointed the aristocracy's expectations. He did not want to be a tool in the hands of the boyars; he acted too independently, worked out his own political plans—in foreign policy very bold and sweeping ones—and sought to raise all the Catholic states of Europe against the Turks, with Orthodox Russia at their head. He occasionally pointed out to his advisers in the Council that they had not seen anything, had not studied anything, and ought to go abroad for some education, but he did it politely, without giving offense. What vexed the great boyars most was the presence near the throne of the Tsar's lowborn relatives on his mother's side[2] and his predilection for foreigners, especially for Roman Catholics. In the Boyars' Council there were one prince Mstislavsky, two princes Shuisky, and one prince Golitsyn, and next to them sat five newly made boyars, nobodies like the Nagoys; and among the nobles of the second rank there were three former clerks! The boyars were even more indignant about the unruly and dissipated Poles with whom the new Tsar inundated Moscow, and the common people shared that feeling.

The Polish hetman Zolkiewski, who took an active part in Moscow affairs during the Time of Troubles, describes in his notes a small incident highly revealing of the state of affairs in Moscow. At the very beginning of 1606 Dimitri's envoy Bezobrazov went to Krakow to inform King Sigismund of the new Tsar's accession. Having delivered his message in proper fashion, Bezobrazov gave a wink to the chancellor as a sign that he would like to speak to him in private. He told his listener that Prince Shuisky and Prince Golitsyn had commissioned him to reproach the King for having given them as tsar a low-bred and frivolous man, cruel, dissolute, and a spendthrift, who was unworthy to occupy the Moscow throne and

---

[2] Ivan IV's fifth wife, Maria, came from a family of obscure country landowners, the Nagoys. [Translator's note.]

did not know the proper way to treat the boyars; that they couldn't think how to get rid of him; that they would rather have for tsar the King's son Prince Ladislas. It was obvious that the chief boyars in Moscow were hatching some plot against Dimitri, and were afraid that King Sigismund might stand up for his nominee.

Dimitri's habits and occasional pranks, especially his casual attitude toward rites and ceremonies, his foreign policy, and some of his other actions and orders, displeased people in various strata of Moscow society and brought much censure upon him. Outside the capital, however, his popularity among the masses did not noticeably decline. The chief cause of his downfall lay elsewhere. It was expressed by the ringleader of the boyars' plot, Prince Vasili Shuisky. At the conspirators' meeting on the eve of the mutiny he candidly declared that he had acknowledged Dimitri solely in order to get rid of Godunov. The boyars needed a pretender so as to depose Godunov, and then they intended to depose their pretender so as to clear the path to the throne for a member of their own set.

This they did, dividing the job between them. The Romanov clique did the first part of it, and the titled circle, headed by Vasili Shuisky, did the second. Both circles regarded the Pretender as their own dressed-up doll, to be kept on the throne for a time and then tossed away when they were through with him. The conspirators did not hope to succeed in their plan without deception, however. The people complained of the Pretender chiefly on account of the Poles, but the boyars did not venture to raise the rebellion against him and the Poles together, and so they divided the two. On May 17, 1606, they led the people to the Kremlin, shouting that the Poles were attacking the boyars and the Tsar. Their purpose was to surround Dimitri under the pretext of defending him and then to kill him.

With the Pretender gone, Vasili Shuisky, the Plotter Tsar, ascended the throne. He was fifty-four years old, purblind, of small stature and unprepossessing appearance, shrewd, cunning

rather than intelligent, an inveterate liar and intriguer, always
ready to listen to infomers, and in great fear of witchcraft.
He had weathered many a storm and would have died on the
scaffold but for the mercy shown him by the Pretender, against
whom he was secretly plotting at the time. He began his
reign by issuing a number of manifestos, broadcast throughout
the country, and each of them contained at least one falsehood.
Thus, in the declaration about taking the oath on his accession
to the throne, he wrote that "it was his good pleasure to kiss
the cross in token that he would not put anyone to death
without first, in council with his boyars, passing true judgment
on the man." But in fact he said something very different when
kissing the cross.

In another manifesto, written in the name of the boyars
and men of all ranks, we read that "as soon as Grishka Otrepiev
was deposed, church dignitaries, boyars, and all sorts and conditions of men were called to choose a tsar "by the whole state
of Muscovy," and they chose Prince Vasili Ivanovich as autocrat
of all Russia. The manifesto clearly speaks of the Tsar's election
by the Zemsky Sobor, but there was no such election. True,
after the Pretender's downfall the boyars did think of summoning townspeople of all ranks to Moscow from all over the
country so as "to choose, by agreement, a tsar who would be
acceptable to all." But Shuisky was afraid of provincial electors,
and it was on his advice that the Zemsky Sobor was dispensed
with. He was acknowledged tsar privately by a few supporters
among the boyars of highest title, and his name was called
out in Red Square [3] by a crowd of Moscow citizens whom he
had set against the Pretender and the Poles. The chronicler
remarks that many people in Moscow knew nothing of what
was happening.

In the third manifesto, issued in his own name, the new
Tsar did not scruple to use a false or forged statement by the
Poles, alleging the Pretender's intention to kill all the boyars

[3] In Russian the same word is used for both "red" and "beautiful." The
name of Red Square was in use long before the Communists came to power
and has no political connotation. [Translator's note.]

and force all Orthodox communicants to adopt the Lutheran
or the Roman faith.

Nevertheless, the accession of Vasili Shuisky is epoch making
in Russia's political history. On mounting the throne he limited
his autocratic power, and in an official document sent to all
the provinces he defined the limitations that he swore, kissing
the cross, to observe faithfully. The document is excessively com-
pressed and vague. It gives the impression of a hastily written
rough draft. At the end of it the Tsar gives all Orthodox Christians a sworn promise of a general character: "to judge them by
true and fair judgment, not arbitrarily, but according to law, and
not at his own discretion." In the text this promise is expounded
more fully. It is the Tsar's solemn duty to consult his boyars
(that is, the duma or Council) when dealing with crimes punishable by death and confiscation of property, and to renounce the
right of confiscating the property of the culprit's family if they
took no part in his crime. Tsar Vasili goes on to say that he
will not listen to false denunciations but will try by every
means to find out the truth, confront the witnesses with the
accused, and punish false informers according to the magnitude
of the charge brought by them against the innocent. This
seems to refer to lesser crimes, dealt with by the Tsar without
the Boyars' Council. The conception of a "fair trial" is defined
more clearly. Thus the statement apparently distinguishes between two kinds of supreme court: trial by the Tsar with
the Boyars' Council, and trial by the Tsar alone. The statement ends with a special pledge by the Tsar "not to lay his ban
on anyone without cause." The ban—the Tsar's disfavor—fell
on those of his officers with whom for some reason he was
dissatisfied. The penalty was proportionate to the person's guilt
and the Tsar's displeasure. It might mean a demotion in the
service, temporary exile from the court (from "the sovereign's
bright eyes"), a lower rank of office, even the loss of a country
estate or town house. In such cases the sovereign used not
his judicial but his disciplinary power in the interests of public
order and efficiency. As an expression of the master's sovereign
will, the ban had no need of legal justification, and since the

old Muscovite standards of humaneness were very low, it sometimes took a savage and purely arbitrary form, and instead of
being a disciplinary measure became a punishment for a criminal
offense. Under Ivan the Terrible, mere doubt of a man's devotion
to his official duties was enough to bring the suspect to the
block. Tsar Vasili gave a solemn vow, which of course he did
not fulfill, to impose a ban only if there was just cause for it,
and to establish a special disciplinary procedure for investigating
alleged misdeeds.

The statement was obviously very limited in scope. The
obligations undertaken by Tsar Vasili were solely intended to
guarantee his subjects' personal and financial security from
arbitrary action by the sovereign, and had no direct bearing
upon the constitution. They did not change or even define
more closely the relations between the Tsar and the chief
governmental institutions, or their respective competence and
significance. The power of the Tsar was limited by the Boyars'
Council as before, but this limitation was binding on him solely
in judicial cases, in dealing with particular individuals.

The origin of the sworn statement, however, is more complex than its content. Behind the scenes it had a history of its
own. The chronicler records that as soon as Shuisky was proclaimed Tsar, he went to Uspensky Cathedral and announced
there, as had never been done in the Muscovite state before,
"I kiss the cross and swear to the *whole country* not to do
any hurt to anyone without the Sobor's consent." The boyars
and men of other ranks advised the Tsar that "he must not
take such an oath, for that was not the custom in Muscovy;
but he would not listen to anyone."

Vasili Shuisky's action evidently seemed to the boyars a
revolutionary prank. The Tsar was offering to share his
sovereign judicial functions not with the Boyars' Council, which
had always helped the tsars to dispense justice and administer
public affairs, but with the Zemsky Sobor, a recent institution,
occasionally called together to discuss some special problem
in the life of the state. Shuisky's action seemed to the boyars
a whim, an unheard-of novelty, an attempt to replace the

Council by the Sobor, to shift the political center of gravity from the aristocracy to the people's representatives. The Tsar who had been afraid to consult the Sobor on his claim to the throne was now venturing to ask its advice in ruling the country!

But Shuisky knew what he was doing. On the eve of the rising against the Pretender he promised his fellow conspirators to rule "by general agreement." Thrust upon the country by a clique of great nobles, he was a party man, a "boyars' tsar," bound to depend upon them. He naturally sought support among the people for his irregular tsardom, and hoped to find in the Sobor a counterbalance to the Boyars' Council. Promising on oath to the whole country not to punish anyone without the consent of the Sobor, he reckoned to escape the boyars' tutelage, to become the people's Tsar, and to limit his power by an institution unaccustomed to that role—that is, to exercise his power unhampered.

In its published form the sworn statement was the result of a compromise between the sovereign and the boyars. According to the preliminary unpublished agreement, the Tsar shared his power with them in all matters of legislation, administration, and jurisdiction. Having won the case for their Council versus the Sobor, the boyars did not insist on publishing all the concessions they had compelled the Tsar to make. Indeed, it would have been unwise of them to publicize how thoroughly they had plucked their old cock. The sworn statement emphasized only the significance of the Boyars' Council as the Tsar's collaborators in the supreme court. That was all the foremost boyars wanted at the time. As a ruling class they had shared power with the sovereigns throughout the sixteenth century, but individual members of it had suffered a great deal from the tsars' tyranny under Ivan the Terrible and Boris Godunov. Now the boyars hastened to seize the opportunity of abolishing this tyranny and safeguarding private persons— that is, themselves—against the recurrence of past troubles by compelling the Tsar to let the Boyars' Council take part in political judicial trials. They were confident that administrative power would remain in their hands as before, on the strength of custom.

In spite of all its deficiencies, Tsar Vasili's sworn statement was a new, hitherto unheard-of thing in Muscovite constitutional practice. It was the first attempt to establish a political system in which the power of the sovereign was formally limited. A new element was introduced that completely altered the nature and meaning of that power. Not only did Tsar Vasili limit his autocracy, but he confirmed this limitation on oath, showing that he was a "sworn-in" ruler, as well as an elected one. The oath by its very nature negated the personal power of the tsars based on the old appanage system idea of the sovereign as the owner of the country. The master of the house does not swear loyalty to his servants and tenants.

At the same time Tsar Vasili renounced three prerogatives in which the personal power of the tsars found its clearest expression. These were (1) "ban without cause," the tsar's disfavor without sufficient reason and solely at his discretion; (2) confiscation of property belonging to the criminal's family and relatives innocent of the crime (abrogation of this right did away with the ancient practice of making the clan collectively responsible for a political offense); (3) special trial, accompanied by torture, on mere denunciation, without confronting the accused with the informers, without the presence of witnesses and the introduction of evidence, and other procedures normally required by law. These prerogatives were an essential part of the Muscovite tsars' power. As Ivan III put it, "I shall give my realm to whomever I like." And his grandson, Ivan IV, said, "We are free to show favor to our servants and are free to put them to death." By swearing to renounce these privileges, Vasili Shuisky became a constitutional sovereign governing his country in accordance with law, instead of being master over slaves.

During the Time of Troubles the aristocracy did not act unanimously. It divided into two sections: the less illustrious members broke away from the foremost boyars and were joined by the Moscow gentry and government clerks. This second layer of the ruling class began to take an active part in the Troubles as soon as Vasili Shuisky ascended the throne. They worked out a different type of constitution, also limiting autocracy, but far wider in scope than Tsar Vasili's sworn statement. Here are the circumstances under which the draft of this constitution was composed:

Few people were content with Tsar Vasili. The chief reasons for this discontent were his irregular accession to the throne and his dependence upon the group of boyars who had elected him and now ordered him about as though he were a child, in the words of a contemporary. If the reigning tsar was unsatisfactory, a new pretender was needed. Pretendership was becoming in Russian political thought a stereotyped form in which all public discontent found expression.

Rumors that the first False Dimitri was still alive began to spread as soon as Vasili Shuisky was made tsar, when there was as yet no second False Dimitri in existence. In the name of that phantom the Seversk district and the towns beyond the Oka, led by the towns of Putivl, Tula, and Riazan, rose against Vasili as early as 1606. Defeated near Moscow by the Tsar's army, the rebels took refuge in Tula, and from there they sent a request to Mniszech,[4] the chief manufacturer of Russian pretenders, to send them any sort of man under the name of Tsarevich Dimitri. A second False Dimitri was found at last, and with the support of Polish, Lithuanian, and Cossack bands established himself in the summer of 1608 at the suburban village of Tushino, quite close to Moscow, thus "laying his thievish hand" on the very center of Muscovy, the region between the Oka and the Volga.

International relations further complicated affairs in Moscow. I have already mentioned the hostility that existed between Sweden and Poland, which arose when the elected king of Poland, Sigismund III, was robbed of his hereditary Swedish kingdom by his uncle, Charles IX. Since the Polish government was obviously though unofficially supporting the second

[4] Palatine of Sandomierz and father-in-law of the first False Dimitri. [Editor's note.]

pretender, Tsar Vasili appealed to King Charles IX for help against the Tushino rebels. Negotiations conducted by the Tsar's nephew, Prince Skopin-Shuisky, resulted in Sweden's sending a detachment to Russia under the command of General De la Gardie. In return, Tsar Vasili had to conclude a permanent alliance with Sweden against Poland and make other onerous concessions.

In answer to such a direct challenge, Sigismund broke off all relations with Moscow, and in the autumn of 1609 he besieged Smolensk. There were many Poles serving in the Tushino camp under the command of Prince Rozhinski, their hetman. The second pretender, despised and insulted by his Polish allies, managed to escape from their strict surveillance and, dressed as a peasant, slipped away to Kaluga in a dung cart. After that Rozhinski made an agreement with King Sigismund, who called him and his Polish bands to take part in the siege of Smolensk. The Russian supporters of the second pretender at Tushino had to follow their example. They sent envoys to Sigismund to discuss with him the election of his son Ladislas to the throne of Moscow. The delegation consisted of one nobleman (Michael Saltykov), several members of the Moscow gentry, and half a dozen prominent government clerks. There was not a single great name among them, but on the whole they were not of plebeian origin.

Stranded in the half-Russian, half-Polish rebel camp at Tushino through either personal ambition or the general political confusion, they took it upon themselves to represent the Muscovite state, the Russian nation. It was sheer presumption on their part, and they had no right whatever to expect that the country would recognize their fictitious claim to be its plenipotentiary envoys. But this does not deprive their action of historical significance. Close contacts with the Poles, their independent habits, and their love of freedom widened the political horizon of these Russian adventurers. As a condition for electing Sigismund's son to the Moscow throne, they demanded that he respect the Muscovite people's ancient rights and privileges, and give them new ones in addition. But while these contacts and the spectacle of Polish liberty were tempting to the Russians, they sharpened their sense of the danger which that liberty might bring to their own religious and national life. Saltykov wept as he spoke to the King about preserving Orthodoxy. The envoys' ambivalent attitude showed itself clearly in the way they tried to safeguard their fatherland from the foreign and non-Orthodox power whose help they were seeking.

The agreement concluded by Saltykov and his comrades with King Sigismund at Smolensk on February 4, 1610, was the most articulate expression of Russian political thought of the period. It stated the conditions on which the Tushino delegates agreed to recognize Sigismund's son, Prince Ladislas, as Tsar of Muscovy. This political document is a fairly well-worked-out plan for a constitution. In the first place, it safeguards the inviolability of the Russian Orthodox faith. Then it goes on to formulate the rights and privileges of the Muscovite people as a whole and of its various classes, and finally it outlines the organization of the supreme power of the state. The rights protecting the subjects' personal liberty against the tyranny of the authorities are stated in far more detail than in Tsar Vasili's sworn statement. Indeed, the very idea of personal rights, scarcely noticeable in Russian political thought before, is for the first time more or less definitely expressed in the agreement of February 4. Everyone has a right to a legal trial, and no one must be punished arbitrarily. Special stress is laid upon this; it is repeated again and again that punishment must not be inflicted on anyone without cause, but only after a fair trial "with all the boyars." Obviously, the habit of settling matters without judicial inquiry and proper trial was a very sore spot in the state organism, and a radical cure was essential.

According to the agreement as well as to Tsar Vasili's sworn statement, responsibility for a political crime was not to fall upon the culprit's innocent brothers, wife, and children, or to involve confiscation of property. Two other conditions relating to the citizens' personal rights are striking in their novelty: men of high rank should not be degraded without cause, and men of humble rank should receive promotion according to their merit; and everyone in Muscovy must be free to go to other Christian countries for the sake of study, and the Tsar must not punish them for it by confiscating their property. The agreement actually contained a suggestion of religious tolerance and freedom of conscience: the King and his son must not compel anyone to forsake the Orthodox Church and join the Roman, for faith is a divine gift, and it is not fitting to convert people by force or to persecute them for their faith; a Russian is free to hold the Russian faith, and a Pole the Polish.

In defining the rights of the different classes, the Tushino envoys showed less fairness and broadmindedness. The agreement made it binding on the Tsar to respect and extend, according to merit, the rights and privileges of the clergy, of clerks of the Council and other government officials, of the Moscow and the provincial gentry, and to some extent of tradespeople. But peasants were not to be allowed to migrate from Russia to Lithuania or vice versa, or to pass from one landowner to another within Russia. The serfs remained the property of their masters, and the sovereign was not to set them free.

The agreement established the structure of the supreme authority in the state. The Tsar must share his power with two institutions: the Zemsky Sobor and the Boyars' Council. Since the Boyars' Council formed an integral part of the Zemsky Sobor, the latter was described in the Moscow version of the agreement (of which something will be said later) as "the Council of the Boyars and of the whole country." The agreement drew, for the first time, a distinction between the political competence of the two institutions. The Zemsky Sobor was to have two functions. In the first place, it was to be responsible for making corrections in or additions to "judicial precedents" and to the law code (*sudebnik*), subject to the sovereign's approval. Precedent and the sudebnik, in conformity with which justice was dispensed in Muscovy, formed part of the constitution; the agreement therefore bestowed upon the Zemsky Sobor the power to modify the constitution. The Sobor was to have legislative initiative as well. If the Patriarch with his synod, the Boyars' Council, and men of all ranks appealed to the Tsar on matters unforeseen in the agreement, the Tsar was to decide on those matters together with the clergy, the boyars, and the whole Russian nation "after the custom of the Muscovite state."

The Boyars' Council had legislative power and, together with the sovereign, issued decrees relating to current affairs. Questions of taxation, of salaries paid to servicemen, and of their hereditary or service estates were to be settled by the Tsar with his boyars and higher civil servants. Without the Council's consent the Tsar was not to introduce new taxes or make any changes in the taxation fixed by former sovereigns. The Boyars' Council was also to have supreme judicial power. Apart from it the Tsar was not to punish, exile, degrade, or deprive anyone of honor. The agreement emphatically repeated that all such cases, as well as questions of succession to the property of persons who died childless, must be decided by the sovereign on the advice of the boyars and government secretaries, and "without them he must not decide anything about these matters."

The agreement of February 4, 1610, was the work of a party or a class—indeed, of several classes—consisting chiefly of the Moscow gentry and government clerks. But subsequent events imparted a wider significance to it. Tsar Vasili's nephew, Prince M. V. Skopin-Shuisky, aided by a Swedish detachment, cleared the northern towns of the Tushino bands and entered Moscow in March 1610. In the people's eyes the gifted young commander was a welcome successor to his old and childless uncle. But he died suddenly. The army sent by the Tsar against Sigismund, who was besieging Smolensk, was defeated by the Polish hetman Zolkiewski. Then the gentry, led by Zakhar Liapunov, deposed Tsar Vasili and compelled him to become a monk. Moscow swore allegiance to the Boyars' Council as a temporary government. The people had to choose between two claimants: Ladislas, whose accession was demanded by Zolkiewski, then advancing on Moscow, and the Tushino pretender, who was also approaching Moscow in the hope that the lower

classes of the capital would be on his side. Afraid of the
Tushino usurper, Moscow made an agreement with Zolkiewski
on the conditions that had been accepted by the King at
Smolensk.

But the treaty on the strength of which Moscow swore
allegiance to Ladislas on August 17, 1610, was not identical
with the agreement of February 4. Most of the articles in it
were fairly close to the original, but others were cut down
in length or expanded. Some were left out altogether, and
some new ones were added. These omissions and additions
were very significant. The foremost boyars left out the paragraph
about promoting men of humble birth according to merit, replacing it by a new condition: "that the Muscovite princely
and noble families should not suffer any detriment to their
honor or titles from foreigners coming into the country." They
also deleted the paragraph giving the Muscovite people the
right to travel to other Christian countries for the sake of
study. The Moscow aristocracy thought that this would be
too dangerous to the sacrosanct traditions at home. The ruling
upper class proved to be on a lower intellectual level than the
middle classes, which were its administrative instruments. This
is the usual fate of social groups that rise too high above the
realities of life.

The agreement of February 4, 1610, was a complete draft
of a constitutional monarchy. It established both the organization of the supreme power and the basic rights of the subjects.
At the same time it was highly conservative and jealously
guarded the old ways, the old traditions, the manner in which
things had always been done in the Muscovite state. People
cling to a written law when they feel that the customs by
which they have lived are slipping away from them. Saltykov
and his friends' were more keenly aware than the higher
aristocracy of the changes that were taking place. They had
suffered more than the latter from the arbitrary rule of those
in authority. Political upheavals and the conflicts with foreigners
that they had experienced impelled them to find some means
against those evils and helped to clarify and broaden their

ideas. They wanted to buttress the tottering ancient tradition by a written law that would give it new meaning.

Like the upper and the middle sections of the Moscow gentry, the provincial gentry too was drawn into the general turmoil. This became noticeable at the beginning of Vasili Shuisky's reign. The first to act were the gentry of the towns beyond the Oka and of the Seversk land—the southern districts bordering on the steppes. The troubles and dangers of life close to the steppes developed a martial and adventurous spirit in the local. population. The first to rise were the gentry of the towns of Putivl, Venev, Kashira, Tula, and Riazan. As early as 1606 the movement was started by Prince Shakhovskoy, the governor of the distant Putivl. Though titled, he was not of ancient lineage. His cause was taken up by the descendants of the Riazan boyars, now ordinary gentry, the Liapunovs, and the Sunbulovs.

A typical representative of this venturesome gentry of the steppes was Prokofi Liapunov, a Riazan landowner, a determined, arrogant, and impulsive man, who felt before others did which way the wind was blowing. But his hand set to work before his head had considered the matter. When Prince Skopin-Shuisky was on his way to Moscow, Liapunov greeted him as tsar while Tsar Vasili Shuisky was still reigning, and thus prejudiced the nephew's position at his uncle's court.

Prokofi's friend Sunbulov organized a Moscow uprising against the Tsar in 1609. The rebels shouted that the Tsar was a stupid and impious man, a drunkard and a lecher; that they were out to defend their own sort, the gentry, whom the Tsar and his accomplices, the foremost boyars, drowned and beat to death. Evidently this was a rising of the lower ranks of the gentry against the aristocracy. In July 1610 Prokofi's brother, Zakhar, and a crowd of his adherents deposed the Tsar, who had the clergy and the foremost boyars on his side.

It is not clear exactly what the political aspirations of the provincial gentry were. Together with the clergy, they helped to elect Boris Godunov to the throne. To spite the high aristocracy they zealously served him as a tsar who was not on

the side of the boyars, though one of them himself, and they
rose in a body against Vasili Shuisky, who was entirely a
"boyars' tsar." They wanted to enthrone Prince Skopin-Shuisky
and afterward Prince V. V. Golitsyn. There exists one document, known as the Instruction, which throws some light on
the political sympathies of this class.

Having sworn allegiance to Ladislas, the temporary government of boyars sent an embassy to Sigismund asking his son
to be tsar. For fear of the Moscow mob, which favored the
second pretender, the "Tushino thief," the temporary government brought Zolkiewski into the capital with his contingent,
but the second pretender's death at the end of 1610 allowed
everyone to go his own way, and there began a strong popular
reaction against the Poles. Towns sent written messages to
one another and united to clear the country of foreigners. The
first to act was, of course, Prokofi Liapunov with his Riazan
followers. But before the newly formed citizen army could
reach Moscow, the Poles had a fierce fight with the citizens and,
setting fire to the city (March 1611), shut themselves up in
the Kremlin and the inner town. The citizen army besieged
them, and elected a temporary government consisting of three
persons: two Cossack leaders, the princes Trubetskoy and Zarut-
sky, and the gentry's leader, Prokofi Liapunov. To guide these
three men, the Instruction was drawn up on June 30, 1611.

The bulk of the citizen army consisted of provincial servicemen, armed and provisioned out of the funds collected from
the urban and rural taxpayers. The Instruction was composed
in the servicemen's camps, but it claimed to be issued by
"the whole land," and states that the three leaders were also
chosen by "the whole land." Thus men of a particular class,
landowning gentry, posed as representatives of the people as
a whole. Political ideas are scarcely discernible in the Instruction, but class pretensions are sharply marked. The three chieftains, who were "to bring order into the land and see to all
civil and military matters," could not, according to the Instruction, do anything without the "whole land" council of the

camp, which was the chief administrative organ and claimed for itself a far greater competence than did the Zemsky Sobor in the agreement of February 4, 1610. The Instruction is chiefly concerned with safeguarding the interests of servicemen, regulating their positions as state servants and landowners. It speaks of estates, hereditary and service, but the only reference made to peasants and house serfs says that those who ran away or were taken out of the country during the Time of Troubles must be returned to their owners.

The citizen army had been encamped close to Moscow for two and a half months and had not yet done anything for the city's deliverance, but it had already assigned to itself the right to dispose of the country at its own discretion. When Liapunov quarreled with his allies the Cossacks, however, the gentry camp was unable to defend its leader and was easily dispersed by Cossack swords.

At last the common people, following and clinging to the provincial servicemen, took part in the general confusion—both those who paid taxes and those who did not. At first they were at one with the servicemen, but gradually they fell away from them and became as hostile to the gentry as to the aristocracy. The ringleader of the gentry's rising in south Russia, Prince Shakhovskoy, "who started all the bloodshed," as a contemporary chronicler says, took as his confederate a man of anything but gentle birth, one Bolotnikov. This Bolotnikov was a man of daring and experience, a former serf in a boyar household, who was taken prisoner by the Tatars, then enslaved by the Turks, and returned to Russia as an agent of the second pretender when that pretender had not yet materialized, but was, so to speak, only a gleam in the conspirators' eyes. Bolotnikov carried the movement started by the gentry to the lower layer of society, where he himself belonged. He recruited his bands among poor townsmen, homeless Cossacks, runaway peasants, and serfs—classes at the very bottom of the social scale—and set them against provincial governors, against the rich and all who had power. Supported by the mutinous gentry of the southern

districts, Bolotnikov with his motley bands made a victorious
march on Moscow, defeating Tsar Vasili's troops more than
once.

But then there came a split between the mutually hostile
social elements united under his banner for a moment through
a misunderstanding. Bolotnikov stopped at nothing. Proclamations from his camp were disseminated in Moscow, calling on
the serfs to kill their masters and take as a reward the masters'
wives and estates, and to slaughter and plunder tradespeople.
Thieves and rogues were promised noble rank, governorship,
honor, and wealth. When Prokofi Liapunov and other gentry
leaders grasped what sort of man they were dealing with and
the kind of people that made up his army, they abandoned
him, went over to Tsar Vasili's side, and helped his troops to
defeat Bolotnikov's rabble.

Bolotnikov perished, but his efforts found support everywhere. In all parts of the country peasants, house serfs, non-
Russian tribes in the Volga region—all the runaways, all the
downtrodden rose in support of this pretender. Their rising
prolonged the Time of Troubles and imparted a different
character to it. Until then it had been a political struggle, a
dispute about the form of government, about the state order.
But when the bottom layer of society asserted itself, the Troubles
became a social struggle, its object the extermination of the
upper classes by the lower. That was the only reason the proposal to elect as tsar Prince Ladislav, a Pole, had a measure
of success. Respectable people reluctantly agreed to accept the
Prince rather than let the throne be occupied by the "Tushino
thief," the candidate of the mob. Polish gentry announced in
the King's council at Smolensk in 1610 that in the Muscovite
state the common people had risen against the boyars and
held almost all the power in their hands. Social disunion was
sharply manifested everywhere. Every important town became
an arena of struggle between the upper and lower classes.
Everywhere, according to a contemporary's testimony, "good"
well-to-do citizens were saying that it would be better to
serve the Prince than be slaughtered by one's own house serfs

or suffer in perpetual thralldom to them; and bad people, together with the peasants, escaped to the Tushino pretender, expecting that he would deliver them from all their troubles.

Their political aspirations are by no means clear, and indeed it is not likely that they thought about the subject at all. They were looking not for any new political system, but simply for a way out of their difficult circumstances, for personal advantage and not for social security. House serfs rebelled in order to escape serfdom and become free Cossacks, peasants to escape duties that bound them to the landowners and to be free of obligations to the state, traders and towns-people to avoid paying taxes and to enter military or civil service. Bolotnikov called under his banner all who wanted to gain freedom, honors, and wealth. The true tsar of all those people was the "Tushino thief," who personified every kind of disorder and lawlessness in the eyes of respectable citizens.

Such was the sequence of events during the Time of Troubles. Let us consider its chief causes and immediate effects.

Chapter
III

The Causes
of Civil Disorder

To explain the causes of the general upheaval known as the Time of Troubles, we must examine the circumstances that gave rise to it and the conditions that prolonged it. We already know the circumstances that called it forth: the old dynasty's violent and enigmatic end, and the artificial attempts to bring it to life again by means of the pretenders. But both the events that gave impetus to the Troubles and its deep-rooted inner causes were effective solely because a favorable soil had been prepared for them by the diligent though shortsighted efforts of Tsar Ivan and Boris Godunov. That soil was the general mood of depression and dull bewilderment created by the blatant violence of Oprichnina and Godunov's sinister intrigues.

The causes of the upheaval are revealed by the course of events. The Troubles began with a purely accidental happening, the end of a dynasty. It constantly happens that a family dies out, either naturally or through violence, and in the case of private persons little notice is taken of it. But it is a different matter when a whole dynasty becomes extinct. At the end of the sixteenth century in Russia that event led to a political and social upheaval. First it was a struggle for the system of government, and then it became a feud between social classes. The conflict between political ideas was accompanied by strife between economic forces. Tsars who replaced one another in rapid succession and pretenders who strove after power were supported by different sections of the community. Each class sought a tsar after its own heart and put forward its own candidate for sovereignty. These tsars and candidates served simply as rallying points in the struggle between conflicting political ideas and different classes. The Time of Troubles was started by the aristocracy's intrigues against the arbitrary power of the new tsars. It was continued by the top layers of the Moscow military gentry, who opposed the oligarchic plans of the foremost nobles and sought political liberty for their own class. They were followed by the rank and file of the provincial gentry, who wanted to rule the country themselves. These, in their turn, attracted to their banners the lower classes, who rose against any state order for the sake of personal advantage—that is, in the name of anarchy. Each stage of the upheaval was accompanied by the intervention of Cossack and Polish bands, the dregs of the Muscovite and Polish settlers on the Don, the Dnieper, and the Vistula, glad of an opportunity for easy plunder in the distracted country.

At first the boyars tried to unite the dissolving community by holding before it the idea of a new political order, but that order did not suit the requirements of other classes. An attempt was then made to avert disaster by artificially reviving the defunct dynasty, which alone had kept mutual hostility at bay and apparently reconciled the irreconcilable interests of the different classes. Pretendership provided a solution. When that failed, having been tried twice, there was left no political bond, no political interest in the name of which the country could be saved from breaking up. But the country did not break up, although the state order tottered. When the political bonds fell apart, there remained the firm national and religious bonds, and it was these that saved the country. The Cossack and Polish bands were slowly but steadily bringing together the population they were ravaging, and at last they compelled the mutually hostile social elements to unite, not in the name of some particular political system, but in the name of national, religious, and civic security, menaced by the Cossacks and the Poles. The Troubles, nourished by the hostility between the various sections of the community, came to an end when the people as a whole rose to fight the outside forces, foreign and antinational, which had interfered in its domestic feud.

The course of events during the Time of Troubles clearly shows that the two facts that had chiefly contributed to it were pretendership and social discord. These facts indicate where the main causes of the Troubles must be sought. I have already had occasion to note (in Chapter I) one misconception in Muscovite political thought: the state as a national union cannot belong to anyone except the nation itself, but both the sovereign and the people of Muscovite Russia regarded it as the hereditary domain of the princely dynasty, whose possessions formed the nucleus of Muscovy. This hereditary-dynastic view of the state was, to my mind, one of the basic causes of the Troubles. The misconception was largely due to the inadequacy or immaturity of political ideas, which lagged far behind the development of the elemental forces of national life.

I repeat, the Muscovite state still preserved in the people's minds its original appanage significance as the Moscow sovereigns' manor, as the family property of Ivan Kalita's descendants, who founded it and for three centuries went on extending and strengthening it. But in fact it was already a union of the Great Russian people, and the idea of the Russian nation as a whole was already glimmering in their minds. But they had not yet risen to the conception of the nation as a political union. The actual union was, as before, held together by the will and the interests of the owner of the land. It should be added that the idea of the state as the sovereign's personal property was not a dynastic pretension of the Muscovite rulers, but simply part of the political thought of the time, inherited from the appanage period. The state had no other meaning than the hereditary domain of the sovereign, who belonged to a certain dynasty. If an average Muscovite citizen of the day were told that a sovereign's power was also a duty, an office, and that in governing his people a ruler served the state, the common welfare, such words would have seemed to him incoherent, a mere confusion of thought. So we can understand how the Muscovites of the time conceived of the sovereign's and the people's relation to the state. They thought that the Muscovite state in which they lived was the property of the sovereign, and not of the Muscovite or Russian people. The two ideas inseparable in their minds were those of the state and the sovereign of a particular dynasty, and not the ideas of the state and the nation. They could more easily imagine a sovereign without a nation than a state without a sovereign.

This view found a highly characteristic expression in the political life of Muscovy. When the relation between the people and the government is determined by the idea of public welfare, and the government fails to secure that welfare, the people become dissatisfied with their rulers and rise against them. When servants or lodgers, whose relation to the house owner is determined by a temporary agreement, find that they are not receiving the promised benefits, they leave the house. Subjects who rebel against their rulers do not leave the country, because they regard it as their own. Servants or lodgers discontented with the landlord do not stay in his house, because they do not regard it as belonging to them. The people of the Muscovite state behaved like dissatisfied servants or lodgers, and not like rebellious citizens. They often grumbled against the actions of the ruling authority, but under the old dynasty popular discontent never reached the point of rebellion against that authority. The Muscovite people developed a peculiar form of political protest. Those who could not put up with the existing order did not rise against it, but "wandered away," escaped from the country. It was as though the people of Muscovy felt themselves to be strangers in their own state, accidental, temporary occupiers of somebody else's house. They thought it permissible, when life became hard for them, to escape from the unsatisfactory house owner, but the idea of rebelling against him or of introducing a new regime in his house did not occur to them. The chief bond that held the Muscovite state together, therefore, was not the idea of public weal, but a ruler belonging to a certain dynasty, and order in the state was thought to be possible only under a sovereign of that particular dynasty. Therefore, when the dynasty became extinct and the state consequently belonged to no one, people lost their bearings, ceased to understand their position, and were reduced to anarchy. Indeed, it was as though they felt they had to be anarchists willy-nilly, that it was their sad but inevitable duty: there was no one left for them to obey, and so they had to be rebellious.

A new tsar had to be elected by the Zemsky Sobor. But such an election was not considered sufficient; it inspired doubts and anxiety. The declaration made by the Zemsky Sobor that elected Boris Godunov anticipated that some people would say about the electors, "Have nothing to do with them, because they made for themselves a tsar of their own," and it called such people "foolish and accursed." A highly popular pamphlet of 1611 tells how its author was given to understand, in a miraculous vision, that the Lord Himself would indicate who was to reign over the Russian land, and that if they elected a tsar of their own will "there would never be a tsar."

Throughout the Time of Troubles people could not accept the idea of an elected sovereign. They thought he would not be a real tsar, and that a true legitimate ruler could only be one born to reign—a hereditary prince, descended from Ivan Kalita. They tried to connect the elected tsars with Ivan Kalita's stock by every kind of device—legal fiction, genealogical surmise, rhetorical exaggeration. After Boris Godunov's election to the throne he was greeted by the clergy and the people as a "hereditary tsar," and congratulated on coming into his "patrimony." Vasili Shuisky, who had formally limited his sovereign power, signed himself in official documents as "autocrat of all Russia," just as the hereditary rulers of Muscovy had done.

While this rigid mentality prevailed in the leading circles, the masses must have regarded the enthronement of an elected tsar not as a sad political necessity, but almost as a violation of the laws of nature. To elect a tsar was, to their minds, as incongruous as to elect one's father or mother. That was why simple minds could not regard as a "true tsar" either Boris Godunov or Vasili Shuisky, and still less the Polish Prince Ladislas. In the people's eyes these were usurpers, while a mere phantom of a "born" tsar, in the person of a trickster of unknown origin, salved legitimist consciences and inspired confidence. The Troubles came to an end only when at last a tsar was found who was connected by kinship, even if indirectly, with the old dynasty. Michael Romanov was securely enthroned not because he was elected by the whole people, but rather because he was second cousin to the last tsar of the old dynasty. Doubt that popular election was a sufficient and legitimate source of sovereign power was one of the factors that helped prolong the Time of Troubles; and that doubt proceeded from the conviction, firmly rooted in the people's minds, that the only true source of sovereignty was hereditary dynastic succession. The nation's inability to grasp the idea of an elected tsar may be said to be one of the contributory causes of the Troubles.

I have pointed out that social discord was one of the most pronounced characteristics of the Time of Troubles. That discord was rooted in the fact that the Muscovite political order was based upon the citizen's obligation to the state—and this was another fundamental cause of the Troubles. An equitable political order presupposes as its essential condition a proper balance between the citizens' rights and obligations, personal or class. The Muscovite state in the sixteenth century exhibited a great variety of social and political relations dating back to earlier epochs. It contained neither free individuals fully possessed of personal rights nor free and autonomous classes. The community, however, was not a uniform mass, as in the Eastern despotic states, where general equality rested upon general absence of rights. It was differentiated into classes formed as early as the appanage period. At that period classes had a purely social significance; they represented differences in economic status, depending upon trade or occupation. Now they acquired a political character. Special state dues were imposed upon them, again according to the people's occupations.

There were as yet no classes in the later sense of the term, but rather different service groups, officially called "ranks." The state service required of them was not the same for all. One kind of service gave the classes upon which it was imposed a greater or lesser power of management and of issuing orders; another kind of service demanded of the classes subject to it simply compliance and obedience. It was the duty of one class to govern, of other classes to act as instruments of the government or to serve as soldiers; still others had various dues and taxes to pay. Unequal value attached to the several kinds of state service created inequality in the political and social positions of the various classes. The lower layers, on which the higher ones rested, carried the heaviest burden and naturally found it irksome. But even the highest ruling class, to which its state service gave the power to command others, had no legal guarantee of its political privileges. It ruled not by virtue of a right conferred upon it, but *de facto*, in accordance with ancient custom. It was its hereditary trade.

Muscovite legislation generally aimed, directly or indirectly, at determining and apportioning state dues. It did not formulate or secure anyone's rights, either personal or communal. The political status of persons and classes was determined solely by their obligations to the state. Clauses that suggested something like class privileges were simply private concessions intended to encourage efficient discharge of duties to the state. And even such concessions were made not to classes as a whole, but to separate local communities in recognition of special conditions. A certain urban or rural community might have its taxes reduced or be exempt from the jurisdiction of a particular court of law, but the need to define the communal rights of the urban or rural population in general found as yet no expression in the law codes. Even local corporate self-government with its elected authorities was based on the same principle of duty to the state and of responsibility, personal or collective, for carrying it out. Local self-government was an obedient tool of the central authority.

Rights are a safeguard of private interests, whether of individuals or of classes. Muscovite political order, determined by the principle of duty to the state, left little room for private interests, which had to be sacrificed to the demands of the central power. Consequently there was no proper balance between rights and duties, either personal or communal, in the Muscovite state. Living under constant menace from foreign enemies, the Russian people put up with the oppressive regime as best they could. They did not as yet sufficiently recognize the value of the individual, and public spirit was but little developed among them. The reign of Ivan the Terrible made them painfully aware of the main defect of the state order. The Tsar's arbitrary rule, his groundless executions, bannings, and confiscations, gave rise to murmurs against him not only among the upper classes, but among the common people as well; "misery and hatred of the Tsar" were widespread. Russian minds became dimly and timidly aware of the need to protect by law people's life and property from the arbitrary decisions of the powers that be.

But this need, accompanied by the general sense of the oppressiveness of the regime, could not have brought about the profound upheaval known as the Time of Troubles had it not been for the extinction of the dynasty that founded the state and was the cornerstone of the political edifice. When it came to an end, the knot that held together all the political relations was cut. Things that had been patiently endured, in obedience to the master's will, appeared intolerable now that the master was gone. In the notes of Ivan Timofeev, a government clerk, there is a picturesque parable of the childless widow of a rich and powerful man whose house is being plundered by his servants, "released from their slavish condition and indulging their self-will." The writer describes under the guise of the helpless widow the position of his native land, left without a "born" tsar and master.

Every class of the community, with its special needs and wishes, rose in revolt to improve its position. But the rising did not take the same form in the upper strata of society as in the lower. The upper classes tried, through legislation, to secure and widen their corporate rights, even at the expense of the lower classes, while the latter showed no sense of community, no desire to alleviate the lot of the broad mass of the working population or to obtain rights for it. Everyone was out for himself, hastening to escape from the irksome conditions created by the stern and unfair distribution of state dues, to find an easier way of life, or to snatch something from the well-to-do. Thoughtful contemporaries observed more than once that the most striking feature of the Time of Troubles was the lower classes' striving to force their way up and push down their superiors. Avraami Palitsyn, the steward of the Troitsky Monastery, wrote that at that time everyone strove to rise above his status: slaves wanted to be masters, serfs sought freedom, simple soldiers behaved like boyars; wise men were humbled by those upstarts and dared not say anything displeasing to them. The encounter between these two conflicting aspirations, one from the upper class and the other from the lower social stratum, inevitably led to fierce class hostility. That hostility was a derivative cause of the Troubles and resulted from the second of its two basic causes.

Contemporary observers put the blame for starting the breakup of social order on the upper classes, in particular on the new, nonhereditary bearers of the supreme power, though indeed Ivan the Terrible had set an encouraging example in this respect by instituting his Oprichnina. Bitterly reproaching Tsar Boris for his arrogant intention to change the state order and reform governmental methods, these observers accused him of raising to high rank men of low birth as a reward for informing against their betters. These men were not used to ministerial work, could not read and write properly, and could scarcely manage to sign an official document, slowly dragging across the paper a shaking hand that did not seem to belong to its owner. By doing this, Boris inspired hatred in the wellborn and experienced officials. The false tsars that followed him acted in the same way. The observers blamed them for it, and regretfully recalled the former "born" tsars, who knew what honors should be given to men of this or that noble family, and for what cause, and did not give promotion to the lowborn. Tsar Boris introduced still greater disorder into the community by encouraging servants to inform against their masters, and by turning out into the street crowds of boyars' house serfs whose masters fell under the Tsar's ban. Deprived of their homes, these men had to live by robbery. Tsar Vasili disseminated sedition right and left, issuing one ukase to attach the peasants to the land and another to restrain the owners' power over their serfs.

The upper classes zealously helped the government to increase social discord. According to Avraami Palitsyn, in Tsar Feodor's reign the foremost nobles, especially Godunov's relatives and supporters, developed a passion for enticing freemen to sell themselves into bondage to them, and used every kind of means to that end. But during three years of famine the owners, unwilling or unable to feed the household staff they had grabbed, turned them out without setting them legally free; and when the hungry bondsmen hired themselves out to other masters, the former owners prosecuted them as runaways.

Unwise behavior of the government and the people, encouraged, as it were, by nature itself, brought about such a disruption in social relations, such a social muddle, that after the end of the old dynasty it was difficult to put things right by the usual official methods. This second, social and political cause of the Troubles greatly helped to prolong them by intensifying the effects of the first cause, the dynastic one, which accounted for the success of the pretenders. Pretendership may therefore be said to be a subsidiary cause of the Troubles, derived from the two basic ones.

The question of how the idea of pretendership had arisen presents no psychological difficulty. The mystery surrounding

Tsarevich Dimitri's death gave rise to contradictory rumors, and the people's imagination chose the most desirable; and what they most desired was that the Tsarevich should prove to be alive and thus provide a happy deliverance from the painful uncertainty that clouded the future. They were disposed, as always happens in such cases, to believe that the evil design had failed, that Providence had once again stepped in to defend the right cause and prepared just retribution for the wrong-doers. The terrible fate of Boris and his family seemed to the perturbed people to be a striking revelation of eternal divine justice, and more than anything else helped the Pretender's success. Moral feeling was reinforced by political instinct, so inarticulate that the masses fully shared in it. Pretendership was the most convenient way of ending the struggle between irreconcilable interests that the extinction of the old dynasty had roused. Forcibly and mechanically it united under the habitual, even if fictitious, authority social elements of a tottering community among which there was no longer any free and organic unity.

Such, then, are the origins of the Time of Troubles. The soil for it was prepared by the harassed state of the people's minds, by a general sense of discontent with the reign of Ivan the Terrible—discontent that increased under Boris Godunov. The end of the dynasty and subsequent attempts to revive it in the persons of the pretenders provided a stimulus for the Troubles. Their basic causes were, first, the people's view of the old dynasty's relation to the Muscovite state and consequently their difficulty in grasping the idea of an elected tsar, and secondly, the political structure of the state, which created social discord by its heavy demands on the people and an inequitable distribution of state dues. The first cause gave rise to the need of reviving the extinct ruling line, and thus furthered the pretenders' success; the second transformed a dynastic squabble into social and political anarchy.

Other circumstances, too, helped to produce the Troubles: the methods and behavior of the rulers who succeeded Tsar Feodor; the boyars' striving for a constitutional monarchy,

which was out of keeping with the character of the Muscovite
sovereigns' power and with the people's view of it; the low
level of public morality as described by contemporary writers;
bans laid on the aristocracy by Boris Godunov; the plague
and famine during his reign; dissensions between different provinces and the Cossacks' intervention. All these things, however,
were only symptoms of the Troubles, conditions that furthered
it or consequences engendered by it, not the causes of it.

The Time of Troubles is the dividing line between two
periods of Russian history; it is connected with the past by its
causes, and with the era to come by its effects. An end was
put to the Troubles by the accession of the Tsar who founded
a new dynasty: that was the first major consequence of the
Troubles.

At the end of 1611 the Muscovite state appeared to be
completely demolished. The Poles held Smolensk, and a Polish
detachment had burned Moscow and was ensconced in the
Kremlin and the inner town. The Swedes occupied Novgorod
and proposed one of their princes as a candidate for the throne
of Moscow. The second False Dimitri was replaced by a third
one, Sidorka by name, in the city of Pskov. The first citizen
army of servicemen dispersed after Liapunov's death. The country was left without a government. The Boyars' Council, which
headed it after the dethronement of Vasili Shuisky, came to an
end when the Poles took the Kremlin with some of the boyars
in it, including the president, Prince Mstislavsky. The state lost
its center and began to disintegrate. Almost every town acted
on its own, busily exchanging messages with other towns. The
state was becoming a kind of formless, turbulent federation.

But at the end of 1611, when no political resources were
left, religious and national forces awakened and came to the
rescue of the disintegrating country. Proclamations issued from
the Troitsky Monastery by Archimandrite Dionisius and Avraami Palitsyn roused the citizens of Nizhni Novgorod, headed
by their elder, a butcher named Kuzma Minin. The call of
Nizhni Novgorod was answered by servicemen who had lost
their work and pay, and often their landed property as well,

and by urban gentry and others. Minin found a leader for them, Prince Dimitri Mikhailovich Pozharsky.

Thus a second citizen army was formed to fight the Poles. From the military point of view it was no better than the first, but it was well equipped, thanks to abundant supplies of money, generously contributed by the townspeople of Nizhni Novgorod and other cities. The citizen army was ready in about four months' time, and spent some six months moving toward Moscow, picking up on the way crowds of servicemen who begged to be taken on at soldiers' pay. A Cossack detachment commanded by Prince Trubetskoy, a remnant of the first citizen army, was encamped near Moscow. Men of the second citizen army feared the Cossacks more than they did the Poles, and in answer to Prince Trubetskoy's invitation they said they would on no account camp together with the Cossacks. But it soon became evident that without the Cossacks' help nothing could be done, and during the three months that the army spent close to Moscow it did nothing of importance.

In Prince Pozharsky's army there were more than forty commanders of good birth and repute in the service, but only two men did anything of real value, and those two were not military men: Avraami Palitsyn, the monk, and Kuzma Minin, the butcher. At Prince Pozharsky's request, Palitsyn persuaded the Cossacks at a decisive moment to support the servicemen, and Minin, having asked Prince Pozharsky for three or four companies, led them in a successful attack against Hetman Chodkiewicz' detachment, which was approaching the Kremlin with provisions for their starving compatriots. Minin's bold assault heartened the men of the citizen army, and with the Cossacks' help they forced Chodkiewicz to retreat.

In October 1612 the Cossacks took Kitay-Gorod (the inner town) by storm. But the citizen army could not bring itself to storm the Kremlin. The handful of Poles in possession of it were reduced by hunger to cannibalism, and finally surrendered voluntarily. At Volokolamsk Cossack chieftains, and not Muscovite generals, drove back King Sigismund, who was advancing toward Moscow to retrieve it for Poland, and forced him to return home. The citizen army of provincial gentry proved once more during the Time of Troubles its lack of efficiency in the work that was both its special calling and a duty imposed upon it by the state.

The leaders of the citizen and Cossack armies and the princes Pozharsky and Trubetskoy sent notices to every town in Muscovy, calling to the capital ecclesiastical authorities and representatives of all ranks to take part in a general council and elect a tsar. In January 1613 chosen representatives of the whole country began arriving in Moscow. It was unquestionably the first Zemsky Sobor in which men of all classes, including townspeople and country dwellers, took part. When all the delegates had gathered, a three-day fast was imposed so that the representatives of the Russian land might cleanse themselves of the sins of the Troubles before starting on their momentous task. When the fast was over, deliberations began.

The first question put to the Sobor, whether they should choose a tsar from among foreign princes, was answered in the negative. It was decided "not to choose for the state of Muscovy either the Polish or the Swedish prince, or anyone else of foreign faith or from non-Orthodox lands," and not to choose "Marinka's son." [1] This decision ruined the plans of Prince Ladislas' adherents. But it was not easy to choose one's own Russian-born sovereign. The more or less contemporary chronicles of the period give a somewhat gloomy picture of the Sobor's deliberations on the subject. There proved to be no unanimity. There was great agitation. Everyone wanted his own way, everyone supported his own choice; some proposed one candidate, others another, all were at variance. The delegates went over and over the possibilities, went through the names of the foremost noble families, but could not agree upon any one. They wasted quite a few days this way. Many great nobles and even commoners tried to bribe the electors, sending them presents and promising favors to come.

After Michael had been elected, a deputation from the Sobor went to ask his mother, a nun, to give her blessing to his

[1] The third pretender. [Editor's note.]

reign. When she said reproachfully that the Muscovite people "could no longer be trusted and had grown mean-spirited," they replied that now they had learned their lesson, had come to their senses and were all of one mind. But the intrigues, underhanded dealings, and dissensions in the Sobor do not bear out its delegates' bland assurances. The Sobor was divided into factions supporting different aristocratic candidates; according to later sources they included Princes Golitsyn, Mstislavsky, Vorotinsky, Trubetskoy, and Michael Romanov. It was said that even Prince Pozharsky, a man of modest character and equally modest lineage, aspired to the throne and spent a good deal of money trying to secure it. The candidate most suitable because of his personal gifts and aristocratic descent, Prince V. V. Golitsyn, was a prisoner of the Poles; Prince Mstislavsky refused to be a candidate; there was no one else to choose from. The Muscovite state emerged from the terrible Time of Troubles without any heroes. It had been rescued by good but mediocre people. Prince Pozharsky was no Boris Godunov, and Michael Romanov was no Skopin-Shuisky. For lack of outstanding personalities, the issue was being settled by intrigue and prejudice.

While the Sobor was split into factions and undecided whom to elect, it suddenly began to receive, in rapid succession, petitions from the gentry, from big merchants, from the towns of the Seversk district, and even from the Cossacks: elect Michael. And it was the Cossacks who settled the matter. Seeing the weakness of the citizen army, they behaved riotously in Moscow, which they had liberated, and did anything they liked, paying no heed to the temporary government of Trubetskoy, Pozharsky, and Minin. But in the matter of electing a tsar they showed themselves zealous patriots. They decisively opposed the idea of choosing a foreigner for the throne and sought a truly Russian candidate. They compared the claims of the second pretender's baby son and of Michael Romanov, whose father, Filaret, was made a metropolitan by the first pretender and a patriarch by the second in his Tushino camp. As the mainstay of the pretenders, the Cossacks naturally wanted to see on the Moscow throne either the son of their Tushino tsar or the son of their Tushino patriarch. The "Tushino thief's" son was not, however, proposed by them in earnest, but rather as a concession to the Cossack tradition, and when the Sobor rejected the proposal, the Cossacks did not insist on their candidate's claim.

There was nothing particularly remarkable about Michael Romanov. He was a boy of sixteen, and personally he could have had little claim to tsardom; and yet it was he who reconciled such hostile elements as the gentry and the Cossacks. This unexpected concord was reflected in the Sobor. Just when the struggle between the opposing factions was at its height, a serviceman from Galich, the supposed birthplace of the first pretender, presented to the Sobor a written statement saying that the nearest kinsman of the old Tsar was Michael Feodorovich Romanov, and that therefore he should be chosen as tsar. Many delegates were against Michael, although he had for some time been regarded as a candidate, and long ago Patriarch Hermogen had pointed to him as a desirable successor to Vasili Shuisky. Many were annoyed at the Galich serviceman's proposal. Angry voices were heard asking, "Who brought this writing? Where does it come from?"

At that moment a Don Cossack chieftain emerged from among the delegates, walked up to the table, and also deposited a "writing" on it.

"What writing have you given us, ataman?" Prince Pozharsky asked.

"About the born tsar, Michael Feodorovich," the chieftain answered.

He is supposed to have settled the matter. "Having read the ataman's writing, all agreed with it unanimously," says one of the chroniclers. Michael was elected tsar.

This, however, was only a preliminary election; it merely indicated the Sobor's candidate. Final decision was left to the country as a whole. Trustworthy men were secretly sent to all the towns to find out who in the people's opinion should be the sovereign of the Muscovite state. The people had, it appeared, been sufficiently prepared. The emissaries came back with the report that all the people, from first to last, had the same thought: "Michael Feodorovich Romanov is to be our sovereign, and we want no other!" This secret inquiry, perhaps including a certain amount of propaganda, was taken by the Sobor as a kind of plebiscite. The solemn day of "the Triumph of Orthodoxy"—the first Sunday in Lent, February 21, 1613— was fixed for the final election. Every rank submitted its own written opinion, and in all the writings the same name appeared—Michael Feodorovich. Then several members of the clergy and a nobleman were sent to Red Square, and almost before they had time to ask whom the people wanted as tsar, the multitude collected round the rostrum shouted, "Michael Feodorovich!"

The unanimous election of Michael had been prepared and supported at the Sobor and throughout the country by various auxiliary means: preliminary agitation, in which numerous kinsmen of the Romanovs took part; pressure from the Cossacks; secret inquiry among the people; the organized acclamation of the Moscow crowds in Red Square. But these electioneering devices proved successful because they found a response in the country's attitude to the Romanovs. Michael was raised to the throne not because of his personal or political popularity, but because of the popularity of the Romanov family, which was at that time loved better than any other among the Muscovite nobility.

The Romanovs were a recent offshoot of an ancient noble family, the Koshkins. Long ago, under Grand Prince Ivan Danilovich Kalita, a certain nobleman called by the Muscovites Andrei Ivanovich Kobyla moved to Moscow from "the Prussian land," as stated in his genealogy. He gained a prominent position at the Muscovite court. His fifth son, Feodor Koshka, was the progenitor of the "Koshkin line," as the chronicles put it. The Koshkins flourished at the Muscovite court in the fourteenth and fifteenth centuries. They were the only nontitled boyar family not submerged by the stream of new titled servants that flooded the Muscovite court in the middle of the fifteenth century. They managed to remain in the foremost ranks of nobility beside the princes Shuisky, Mstislavsky, and Vorotinsky.

At the beginning of the sixteenth century a prominent place at the court was held by Roman Iurievich Zakharin, a descendant of Koshkin's grandson Zakhary and the progenitor of the new branch of the family, the Romanovs. Roman's son Nikita was the brother of Tsaritsa Anastasiia [2] and the only Muscovite boyar of the period who was affectionately remembered by the people. His name is preserved in popular songs about Ivan the Terrible, and he is depicted in them as a good-natured mediator between the people and the wrathful tsar. The most distinguished of Nikita's six sons was the eldest, Feodor. He was very kindhearted, gracious in his manner, and elegant in appearance. He had an inquiring mind and a love of knowledge. Horsey, an Englishman who lived in Moscow at the time, says in his memoirs that this nobleman was eager to learn Latin, and at his request Horsey compiled a Latin grammar for him, writing Latin words in Russian letters.

The Romanovs' popularity, won by their personal character, was greatly increased by the persecution they suffered under the suspicious Godunov. Avraami Palitsyn numbers this persecution among the sins for which God visited the Troubles upon the Russian land. The Romanovs' hostility to Tsar Vasili and their connection with Tushino brought them the favor of the second pretender and popularity in the Cossack camp. The family's ambiguous behavior in the years of the Troubles had thus secured for Michael the support both of the countryside and of the Cossacks. But what helped him most at the Sobor election was the Romanovs' kinship with the old dynasty.

During the Time of Troubles the Russian people had been so often unfortunate in their choice of new tsars that now they felt the only safe thing to do was to elect someone connected, however remotely, with the former reigning house. They saw in Michael not the sovereign elected by the representative sobor, but a cousin of Tsar Feodor, a born hereditary tsar. A contemporary historian plainly says that Michael was asked to reign "because of the bond of kinship between royal offspring." It is

[2] The first wife of Tsar Ivan the Terrible. [Translator's note.]

significant that Avraami Palitsyn calls Michael "God's elect before his birth," and clerk Ivan Timofeev, in writing out an unbroken series of hereditary tsars, puts Michael directly after Feodor Ivanovich, ignoring Godunov, Shuisky, and all the pretenders. Tsar Michael himself in his proclamations usually called Ivan the Terrible his grandfather.[3]

It is hard to tell how far Michael's election was helped by the rumor that on his deathbed Tsar Feodor orally bequeathed the throne to his cousin Feodor Romanov (Filaret), Michael's father. But there was another consideration that must have favored Michael in the eyes of the boyars who directed the course of the election, a circumstance to which they could not have been indifferent. It is reported that F. I. Sheremetev wrote to Prince Golitsyn, who was in Poland: "Misha Romanov is young, his reason is immature, and he will suit us." Sheremetev knew, of course, that the throne would not deprive Misha of the capacity to grow, and that youth would not be his permanent condition. But his other characteristics seemed to promise that the nephew would be a replica of his uncle, resembling him in intellectual and physical weakness, so that he would be a kind, gentle tsar under whose rule there would be no repetition of the trials that the nobles had gone through in the reigns of Ivan the Terrible and Godunov. They wanted to elect not the most gifted candidate, but the most convenient. That was how the founder of the new dynasty came to the throne, putting an end to the Time of Troubles.

[3] A granduncle is called in Russian by the same word as a grandfather. [Translator's note.]

Chapter
IV

Political Reconstruction

Let us turn to the immediate consequences of the Time of Troubles, responsible for the political and moral environment in which the first tsar of the new dynasty had to act. The fourteen stormy years that the Muscovite state had gone through had left their traces. This became apparent at the very beginning of Michael's reign. The Time of Troubles brought about two great changes: In the first place, the old political tradition upon which the state order had been based in the sixteenth century was shattered; second, the hostile relations that now existed between Muscovy and its neighbors imposed a greater strain upon its national resources than it had ever known in the sixteenth century. These two changes gave rise to a number of new political ideas that gained possession of the people's minds, and also to a number of new political facts that formed the basic content of Russia's history in the seventeenth century. Let us examine both of them.

The Time of Troubles gave the people of Muscovy an abundant supply of political ideas, unknown to their fathers in the sixteenth century. It is a sad advantage of anxious times that, while depriving men of peace and contentment, they provide new conceptions and experiences. A storm turns the leaves on the trees the wrong side upward; similarly, times of unrest and confusion break down the façades and expose the back-yards, at the sight of which people accustomed to look at the face values of life begin to reflect that there is much they have never seen before. This is how political thought begins. The best school for it, though a severe one, is a national revolution. That is why political thought is, as a rule, most active during social upheavals and immediately after them.

The ideas that had enriched Russian minds during the Time of Troubles profoundly changed their old habitual attitude to the sovereign and the state. We already know what that attitude was. Muscovite people of the sixteenth century regarded their sovereign as the owner of the state territory rather than as the guardian of public weal, and thought of themselves as strangers and sojourners, dwelling on that territory by political accident. The sovereign's personal will was the only motive power in the life of the state, and his personal or dynastic interests were its only purpose. The person of the sovereign blotted out the state and the people. The Time of Troubles undermined this firmly established attitude. During those trying years the people were more than once called upon to choose their sovereign. Some years there was no sovereign at all, and the nation was left to its own resources.

From the very beginning of the seventeenth century Muscovite citizens found themselves in such situations and saw such things as would have seemed impossible, indeed unthinkable, in their fathers' day. They saw the downfall of tsars who were not supported by the people; they saw that the state left without a sovereign did not fall to pieces, but gathered its forces and chose a new one. It had never occurred to the people of the sixteenth century that such things could happen. In the old days it seemed inconceivable that the state could exist apart from the sovereign; he was its complete embodiment. During the Troubles, when at times there was no tsar at all, or no one knew who was tsar, the ideas that had once been inseparable began to fall apart. The words "the State of Muscovy" used in the documents of the Time of Troubles grew comprehensible as expressing not merely something conceivable, but something that existed as a fact—even without a tsar. The idea of the state as distinct from the person of the sovereign slowly dawned on Muscovite minds, and gradually merged with the idea of the nation. In official documents of the period the old formula "sovereign ruler, Tsar and Grand Prince of All Russia," is often replaced by the expression "the people of the Muscovite state."

We have seen how difficult it was for Russians to grasp the idea of an elected tsar. This was because it had not occurred to them that, in case of need, the will of the people could be a sufficient basis for lawful sovereignty; and the reason they failed to understand this was that they had never thought of the nation as a political power. All the tsar's subjects were regarded as his bondsmen, his serfs, or as orphans, homeless people without kin who lived on his land. What kind of political will can bondsmen or orphans have, and how can it be the source of the divinely ordained authority of God's anointed? The Time of Troubles for the first time profoundly disturbed this stagnant political attitude and made people painfully aware of how unprepared they were for dealing with the formidable tasks so suddenly thrust upon them by the elemental forces of national life. Left to itself, the community was willy-nilly learning to act consciously and independently, and there began to germinate in it the thought that the community, the people, were not strangers and sojourners in somebody else's land, and that the politically accidental element in the state was not the people, but the dynasty. In the course of the fifteen years that followed Tsar Feodor's death, four unsuccessful attempts had been made to found a new dynasty, and only the fifth proved successful.

The tsar's will was often supported, and sometimes replaced, by another political power—the will of the people. It found expression in the decisions of the Zemsky Sobor, in the Moscow crowds' proclamation of Vasili Shuisky as tsar, and in the conferences of delegates from different towns rising against the Tushino pretender and the Poles. Thanks to all this, the idea of the tsar as a landlord began to recede, or at any rate to combine in the people's minds with a politically new idea: the tsar as the people's elect. Thus a different relationship came to be recognized among the basic elements of state order: the state, the sovereign, and the people. Formerly, the idea of the sovereign obliterated that of the state and the people. It seemed easier to imagine a tsar without the people than a state without a tsar. Now experience had shown that a state could, at least for a time, exist without a sovereign, but neither a sovereign nor a state could exist without the people.

Similar conclusions were drawn from another, negative point of view by contemporary publicists who wrote about the Time of Troubles—Avraami Palitsyn, Ivan Timofeev, and others who have not left their names. They thought that at the root of the calamity was the lack of manly courage in the community, the people's inability jointly to oppose vested authorities when they violated law and order. When Boris Godunov was "behaving lawlessly" and "destroying great pillars which adorned the country, all the noblest turned dumb, were mute as fishes; no strong man was found in Israel, no one dared to tell the truth to the ruler." It was for this social connivance, for "the foolish silence of the whole community," as Avraami Palitsyn put it, that the country was punished.

True, at the Sobor of 1613, amidst general dissension and confusion, the old traditional idea of a "born tsar" had won the day, and Michael owed his election to it. This retrograde movement showed that the mind of the nation, represented at the Sobor by chosen delegates, was not equal to dealing with the new situation and preferred to return to the old tradition, to the "foolish silence of the whole community." We shall see more than once later on how the stream of social consciousness was muddied by atavistic elements in the nation's life. But in various sections of the community the idea that the people should take an active and organized part in public affairs found utterance throughout the Time of Troubles, sometimes with great force. If one considers all the implications of this idea, and the difficulty people generally have in acquiring any new political ideas, one can see what a radical change must have taken place in the Muscovites' mental outlook; and it was bound to have a lasting effect.

Traces of it are apparent in certain incidents of that period. In 1609 Sunbulov, one of the rebellious servicemen from Riazan, collected a crowd of people in a Moscow square and demanded that the boyars depose Tsar Vasili. But some of the men in the crowd said to the rebels: "Even if you are displeased with a tsar, you cannot depose him without the foremost boyars and the assembly of all the people." Clearly a general assembly headed by the boyars was considered the only institution entitled to settle matters of such importance. The new governments acknowledged and upheld the principle of the people's will in deciding vital political questions. The argument addressed to the rebels by the reasonable citizens in the Moscow square was repeated by Tsar Vasili himself. When Sunbulov and his accomplices broke into the palace, the Tsar met them with the words "Why have you traitors come to me with such shouting and effrontery? If you want to kill me, I am ready to die. But if you want to depose me, you cannot do it until all the great nobles and men of all ranks are assembled, and whatever the whole country's verdict is, I am prepared to accept it."

The community had more than once been called upon to decide important questions of state policy, and in time people became inclined to think that a properly constituted Zemsky Sobor was entitled not only to elect a tsar, but on occasion to pass judgment on him. This idea was actually officially expressed by a representative of Tsar Vasili Shuisky's government. At the very beginning of his reign a certain prince named Grigori Volkonsky was sent to Poland to justify before the Poles the assassination of the first pretender and his Polish supporters. The envoy was given official instructions to tell the King and his nobles that the people of the Muscovite state, having justly condemned the False Dimitri, had a right to punish such a tsar for his evil deeds, which were an abomination to the Lord. Prince Grigori took an even bolder step: in developing the ideas contained in his instructions, he said that even if Dimitri himself, the true Tsarevich, were to appear now, he could not force himself on the country as tsar if the people did not want him to reign over them. In the sixteenth century such political heresy would have terrified even the liberal Prince Kurbsky.

The events of the Time of Troubles not only instilled new ideas in the people's minds, but actually changed the composition of the ruling class with the help of which the old dynasty reigned, and this change greatly furthered the growth of the new ideas. The old Muscovite sovereigns ruled the country with the aid of the boyars, well organized as a class, imbued with aristocratic spirit, and accustomed to power. The political significance of this class was not safeguarded by law, but rested upon ancient custom. The custom, however, was indirectly supported by two circumstances: in the first place, a paragraph in the law code (sudebnik) of 1550 confirmed the legislative authority of the Boyars' Council, in which the foremost boyars played the chief part; secondly, the law of precedence made government appointments subordinate to genealogical considerations, and thus greatly helped the aristocracy to climb higher and higher. The first of these two indirect supports upheld the status of the boyars as the chief legislative corporation, and the second its status as the ruling class.

In Michael's reign one of the most aristocratic representatives of that class, Prince I. M. Vorotinsky, described the position of the boyars in the old days as follows: "The former tsars sometimes imposed a ban on us, but we were not deprived of our governing power; we had the management of public affairs throughout the country and were not dishonored by the lowborn." In other words, individual members of the boyar class sometimes suffered cruelly from the tyranny of the former sovereigns, but the boyar class itself never had its administrative functions taken away from it, nor was precedence given to men of low birth. Prince Vorotinsky well expressed the status of boyars as a ruling class in spite of the political helplessness of its members.

It was this class that began to disintegrate at the Time of Troubles, though the process had been set in motion by Ivan the Terrible. The compact ranks of boyar families grew thinner and thinner, and the gaps were filled by aggressive lowborn men, unaccustomed to power, with no family tradition or political training. A whole series of aristocratic old families that had held high office for generations disappeared from the court of the new sovereigns. Under tsars Michael and Alexei there were no longer any princes Kurbsky or Kholmsky or Mikulinsky or Penkov. Princes Mstislavsky and Vorotinsky were soon to disappear also. The list of boyars and Council members for 1627 includes the last of the princes Shuisky, and not a single prince Golitsyn. Nor are there in the top ranks any of the untitled Muscovite families of ancient lineage: no Tuchkovs, no Cheliadnins, Saburovs, Godunovs. Their places are occupied by men of new families, unknown or scarcely known in the sixteenth century: the Streshnevs, Naryshkins, Miloslavskys, Lopukhins, Boborykins, Iasykovs, Chaadaevs, Chirikovs, Tolstoys, Khitrys, and so on; among the titled families there are Prozorovskys, Mosalskys, Dolgorukys, Urusovs. Many good old families survived only in their less distinguished branches.

This change in the composition of the ruling class was noticed both at home and abroad. At the beginning of Michael's reign the remainder of the old Moscow boyars complained that during the Time of Troubles many of the lowest born had risen to the top—peasant traders and provincial servicemen of humble origin, to whom "accidental" tsars and pretenders gave high posts, raising them to the ranks of *okolnichi*, members of the Boyars' Council, and clerks. In 1615 Polish commissioners negotiating with the Muscovite envoys taunted them by saying that "for their sins, it was now the practice in Muscovy to pass over many princely and boyar families, and improperly allow simple peasants, priests' sons, and loutish butchers to deal with important matters of state." Under the new dynasty these political novices made their way up more and more boldly, and actually penetrated into the Boyars' Council, which had thinned out noticeably and had fewer and fewer boyars in it. These novices were the forerunners and harbingers of the eighteenth-century politicians whom their contemporaries rightly described as "chance men," men whom chance favored. And so, I repeat, sovereigns of the old dynasty ruled with the help of a whole ruling class, but in the seventeenth century the sovereign began to reign with the help of individual men who happened to have risen to the top. These new men, free of governmental traditions, became the bearers and champions of the new political ideas that had penetrated into Muscovite minds during the Time of Troubles.

The intrusion of so many new people into the aristocratic ruling circles brought confusion into the calculations of precedence. The boyar aristocracy formed a locked chain of individuals and families, which resulted in a complicated network of official and genealogical relations. Two claimants to the same post, not knowing what their relationship to each other was, determined their relative genealogical position, involving a third, a fourth, a fifth person, and so on; and if one of the rivals made a mistake, either unwittingly or through not insisting on his rights, he put a slur upon those persons' family honor, and they interfered in the case in self-defense. Prince D. M. Pozharsky was on one occasion pronounced to be beneath B. Saltykov. The Boyars' Council argued this way: Pozharsky was a relative and an equal of Prince Romodanovsky, and both were descendants of the princes Starodubsky; Romodanovsky held a lower place than M. Saltykov, and M. Saltykov occupied a lower place in the family tree than B. Saltykov; therefore, Prince Pozharsky was lower than B. Saltykov.

Newcomers broke this chain of precedence, into which they did not fit. They entered the ranks of the old nobility through personal merit or under the pretext of having deserved well of the state. But the law of precedence did not recognize heroic deeds. What did it care about meritorious service to the fatherland? It took account of a man's ancestry, and the family tree, and the register of official posts held by this or that person. It had a fatherland of its own—family honor. But the new people were not going to have their merits and achievements overlooked, and hardly any period in Muscovite history is so full of petty quarrels over precedence as the reign of Michael.

The most important of the newcomers, Prince D. M. Pozharsky, had to bear the full brunt of these conflicts. It did not matter that he had cleared the state of the rowdy Cossacks and the country's enemies, the Poles; it made no difference that he, a *stolnik* [1] of humble birth, had been created a boyar and granted "big estates"; he was found fault with on every occasion. It was said over and over again that the Pozharskys were not of high rank, had never held important posts, had served only as city prefects and provincial magistrates. When he was pronounced inferior to Saltykov, he made no objection, but he did not obey the Tsar's ukase and the boyars' verdict. Then Saltykov sued him for having dishonored him, and the savior of the country was "surrendered" to his utterly insignificant but aristocratic rival and went through the humiliating rite of being solemnly and ignominously led under guard—two men holding him by the arms—from the Tsar's courtyard to the front steps of Saltykov's house. But Tatishchev, who sent in a presumptuous complaint against the same Prince Pozharsky, was scourged and "surrendered" to Pozharsky.

The breakup of the law of precedence began with the conflict between the ideas of lineage and personal merit. Eventually the idea of aristocratic birth as the ground for precedence was rejected. Personal merit, high rank obtained as a reward for service, did not make a man an aristocrat. The basic principle of the law of precedence was that the tsar rewarded service by gifts of money and estates, but could not ennoble a man. When litigation about precedence increased inordinately, and most official appointments were accompanied by wrangling and disobedience, the government tried to avoid the harm thus caused to administrative efficiency by giving posts hitherto held only by men of ancient lineage to men of plebeian origin, who were not supposed to argue about precedence. But having received aristocratic appointments, the plebeians imagined themselves to have been ennobled, and wrangled with one another about precedence just as much as the nobles. Sometimes they actually claimed precedence over real aristocrats. In punish-

[1] A minor court functionary whose duty it was to oversee the tsar's table. [Editor's note.]

ment they were deprived of rank, imprisoned, flogged with the knout, but they persisted in their course. Once during a sitting of the Boyars' Council one of the members and a secretary, exasperated by having endlessly to deal with futile and vexatious disputes, thrashed an obstinate lowborn litigant with their sticks, repeating as they did so, "So much for your foolish claim! You should know your place!"

The plebeians' constant recourse to litigation was the result of circumstances. The Time of Troubles brought about a great reshuffling of the service-gentry families. The status of some had risen, that of others had fallen. Service rank as such was of little account in questions of precedence and did not confer nobility; but a titled nobleman of ancient lineage was generally given high rank in the service as a token of his noble birth. Lowborn men who had attained high rank in the service during the Troubles attempted to transform the sign of membership in the nobility into the source of it; they began to think that by giving high office to a plebeian, the tsar made him an aristocrat. This idea, destructive of the fundamental principle of the law of precedence, was one of the new political conceptions formed during the Time of Troubles. It was clearly expressed by a humble serviceman who said to his highborn rival, "Both great and small live on the Tsar's bounty." That idea led to the repeal of the law of precedence in 1682 and provided the basis for Peter's Table of Ranks in 1722. More than any other measure, it furthered the amalgamation of the old boyar aristocracy with the bureaucratic gentry.

New political ideas born in the people's minds during the Troubles had a direct and noticeable influence upon the state order under the new dynasty—that is, upon the part played by the supreme power in ruling the country. The change that took place was, however, merely a continuation or realization of the strivings that had made themselves felt at the Time of Troubles. I have said more than once that the relations between the sovereign and the nobility as a class were determined by custom, by tradition, and not by law. They depended on chance or the tsar's arbitrary will: the master of the house—the sovereign—could discuss with his servants—the nobles—the conditions of their work, but not the management of the house. With the end of the old dynasty, these household relations were inevitably put on a political basis. An elected tsar, whether a Russian or a foreigner, could not regard the state as his hereditary property, and the nobles—his bailiffs—wanted to take part in the management.

During the Troubles the boyars and upper gentry tried more than once to establish a state order based upon a written agreement with the tsar; that is, they wanted formally to limit his power. An attempt to do so was made on Vasili Shuisky's accession, and in Saltykov's treaty of February 4, 1610. These attempts were a consequence of the break in the Muscovite political tradition after the end of the dynasty. But even when the Troubles were over, the boyars did not relinquish their hopes. On the contrary, the political ferment engendered by the reigns of Ivan the Terrible and Godunov developed into a burning need. Michael's father, the Metropolitan Filaret, on hearing of the electors' assembly in Moscow, wrote from Poland, where he was a prisoner, that the reestablishment of the power of former tsars would expose the country to the danger of final ruin, and that he would rather die in a Polish prison than witness such a disaster. He never suspected that on returning to Russia, where he was to share his son's power and title of sovereign, he would have to reckon with the consequences of his idea of a constitutional monarchy.

Something that was in keeping with that idea happened on Michael's accession to the throne. Various witnesses testified that a new attempt was made to limit the Tsar's power, but later on it somehow faded both from people's minds and from the state order. It is mentioned by a contemporary, a citizen of Pskov, who wrote quite a good account of the Time of Troubles and of Michael's enthronement. He speaks with indignation of how, after Michael had been elected, the boyars managed the country, ignoring the Tsar and having no fear of him. He adds that on Michael's accession the boyars made him kiss the cross and promise on oath that he would not execute anyone belonging to an illustrious and noble family for any crime whatsoever, but merely banish him or keep him in confinement.

A fuller and clearer account of what happened is given by a man of a later generation, a clerk in the Department of Foreign Affairs, Grigori Kotoshikhin. He escaped from Russia in 1664 and while living in Sweden wrote a description of the Muscovite state. Having left Moscow nineteen years after the accession of the second tsar of the new dynasty, he could remember most of Michael's reign, and he had other people's reminiscences to draw on. In his description he puts this sovereign alongside others who ascended the throne after the end of the old dynasty, not by hereditary right, but through popular election. Kotoshikhin thought that on accession all those tsars had their power limited. According to him, the conditions they promised to observe, "signed by them in writing," were that they would "not be cruel and wrathful," would not put anyone to death for any reason without a fair trial, and would consult with the boyars and other members of the Council on all matters of state and do nothing without their knowledge, either secretly or openly. Kotoshikhin adds that although Tsar Michael styled himself "autocrat," he could do nothing without the Boyars' Council.

This is confirmed by an eighteenth-century historian, Tatishchev, who made use of documents unknown to us. Apropos of the Council's attempt of 1730,[2] he wrote a short political-historical essay in which he said that although Tsar Michael was elected to the throne by a properly constituted Zemsky Sobor, he had to make the same written declaration as Tsar Vasili Shuisky, and consequently "could do nothing, but was glad to be left in peace"; in other words, he left the business of governing to the boyars. In another of his works, however, Tatishchev throws doubt on the existence of such a declaration. Discussing a reference made to it by Strahlenberg, a Swede who lived in Russia under Peter I, Tatishchev says that he knows of no written or verbal testimony to such a document. Strahlenberg, in his

[2] The attempt to limit the power of Empress Anna Ivanovna on her election to the throne. [Translator's note.]

description of Russia published in 1730, made use of memoirs and verbal accounts about the seventeenth century still fresh in people's minds. He learned from these that on Michael's accession he had to make the following promises in writing and confirm them on oath: He was to observe and defend the Orthodox faith; to forget family feuds and dissensions of the past; to refrain from issuing new laws, changing old ones, declaring war, and making peace at his own discretion; to settle important legal cases according to law, in the regular manner; and finally to give his private hereditary estates to his relatives or join them to the crown lands. Michael's sworn declaration is not known, and the obligations undertaken by him cannot be traced in the official documents of the time.

The long statutory act by which the Zemsky Sobor confirmed Michael's election and the statement on the strength of which the oath of allegiance was taken contain three points referring to the new Tsar's power: (1) He was elected because he was a nephew of Feodor, the last Tsar of the old dynasty; (2) the Sobor swore allegiance not only to him, but also to his future consort and children, indicating that he was regarded as the founder of a new dynasty; (3) servicemen gave a promise not to oppose any of the sovereign's decisions and to remain at their posts at his command.

The formal limitations of Michael's power may be called in question; but the report that it was limited dates back to Michael's contemporaries and persisted for more than a century. Vague hints enable us to guess what really happened. The Pskov version inspires most confidence, for it tells the story in the form it took before rumor transformed it into a political legend. During the first five years of Michael's reign, while his father was still a prisoner of the Poles, everything at the court was managed by the Romanovs' relatives—Saltykovs, Cherkasskys, Sitskys, Lykovs, Sheremetevs. But there still remained some great boyars —the Golitsyns, Kurakin, Vorotinsky—who had forced the sworn charter on their confrere Tsar Vasili Shuisky, and afterward, with Mstislavsky at their head, swore allegiance to Prince Ladislas. They might be dangerous to the Romanov party and start fresh trouble if they were not given a share of the booty. And for Michael's own partisans, power obtained accidentally or by doubtful means would be a bone of contention for which they might, if the occasion arose, fly at each other's throats. It was to the interest of both parties to safeguard themselves from the repetition of the unpleasant experiences of the past, when the Tsar or some favorite of his could treat the nobles as serfs. Thus, while the Sobor was at work, a secret arrangement behind the scenes was made by the courtiers, similar to the one that was wrecked by Godunov and which succeeded under Shuisky.

The immediate purpose of the agreement was to safeguard the nobles' personal security from the Tsar's tyranny. It was easy enough to bind a meek boy like Michael by a sworn obligation, especially with the help of his mother, the nun Martha, a capricious intriguer who kept a tight hold on her son. It is hard to say whether Michael had to give the promise in writing. The story makes no mention of a signed document and speaks only about the oath. The first years of Michael's reign confirm the idea of such an agreement. People saw and spoke of how the ruling men did what they liked throughout the country, "despising" their sovereign, who was compelled to turn a blind eye to their behavior. We can understand, too, why the Tsar's "sworn statement"—if it ever existed—was not made public. From the time of Vasili Shuisky, an elected tsar with limited power was regarded by the people as a representative of a party, an instrument of the boyar oligarchy. While the Zemsky Sobor of 1613 was sitting, it would have been especially awkward to bring to light an arrangement that was definitely partisan. A secret limitation of his power, in whatever form, did not of course keep Michael from retaining the title of autocrat and even putting it on the new royal seal that he ordered.

The ruling circles that had made the secret pact had for their highest governing organ the Boyars' Council. But in Michael's reign this council was not the one supreme governmental institution. Side by side with it we often find another of equal authority—the Zemsky Sobor. Its composition had greatly changed by this time; it had become truly representative. Michael's reign was a time of great activity on the part of the government together with the Zemsky Sobor. Never before or after did the elected representatives of all the ranks in the Muscovite state assemble so often. Almost every important question of foreign or domestic policy made it imperative for the government to seek the people's cooperation. There is documentary evidence that in Michael's reign as many as ten Zemsky Sobors were called. Even more important, the Sobor's competence became much wider than before, even wider than Saltykov's treaty would have made it. It now dealt with matters that in the old days were within the competence of the Boyars' Council alone—current business such as questions of taxation, for example. In Saltykov's treaty such matters were for the Tsar and the Council to settle. The Sobor thus took a direct part in the Council's activities, but it stood in a peculiar relation to the Tsar. As a temporary government the Sobor, headed by the boyars, managed all the affairs of the country until the newly elected Tsar arrived in Moscow; and yet it was not the Sobor that set conditions for its nominee, but he that set conditions for it.

The tone of the Tsar's—or rather his mentors'—communications with the Sobor became more and more peremptory. "We became tsar at your request and not of our own wish. We have been chosen by the whole state to reign over you. You swore allegiance to us of your own free will, you promised to serve and to do right by us, and to live in concord, but now there are robberies and murders everywhere, and various disorders of which we receive complaints, so you must remove all these vexations from us and put everything in order." This was said to delegates of the Sobor, sometimes "with great anger and tears." The general tenor of the Tsar's speeches was: "You yourselves asked me to reign, so give me the means of doing so, and don't lay more burdens upon me."

The Sobor of 1613 somehow became administrative, and responsible to the person to whom it had given power. Putting all the available information together, we can only say that Tsar Michael's power was limited by conditions similar to those imposed upon Tsar Vasili Shuisky; that is, it was limited by the

Boyars' Council. But after the Time of Troubles, when it was essential to restore order in the country, the Council kept encountering difficulties it could not surmount by itself, so that it had to seek the Sobor's cooperation. Direct participation of the people in the government during the Troubles could not come to an end the moment the Time of Troubles was over. A tsar elected by the common will of the people, by the whole country, naturally had to rule with the help of the people, of the representatives of the land. The Boyars' Council restrained the power of the Tsar, and the Zemsky Sobor, coming to the aid of the Council, curbed the Council's power; it was, so to speak, a counterbalance to it.

Thus, under the continuing influence of political ideas and needs called forth by the Troubles, the Tsar's power acquired a highly complex and conditional character and became something of a compromise. This power was twofold, and it was ambiguous both in its origin and in its structure. Its actual source was popular election, but it appeared under the guise of hereditary succession based on kinship—a political fiction. It was limited by a secret contract with the upper ruling class, which governed through the Boyars' Council, but publicly and officially it was autocratic in a vague sense, titular rather than juridical, which did not prevent even Vasili Shuisky's styling himself an "autocrat" in important state documents. And so the new Tsar's power rested upon two parallel ambiguities: in origin it was both hereditary and elective, and in structure both limited and autocratic.

This could not be a final and permanent position of the supreme power. It could last only until the conflicting interests and relations, thrown into confusion at the Time of Troubles, had settled down. And indeed such a position was merely an episode in the history of the Muscovite state. The structure of the supreme power was gradually simplified and its heterogeneous constituents assimilated with one another. So far as we can tell, the political obligations accepted by Tsar Michael were observed by him throughout his reign. The Tsar's father, on returning from Polish captivity, was raised to the rank of patriarch and cosovereign, and took the helm of the state with a firm hand. He did not always consult the boyars, but so long as Filaret lived, government was carried on jointly by the two sovereigns with the participation of the Boyars Council and the Zemsky Sobor.

The diarchy was a compromise between family traditions and political considerations. It was unseemly for the father to become simply a subject of his son, and the son needed constant guidance, which it was natural to entrust to the father with the title of cosovereign. The idea of the indivisibility of supreme power was dealt with dialectically. The question as to which of the two sovereigns took precedence was settled this way: "Such as the sovereign is, such is his, the sovereign's, father; their sovereign majesty is indivisible."

Tsar Michael left no testament, and we can understand why. Under the new dynasty the state ceased to be the sovereign's hereditary estate, and the former legal way of bequeathing power by last will and testament was no longer valid. But there was no law of succession, and therefore Tsar Alexei, like his father, ascended the throne in a different way than did the tsars of the old dynasty. He acceded to power, so to speak, on two juridical grounds: inheritance without a will and election by the Zemsky Sobor.

In 1613 the country swore allegiance to Michael and his children. Tsar Alexei ascended the throne as his father's successor, and his contemporaries called him a "born" tsar; that is, a hereditary one. But the Zemsky Sobor had more than once been called to elect a tsar, and an election as a substitute for a testament was an established precedent. Now this method was employed again, so as to make it a permanent rule. The Sobor's election merely confirmed the legal inheritance established by the Sobor's sworn decision of 1613. Contemporaries testify that after Michael's death in 1645 a properly constituted Zemsky Sobor was called, and that it elected to the throne his son Alexei, aged sixteen, and swore allegiance to him. A foreigner, Holstein's ambassador Olearius, in his description of the Muscovite state says that Tsar Alexei ascended the throne with the unanimous consent of all the boyars, highborn gentry, and all the people. Kotoshikhin, a Moscow clerk who has already been mentioned, also clearly speaks of the Sobor's being called to elect Tsar Alexei. He writes that after Michael's death his son was elected as tsar by the clergy, the boyars, the gentry, merchants, tradespeople, men of all ranks, and the lower orders, by which he probably meant the common people of Moscow, who were asked to assemble in Red Square to voice their wish in the matter of the new tsar. But the obligations undertaken by Michael were not imposed upon his son. In another passage Kotoshikhin remarks, "The present Tsar was elected to the throne, but he did not give any promises in writing, as former tsars did, and it was not asked of him, because he was believed to be very gentle, and so he is styled autocrat and rules the state after his own will."

The Zemsky Sobor did not limit the tsars' power, and only the boyars could have asked Alexei for a contract in writing. Evidently in 1645 the repetition of a deal behind the scenes was still considered possible, but it was found unnecessary. Tsar Alexei justified the confidence placed in him by his boyars, who did not seek to impose any conditions on him at his accession. He did not take advantage of his autocratic power and lived in complete concord with the boyars. Political tendencies that after the Time of Troubles had led to the secret contract of 1613 had by now evaporated from the minds of the new generation with which Alexei had to deal.

While the idea of a tsar's political obligations was gradually fading out, Tsar Alexei made an attempt to transform popular election into a merely symbolic rite. Some eighteen months before his death, on September 1, 1674, the Tsar, in the presence of church hierarchs, members of the Boyars' Council, and foreign envoys resident in Moscow, announced to the people in Red Square that his eldest son, Feodor, was heir to the throne. This solemn declaration was a formal way of handing down his power as tsar to his son after his own death. It was the only action that legalized, as it were, the accession of Feodor, who, being Michael's grandson, was not included in the 1613 treaty.

But this "demonstrational" method of transferring power in the presence of the people did not take root. When Alexei's eldest son, Tsar Feodor, died without male issue, an election to the throne was needed again, but this time it was held in a simplified, or rather in a distorted, form. In April 1682, as soon as Feodor had breathed his last, the Patriarch, the bishops, and the boyars who had come to take leave of the dead Tsar assembled in one of the palace rooms to discuss which of Alexei's two remaining sons was to reign. They decided that the question must be submitted to the people of all ranks in the state. Then and there the Patriarch, bishops, and boyars went out onto the front steps of the palace, ordered that men of all ranks be assembled in the palace yard, and put the question before them. By a majority of votes, though not an overwhelming majority, the younger Tsarevich, ten-year-old Peter, was proclaimed tsar over his older brother, the feeble-minded Ivan. The same question was addressed by the Patriarch to the bishops and boyars standing beside him on the steps, and they also voted for Peter. Immediately the Patriarch went into the palace and blessed Peter as tsar.

I mention these details to show how simply matters of such importance were settled in Moscow in those days. It is obvious that no elected representatives of the people were present at that casual meeting and no general consultations were held. The matter was settled by the crowd of men of various ranks who had gathered in the Kremlin on the occasion of the Tsar's death. It is obvious that the people, headed by the Patriarch, who were at that moment deciding the destiny of the state had no conception of state law, of the meaning of the Zemsky Sobor, or indeed of the state as such. They found such ideas superfluous in the present case. But after the meeting of May 15, 1682, the streltsy, incited by Tsarevna Sofia's party, responded to the action of the ruling authorities by demanding a new parody of the Zemsky Sobor, which forthwith elected both tsareviches to the throne. In the records of this second irregular election we read that all the ranks of the state petitioned that "for the sake of general appeasement both brothers should be enthroned as tsars and wield autocratic power together."

We have traced the changes in the position of the supreme power under the first three tsars of the new dynasty, and the result to which these changes led after the death of the third tsar. The century that began with the ruling classes' strenuous efforts to establish fundamental laws and a constitutional government ended with the country's having no fundamental laws at all, no properly regulated government, and not even a law of succession to the throne. Incapable of framing such a law, those in authority had recourse to court intrigue, to symbolic ceremony, to a counterfeit of the Zemsky Sobor, and finally to open mutiny.

The nobles, however, clung to their political tradition. At the end of 1681, when it was proposed to abolish the law of precedence, on which the political significance of the nobility was largely based, they covertly made one more attempt to save their position. Disappointed in their long-cherished hopes of dominating the central government, they tried to ensconce themselves in the provinces. They drew up a plan for dividing the state into large sections that had histories of their own and which had once been independent principalities, and for members of the Muscovite aristocracy to be appointed as their permanent, lifelong governors. There would thus be created plenipotentiary local rulers "of boyar rank"—governors of the state of Kazan, of the state of Siberia, and so on. Tsar Feodor gave his consent to this plan of aristocratic decentralization of government, but the Patriarch, to whom it was submitted for his blessing, vetoed it, pointing out the dangers in which it would involve the state.

The change in the composition and the significance of the Zemsky Sobor was one of the most important consequences of the Time of Troubles. In the sixteenth century only civil servants, officials in the central and local administration, were summoned to it. But the Sobors of 1598 and 1605 included a number of the "common" people's delegates. In the conditions created

by the Time of Troubles, elected delegates considerably outnumbered officials, and the Sobor thus acquired the character
of a truly representative body. Circumstances compelled the
people to take a direct part in public affairs, and the government
encouraged them to do so, appealing to them for help or
exhorting them to defend the Orthodox faith. Pamphlets on
current affairs, with a dash of the miraculous added, were
solemnly read to the congregations in the cathedrals. Phrases
hitherto unfamiliar, such as "the council (*soviet*) of the whole
land," "the people's general assembly," "taking thought *in common*," and so on, became usual expressions of the new ideas that
had gained possession of the people's minds.

The idea that had most effect was that of electing the sovereign by "the council of all the land." It was gradually extended
to all matters of national importance. All public business had
to be earnestly thought over "in common," and to this end
the towns organized conferences, electing the "best men" of all
ranks from the local population. When the country was being
torn between the rival tsars, Vasili Shuisky and the second
False Dimitri, the idea of the state as a unity awakened in
people's minds, and they recalled the calamities of the appanage
period. They did not venture on any important step without
the elected representatives of all the ranks. The embassy of
Metropolitan Filaret and Prince V. V. Golitsyn to King Sigismund in 1610 was accompanied by a retinue that included more
than a thousand such representatives. On his march to Moscow,
Prince Pozharsky issued proclamations to the towns, calling
elected men of all ranks to join his camp. It was the common
wish that every enactment of state importance should be wit-
nessed, as far as possible, by the whole country through its
representatives. Their presence testified that the whole business
was conducted openly and honorably, and not by secret, behind-
the-scenes conspiracy, as was the practice of Maliuta Skuratov,
Boris Godunov, and Vasili Shuisky himself. Their methods were
now considered the main cause of the country's calamities. Thus
the idea of an elective Zemsky Sobor took shape in people's

minds, and had been partly put to the test before the convocation of the electoral Sobor of 1613, which may be regarded as the first real instance of true popular representation.

Having cleared Moscow of the Poles, the boyars and the military leaders of the second citizen army summoned for communal consultation and election of a sovereign "the best men, wise and steadfast," chosen to represent all the ranks, including townsmen from every district, provincial tradesmen, artisans, and peasants. The last two classes were not represented at the sobors of the sixteenth century. The leaders of the citizen army wanted to carry out to the letter the idea of an ecumenical or universal council, as the documents of the period expressed it; that idea had grown in people's minds during the Time of Troubles. The change in the composition of the Sobor was accompanied by a change in its significance. In the sixteenth century the government summoned sobors of civil servants in order to find among their members responsible executors of the Sobor's decisions or of the Tsar's decrees. The leaders of the second citizen army wrote in their circular letter to the towns that a state cannot be built without a sovereign.

We have already seen that the elective Sobor of 1613, having accomplished its main task, the choice of a tsar, became an administrative commission, which, under the guidance and at the request of the newly chosen Tsar, took preliminary measures for establishing order in the country before a permanent system of administration was formed. As soon as that was done, the Sobor had another task assigned to it. In 1619 it was decided, for the sake of establishing order in the country, to summon to Moscow chosen delegates from every town, "good and reasonable" men of every rank, able to give an account of all the injustice, violence, and pillage they had suffered. After hearing the petitions presented by them about "their needs, hardships, destitution, and all manner of deficiencies," the Tsar in council with his father the Patriarch would take thought about the state so as to arrange everything for the best." In this way the delegates, by making petitions, were able to ask for legislative action, while the supreme power of the state reserved for itself the right to decide the questions that had been raised. The Zemsky Sobor was no longer the bearer of the people's will. It became the mouthpiece of their complaints and desires, which is by no means the same thing. In our further study of the seventeenth century we shall have occasion to see the effect of this change upon the organization, the activities, and the fortunes of the sobors.

The above mentioned consequences of the Troubles—new political ideas, new elements in the composition of the ruling class, new status of the supreme power, new character acquired by the Zemsky Sobor—all seemed to promise well for the development of the state and the community, and provided the new dynasty with abundant spiritual and political resources that the old dynasty had never possessed. But sharp changes in ideas and customs always carry with them the danger that the people will not know how to make proper use of them, and will turn the new possibilities into a source of new difficulties for themselves. The consequences of the Time of Troubles showed that the old political tradition was disrupted and the customary political order had vanished; and however thoroughly the people may grasp the ideas corresponding to the changed conditions, they will walk unsteadily until those revolutionary ideas themselves become a firm tradition.

The change in the position of the supreme power at the end of the seventeenth century shows that this danger was very real for the Muscovite state. That danger was increased by a number of other, highly unfavorable consequences of the Time of Troubles. The storms of that period wrought havoc both in the economic life of the country and in the general mood of the Russian people. The country was devastated. Foreigners visiting Muscovy shortly after Michael's accession (1613) drew a terrible picture of abandoned or burned-out villages and derelict huts filled with corpses. The stench compelled the travelers to spend winter nights out of doors in the frost. People who had survived the Troubles sought refuge wherever they could. Civic order was disrupted, all social relations were in a tangle. Much concerted effort was needed to reestablish order, to collect the runaways and bring them back to their old homes and the regular manner of life. There have come down to us from the time of Tsar Michael a good many lists of servicemen in various districts and land registers describing the economic position of the landowning servicemen and of the peasantry. They give a vivid picture of the economic plight of the state and the people of Muscovy under the first tsar of the new dynasty.

To begin with, there was a noticeable change in the composition of the rural peasant population, which was the chief source of state revenue. The sixteenth-century registry books show that the peasantry was divided, on a property basis, into two classes: peasants proper and the *bobyls*. The latter were poor peasants who cultivated smaller plots of land than peasants proper, or had no land at all and owned only their homesteads. In the sixteenth century the peasants greatly outnumbered the bobyls, but according to the registers of Michael's reign these positions were changed, and in some districts actually reversed: the number of peasants equaled that of the bobyls or was considerably below it. Thus in 1622, on the estates of servicemen in the districts of Belev, Mtsensk, and Elets, there were 1,187 peasants and 2,563 bobyls. This means that during the Troubles a tremendous number of peasants had to give up their land or retain only a part of it. An increase in the number of bobyls indicated an increase in the amount of wasteland, land that had gone out of cultivation. There is nothing exceptional in the statement made in an agrarian register for 1616 that in a certain sector of the Riazan district the area of wasteland was twenty-two times larger than that of cultivated land.

The steward of the Troitsky Monastery, Avraami Palitsyn, who was a good manager of the monastery land and well informed about the economic conditions of the country, gives interesting confirmation of this state of things. He writes that during the three years of bad harvests in Boris' reign many people had enormous quantities of grain left from former years in their barns, and stacks of unthreshed grain in the rickyards. The owners and other people subsisted on these old supplies during the fourteen years of Troubles, when "plowing and sowing and harvesting were abandoned, for the sword was always at men's throats." This statement testifies to the development of agriculture before the Time of Troubles, shows that there was little market for grain, and indicates the subsequent decline in the cultivation of land.

This decline, involving a profound change in the composition of the rural population, was bound to have an adverse effect on the economic position of private landowners, especially of the provincial gentry. I shall mention a few data referring to different districts taken at random from the registers of servicemen for 1622. The military fitness of servicemen as a class depended upon the income from their estates and upon the number and the prosperity of the peasants living on those estates. Few of the provincial gentry had hereditary estates; the great majority lived on the income from the land they had on military tenure. Thus in the Belev district hereditary estates formed only one quarter of the local gentry's land, in the district of Tula a little more than one fifth, in Mtsensk one seventh, and in Elets one part in 157. In the Tver district even the richest of the gentry held only one quarter of its land as hereditary property. The military service estates of the provincial gentry were as a rule very small and scantily populated. An average military service estate in the district of Tula contained 135 *desiatinas* [3] of arable land, of Elets 124, of Mtsensk 68, of Belev 150. The number of agricultural workers in those four districts averaged one to every 60 desiatinas. But it must not be imagined that all this arable land was actually cultivated by the peasants and bobyls. Only a small part of it was tilled, and not by them alone. In the district of Tver a well-to-do member of the upper provincial gentry cultivated only 95 desiatinas out of the 900 that belonged to him, either by inheritance or as a reward for service. Of these 95 desiatinas, 20 were tilled for him by his serfs and the remaining 75 were used by 28 peasants and bobyl householders living in 19 homesteads, so that on the average each homestead had 4.6 desiatinas attached to it. It was comparatively rare for a peasant household to have more land than this under the plow. Besides, in Elets and the three

[3] About 370 acres. One desiatina equals 2.7 acres. [Translator's note.]

other districts just mentioned there were many landless servicemen who possessed homesteads but had no peasants, and many
who had no homesteads. Out of 878 servicemen in the district
of Elets, 429 were either altogether landless or had homesteads
only. Some of the gentry abandoned their estates and joined
the Cossacks, pledged themselves as bondsmen to a boyar household, became lay brothers in monasteries, or, as the registers put
it, "hung about pothouses."

As the servicemen's farming deteriorated, the need to increase
their salaries so as to make them fit for service grew more
and more urgent. But an increase in salaries meant an increase
in taxes, payable by the peasants, whose assessment depended
on the size of the areas they had under cultivation. The peasants,
unable to bear the burden of ever increasing taxation, reduced
their tillage so as to have less to pay. The Treasury was thus
involved in a vicious circle.

The government's difficulties were intensified by the profound
change in the country's mood. The new dynasty had to do with
a different kind of community than the one the former tsars
had ruled. The alarming experiences of the Time of Troubles
had a disruptive effect on the political habits of the people. With
the enthronement of the new dynasty all classes of society
throughout the seventeenth century ceaselessly complained of
their miseries, impoverishment, ruin, of the abuses of the authorities—things they had suffered before, but which they had endured in silence. Discontent became the predominant note in
the mood of the masses and remained so till the end of the
century. The stormy Time of Troubles made the people far
more impressionable and irritable than before. They lost their
power of political endurance, at which foreign observers used
to marvel in the sixteenth century, and were no longer resigned
and obedient tools in the hands of the government. This change
found expression in a way that had hitherto not been observed
in the history of the Muscovite state. The seventeenth century
was a time of popular uprisings. This is all the more surprising
because it happened under tsars whose actions and personal
character apparently gave least justification for it.

Chapter
V

Muscovy, Eastern Europe and the Ukraine

We have dwelt at some length on the consequences of the Time of Troubles as reflected in the internal life of the state and the community. Let us turn now to another set of events springing from the same source—the external relations of the state under the new dynasty.

The international position of Muscovy underwent a great change after the Time of Troubles and became incomparably worse than before. For a century and a half the old dynasty had unswervingly followed one line in its foreign policy. It acted aggressively, increasing the area of the state slowly but constantly as it gathered together the scattered portions of Russian territory. As soon as Great Russia was politically united, further tasks for its foreign policy became apparent. Ivan III, while taking possession of the last independent regions of Russia, declared in his struggle against Poland that united Great Russia would not lay down its arms until it had regained all the remaining parts of the Russian land wrested from it by its neighbors and gathered the whole nation together.

His grandson, Ivan IV, sought to expand the territory of the Russian state to the natural geographical boundaries of the Russian plain, occupied by hostile tribes and nations. Thus Moscow foreign policy had two tasks before it: to complete the political unification of the Russian people and to expand the territory of the state to the boundaries of the Russian plain. The old dynasty did not carry out these tasks, neither the national nor the territorial, but it achieved considerable success in dealing with them. Ivan IV's father and grandfather regained the Seversk and Smolensk lands, thus pushing their way to the Dnieper. Tsar Ivan IV, the Terrible, initially moved in the opposite direction and gained possession of the regions of the middle and lower Volga, extending the eastern frontiers of the state to the Ural Mountains and the Caspian Sea. His campaigns in the west were less successful. He wanted to acquire Livonia and reach the eastern shore of the Baltic, which was the natural boundary of the Russian plain. But he did not succeed in gaining the entire course of the western Dvina, and in the war with Stephen Batory he actually lost ancient Russian towns on the shore of the Gulf of Finland and Lake Ladoga—Iam (Iamburg), Koporye, Korela (Keksholm), and Ivangorod.

His son, Tsar Feodor, after a new war with Sweden (1590–95), retrieved his father's losses and managed to regain the shore of the Gulf of Finland, which had once belonged to Novgorod. But during the Time of Troubles Moscow again lost the western foothold it had acquired in the sixteenth century. The Poles took back from Muscovy the Smolensk and Seversk regions, cutting Muscovy off from the Dnieper, and the Swedes pushed it off the shores of the Baltic. The first tsar of the new dynasty had to cede to Sweden by the Stolbovo Treaty (1617) the above mentioned towns as well as Oreshek (Schlüsselburg), and to Poland, by the Treaty of Deulino (1618), the Smolensk and Seversk lands. Muscovy was compelled once more to retreat a long way from its former western boundary. The new dynasty made a bad beginning. It did not merely renounce the national task of the old dynasty, but it lost much of what it had inherited from it.

The external position of the state was made worse by the contempt in which its neighbors held it after the Troubles. The Muscovite boyars wrote in a circular letter sent to the towns in 1612: "Enemies are pillaging the state of Muscovy on every side; the neighboring sovereigns put us to shame and reproach." In order to retrieve its losses, the new dynasty had to strain the resources of the nation even more than the old one had done; it was both its national duty and the condition of its security on the throne. And so from the very first it engaged in a series of wars for the sake of retaining what it possessed and regaining what had been lost. The strain upon the nation increased when these wars, defensive in their origin, imperceptibly and unintentionally on the part of the Muscovite "politicians" became wars of aggression—a direct continuation of the unifying policy of the old dynasty, a struggle for Russian territory that had never belonged to the Muscovite state.

International relations in eastern Europe at that time gave Moscow no respite after its first unsuccessful efforts, so that it could not prepare itself for further action. In 1654 the Ukraine rose against Poland and put itself under the protection of the Muscovite Tsar. This involved the state in a new struggle against Poland. The problem of the Ukraine complicated still further the old tangled accounts between Moscow and Poland concerning the Smolensk and Seversk regions, and was the starting point of Muscovite foreign policy from the middle of the seventeenth century onward. It is connected with the history of western Russia, but I shall touch upon this only to show how the problem first arose. In 1648 a Cossack chief, Bohdan Khmelnitsky, headed a rising against Poland. He was unanimously supported by the peasantry, which rose against its masters, the Polish and Polonized Russian gentry. The "registered" Cossacks also took Khmelnitsky's side. A formidable army was formed, and in some five or six months' time he had almost the whole of the Ukraine in his hands. To understand the causes of the Ukrainian uprising of 1648 we must make clear what Poland was like, the Ukraine's place in it, how Polish gentry came to be in the Ukraine, how the Cossack host originated, and why the Ukrainian peasantry supported its rebellion against Poland.

Reunion with western Russia was the hardest task that Muscovite foreign policy had to face. It involved a number of difficulties that had gradually developed out of the political transaction between the Polish gentry and the Lithuanian Grand Prince Jagiello in 1386. On the strength of this transaction Jagiello acquired the Polish kingdom together with the hand of the Polish queen, Jadwiga. This arrangement was to the advantage of both sides. Jagiello hoped that through becoming king and accepting Catholicism for himself and his people, he would gain the support of Poland and of the Pope against the dangerous Teutonic order; and the Poles wanted, through Jagiello, to obtain control of the resources of Lithuania and especially of western Russia, Volhynia, Podolia, and the Ukraine. A dynastic bond was thus established between the neighboring kingdoms of Poland and Lithuania, a purely mechanical union of two heterogeneous and indeed hostile states. It was a diplomatic deal, resting upon mutual misunderstanding, rather than a political act based on an identity of national interests.

Nevertheless, the union brought about important changes in the position of western Russia. When that part of the country was conquered by Lithuanian princes, Lithuania came under Russian influence. At the beginning of the fifteenth century Russian provinces annexed by Lithuania—Podolia, Volhynia, Kiev, Smolensk, and the Seversk region—were far more extensive and more thickly populated than the country that conquered them. Ethnically and culturally this Russo-Lithuanian principality was more Russian than Lithuanian. The Russian language, laws, and customs, as well as the Orthodox faith, had for about a century been spreading in semibarbarous, pagan Lithuania. Cultural amalgamation of the two nationalities under the predominant influence of the Russian—the more developed one—was making such progress that within two or three generations, by the beginning of the sixteenth century, Lithuania would have been completely merged with western Russia. But after the union between Lithuania and Poland, the Russian influence in the Lithuanian part of the kingdom was gradually replaced by the Polish, which penetrated there in various ways.

To begin with, there were the *seyms* (diets) at which the common affairs of both the allied states were dealt with. The Russo-Lithuanian magnates met there with the Polish gentry and became acquainted with their political ideas and the social order prevalent in Poland. Polish influence was also introduced into Russo-Lithuania by the charters granted by the Lithuanian princes, which established in Lithuania the same system of administration, the same rights and relations between the classes, as in Poland. Infiltrating into the country in these ways, the Polish influence profoundly changed both the administrative system and the social structure of the Russian provinces that formed part of the Lithuanian principality.

Russian princes owned these provinces in accordance with the old hereditary principle, like their ancestors in the eleventh and twelfth centuries. In submitting to the power of the Grand Prince of Lithuania, they promised to serve him faithfully and to pay tribute on their possessions. He, on his part, granted them their princedoms as hereditary property, though sometimes only for temporary possession "until he should declare his will." This practice was destructive of the old hereditary principle of ownership. By the beginning of the sixteenth century the princes had become service landowners, complete masters of their princedoms, and, together with the foremost nobles and Lithuanian magnates, constituted a landed aristocracy similar to the Polish, and even more influential. Members of this aristocracy, the *pans*, formed the governing council, or *rada*, of the grand prince, which considerably limited his power. In accordance with Grand Prince Alexander's charter of 1492, a Lithuanian sovereign could not conduct relations with foreign states, issue new laws or change the old, dispose of state income and expenditure, or appoint state officials without the rada's consent. The sovereign was bound by the rada's decisions. Even if he disagreed, he obeyed them "for his own and the common benefit." Meanwhile there were introduced in Lithuania the same higher administrative posts as in Poland, which in time became lifetime appointments: hetman, the chief military commander; chancellor, the keeper of the state seal; two ministers of finance; deputy treasurers in charge of the state revenue and expenditure; and the court chamberlain. Provinces that had been ruled by Russian princes by agreement with the free cities were now put under the rule of *voevodas* (governors), assisted by city commandants and chiefs of the rural districts into which the provinces were divided. Thus the central and provincial governments of Russo-Lithuania came to resemble the Polish, and acquired an oligarchic structure.

The charters, given either to the principality as a whole or to separate districts, were a means of establishing in Lithuanian Russia class relations and rights similar to those that obtained in Poland. The Horodlo seym of 1413, which confirmed the union between Poland and Lithuania, issued a charter conferring on the Lithuanian nobles, if they became Roman Catholics, the rights and privileges of the Polish gentry. In 1447 King Casimir extended the same privileges to the Orthodox aristocracy. The Russo-Lithuanian landowners were granted the same rights as the Polish to own hereditary and service estates, and were exempted from taxes and dues, except some light ones that were of symbolic rather than financial value, as tokens of subjection. The landowners' peasants were removed from state jurisdiction and made subject only to their masters. Casimir's charter forbade the peasants to migrate from private owners' lands to those belonging to the sovereign, and vice versa. These enactments marked the beginning of serfdom in Lithuania, after the pattern of Poland, where it had been established as early as the fourteenth century.

The general and local charters gradually equalized the rights and liberties of the Russo-Lithuanian and Polish gentry. The gentry had extensive powers over the peasant population, and played an important part in legislation, dispensation of justice, and general administration. This status of the Russo-Lithuanian gentry was confirmed in the sixteenth century by the law code of the Lithuanian principality, the Lithuanian Statute. The first edition of the statute appeared in 1529, under Sigismund I. Later it was frequently revised and enlarged, so as to bring it into line with Polish law. Consequently, the statute was strongly influenced by Polish legislation, mingled with ancient Russian juridical customs that lingered in Lithuanian Russia from the times of *Russkaia Pravda*.[1] In its final version the statute was published in Russian under Sigismund III in 1588. The second edition of the statute, confirmed by the Vilna seym in 1566, introduced in the Lithuanian principality district assemblies of the gentry, similar to the Polish, which met in each district to elect local judges as members of the gentry class tribunal, and also two representatives of the district gentry to sit in the general seym.

The Lithuanian seym, as established by the Horodlo Treaty, originally consisted only of Lithuanian princes and magnates. The Lithuanian aristocracy, by now mostly Roman Catholic, was thus given a privileged position as compared with the Russian Orthodox. Consequently, the Russian provinces annexed by Lithuania rose against the Lithuanian government when, after Vitold's death in 1430, a fresh feud broke out between Gedymin's descendants. In this struggle the Russian princes and boyars won for themselves the same rights as the Lithuanian magnates, and about the middle of the fifteenth century they were admitted to the general seym. But even after this the seym retained its aristocratic character. The Russian provinces were represented in it only by princes and pans, who were summoned individually and had a decisive vote. In the first half of the sixteenth century, under Sigismund I, the Russo-Lithuanian gentry engaged in a lively struggle against their own native aristocracy and won the right of also being summoned to the general seym. By the statute of 1566 the gentry of the former Russian provinces were admitted to the Lithuanian seym in the same way as the Polish were to their own. The Russo-Lithuanian gentry was in favor of a permanent union with Poland, and when in 1569 the Lublin Treaty merged the seyms of the two

[1] The law code of Grand Prince Iaroslav (1019–54). [Editor's note.]

countries, the political rights of the Russo-Lithuanian gentry were made fully equal to those of the Polish.

While the gentry in the Lithuanian principality gained more power, the ancient cities of western Russian weakened. In Kievan Russia, provinces with their district towns formed self-contained units, subordinated to the senior town's *veche* (town assembly). But when government by crown officials was introduced, the chief provincial towns were severed from their respective provinces. Instead of a veche, there was now a voevoda appointed by the grand prince and assisted by numerous underlings. Rural and urban self-government was replaced by crown administration. Suburban lands, used by town communities jointly, were distributed by the grand princes to private owners in return for military service. Boyars, service landowners, and small landed proprietors who had formerly belonged to urban communities now, on the strength of their gentry privileges, set themselves apart from the trading and industrial urban population and, leaving the towns, began to settle on their hereditary estates or those granted to them in reward for service.

The ancient domains of the self-governing Russian cities gradually broke up into private estates of the aristocracy and the gentry. The cities, drained of their resources, remained isolated among these new and often hostile landowners who had robbed them of their original heritage. The voice of the veche was confined within city walls and did not reach the outlying districts. The grand prince's officials had their way with the urban population.

To improve the position of the towns, the sovereigns of Poland and Lithuania gave them the German form of municipal self-government, the so-called Magdeburg Law, which was introduced into Poland in the thirteenth and fourteenth centuries by German colonists who came in swarms to Polish towns. As early as the fourteenth century the Magdeburg form of self-government was instituted in the towns of Galicia when that province was added to Poland by Casimir the Great in 1340. In the second half of the fifteenth century the Magdeburg Law spread to other towns of western Russia. It gave the burghers certain

trading privileges, relieved them of some of the state impositions, and exempted them from the jurisdiction of voevodas
and other crown officials. According to the Magdeburg Law,
the town was governed by two councils or *collegia*: the *lava*,
the members of which, under the chairmanship of a *voit* (German *Vogt*) appointed by the king, dispensed justice to the
burghers, and the rada, consisting of the burghers' elected representatives and headed by burgomasters who looked after the
city's finance, trade, good order, and good behavior.

In the fifteenth century and the first half of the sixteenth,
the political influence of Poland over Lithuania assimilated
the Russo-Lithuanian regime with the Polish and helped to preserve the dynastic union, frequently renewed by fresh treaties,
between the two states, which sometimes had separate sovereigns
and sometimes were united under the power of one. In the
sixteenth century a new combination of circumstances strengthened the bond between Poland and Lithuania, bringing them
into a closer unity, and produced results of the utmost importance for the whole of eastern Europe and particularly for
southwestern Russia. I have in mind the great church schism in
western Europe in the sixteenth century, the Reformation.

One would have thought that eastern Europe would care
nothing about a German scholar, Martin Luther, who in 1517
began arguing about the true source of Christian doctrine, about
salvation by faith and other theological matters. And yet the
ecclesiastical revolution in western Europe left its mark upon
eastern Europe too. It did not affect it directly, by its religious
and moral implications, but, so to speak, obliquely, like a distant
echo. Certain freethinking trends in Russian ecclesiastical circles
in the sixteenth century were rather closely connected with the
Reformation and found support in ideas coming from the Protestant West. But I would not venture to say whether it was in
the west or in the east of Europe that the Reformation had
most effect on international relations. It certainly proved to be of
some importance for the history of the Russian state.

Speaking generally, I accept with many reservations the idea
that ancient Russia was completely isolated from western Europe,

ignoring and being ignored by it, impervious to its influence
and exercising no influence upon it. Western Europe knew
ancient Russia no better than it knows the modern, but Russia,
both in our time and three or four centuries ago, has always
felt the impact of events in the West, even if it misinterpreted
them and reacted to them sometimes more strongly than it might.
That is what happened in the sixteenth century. In order to
consolidate the dynastic bond between Poland and Lithuania,
the Polish government, under the clergy's leadership, began
vigorous propaganda for Catholicism in Orthodox Lithuanian
Russia. The campaign was particularly intense in the reign of
the third of the Jagiellonian kings, Casimir, in the fifteenth century, and met with strong resistance on the part of the Orthodox
Lithuanian population. As a result, by the end of the fifteenth
century the Lithuanian principality began to disintegrate. Orthodox Russian and even Lithuanian princes gradually left the
country and entered the service of the Grand Prince of Muscovy.

The Reformation brought about a sharp change in the relations between the states. Protestant doctrines found in Poland
a fruitful soil, prepared by close cultural relations with Germany. A number of young Polish men studied at Wittenberg
and other German universities. In 1520, three years after the
Wittenberg dispute, the Polish clergy held a conference at
Piotrkow and forbade the Poles to read German Protestant
writings, which were rapidly spreading throughout the country.
In support of the clergy, the Polish government at the Torun
convention of the same year issued a decree menacing with
confiscation of property and perpetual exile all who imported,
sold, or distributed Luther's or other Protestants' writings in
Poland. These prohibitions grew sterner and sterner. After a
few years the threat of confiscation of property was replaced
by that of capital punishment. But all this was of no effect.
Protestantism was growing among the Polish population; even
the bishop of Kiev, Pac, openly advocated Lutheran ideas.

From Poland and other neighboring countries Protestantism
penetrated into Lithuania. About the middle of the sixteenth
century, its seven hundred Catholic parishes retained only a

thousandth part of their parishioners. The rest had become Protestants. In 1525 the Prussian Teutonic order seceded from the Roman Church, and its grand master, Albert, accepted the title of duke. This order began publishing Lithuanian translations of Protestant works. The man who did most to spread Protestantism in Lithuania was Avraam Kulva, a Lithuanian who had studied in north Germany and obtained his doctorate there. He found a successor in a German pastor named Winkler, who also preached Luther's doctrines. Calvinism met with even greater success. Its chief supporter was an influential Lithuanian magnate, Nicholas Radziwill the Black, first cousin to Queen Barbara, originally the secret and later the officially recognized wife of King Sigismund Augustus. In the fifties of the sixteenth century the great majority of the Catholic gentry were converted to Protestantism, and their example was followed by some of the Orthodox Russo-Lithuanian aristocracy—the Vishnevetskys (Wisniowieckis), Chodkiewiczes, and others. It was these successes of Protestantism that had prepared the ground for the Lublin union of 1569.

The Protestant influence weakened the Catholic propaganda in Lithuanian Russia. The last Polish kings of the Jagiellonian dynasty, Sigismund I and Sigismund II Augustus (1506–72), were indifferent to the religious struggle waged in their united realm. Sigismund Augustus, kindly, pleasure-loving, and indolent, brought up in the new climate of thought, actually patronized the new doctrines, so far as his position in the kingdom allowed him to do so. He lent people Protestant books from his own library and did not object to having sermons with a Protestant flavor preached in the court chapel. When he left the palace to attend religious services on feast days, he did not care whether he drove to church or chapel. While supporting the Protestants, he also showed favor to the Orthodox. In 1553 he issued an interpretation of the Horodlo seym's decree of 1413 (excluding the Orthodox from government and public posts) that practically canceled it.

With the decrease of Catholic propaganda, supported by former kings, the Orthodox population of Lithuania lost its fear of the Polish government and was no longer hostile to it. This change in popular attitude made it possible to continue the political union between Lithuania and Poland. Sigismund Augustus was childless. At his death the Jagiellonian dynasty would end, and with it the dynastic union between the two states. So long as Catholic propaganda, encouraged by Polish governments, was extremely active in Lithuania, the Orthodox population of that country would not even think of preserving the union. The question of future relations between Lithuania and Poland was causing anxiety. But thanks to Sigismund Augustus' tolerance or benevolent indifference, the Orthodox ceased to fear the idea of remaining united to Poland. The only people likely to be against it were the Lithuanian magnates, who were afraid of being swamped by the Polish service gentry. But this was just what the Russo-Lithuanian service gentry wished to happen, and for that very reason they wanted a permanent union with Poland.

In 1569 the seym assembled at Lublin to decide whether the union should be continued. When the Lithuanian aristocracy proved to be against it, the King won over to his side the two most influential magnates in southwestern Russia: the Kiev voevoda, Prince Constantine Ostrozhsky, a descendant of Riurik, and Prince Alexander Czartoryski, voevoda of Volhynia and a descendant of Gedymin. Prince Ostrozhsky was owner of extensive lands. Although he recognized the King as his sovereign, he was richer and more influential than Sigismund Augustus. His vast estates included almost the whole of what is now the province of Volhyn, and considerable portions of the Podolsk and Kiev provinces. There were thirty-five towns in them and seven hundred villages, which brought him in some ten million zlotys (more than ten million rubles in our currency [2]). These two magnates carried over with them the local Russian gentry, who already had a leaning toward Poland. The Lithuanian gentry followed them, and this decided the question of the union. The Lublin seym declared the political fusion of the two

[2] Russian currency toward the end of the nineteenth century. [Translator's note.]

states to be unseverable, even after the extinction of the Jagiellonian dynasty.

At the same time the constitution of the united state was finally determined. Poland and Lithuania were united on an equal basis as two halves of a single state, the first half being called a kingdom and the second a principality. The two together received the name of *Rzecz Pospolita (Res Publica)*. It was an elective monarchy organized as a republic. The government was headed by the King, elected by the general seym of the kingdom and the principality. Legislative power belonged to the seym, composed of "land envoys"—representatives of the gentry (and only of the gentry)—and to the senate, consisting of the highest officials, lay and clerical, from both parts of the realm. While the supreme power rested with the King, the seym, and the senate, the kingdom and the principality retained their separate administrations, their own ministers, armies, and laws. The Lublin seym allotted to the kingdom of Poland certain provinces that had formed part of the principality of Lithuania, and this proved to be of momentous significance for the subsequent history of southwestern Russia. The provinces in question were Podolia (the western part of Grodno province), Volhynia, and Ukraine (that is, the provinces of Kiev and Poltava, and parts of Chernigov and Podolsk provinces). That was how the Lublin union was concluded. It involved consequences of great political, national, and religious importance for southwestern Russia and eastern Europe as a whole.

For western Russia the enactments of the Lublin seym were the high-water mark of the Gedymin dynasty's rule and of the Polish influence it furthered. The Poles attained the aim they had pursued for almost two hundred years—permanent union of their state with Lithuania and annexation of the highly desirable southwestern Russian provinces, rich in natural resources. Gedymin's descendants, influenced by Poland, did away with many ancient customs and institutions in the Russian provinces over which they ruled, and introduced much that was new.

The old Kievan Russia was ruled by princes of the Riurik

line, with their fighting men, by agreement with the senior self-governing towns of the districts. Private ownership of land was but little developed, and the rulers' social and economic relations with the provinces governed by them were unstable. Under Gedymin's descendants this shifting ruling class was replaced by an aristocracy of big landowners, which included Russian and Lithuanian princes and noblemen, permanently settled on their estates. As the regime became stabilized, this aristocracy gave way to the military class of small landowners, service gentry. The ancient provinces or lands of Kievan Russia, politically centered around their senior towns, were broken up in Lithuanian Russia into administrative districts ruled by the grand prince's governors and united not by local bonds, but by a common government center. The senior towns, which through their veches represented their provinces in dealing with the princes, were severed from the provincial community by state administration and private landowners. The Magdeburg Law, which replaced the veches, transformed them into strictly limited class communities of tradesmen and artisans living within the narrow confines of the cities. The old provincial capitals were thus deprived of all national significance and participation in the political life of the country. Domination of the gentry, officials with lifetime and sometimes hereditary appointments, and the Magdeburg Law—these were the three innovations introduced into Lithuanian Russia under the Polish influence. The consequences of the Lublin union greatly helped to introduce the fourth innovation, serfdom, for which the Polish influence had already prepared the way.

From the middle of the sixteenth century onward the lands along the middle reaches of the Dnieper, long uninhabited, rapidly became populated. The beautiful open steppes were a natural attraction to settlers. The growth of serfdom in Lithuania swelled their numbers. At the beginning of the sixteenth century the rural agricultural population of those parts could be divided into several sections, according to their dependence upon the landowners. There were "migrating" peasants; peasants settled with or without a loan from the landowner and having the right to move elsewhere; and serfs working as agricultural laborers. Between 1529 and 1566 (when the first and the second statutes were issued), as the political power of the gentry increased, the status of these different sections of the peasantry was more and more equalized and their liberty restricted. The Lublin union of 1569 hastened this process. Under the elected kings of the Rzecz Pospolita, its legislation and the whole of its political life came under the direct influence of the Polish-Lithuanian gentry, the country's ruling class, which lost no opportunity to exploit its political predominance at the expense of the rural population subject to it.

When Russian provinces on both sides of the middle reaches of the Dnieper were taken over by Poland, Polish administration penetrated there, ousting the Russian, and under its protection the Polish gentry came also, buying land and introducing serfdom, which was firmly established in Poland. The local Russo-Lithuanian gentry readily adopted the ideas and customs of their new neighbors from the Vistula and western Bug districts. To some extent the law and the government regulated the tributary relations between the peasants and the landowners in the interests of the Treasury, but as a person, the peasant was entirely at the discretion of his master. The gentry assumed the rights of life and death over their peasants. For a member of the gentry to kill a serf was the same as to kill a dog—so the modern Polish writers tell us.

Escaping from slavery, which was like a noose tightening around the peasant neck, the rural population migrated in ever increasing numbers from the central provinces of Poland and Lithuania to the boundless steppes of the Ukraine. They went farther and farther down the Dnieper and the eastern Bug to areas where the gentry had not yet found their way. Speculation in land soon began to take advantage of this migration, thereby giving it a fresh impetus. Members of the aristocracy and of the service gentry applied for lifetime appointments as supervisors of the Ukrainian frontier towns—Bratslav, Kanev, Cherkassy, Pereiaslav—surrounded by extensive wastelands. They obtained grants of large areas of the boundless steppes that had never been measured by anyone, or simply took possession and hastened to populate their new estates, attracting runaway peasants and artisans by promises of various privileges and exemptions from taxes. The Ukrainian steppes at that period were dealt with in the same way as, in more recent times, the Bashkir lands or the eastern shores of the Black Sea. The most illustrious and highly placed members of the aristocracy, the princes Ostrozhsky and Vishnevetsky, the Potockis, Zamoyskis, and so on and so on, did not scruple to take part in the greedy scramble for uncultivated crown lands along the Dnieper and its steppe tributaries on either side. But the land speculators of that time were, after all, more conscientious than their modern imitators in the Urals and the Caucasus. Thanks to them, the Ukraine of the steppes soon came to life. Within a short time there appeared dozens of small towns, hundreds and thousands of homesteads and villages.

Meanwhile, the steppes were being fortified, for otherwise the settlers could not live there. Beyond the line of ancient cities—Bratslav, Korsun, Kanev, Pereiaslav—a series of new castles was built, under the protection of which small towns and villages grew up. Constant struggle with the Tatars made these settlements into military communities, somewhat similar to the "warriors' outposts" that defended the steppe boundaries of Kievan Russia in the tenth and eleventh centuries. It was from these settlements that the Ukrainian Cossack host was gradually formed.

Originally the Cossacks were a social class not confined to any particular part of the country. As early as the sixteenth century the name of Cossacks was given to hired laborers working for a season in peasant homesteads, men without any definite occupation or fixed residence. That was the original meaning of the term. Later on, in Muscovite Russia, this wandering, homeless class of people received the name of "free vagrant men" or simply "freemen."

Southern Russia, on the borders of the steppes, was a particularly favorable soil for producing such people. The conditions of life imparted a special character to the people living there.

When the horror of the Tatar invasion had been almost forgotten, a permanent feud began between the Russians living in the borderlands and the Tatars wandering over the steppes. The fortified frontier towns were the starting points and bases of support for this struggle. There sprang up in those parts a class of men who gained their living by going into the steppes to hunt and fish. These armed hunters and fishermen, poor and adventurous, probably obtained the equipment for their dangerous occupation from local tradesmen to whom they sold their prey. In that case they belonged to the category of hired workmen, employed by their masters. As they were used to steppe warfare, they might also have been supported by the grand prince's local officials. These men, who had constant skirmishes with Tatar hunters in the steppes, received the Tatar name of Cossacks, which afterward was applied to the free vagrant laborers in northern Russia as well. In the southeast region of the steppes such skirmishing began earlier than elsewhere. That, I think, is the reason the earliest reference to Cossacks mentions the Cossacks of Riazan, who helped their town against the Tatars in 1444.

In Muscovite records of the sixteenth and seventeenth centuries we find references to things that could have happened only when Cossack organizations were just beginning to be formed. In the service registers in the steppe districts we come across entries saying that this or that impoverished young man "wandered off to the steppes," "went to be a Cossack." This does not mean that he joined some regular Cossack community, for instance on the Don. He simply happened to have found companions and, leaving the service and his estate, went off with them to the steppes to live a free life, take up for a time some free occupation in the steppes, have a brush with the Tatars, and then come home and settle down somewhere. The Elets register of 1622 mentions a whole party of Elets landowners who abandoned their hereditary estates and went off to be Cossacks. Afterward they became bondsmen to noblemen or lay brothers in monasteries.

It may be said that the original home of the Cossacks was

along the line of Russian towns bordering on the steppes and extending from the middle Volga to Riazan and Tula, then turning sharply south via Putivl and Pereiaslav and ending at the Dnieper. Soon the Cossacks took another step in their advance upon the steppes. That happened when the Golden Horde had split up and the Tatars had weakened. Town Cossacks, probably those of Riazan in the first instance, began settling in small military self-employed communities in the open steppe in the upper Don region. The Don Cossacks may well be regarded as the prototype of the steppe-dwelling Cossacks. At any rate, in the second half of the sixteenth century, when the Zaporozhye Cossacks were just beginning to form their military community, those of the Don were already organized. They included some Christianized Tatars. There has been preserved a petition of a newly baptized Crimean Tatar, who left the Crimea for the Don in 1589, and there served the Muscovite sovereign for fifteen years, "waging war against the Crimean people and together with the Don Cossacks attacking their villages." From the Don he went to Putivl. He petitioned the Tsar to exempt his homestead at Putivl from dues and taxes, and to let him carry on his service to the Tsar together with other men who had been exempted.

The Cossacks of the Dnieper are first mentioned in the records at the end of the fifteenth century, later than those of Riazan. Their origin and initial social status were as simple as elsewhere. Parties of young men from towns in the Kiev region, in Podolia and Volhynia, set out for the wild steppes "to lead a Cossack life" and make a living by beekeeping, hunting, fishing, and skirmishing with the Tatars. In spring and summer these newcomers worked at their trades along the Dnieper and its steppe tributaries, and in the autumn they moved to the local towns with their booty and made their homes there, especially in Kanev and Cherkassy, which became the main haunts of the Cossacks. Some of them, as in northern Russia, hired themselves out to work for the townspeople or the landowners. But local geographical and political conditions brought complications to the Ukrainian Cossacks. They were caught in the whirlpool of international conflicts between Russia, Lithuania, Poland, Turkey, and the Crimea. The part they had to play in these conflicts gave them a historical significance.

I have mentioned that the intensive colonization of the lower reaches of the Dnieper increased the numbers of the local Cossacks. They were needed in the region and in the state as a whole, but they were restless men, causing many difficulties to the Polish government. Accustomed to fighting, those steppe adventurers were the country's best defense against Tatar raids. But it was a double-edged weapon. One of the Cossack pursuits in the steppes—indeed, the chief one—was to make retaliatory raids on Tatar and Turkish lands. The attacks were made both from land and from the sea. At the beginning of the seventeenth century, light Cossack craft ravaged Tatar and Turkish towns on the northern, western, and even southern shores of the Black Sea, and actually reached the Bosporus and Constantinople. In return, the Turks threatened Poland with war, which the Poles feared more than anything else.

As early as the beginning of the sixteenth century it was planned in Warsaw to make the Cossacks harmless without hindering their usefulness. The plan was to pick the most dependable men out of the disorderly and ever increasing mass of the Cossacks and engage them in salaried government service under the obligation to defend the Ukraine. The rest were to be returned to their former condition of life. It is on record, however, that at the very beginning of the sixteenth century Cossack detachments had already been recruited for frontier service. Probably that was one of the experimental attempts to organize a corps of frontier guards from the armed traders of the steppes. Only in 1570 was a permanent detachment of three hundred "listed" or "registered" Cossacks formed. Under King Stephen Batory their number was increased to five hundred, and it went on increasing until in 1625 it amounted to six thousand. But this did not in the least help to diminish the number of unregistered Cossacks. Local officials and landowners did their best to make these irregular Cossacks, mostly of peasant origin, return to their peasant status and former duties, but men who had had a taste of free Cossack life wanted no part of that. They considered that they had a right to disobey, for the same government that was thrusting them back under the landowners' yoke as peasants turned to them for help in wartime and called them to the banners by the tens of thousands, and never mind the registers. Such double dealing on the government's part angered the irregulars, and trouble was ready to flare up the moment an adroit leader appeared among them.

Meanwhile, on the lower reaches of the Dnieper, a Cossack nest was being built in which the Ukrainian malcontents could find refuge and a training ground for open rebellion. That was the Zaporozhye.[3] It grew imperceptibly out of the pursuits of the free steppe traders "cossacking afield." From the frontier towns of the Ukraine they went far down the Dnieper, beyond the rapids. Professor Liubavsky has suggested that the first beginning of the Zaporozhye Sech (fortress) can be traced to a large company of Cossacks who plied their various trades beyond the rapids, close to Tatar encampments, toward the end of the fifteenth century. When the town Cossacks began to suffer from restrictions imposed upon them by the Polish government, they fled to the familiar places beyond the rapids, where neither the Polish commissioners nor punitive detachments could reach them. There, on the islands formed by the Dnieper as it escapes from the narrows into the open steppe in a broad sweep of water, the fugitives made fortifications for themselves. In the sixteenth century their chief settlement was on the island of Khortitsa, nearest to the rapids. That was the Zaporozhye Sech, famous in its time. Later on it was transferred from Khortitsa to other islands. It was a fortified camp surrounded by ramparts of tree trunks and provided with artillery, consisting of small cannons captured from Tatar and Turkish fortresses. Single men from all parts of the country formed there a quasi-military association, practicing various trades and styling themselves the "knightly host of Zaporozhye."

Members of the sech lived in open tents made of dry brush-

[3] "The place beyond the rapids"; from *za* (beyond) and *porog* (a rapid). [Translator's note.]

wood and covered with horsehide. They had different occupations. Some were mainly booty seekers, and lived on their gains
in warfare. Others occupied themselves with hunting or fishing,
and supplied the former with provisions. Women were not
allowed in the sech. Married Cossacks lived apart and tilled
the land, providing the sech with grain. Until the end of the
sixteenth century the Zaporozhye remained a mobile community
with a floating population. In the autumn it dispersed to spend
the winter in Ukrainian towns, leaving in the sech a few hundred men to guard the artillery and other communal property.
In quiet times in the summer there were about three thousand
men in the sech. But it was overcrowded when the Ukrainian
peasantry were driven to desperation by the Tatars or the Poles,
or when something else was astir in the Ukraine. Then all who
were discontented or persecuted or caught in some misdemeanor
fled to the Zaporozhye. A newcomer to the sech was not asked
who he was, or what his religion was, or where he came from,
or who his father was. Everyone who seemed suitable as a
comrade was accepted.

At the end of the sixteenth century the Zaporozhye showed
signs of a military organization, as yet unstable, but later more
clearly defined. The military brotherhood of Zaporozhye was
ruled by an ataman, elected by the Cossack assembly, which
also elected a judge and a secretary. These were the elders of
the sech. The brotherhood was divided into detachments that
eventually came to number thirty-eight. They were commanded
by elected atamans, who were also included among the elders.
The Cossacks prized comradely equality above all. Everything
was decided by the assembly, which did not stand on ceremony
with its elders; the assembly elected and changed them, and,
when displeased, punished them by plunging them into the
river with a heavy load of sand in their shirts.

In 1581 a grand gentleman from Galicia, Zborowski, a reckless
adventurer, appeared at the sech to urge the Cossacks to make a
raid on Moscow. The "knightly host," bored with inaction and
lacking money, joyfully accepted his suggestion and at once
elected him ataman. On the march the Cossacks kept asking him

whether, when they returned from Moscow, God grant, safe and sound, he might find another profitable job for them. But when, giving up the idea of attacking Moscow, he offered instead to lead a campaign against Persia, they very nearly killed him, after quarreling violently among themselves.

Eagerness for military gain, or more simply for plunder and booty, increased during the sixteenth century in proportion to the growing number of Cossacks. They could no longer subsist by hunting and fishing in the steppes, and wandered about by the thousand in the Ukrainian lands on the right bank of the Dnieper, robbing the inhabitants. The local authorities could not get rid of the unemployed Cossacks, who did not know what to do with themselves and readily followed any leader who called them against the Crimea or Moldavia. The bands that attacked Muscovy during the Time of Troubles consisted of Cossacks of this type. Raids against the neighboring countries were at that time called in the Ukraine "Cossacks' bread." They cared for nothing except booty, and when Zborowski talked to them about loyalty to the king and to the fatherland, they answered with the popular saying that "men live while they have enough to eat." But the Cossacks did not always feed on other countries, on the Crimea or Moldavia or Muscovy. In the seventeenth century it was the turn of their own land to be pillaged. The inexhaustible supply of newcomers to the sech made the Zaporozhye a hotbed of Cossack rebellions against the Rzecz Pospolita itself.

And so the Lublin union brought with it to southwestern Russia three closely interconnected consequences: serfdom, an increase in the peasant colonization of the Ukraine, and the transformation of the Zaporozhye into a rebellious refuge for the enslaved Russian population.

Chapter VI

The Cossacks

We have traced in its general outline the history of the Ukrainian Cossacks in connection with Lithuanian Russia up to the beginning of the seventeenth century, when a radical change in their position took place. We have seen how some of the free bands of steppe traders developed into armed detachments that lived by raiding neighboring territories, and how the government recruited its frontier guard from these detachments. All the different sections of the Cossack population looked to the steppes for booty, and in their search for it they more or less helped to defend the vulnerable southeastern boundary of the state. But after the Lublin union they changed their bearings and turned against the state they had hitherto defended. The international position of the Ukraine demoralized this composite and vagrant mass and prevented its developing any civic sense. The Cossacks were accustomed to regard neighboring countries—the Crimea, Turkey, Moldavia, and even Muscovy—as sources of booty, as "Cossacks' bread." They began adopting the same attitude toward their own state when Polish and Lithuanian landowners came to settle on its southwestern border, introducing serfdom there. Their own state was now in their eyes a worse enemy than Turkey or the Crimea, and from

the end of the sixteenth century onward they attacked it with redoubled fury.

Thus the Ukrainian Cossacks were left without a fatherland and consequently without a religion. In those days the whole moral world of an average eastern European rested on these two inseparable bases: the fatherland and the fatherland's God; the Rzecz Pospolita gave the Cossacks neither the one nor the other. Their Orthodox heritage was to them a vague memory of childhood or an abstract idea that laid no obligations upon them and was utterly inapplicable to their manner of life. In wartime they treated the Russians and their churches no better than they treated the Tatars, and worse than the Tatars would have done. An Orthodox Russian pan, Adam Kissel, a commissioner who had to deal with the Cossacks and knew them well, wrote in 1636 that they were devoted to the Orthodox Church and its clergy, although with regard to religion they were more like Tatars than like Christians.

The Cossacks lived, so to speak, in a moral and spiritual void. In the Rzecz Pospolita there was probably no other class that stood on so low a level of civic and moral development as they. Perhaps only the hierarchs of the Ukrainian church before the Union of Brest could vie with them in this respect. The slow-witted Cossacks had not yet come to recognize their own Ukraine as their fatherland. This was partly due to the motley composition of the Cossack host. A listed detachment of five hundred registered Cossacks, recruited in the reign of Stephen Batory, included men from seventy-four towns and districts of Lithuania and western Russia, even from such distant ones as Vilna and Polotsk, men from seven Polish towns—Cracow, Poznan, etc.—Muscovites from Riazan and from somewhere on the Volga, Moldavians, and, in addition to all these, one Serb, one German, and one unbaptized Tatar from the Crimea. What could have united this motley crew? A pan sat astride its neck and a sword dangled at its belt. Cut down the pan and hire out the sword—that summed up a Cossack's political outlook. It was all the social science he learned at the sech—the Cossack academy, the highest school of valor for a good Cossack, "the mutineers' den," as the Poles called it. The Cossacks offered their services for an appropriate fee to the German emperor against the Turks, to the Polish government against Muscovy and the Crimea, and to Muscovy and the Crimea against the Poles.

The early rising of the Cossacks against Poland were of a purely social and democratic character, with no religious or national tinge. Their starting place was, of course, Zaporozhye, but even the leader of the first rising was an alien belonging to a class hostile to the Cossacks, a traitor to his rank and country —a ruined Polish landowner, Christopher Kosinski. He somehow attached himself to the Zaporozhye, and with a detachment of his fellow Cossacks contracted to serve the King. But in 1591, for the sole reason that the mercenaries had not received their wages at the proper time, he collected a band of the Zaporozhye Cossacks and all kinds of Cossack riffraff and began pillaging and burning Ukrainian towns, villages, and the gentry's estates, big and small, particularly those of the princes Ostrozhsky, the richest landowners in the country. Prince C. Ostrozhsky defeated him, took him prisoner, then pardoned him and his Zaporozhye comrades on their oath to keep the peace in their home beyond the rapids. But a couple of months later Kosinski raised another rebellion, swore allegiance to the Tsar of Muscovy, and boasted that with Turkish and Tatar help he would turn the whole of the Ukraine upside down and butcher all its gentry. He besieged the town of Cherkassy, planning to slaughter all the inhabitants including the governor, Prince Vishnevetsky—the man who had persuaded Prince Ostrozhsky to have mercy on Kosinski. At last he was killed in combat with this governor. Kosinski's work was continued by Loboda and Nalivaiko (Nalewajko), who went on pillaging the Ukraine west of the Dnieper till 1595. And it was this mercenary band, without God or fatherland, that had thrust upon it, by the force of circumstances, the national and religious banner and the lofty task of defending Orthodoxy in western Russia.

This unexpected role had been prepared for the Cossacks

by another union, an ecclesiastical one, which took place twenty-seven years after the political union. I shall briefly mention the main circumstances that led up to it.

Roman Catholic propaganda, renewed in 1569 with the appearance of the Jesuits in Lithuania, soon demolished Protestantism there, and attacked Orthodoxy. It met with strong opposition, first from Orthodox magnates headed by Prince C. Ostrozhsky and then from the urban population and the brotherhoods. But the leading hierarchs of the Ukrainian Orthodox Church, demoralized, despised by their own flock and persecuted by the Catholics, reverted to the old idea of union with Rome, and at the Brest Council of 1596 the Russian church community split into two mutually hostile factions, the Orthodox and the unionists. The Orthodox faction ceased being the lawful church, recognized by the state. The rank and file of the Russian Orthodox clergy were to be left without bishops, after the death of the two who had not accepted the union. Russian townspeople lost the political support of the Orthodox aristocracy, which was rapidly becoming Catholic or unionist. The only power that could come to the rescue of the clergy and the townspeople was the Cossacks and their reserves, the Russian peasantry. These four classes had different interests, but in view of the common enemy the differences were forgotten. The ecclesiastical union did not unite these classes, but it gave a new stimulus to their common struggle and helped bring them to a better mutual understanding. It was easy to make a Cossack or a serf believe that the union was an alliance between the Polish king, the pans, the Catholic priests, and their common agents the Jews against the Russian God, whom every Russian was duty bound to defend. If a downtrodden serf or an unruly Cossack, half inclined to make an end to the pan on whose land he lived, were told that this would help the cause of the abused Russian God, that was enough to salve a conscience vexed by a vague feeling that a massacre was not a good deed, whichever way you looked at it.

The first Cossack uprisings at the end of the sixteenth century had, as we have seen, no religious or national character. But from the beginning of the seventeenth century the Cossacks gradually went over to the Orthodox resistance movement. The Cossack hetman Sahaydachny (Sahajdaczni), with the whole Zaporozhye host, joined the Kiev Orthodox brotherhood. In 1620, through the Patriarch of Jerusalem and without the Polish government's consent, he reinstated the Orthodox hierarchs, who carried on their work under the Cossacks' protection. In 1625 the head of this hierarchy, the Metropolitan of Kiev, called on the Cossacks to defend the Orthodox population of the city, and the Cossacks duly drowned in the Dnieper the voit who had persecuted the Orthodox.

That was how the Cossacks took up the banner that bore on its front side a call to fight for faith and the Russian people, and on the reverse side a call to exterminate the magnates and gentry or expel them from the Ukraine. But this banner did not unite all the Cossacks. As early as the sixteenth century there appeared economic differences among them. Those who had once sought shelter in frontier towns and earned their living by going to the steppes in pursuit of various trades began to settle down there, to build farms and plow the land. At the beginning of the seventeenth century some of the frontier districts, for instance that of Kanev, were already full of Cossack homesteads. As usually happens when vacant lands are colonized, occupancy confers the right of ownership. It was chiefly from these Cossack settlers that the Polish government recruited the registered Cossacks, who were put on salary. In the course of time these were drafted into territorial units or regiments, attached to the urban administrative centers of the districts inhabited by the Cossacks. According to the agreement made by the Cossacks with the King's hetman Koniecpolski in 1625, their registered host was to number six thousand; it consisted of six regiments (those of Belaia Tserkov, Korsun, Kanev, Cherkassy, Chigirin, and Pereiaslav). In Bohdan Khmelnitsky's time there were already 16 regiments containing over 230 squadrons.

The division into regiments dates back to the time of Hetman Sahaydachny (d. 1622), who did much to organize the Cossacks of the Ukraine. This hetman's methods brought to light the cleavage inherent in the very structure of the Cossack community. Sahaydachny wanted to draw a sharp line between the registered Cossacks as a privileged class and the simple peasants who took up a Cossack's vocation, and people complained that he made things hard for the peasants. Belonging to the gentry by birth, he brought to the Cossacks the ideas of his class. The Cossacks' struggle with the Ukrainian gentry thus acquired a special character. It now aimed not at liberating the Ukraine from the power of the alien gentry that had planted itself upon it, but at replacing that gentry by a native privileged class. The registered Cossacks were to be the gentry of the future.

But the real strength of the Cossack force did not lie with the registered men. The registered Cossacks, even reckoning them at six thousand, were not one tenth of the men who regarded themselves as Cossacks and claimed a Cossack's rights. Generally speaking, they were poor, homeless men. A considerable part of them lived on the gentry's estates and, as free Cossacks, were unwilling to have the same duties imposed on them as on the peasants. Polish landowners and their bailiffs would not recognize these people's liberties, and tried to return them to their peasant status. When the Polish government needed the Cossacks' help in war, it allowed all of them to join the army, whether they were registered or not, but as soon as the need was over it deleted the superfluous men from the register, so as to make them return to their former positions. These deleted men, threatened with serfdom, congregated in their refuge, the Zaporozhye, and organized rebellions. That was how the Cossack uprisings began. They started in 1624 and continued for fourteen years under the leadership of Zhmailo, Taras, Sulima, Pavliuk, Ostranitsa, and Gunia. The registered section of the Cossacks was either divided between the opposing sides or took the part of the Poles.

All these uprisings were unsuccessful. When they ended in 1638, the Cossacks had lost their chief privileges. The register was revised and the listed Cossacks were put under the command of Polish officers. The ataman was replaced by a government commissioner. The settled Cossacks lost their hereditary lands. The unregistered ones were returned to serfdom. There were no free

Cossacks left. As a Ukrainian chronicler put it, all freedom was taken away from the Cossacks; heavy taxes, unheard of before, were imposed upon them, and the churches were leased to the Jews.

Poles and Russians, Russians and Jews, Catholics and unionists, unionists and Orthodox, brotherhoods and bishops, gentry and peasantry, peasants and Cossacks, Cossacks and townspeople, registered Cossacks and indigent free Cossacks, town Cossacks and the Zaporozhye, Cossack elders and Cossack rank and file, Cossack atamans and Cossack elders—all these social groups in their conflicting relations with one another were split into mutually hostile pairs. This internecine hostility, latent or open, was a stranglehold on the country's life, and none of the wise politicians in Kiev or Warsaw was able to unravel the tangled and ever tightening knot. Bohdan Khmelnitsky attempted to cut it with the Cossack sword. It is hard to say whether his rebellion and the inevitable need to intervene in it had been foreseen in Moscow. Russian attention was riveted on Smolensk and the Seversk land, and after the unsuccessful war of 1632–34 Muscovy was preparing quietly to regain its losses at the first opportunity. The Ukraine lay as yet far beyond the horizon of Muscovite politics, and besides, the memory of Sapiegha's and Lisovski's Cossack hordes was still fresh in people's minds. True, messages had been sent to Moscow from the people of Kiev expressing their readiness to serve the Orthodox Tsar of Muscovy, and even begging him to take the Ukraine under his mighty protection, for the people of the Ukraine had no one to turn to but him. Moscow's cautious answer was that should the Poles begin to interfere with religion, the Tsar would consider how best to defend the Orthodox faith from the heretics.

From the very beginning of Khmelnitsky's rebellion the relations between Muscovy and the Ukraine became ambiguous. His success surpassed his own expectations. He had never thought of breaking away from Poland; he only wanted to give a shock to the arrogant pans—and suddenly after three victories the whole of the Ukraine was in his hands. He himself confessed that he had succeeded in doing something he had never dreamed of.

Success intoxicated him, especially at dinner one night when envoys from Moscow were present. He pictured to himself the Ukrainian principality ruled by Grand Prince Bohdan and extending beyond the Vistula. He called himself "monarch and autocrat of Russia," threatened to turn all the Poles upside down, to drive all their gentry beyond the Vistula, and so on. He was greatly annoyed with the Tsar of Muscovy for not having helped him from the first, and attacked Poland then and there. In his anger he said "unseemly things" to the Muscovite envoys, and toward the end of dinner threatened to demolish Muscovy and get at the man who ruled it. Simplehearted boasting was succeeded by abject, but not simplehearted, contrition.

This changeability of mood was due not only to Bohdan's temperament, but to his feeling that he was in a false position. He could not prevail over Poland with the Cossack forces alone, and as the longed-for help from Moscow was not forthcoming, he had to hold on to the Khan of the Crimea. After his first victories he hinted that he would be ready to serve the Tsar of Muscovy if the Tsar supported the Cossacks. But Moscow was delaying, as people do when they have no plans of their own, and waiting upon the course of events. Moscow did not know what to do with the rebellious ataman—whether to accept his allegiance or merely to help him covertly against the Poles. Khmelnitsky was less convenient as a subject than as an unofficial ally. A subject must be defended, but an ally may be deserted when he is no longer needed. Besides, to give open support to the Cossacks would draw Muscovy into war with Poland, and entangle it in all the Ukrainian domestic troubles. But to remain indifferent to the struggle meant abandoning the Orthodox Ukraine to its enemies, and making an enemy of Bohdan. He threatened that if Moscow gave him no support, he would join with the Crimean Tatars in an attack on Muscovy, or else make peace with the Poles and turn with them against the Tsar.

Soon after the Zborov Treaty, feeling that a new war was inevitable, Bohdan told the Muscovite envoy that in case of defeat he would like to move with all his Zaporozhye host into

Muscovite territory. Only eighteen months later, when Khmelnitsky had failed in his second campaign against Poland and lost
nearly all the advantages he had gained in the first, it was recognized at last in Moscow that his plan presented a way out of the
difficulty, and he was invited to move with all his Cossack host
to the Tsar's fertile and extensive lands along the rivers Donets
and Medveditsa and other suitable parts of that region. Such a
migration did not entail a war with Poland, did not drive the
Cossacks under the yoke of the Turkish sultan, and provided
Muscovy with a good frontier guard along its steppe boundary.

But events moved at a swifter rate than the sagacious Muscovite politicians had calculated. Khmelnitsky was forced to begin
a third war with Poland under unfavorable conditions, and now
he implored the Tsar to accept him as a subject, since his only
alternative was to put himself under the protection of the
Sultan or of the Khan of the Crimea, who had long been woo-
ing him. At last, early in 1653, Moscow decided to accept the
Ukraine as a subject province and go to war with Poland. But
even then it let the business drag on for almost a year. Khmelnitsky was not informed of Moscow's decision till the summer.
In the autumn the Zemsky Sobor was called to discuss the matter,
"as was proper"; then Moscow waited a little longer, until the
ataman suffered a new defeat, betrayed again by his ally the
Khan—and only in January 1654 were the Cossacks able to take
the oath of allegiance.

After capitulating in 1634 at Smolensk, the Russians waited
thirteen years for an opportunity to wipe away the disgrace. In
1648 the Ukrainian Cossacks rebelled against Poland. Poland was
in a desperate position. The Ukrainians asked Moscow to help
by taking them under its rule so they could dispense with the
treacherous Tatars. Muscovy did not budge, afraid of breaking
the peace with Poland. For six years it watched with phlegmatic
interest how Khmelnitsky's campaign, ruined by the Tatars at
Zborov and Berestechko, was going from bad to worse, how the
Ukraine was being devastated by its allies the Tatars and by a
brutally savage civil war. At last, when the country was completely exhausted, it was taken under Muscovy's mighty pro-

tection—with the result that the Ukrainian upper classes changed from rebels against Poland to embittered subjects of the Muscovite Tsar. All this could have happened only because neither side understood the other. Moscow wanted to get hold of the Ukrainian Cossacks even without their territory, and would take the Ukrainian towns only on condition that they be administered by Muscovite voevodas with their secretaries. Khmelnitsky, on the other hand, reckoned to become something like the Duke of Chigirin, ruling the Ukraine under the remote supervision of the Muscovite sovereign and with the help of the Cossack aristocracy—ataman's assistants, colonels, and other elders.

Both sides misunderstood and distrusted each other, and said things they did not mean and did things they did not wish. Bohdan expected Moscow openly to break with Poland and attack it from the east, so as to free the Ukraine from Poland and take it under its wing. But the subtly calculating Muscovite diplomats waited for the victorious Cossacks to bring the Poles to such a pass that they would abandon the rebellious Ukraine, which could then be united to Great Russia legally, without violating "perpetual peace" with Poland.

Two months before the Zborov affair, which was to settle the fate of Poland and the Ukraine, Bohdan humbly begged the Tsar "to give a blessing" to an attack by the Russian army against the Poles, their common enemy, while he, Bohdan, "in God's good time" would attack them from the Ukraine, praying that "the just and Orthodox sovereign would be tsar and autocrat of the Ukraine." Moscow's answer to this evidently sincere petition must have sounded like a cruel mockery to Bohdan. It said that "perpetual peace" with Poland could not be violated, but if the King released the ataman and the whole Zaporozhye host from their allegiance, the Tsar would show favor to the ataman and all the Zaporozhye host, and command that they be taken under his sovereign protection. Misunderstanding and distrusting each other, both sides badly knocked their heads against something they had failed to see in time.

Bohdan was a brave swordsman and a wily diplomat, but he was not a statesman. Once when he had taken a drop too much he expressed the basic principle of his domestic policy to Polish commissioners by saying, "If a prince commits a crime, cut his head off. If a Cossack commits a crime, do the same to him. That will be justice." He regarded his rebellion merely as a struggle of the Cossacks against the Polish gentry, who treated them "as the lowest of slaves," and he admitted that he and his Cossacks bitterly hated the magnates and the gentry. But he did nothing to abolish or even to lessen the fatal social discord latent among the Cossacks themselves, although he was vaguely aware of it. It had begun before his time and manifested itself sharply after him; it was the rift between the Cossack elders and the Cossack rank and file, the common Cossacks in the towns and at Zaporozhye. The hostility between them caused endless strife, and as a consequence the Ukraine west of the Dnieper fell prey to the Turks and became a wilderness.

Moscow, too, received due retribution for its subtle and cautious diplomacy. It looked upon the union with the Ukraine from its traditional political point of view, as a further step in gathering together the Russian lands. A large tract of Russian territory was wrested from Poland and restored to its hereditary owner, the Tsar of Muscovy. After the conquest of White Russia and Lithuania, the Tsar's title was immediately revised, and he was styled "the autocrat of all Great and Little and White Russia, of Lithuania, Volhynia, and Podolia." But in Moscow they understood very little about relations between the different social groups in the Ukraine and took little notice of them, as being of no importance. The Moscow boyars wondered why Ataman Vyhovsky's envoys spoke with such contempt about the Zaporozhye Cossacks as gamblers and drunkards, while all the Cossack population, including the ataman, was called "the host of Zaporozhye." They questioned the envoys with interest, asking them whether the former atamans lived in towns or at Zaporozhye, and from what ranks they were elected, and where Bohdan Khmelnitsky himself came from. Evidently the Muscovite government, having annexed the Ukraine, found that it knew nothing whatever about its internal relations. In consequence, the Ukrainian question, so crookedly presented by both

sides, impeded and defeated Moscow's foreign policy for years
to come, entangled Muscovy in the hopeless Ukrainian squabbles,
split its forces in the struggle against Poland, compelled it to renounce Lithuania and White Russia with Volhynia and Podolia,
and barely permitted it to keep Ukrainian lands east of the
Dnieper, with Kiev on the opposite bank. After these losses
Moscow could apply to itself Bohdan Khmelnitsky's words when
he reproached it, weeping, for not having helped him in time: "It
was not this that I wanted, and this isn't the way things should
have happened."

The Ukrainian question directly or indirectly complicated
Moscow's foreign policy. Tsar Alexei began the war with Poland for the Ukraine in 1654, and soon gained the whole of
White Russia and a considerable part of Lithuania with the
towns of Vilna, Kovno, and Grodno. While Muscovy was an-
nexing Poland's eastern provinces, another enemy, the Swedish
King Charles X, attacked the country from the north and, moving as quickly as the Russians, occupied all Great and Little
Poland with Cracow and Warsaw, drove out King Jan Casimir,
and proclaimed himself king of Poland. Finally he tried to rob
Tsar Alexei of Lithuania. Thus the two enemies who had been
attacking Poland from different sides collided and quarreled
over the booty. Tsar Alexei recalled Ivan IV's idea about the
shores of the Baltic and Livonia, and the war with Poland was
interrupted in 1656 by war with Sweden. The forgotten idea of
expanding the Muscovite territory to its natural boundary, the
Baltic Sea, came to the fore again. The question remained as far
from solution as ever. The Russians did not succeed in taking
Riga, and the Tsar soon stopped military operations and finally
made peace with Sweden in 1661, giving back all he had gained
from it. The war proved fruitless and indeed harmful to Muscovy, because it gave Poland a chance to recover from the Swedish onslaught; but it did something to prevent the union of the
two states under the same king. They were equally hostile to
Muscovy but constantly weakened their own powers by opposing each other.

Bohdan was nearing his end, but once more he stood in the

way of both his friends and his enemies, of both the state he had betrayed and the one he had sworn to serve. Alarmed by the rapprochement between Russia and Poland, he made an agreement with King Charles X of Sweden and the Transylvanian Prince Rakoczy to divide Poland among the three of them. A true representative of the Cossacks, who were accustomed to serve any number of customers, Bohdan had been a servant or an ally or sometimes a traitor to all the neighboring sovereigns— the King of Poland, the Tsar of Muscovy, the Khan of the Crimea, the Sultan, the ruler of Moldavia, and the Prince of Transylvania. Finally he hatched out a plan to be an independent prince of the Ukraine under Charles X, who wanted to be king both of Sweden and of Poland. It was these intrigues of the dying Bohdan that made Tsar Alexei end the war with Sweden as best he could.

The Ukraine was also responsible for involving Moscow for the first time in direct conflict with Turkey. After Bohdan's death there began an open struggle between the Cossack elders and the rank and file. His successor, Ataman Vyhovsky, went over to the Polish king, and together with the Tatars destroyed Tsar Alexei's best army at Konotop. The Poles, encouraged by this, and freed from the Swedes with Moscow's help, refused to give Moscow any of its war gains. There began a second war with Poland, bringing with it two military disasters to Muscovy: Prince Khovansky's defeat in White Russia and Sheremetev's capitulation at Chudnovo in Volhynia because of the Cossacks' treachery. Lithuania and White Russia were lost. Vyhovsky's successors, Bohdan's two sons, Iuri and Teteria, proved to be traitors. The Ukraine split into two hostile halves. The area east of the Dnieper belonged to Muscovy, and the area west of the Dnieper belonged to Poland. The King had seized almost the whole of the Ukraine.

Both warring states became completely exhausted. Moscow had no money left to pay its soldiers, and issued copper coinage at the value of silver, which caused a riot in 1662. Great Poland, under the leadership of Lubomirski, rebelled against its king. Muscovy and Poland seemed prepared to drain each other to the last drop of blood. They were saved by their common enemy, Ataman Doroshenko, who surrendered himself and the Ukraine west of the Dnieper to the Sultan in 1666. Menaced by a formidable enemy, Poland and Muscovy concluded an armistice at Andrusovo in 1667, and that put an end to the war. Moscow retained the Smolensk and Seversk regions and the eastern Ukraine with Kiev. It now occupied an extended front line along the Dnieper from its upper reaches down to Zaporozhye, which, true to its historical character, remained a halfway house, serving both Poland and Muscovy.

The Treaty of Andrusovo resulted in a sharp change in Moscow's foreign policy. From the cautiously shortsighted B. I. Morozov, leadership passed to A. L. Ordin-Nashchokin, the author of the treaty, who was capable of looking ahead. He began working out a new political combination. Poland no longer appeared dangerous. The perennial struggle with it was discontinued for a long time, for a whole century. The Ukrainian question was crowded out by other problems to which it had given rise: those of Livonia—that is, of Sweden—and of Turkey. In order to contend with them, it was essential to have an alliance with Poland, menaced by both these countries. Poland itself eagerly sought the alliance. Ordin-Nashchokin developed the idea as part of a system. In a note that he submitted to the Tsar before the Andrusovo Treaty, he used three arguments to prove that such an alliance was necessary: it alone could make it possible to protect the Orthodox population in Poland; only a close alliance with Poland could restrain the Cossacks from beginning a cruel war against Muscovy at the instigation of the Crimean Khan and the Swedes; and finally, if this alliance were concluded, the Moldavians and Walachians, now separated from Orthodox Russia by a Poland hostile to it, would be able to join Russia and forsake the Turks. Then all the Walachians from the Danube and the Dniester regions, all Podolia, Red Russia, Volhynia, the Ukraine, and Great Russia would form one great and numerous Christian people, children of the same mother—the Orthodox Church.

This last argument must have particularly appealed to Tsar

Alexei, who had long been concerned about the Christians in Turkey. At Easter in 1656, in church, having exchanged Easter greetings with Greek merchants who lived in Moscow, the Tsar asked them whether they wished him to free them from the Turkish yoke. They naturally answered in the affirmative, and he continued: "When you return to your country, ask your bishops, priests, and monks to pray for me, and through their prayers my sword will sever my enemies' necks." Then, turning to the boyars, he said with copious tears that his heart was aching for those poor people enslaved by the infidels, and that on the Day of Judgment God would call him to account if, although he had the chance to free them, he neglected to do so; but that he had vowed to sacrifice his army, his treasury, and his very blood in order to save them. This was reported by the Greek merchants themselves. In the treaty of 1672, shortly before the Sultan's invasion of Poland, the Tsar promised to help the King in case of a Turkish attack, and to send envoys to the Sultan and the Khan to dissuade them from waging war on Poland.

The views of the two parties to the unusual alliance by no means coincided. Poland cared above all for its external security, while Moscow was equally concerned about its coreligionists. That problem had two sides to it. Russia thought of Turkish Christians, and Turkey of Russian Moslems. Religious relations in eastern Europe cut across one another as early as the sixteenth century. Tsar Ivan IV conquered two Moslem khanates, Kazan and Astrakhan. The conquered Moslems turned with hope and supplication to their spiritual head, the successor of the caliphs, the Sultan of Turkey, appealing to him to free them from the Christian yoke. At the same time there lived in the Balkans under the power of the Sultan a numerous population of the same roots and religion as the Russian people. These people turned, also with hope and supplication, to the Tsar of Muscovy as the protector of the Orthodox East, appealing to him to free Turkish Christians from the Moslem yoke.

The thought of fighting the Turks with Moscow's help was spreading rapidly among the Balkan Christians. As stipulated in the treaty, the Muscovite envoys went to Constantinople to dissuade the Sultan from invading Poland. They brought back some significant information. Traveling through Moldavia and Walachia, they heard people say, "If God would only grant the Christians even a small victory over the Turks, we'd begin at once making profit out of the infidels." In Constantinople the Muscovite envoys were told that recently envoys from the Kazan and Astrakhan Tatars and Bashkirs had been there, asking the Sultan to accept under his sovereignty the states of Kazan and Astrakhan, and complaining that the Muscovites, out of hatred for their Moslem faith, beat many of them to death, and plundered them constantly. The Sultan bade the Tatars be patient a little longer, and presented their envoys with new tabards.

Thus the Ukrainian question entailed two others, the Baltic and the eastern—the question of acquiring the shores of the Baltic sea and of relations with Turkey on account of the Balkan Christians. The second question was at the time merely theoretically developed in the benevolent thoughts of Tsar Alexei and Ordin-Nashchokin. The Russian state was not yet strong enough to approach it directly and practically, and meanwhile all the Muscovite government could do was struggle with the enemy that blocked the way to Turkey—the Crimea. For Muscovite diplomacy this Crimea was a thorn in the flesh. It entered as a vexatious hindrance into every international combination. At the very beginning of Tsar Alexei's reign, when there had not yet been time to settle outstanding accounts with Poland, Moscow was already urging Poland to conclude an offensive alliance against the Crimea. When in 1686 the Andrusovo armistice was replaced by a permanent peace treaty, the Muscovite state entered for the first time a European coalition—a quadruple alliance with Poland, the Holy Roman Empire, and Venice against the Turks. It chose for itself the part that was most familiar to it—struggle with the Tatars, attack upon the Crimea. Thus every new step made Muscovy's foreign policy more complex. The government established new ties or reestablished old ones with many states that could help it against hostile neighbors, or which needed its help in their European relations.

Muscovy proved to be of some value to Europe. Even at the time of its worst international humiliation, soon after the Troubles, it retained some diplomatic weight. International relations in the West were for the moment favorable to it. They were becoming unstable, for the Thirty Years' War had just begun, and every state was seeking outside support, afraid of isolation. Although Muscovy was politically weak, its significance for the Orthodox Church and its geographical position gave it power. The French ambassador Courmenant—the first ambassador sent by·France to Moscow—called Tsar Michael "chief of the eastern land and of the Greek religion," and it was not simply out of French politeness that he did so.

Muscovy stood at the rear of all the states between the Baltic and the Adriatic. When their mutual relations grew entangled and war spread over the western half of the European continent, each of these states was anxious to safeguard its eastern boundary by making an alliance with Muscovy or desisting from hostilities against it. That was why, after the accession of the new dynasty, the circle of Muscovy's external relations began to expand, even without any effort on the part of its government. Moscow was drawn into various political and economic combinations that were being formed in Europe. England and Holland helped Tsar Michael to come to terms with hostile Poland and Sweden, because Muscovy was a good market for their merchandise and a convenient route to the East, to Persia and even to India. The French king offered Michael an alliance because France had commercial interests in the East, rivaling those of England and Holland. The Sultan himself invited Michael to fight with him against Poland. The Swedish king, Gustavus Adolphus, who by the Stolbovo Treaty had robbed Muscovy of its war gains, had enemies in common with Muscovy in Poland and Austria, and so he suggested to the Muscovite diplomats the idea of forming an anti-Catholic alliance. He tempted them with the prospect of making their humiliated fatherland an organic and independent member of the political world of Europe, and called the victorious Swedish army fighting in Germany the advance guard that defended the state of Muscovy. He was the first to appoint an ambassador to reside in Moscow. Under Tsar Michael the Muscovite state was weaker than under Ivan IV and Feodor, but it was much less isolated from Europe. This was even more the case in Tsar Alexei's reign. The arrival of foreign envoys in Moscow became quite a familiar event, and Muscovite envoys went to various European courts, including those of Spain and Tuscany.

Muscovite diplomacy had never before had such a wide field of activity. But while it sometimes gained and sometimes suffered loss on its western frontiers, Muscovy unfailingly advanced eastward. As early as the sixteenth century Russian colonization spread beyond the Urals, and in the course of the sixteenth century it went far into the depths of Siberia, reaching the Chinese frontier. By the middle of the seventeenth century Muscovite territory had increased by at least seventy thousand square miles, if indeed one can apply any geometrical measure to its acquisitions there. These successes of Russian colonization in the east eventually brought the Muscovite state into conflict with China.

And so the external relations of the state grew more complex and difficult. They had a many-sided effect upon its internal life. As wars became more frequent, Moscow was made to feel more and more the shortcomings of the Russian ways of life and the need to learn more about other countries. As visits of foreign envoys grew more frequent, opportunities for making instructive comparisons increased also. Closer contacts with western Europe opened a way out of the narrow circle of tradition-bound ideas and prejudices, if only for the Muscovite ruling class. But, above all, wars and new experiences made people aware of the paucity of their material means, of the antiquated deficiencies of their military equipment, the meager productivity of labor, and the inability to make a profitable use of it. Every new war, every defeat brought the government new cares and difficulties, and new burdens to the people. The external policy of the state imposed an ever increasing strain upon the national resources. A brief enumeration of wars waged by the first three tsars of the new dynasty is sufficient to show how great that strain was.

Under Tsar Michael there were two wars with Poland and one with Sweden—all three unsuccessful. Under his successor, Tsar Alexei, there were again two wars with Poland over the Ukraine and one with Sweden. Both of them were also unsuccessful. Under Tsar Feodor there was a trying war with Turkey, begun in his father's reign in 1673 and ended by the futile Bakhchisarai armistice in 1681. The western Ukraine beyond the Dnieper remained in Turkish hands. If you consider the length of all these wars, you will see that out of some seventy years from 1613 to 1682, thirty were spent in war, sometimes against several opponents at once.

Chapter
VII

Law and Society

Let us turn again to the internal life of the Muscovite state. A survey of its foreign policy and of the immediate consequences of the Time of Troubles has shown that the government of the new dynasty was faced with difficult external problems, while its material and moral resources were well-nigh exhausted. We must now consider where and how it was to find the means it lacked.

In answering this question we shall go over the most conspicuous events in Russia's internal life. They are very complex and move along different lines, which sometimes meet and sometimes go in opposite directions. Yet we can discern their common source—the profound changes brought about by the Time of Troubles in the people's mentality and their mutual relations. Custom, which under the old dynasty had been the mainstay of the state order, lost its stability; tradition, which had guided the builders and guardians of that order, was broken. When people cease to act from habit and lose the thread of tradition, they begin to think hard and fretfully. This renders them suspicious and hesitant, and makes them timidly try various methods of action. Such timidity was characteristic of Muscovite statesmen of the seventeenth century. They had plenty of new ideas, the fruit of painful experience and hard thinking, but they moved with an unsteady gait, as though uncertain of their bearings—a sign that they were unused to the new situation. They recognized that the means at their disposal were inadequate for dealing with the problems they had to face, and at first they tried to find new means in the old national sources, and by putting more strain on the people to repair, complete, or reestablish the state order bequeathed to them by their fathers and forefathers. Then, observing that domestic supplies were exhausted, they anxiously rushed in another direction and called in foreign aid to support their flagging forces; but after a time they again succumbed to timorous reflections, wondering if they had deviated too far from ancestral tradition, and might after all manage with domestic remedies, without outside help. For a time these changes alternated. In the second half of the seventeenth century they ran concurrently. At the end of it they came into conflict and produced a number of political and ecclesiastical upheavals. With the beginning of the eighteenth century Peter's reforms forced them into a single channel, directed toward the same goal. Such, in general outline, was the course of Muscovy's internal life from the end of the Time of Troubles to the beginning of the eighteenth century. Let us turn now to its separate stages.

However much the new dynasty strove to act in the spirit of the old one, so as to make people forget that it was new and therefore less legitimate, it could not dispense with innovations. The Troubles had broken down so much of the past that the very restoration of the ruins inevitably acquired the character of reform, of innovation. Innovations continued in a broken series from the first reign of the new dynasty to the end of the century, preparing the ground for Peter the Great's reforms. As I have just mentioned, we can discern in the stream of these preparatory innovations two trends of different origin and character, which at times ran concurrently and indeed seemed to merge. One series of reforms was introduced without foreign help, by domestic means, as suggested by one's own reason and experience. And since domestic means consisted solely in increasing the power of the state at the expense of civic liberty, and in restricting private enterprise for the sake of the state's requirements, every reform of that kind involved a heavy sacrifice of the people's prosperity and freedom. But human affairs follow a law of their own, independent of men's intentions; it is what is usually called "the force of things." Recourse to homemade reforms was soon felt to be insufficient or completely useless, and the more apparent this became, the stronger grew the conviction that it was necessary to learn from other nations and to borrow from outside.

The purpose of the homemade innovations was to preserve or to reestablish the order disturbed by the Time of Troubles, and accordingly they were marked by typically Muscovite caution and halfheartedness. They introduced new forms, new methods of action, but no new principles. The general tendency of this innovatory activity may be described as an endeavor to overhaul the state order without making any radical change in it, to make partial repairs without rebuilding the whole. In the first place it was necessary to organize social relations, disturbed by the Troubles, to fit them into a firm framework, and to regulate them by hard and fast rules. In this respect Tsar Michael's government had to struggle with endless difficulties. The whole mechanism of the state was shattered, so that everything had to be renewed and almost completely rebuilt. The author of the Pskov record of the Time of Troubles, to whom I referred earlier, says bluntly that under Tsar Michael, "the state began being built afresh." His reign was a time of lively legislative activity, concerned with the most diverse aspects of public life.

Toward the beginning of his successor's reign a fairly large number of new laws had accumulated, and it was felt that they ought to be sorted out. In accordance with the established procedure, new laws were issued chiefly in response to questions from this or that government department in connection with its juridical and administrative work, and were sent to the department in question for guidance and information. There the new law was added to the Sudebnik of 1550, as required by one of its articles. Thus the basic code, like the trunk of a tree, put forth fresh branches in the different ministries. Their books of edicts were continuations of the sudebnik. These departmental continuations had to be unified and included in one comprehensive code, to avoid the repetition of an incident, probably unique of its kind, that happened in Ivan the Terrible's reign. Adashev raised in the Boyars' Council a legislative question from the Department of Petitions. The same question had already been asked by the Treasury and been settled, but the Boyars' Council seemed to have forgotten this; it ordered that its decision be registered in the book of edicts of the Treasury Department once more. It also happened sometimes that one governmental department would search the registers of others for the record of a law that had been duly entered in its own book of edicts. Obviously, an ignorant clerk could make a hopeless muddle of things, and a clever one could twist them as he pleased.

The need for codification, made all the more urgent by the officials' malpractices, was chiefly responsible for the appearance of the Ulozhenie, the new code of law; indeed, to some extent it actually determined its character. Other circumstances no doubt influenced it as well. The unusual position in which the state found itself after the Time of Troubles inevitably created new demands and set unprecedented tasks to the government. The country's needs, rather than new political ideas acquired during the Troubles, speeded up the government's legislative activity and gave it a new direction in spite of the new dynasty's efforts to be faithful to the past.

Before the seventeenth century, Muscovite law had consisted of a body of case law. It answered particular questions raised by administrative practice, and did not touch upon the basic principles of state order, which rested not upon written law, but upon ancient tradition, familiar to all and universally recognized. As soon as the tradition was broken and the state began to deviate from its habitual course, there arose an urgent need to replace custom by clearly formulated law. That was why legislation became more systematic under the new dynasty, and was no longer confined to particular instances of state organization; it began to concern itself with state order as such, trying, though unsuccessfully, to clarify and express the principles that lay at the basis of it.

It is not easy to determine what relation the Ulozhenie had to the Moscow mutiny of 1648, which took place some six weeks before the Tsar and his council had decided to compile a new law code. The mutiny threw a clear light on the new dynasty's position. Its first two tsars did not enjoy the people's respect. In spite of its elective origin, the new dynasty soon acquired the habits of the old one. It began to look upon the state as its hereditary property and to rule it in an offhand way, with the good-natured carelessness of a country squire. Generally speaking, it successfully copied the defects of the old dynasty—perhaps because there was nothing else in it to copy. The poor remains of the shattered nobility, with an admixture of new people who were no better, formed the court circle, ardently aspiring to become the ruling class. The most influential part of that circle consisted of the Tsar's, and especially the Tsaritsa's, relatives and minions. For years to come the new dynasty's throne was enveloped in a fog of favoritism. A long series of men wielding power through the Tsar's favor stretches throughout the first three reigns. Under Michael there were the Saltykovs, Prince Repnin, and again the Saltykovs; under Alexei there were Morozov, the Miloslavskys, Nikon, Khitrovo; under Feodor there were Iazykov and Likhachov. Patriarch Filaret himself, styled "the second great sovereign," behaved not like the courteous nobleman he had once been, but like any other man in power, and appointed as his successor to the patriarchate a man whose only merit was to have been a bondsman of Filaret's. To make matters worse, the first three tsars acceded to the throne as minors—the first two at the age of sixteen and the third at fourteen. Taking advantage first of their youth and later of their lack of firmness, the ruling circles encouraged arbitrariness and graft in the administration to an extent that would have been envied by the worst officials of Ivan IV's time, who "fed the Tsar on one half of the state revenue and kept the other for themselves," in the words of Muscovite *émigrés* of the period.

Administrative malpractice was all the easier because the culprits were in a privileged position with regard to punishment. As
we know, Tsar Michael bound himself not to put men of noble
lineage to death for any crime whatsoever, but only to sentence
them to exile and strict confinement. Under Tsar Alexei it sometimes happened that for the same kind of crime persons of high
rank were punished merely by the Tsar's displeasure or by dis-
missal from their posts, while lower officials and common people
had a hand or a foot cut off. Commitments secretly made by
the tsars to the nobility put the new dynasty into a radically
false position, and created an impression of conspiracy between
the sovereign and the nobles against the people. Kotoshikhin's
words about Tsar Michael are revealing in this connection: "Although he styled himself an autocrat, he could do nothing without the boyars' advice"—and was glad to be left in peace, adds
Tatishchev; in other words, he left the government to the
boyars.

The people instinctively understood this, and with the accession of the new dynasty there began an era of popular uprisings.
Alexei's reign in particular was a "rebellious time," as people
said. By then the type of the "strong man," or a man temporarily
in power, was firmly established in Muscovite society and administration. The term meant a person in authority, a privileged
landowner, lay or clerical, or an official favored by the court
and sure that he could do with impunity anything he liked, sufficiently unscrupulous to take advantage of the general lack of
rights and use his power against defenseless people, "oppressing
them and wronging them with many wrongs." This was perhaps
the most characteristic and successful product of the new dynasty's domestic policy, worked out by the Muscovite ruling
circles in full confidence that the Tsar was in their hands and
could not manage without them.

The common people hated those powerful upstarts wholeheartedly. The Moscow rebellion of June 1648, which had many
repercussions in other towns, was a clear expression of that
feeling. The common people in the capital, more than in other
towns, suffered from the strong men, lay and clerical. The Pa-

triarch, bishops, and monasteries were no better off than the laity. Pastureland around Moscow was taken over and occupied by new settlements, suburban houses, and kitchen gardens. By-roads to the surrounding woods were plowed up, so that a towns-man had nowhere to graze his cattle and could not drive to the forest to get fuel—something that had never happened under former sovereigns. The June riots were a rebellion of the common people against the strong. "The rabble rose against the boyars," began plundering their houses and those of the gentry and government clerks, and attacked the most hated of the high officials.

The lesson had a considerable effect. The court was greatly alarmed. Steps were taken to mollify the Muscovite soldiery and the mob. At the Tsar's command the streltsy were treated to drinks. For several days the Tsar's father-in-law entertained delegates from the taxpaying population of the capital in his home. The Tsar himself, during a church procession, addressed the people with a speech that sounded like an apology, and with tears in his eyes "begged the rabble" to spare his dear friend and relative Morozov. Promises were lavishly given. The rulers began to fear the community. Rumors went about that the Tsar had become gracious and was driving the strong men out of his realm, that they were being stoned and beaten. Under the old dynasty Moscow had never experienced such stormy manifestations of popular resentment against the ruling classes, had never seen such a rapid transition from contempt for the people to pandering to them or heard such unseemly speeches about the Tsar as spread through the city after the riots. "The Tsar is a fool. He does what the boyars Morozov and Miloslavsky tell him. They are the real masters, and the Tsar himself knows it, but he says nothing. The devil robbed him of his wits."

It was not the Moscow riot of June 1648, soon reenacted in other towns, that prompted the idea of compiling the new law code—there were other reasons for this—but it caused the government to invite representatives of the people to take part in the work. The Zemsky Sobor, called for September 1 of the same year to hear and confirm the new code, was regarded by the government as a means of pacifying the people. We may well believe Patriarch Nikon, who wrote, as though it were a matter of common knowledge, that the Zemsky Sobor was summoned "out of fear of the common people and of civil strife, and not for the cause of truth." There is no doubt that although the riots were not the original reason for undertaking the work of codification, they affected the course of it. The government's alarm interfered with the work.

The idea of compiling a new law code came in the first instance from the Tsar, with a small advisory assembly consisting of the Patriarch's synod and the Boyars' Council. Proclamations sent to the provinces in the summer of 1648 said that a statute book was to be written at the command of the Tsar and the Patriarch, the decision of the boyars, and the petition of stewards, clerks, and men of all ranks. It is hard to say when and how such a petition was presented to the government, and indeed whether it was presented at all. It was a habit of the Muscovite governments that replaced one another after the end of the old dynasty to speak in the name of "all the land." Under the new tsars "petitions from men of all ranks" became a stereotyped formula used indiscriminately to sanction every important governmental action. It was sufficient for an accidentally formed group of men of different ranks to address a petition to the Tsar, and a ukase would follow "in accordance with the petition of men of all ranks." This official counterfeit of the people's will became a kind of political fiction, preserved to this day as a survival from the past and used on special occasions with a purely conventional meaning.

In any event, it is certain that on July 16, 1648, the Tsar with the Boyars' Council and the Holy Synod decreed that passages should be chosen from apostolic and patristic rules and Byzantine emperors' laws applicable to state and civic affairs. Decrees of former Russian sovereigns and boyars' verdicts should be collected and compared with the old law codes. If there were no decrees or verdicts on some matters, new articles were to be written. All this was to be done "by general consultation." A special codifying committee was entrusted with drafting the plan of the Ulozhenie. It consisted of five members—the princes Odoevsky, Prozorovsky, and Volkonsky, and two secretaries, Leontev and Griboedov. They were not particularly influential men and did not stand out in any way from other courtiers and officials. The Tsar himself, sharing the general opinion, thought poorly of Prince Odoevsky. Only the clerk Griboedov left a trace in Russian letters; at some later date he wrote a textbook of Russian history, probably for the Tsar's children. The author traced the descent of the new dynasty, through Tsaritsa Anastasiia, to the son of a nonexistent Romanov styled "sovereign of the Prussian land," a reputed relative of the Roman Caesar Augustus.

The three chief members of the committee sat in the Boyars' Council, so "Prince Odoevsky's and his comrades' department," as it is called in the documents, was evidently the Council's committee. It had to select passages from the sources indicated to it and compose new articles. Both were written out and submitted for consideration to the Tsar and the Boyars' Council. Meanwhile, by September 1 delegates of every rank had been summoned to Moscow: servicemen, tradesmen, townsmen. The rural and provincial population as a whole was not represented. From October 3 onward the Tsar, with the clergy and members of his council, listened to the draft of the Ulozhenie prepared by the committee. At the same time it was read to all the delegates, so that after "general consultation, the whole of the Ulozhenie should be secure and unchangeable." Then the Tsar bade the church hierarchs, the members of the Boyars' Council, and the delegates to confirm the text of the code by signing it. It was printed in 1649 with the signatures of the Sobor's members and sent to all the government offices in Moscow and the provinces, so that "all business should be carried on in accordance with the Ulozhenie."

Such is the history of the new law code as it is told in its official preface. The committee had a twofold task laid upon it: first it had to collect, sort out, and codify current laws that had been issued at various times, did not tally with one another, and were recorded by some departments and not by others; second, it had to classify cases not foreseen in those laws.

The second task was particularly difficult. The committee could not rely solely on its own judicial foresight and judgment in picking out such cases and deciding to which category they belonged. It was essential to have a knowledge of social needs and relations, to study the national conception of justice and the practice of legal and administrative institutions. At any rate, that is how we would approach the task at the present time. In dealing with its first task the committee could obtain information from the delegates. In dealing with the second it would have to look through the files of government offices in order to find precedents or suitable instances and discover how cases unforeseen by the law had been settled by provincial governors, central departments, and the Tsar himself with the Boyars' Council. It was a tremendous work, requiring many long years.

Such an ambitious undertaking, however, was not contemplated. It was decided to compile the Ulozhenie by a quick method on a simplified program. The Ulozhenie was divided into twenty-five chapters containing 967 articles. By the end of September 1648—that is, in two and a half months' time—the first twelve chapters, almost half of the whole code, were drafted, and from October 3 onward the sovereign had them read to him and his Council. The remaining thirteen chapters were compiled, heard, and ratified by the end of January 1649, when the committee's and the Sobor's work had been finished and the text of the Ulozhenie had been written down. That means that the fairly large volume was compiled in about eighteen months. To understand why the legislative work was done so rapidly we must bear in mind that while the Ulozhenie was being drawn up, alarming news of riots came from Solvychegodsk, Kozlov, Talitsk, Ustiug, and other towns, following the Moscow mutiny in June. In January 1649, when the committee was completing its task, there were rumors of a new rebellion brewing in Moscow. The work was being done in a hurry so that the delegates could hasten to their respective towns and tell the people of the new course being taken by the government and of the Ulozhenie, which promised everyone equal and fair judgment.

The Ulozhenie was indeed compiled hurriedly and haphazardly, and it bears traces of that hurry. The committee did not attempt to study all the legal material accumulated in various government departments, but confined itself to the main sources indicated to it in the instruction of July 16. These were the Kormchaia (the second part of it), containing the codes and decrees of the Byzantine emperors, the Muscovite sudebniks, the Sudebnik of 1550, and the decrees and boyars' verdicts complementary to it—that is, the books of edicts of the different departments. These books were the richest sources of the Ulozhenie. A number of chapters in it are compiled from them and are full of extracts, paraphrased or copied out word for word. Thus, two chapters on hereditary and service estates are made up from the books of the Department of Estates. The chapter on the bondsmen's court of justice comes from the books of the Department of Justice, the chapter on brigands and thieving from the books of the Brigandage Department.

In addition to these main sources, the committee used auxiliary ones. It makes a somewhat peculiar use of a foreign code, the Lithuanian Statute of 1588. In the original text of the Ulozhenie, still extant, we find constant references to it. The committee members followed the statute, especially in the early chapters, in the arrangement of subject matter, the order of articles, the choice of cases requiring legal definition, and the framing of legal questions; but they always sought the answers in their own native jurisprudence. They borrowed, so to speak, the schemata of juridical situations in so far as these were common to both the Lithuanian and the Russian law or made no difference to either, but they left out all that was unnecessary or foreign to the Muscovite conception and practice of legal justice. They made a new version of everything that they borrowed, so that the statute was not so much a source of the Ulozhenie as a help for codifying it and providing its compilers with a ready-made program.

The committee had to use another auxiliary source, all the more important because it was a living source, not provided by the archives: I mean the Sobor itself, or, more exactly, the elected delegates who were called to listen to the reading of the Ulozhenie and to sign it. We have seen how the code came into being. The initiative came from the Tsar and the Boyars' Council; the draft was prepared by the Council's committee with the help of the governmental departments, which provided the material and the references, was examined, corrected, and confirmed by the Council, and then was read to the delegates for their information and signature. The country's representatives, however, were not merely passive listeners to a code that had been drawn up independently of them. True, there is nothing to show that the delegates discussed the articles of the Ulozhenie while it was being read to them. They were not asked to say yes or no to each article after they had listened to it. Nevertheless, they were able to take a considerable part in the work, and they did so in several different ways.

The decree of July 16 did not call for a new law code. It merely charged the committee with collecting and coordinating the existing supply of government enactments, and establishing agreement between the old law codes, the Tsar's decrees, and the boyars' verdicts. The committee introduced new articles merely to fill the gaps in the existing laws. It had to do its work in general consultation with the country's elected representatives, who were summoned to Moscow "to do the Tsar's and the country's business" together with the boyars, Prince Odoevsky, and his colleagues, and "be in their department." Evidently the country's representatives formed part of the codifying committee or were attached to it. As they became familiar with the draft in the course of preparation, the delegates, being well-informed people, pointed out to the codifiers what changes and additions should be made, and stated their own needs. The committee gave these statements and recommendations the form of petitions from the people and submitted them to the Boyars' Council, which passed its verdict on them. The Council's decisions were announced to the delegates as laws and entered in the Ulozhenie. In this way the delegates could take part in the actual drafting of the code.

It is hard to say whether these committee consultations were held at the general meeting of the delegates, who numbered no less than 290, or in smaller groups. We know that on October 30, 1648, delegates of servicemen and commercial townspeople submitted two separate petitions asking for the imposition of a tax upon suburban villages, town houses, and trading establishments belonging to untaxed owners. The committee put these petitions together and submitted them to the Council as the general request from "the whole land." These petitions, reports, citations, and references and the Council's verdicts upon them eventually formed a body of rules on the composition of urban communities and their relations with outsiders pursuing a trade in the town. Chapter XIX of the Ulozhenie consists of these rules.

Advisory directions to the committee members and petitions submitted through them to the Council were two means by which the delegates took part in compiling the Ulozhenie. There was a third way, the most important of all: the delegates could come into direct contact not with the committee, but with the Tsar's council itself. This happened when the sovereign and his councilors appeared among the delegates to discuss the subject under discussion. The Ulozhenie mentions one such case, though it was not the only one; the elected representatives of all ranks petitioned on behalf of the whole country to take away from the church such lands as came into the clergy's possession contrary to the law of 1580. In Chapter XVII of the Ulozhenie, dealing with hereditary estates, a new article (42) was inserted saying that the Tsar, after consultation with the Holy Synod, members of the Boyars' Council, and elected representatives of servicemen, decided "jointly with the Sobor" to forbid transferring hereditary estates to the church. The delegates were thus given a direct share in legislation; not all of them, only servicemen, as representatives of hereditary landowners whose interests were involved. The petition, however, came from the whole country, "from men of all ranks." The central government proved to be on a lower level of political consciousness than the elected representatives. It was concerned with class interests only, while they thought of the country as a whole.

Two other decisions of the Sobor in which the delegates took part are known to us from documents, though they are not directly mentioned in the Ulozhenie. At the petition of the serviceman delegates, the Tsar with his Council and the petitioners decided to abolish the time limit for returning runaway peasants to their owners. This decision is set forth at the beginning of Chapter XI of the Ulozhenie, "Concerning Peasants." Still more important is Chapter VIII, "On Ransoming Captives"; it introduces a general tax per household for ransoming prisoners and states the tariff at which ransom was to be paid. This chapter repeats the decree jointly issued by the Tsar, his Council, and "elected men of all ranks." On that occasion all the elected members of the Zemsky Sobor shared in its legislative power.

Finally, one particular case clearly shows both the attitude of the delegates to the work of compiling the Ulozhenie and the attitude of the government to the people's petitions. A delegate of the Kursk gentry, Malyshev, before going home at the end of the Sobor's session, obtained at his urgent request a safe-conduct from the Tsar to defend him—from whom, do you think? From his own electors! He was afraid they would "do him harm" for two reasons: first, because he had not succeeded in getting all their demands dealt with in the Ulozhenie, and second, he had been overzealous in the cause of piety, and in a special petition to the Tsar "said evil things" of his Kursk fellow citizens, accusing them of spending Sundays and holy days "in unseemly fashion." With regard to the first point, the safe-conduct cleared him of the charge of having failed to introduce into the Ulozhenie his electors' "various whims." As to the second point, Malyshev puts the blame on the government and the Tsar himself, complaining that the Ulozhenie merely indicated the hours of work and business on Sundays and holy days (Chapter X, Article 25), but did not prohibit or punish "wrong conduct on feast days," as he had asked in his petition. The Tsar took heed of the moralist's persistent request and commanded that rescripts be issued "with strict prohibitions" about the proper manner of spending holy days, but he made no addition to the Ulozhenie.

We can now form an idea of the way in which the Ulozhenie was compiled. It was a complicated process in which the following aspects may be distinguished: codification, consultation, revision, legislative decision, and ratification by the signatories as the last stage indicated in the decree of July 16. The various functions were distributed among the various components of the Sobor; the Boyars' Council and the Holy Synod, headed by the sovereign; Prince Odoevsky's committee of five; and elected representatives attached to the committee rather than to the Council. All these taken together formed the 1648 Zemsky Sobor.

Codification was the business of Prince Odoevsky's department, and consisted in choosing and classifying legal enactments from the sources indicated to him. His committee had also to edit the delegates' petitions.

Consultation was the delegates' contribution to the committee's work. Their part in it consisted, as we have seen, in presenting petitions that served as debates and replaced verbal discussions. A case is recorded in which the delegates' petition was a direct expression of protest and resulted in the annulment or alteration of the Tsar's ukase, which they opposed. I have already mentioned the delegates' petition to impose a tax on privileged suburban villages belonging to private owners. A decree was issued that these villages should be taxed and transferred to crown ownership after preliminary inquiry as to the place the inhabitants had originally come from and the date of their coming, if it was after 1613. The delegates, afraid of the Muscovite officials' usual procrastination and underhanded dealings, sent in another petition asking that the suburban villages be transferred to the crown "without dates and without inquiring where the people were living at present." The petition was put before the Tsar that very day and fully granted.

Revision and legislative decisions were left to the Tsar and his Council. Revision consisted in looking through the current laws as codified by the committee. The decree of July 16 sus-

pended, as it were, the action of these laws, reducing them to
the level of temporary regulations until they received new legislative sanction. While the Ulozhenie was being compiled, the old
laws lost their binding power, but they still remained the basis
of legal norms. The Boyars' Council either revised their wording
or reconsidered their subject matter and altered or canceled
them. Most frequently it added to the proposed draft some old
decree overlooked by the committee, or a new regulation to
meet some unforeseen case. Thus revision was combined with
editing. I shall confine myself to one instance mentioned in the
Ulozhenie. At the beginning of Chapter XVII, "On Hereditary
Estates," the committee included the decrees of Tsar Michael
and Patriarch Filaret on the order in which heirs should succeed to hereditary estates or to those awarded for service. The
Council confirmed these articles of the draft but made an addition to it specifying cases in which mothers and childless widows
of landowners should gain maintenance from the service estates.

Revision was entirely in the Council's hands, but in issuing
decisions on matters of law it shared its legislative power with
other sections of the Sobor, according to the nature of the case.
Sometimes the verdict was pronounced only by the Tsar with
the Boyars' Council, sometimes with the Holy Synod as well;
occasionally delegates from certain ranks were called in, and
more seldom the question was decided by the whole Sobor,
representative of men of all ranks. The intention was to make
the Ulozhenie "stable and unchangeable in time to come," but
it was being drawn up by a gathering that had nothing "stable
and unchangeable" about it. The common and binding task of
the Sobor, for which it had really been summoned, was to ratify
the law code by the signatures of all its members, both official
and elected. This was to be a guarantee on the part of the
rulers and of the people's representatives that they acknowledged
the Ulozhenie to be equitable and adequate to their requirements, and that they would conduct "all business in accordance
with it." Patriarch Nikon was quite wrong when he reviled the
Ulozhenie, calling it "an accursed book, the devil's law." In that
case, why had he said nothing while listening to that accursed

book and signing it in 1649, when he was archimandrite of the Novospassky Monastery?

The Ulozhenie was apparently intended to be the last word on Muscovite jurisprudence, a complete code of all legal enactments accumulated in Moscow government offices by the middle of the seventeenth century. This intention can be detected in the Ulozhenie, but it is not very successfully carried out. Considered from the technical point of view as a work of codification, it is no better than the old sudebniks. The arrangement of subject matter shows a desire to represent the state order by a vertical selection, with the church and the Tsar and his Council at the top, and the Cossacks and village taverns (dealt with in the last two chapters) at the bottom. At the cost of much effort the chapters of the Ulozhenie can be grouped into sections dealing respectively with constitutional law, with the organization and administration of justice, and with civil and criminal law. But the codifiers did not succeed in grouping them systematically. They did not make full and methodical use of the material at their disposal. Articles taken from various sources were not always correlated, and sometimes were wrongly placed; they were put together in a heap, rather than sorted out.

The fact that the Ulozhenie was in force for nearly two centuries, until it was replaced by the Code of 1833, does not testify to its merits, but only shows how long we Russians can manage without satisfactory law. But as a record of legislation the Ulozhenie was a considerable step in advance of the sudebniks. It was not merely a practical guide for judges and administrators, setting forth the procedure of reestablishing rights that had been violated and saying nothing about rights as such. True, the Ulozhenie, like the sudebniks, dwells chiefly on formal justice. Chapter X, "On Courts of Law," has more articles in it than any other, and forms almost a third of the code. There are important though quite intelligible gaps in the treatment of material justice. It contains no constitutional law, of which the Muscovite people of the period had no inkling; the sovereign's will and the pressure of circumstances were sufficient for them. There is no systematic exposition of family law, closely connected with common and ecclesiastical law. The legislators did not venture to impinge either upon custom, which was much too rigid and torpid, or upon the clergy, who were much too sensitive and jealous of their spiritual monopolies.

Nevertheless, the legislative scope of the Ulozhenie is far wider than that of the old sudebniks. It attempts to analyze the component elements of the community and define the positions and mutual relations between the different classes. It speaks of servicemen and service landownership, of peasants, townspeople, bondsmen, the streltsy, and the Cossacks. Most attention, of course, is paid to the gentry, as the dominant military and land-owning class. Almost half of the articles of the Ulozhenie are directly or indirectly concerned with its interests and position. There as elsewhere the compilers of the code strive to face reality.

In spite of its generally conservative character, the Ulozhenie could not help reflecting two reformative tendencies indicative of the direction in which the life of the community would develop or was already developing. In the decree of July 16 one of these tendencies found expression in the charge to the codifying committee to draw up such a law code that "in all matters judgment and penalties should be the same for men of all ranks, from the highest to the lowest." This did not mean general equality before the law and the same rights for everyone; it meant equal legal justice for all, without special immunity from this or that particular jurisdiction, without departmental distinctions, class privileges, and exemptions, which abounded in Muscovite legal practice. What the legislators had in view was fair and impartial judgment for both the nobility and the common people, the same jurisdiction and legal procedure for all, though the degrees of punishment might differ. Everyone, even a foreigner, was equally entitled to a fair trial, "regardless of the wrong," which had for its object to "save the wronged from the hand of the wrongdoer." Such is the injunction given in Chapter X, in which an attempt is made to establish equitable administration of justice. The idea of a fair trial followed from the general principle, adopted in the Ulozhenie, of doing away with all privileged positions and relations in so far as they were prejudicial to the interests of the state, and especially of the Treasury.

Another tendency proceeding from the same source was reflected in chapters about the different classes of society, and involved a new conception of a free person's relation to the state. To see the full meaning of this tendency we must put aside for a moment modern ideas about personal liberty. For us personal liberty and independence are not only inalienable rights, safeguarded by law, but moral duties. None of us would want to become bondsmen by contract, and indeed could not do so, because no court of law would countenance such a contract. But we must not forget that we are studying Russian society of the seventeenth century—a serf-owning society. There were different forms of bondage, and at the time the Ulozhenie was being compiled a new form was about to be added to them: peasant serfdom.

In those days the legal definition of personal freedom included a free person's right to surrender his freedom to another for a time or forever, without having the right to terminate the bondage of his own will. In ancient Russia the right to dispose of one's freedom was the basis of several varieties of thralldom. But until the Ulozhenie came into force, there existed a type of personal dependence that did not involve lifelong bondage. A man could give himself in pledge (*zaklad*) to another person. This meant that as security for a loan or in exchange for some favor—for example, for remission of a task or defense in a court of law—a man could put his person and his labor at the disposal of another person, retaining, however, the right to end his service at will—as soon, of course, as he had fulfilled his contract. Such dependents were called zakladchiks.

Obtaining a loan on the security of one's labor was the most profitable way in which a poor man could invest his labor in ancient Russia. But although the zakladchiks were distinct from bondsmen, they began taking advantage of the bondsman's privilege of exemption from state dues. This was an abuse that set the law against both those who thus pledged themselves and those who accepted them as pledgers. The Ulozhenie imposed taxes on the zakladchiks (Chapter XIX, paragraph 13), and if they pledged themselves again threatened "to punish them cruelly" with the knout and exile to Siberia, beyond the Lena. Their receivers would be punished by "the sovereign's great displeasure" and confiscation of the lands "where the zakladchiks shall live in the future."

For many poor people, bondage, and especially self-pledging, was a way out of serious economic difficulties. People set little value on personal freedom in those days, and in view of the general lack of personal rights, the benefits of a powerful receiver's patronage were greatly prized. The abolition of self-pledging was therefore a heavy blow to the zakladchiks, so much so that in 1649 they were planning a new rebellion in Moscow, "reviling the Tsar with every kind of unseemly abuse."

We can understand their feelings without sharing them. If a free person, a serviceman or a taxpayer, sold himself into bondage or became a zakladchik, he was lost to the state. By curtailing or forbidding such transactions, the Ulozhenie expressed the general principle that a free person who was under an obligation to pay taxes or to give his service to the state had no right to discard the duties incumbent upon free men by renouncing his freedom. A person must belong to and serve the state alone, and could not be anyone's private property: "no one is permitted to sell Christian people" (Chapter XX, paragraph 97). Personal freedom was thus becoming obligatory and was enforced by the knout.

But a right that people are compelled to exercise becomes an obligation. This obligation is not a burden to us, because in forbidding us to be bondsmen, or even half bondsmen, the state safeguards our most precious possession—human personality. As moral and social beings we wholly support the restriction imposed upon us by the state, and it is dearer to us than any other privilege. But in the Russian society of the seventeenth century this universal human obligation to preserve one's freedom was not recognized either by individual minds or by the communal consciousness. A blessing that to us is beyond all price had no value whatsoever for a Russian working man of the seventeenth century. And indeed, in forbidding a man to sell himself to a private owner the state was safeguarding him not as a human being and a citizen, but only as a potential soldier or taxpayer in its own interests. The Ulozhenie did not abolish personal bondage in the name of liberty, but transformed personal liberty into bondage in the interest of the state.

The strict prohibition against selling one's liberty was only one aspect of the general policy set forth in the Ulozhenie. The aim of that policy was to control social groupings by confining people to tightly circumscribed class enclosures, to fetter their work by squeezing it into the narrow frame of state requirements, which dominated all private interests. The zakladchiks were simply the first to feel the burden that was falling upon other classes as well. The position of the state forced sacrifices upon the people as a whole. We shall see this in studying the administrative and class structure after the Time of Troubles.

The Ulozhenie completed the legislative work of former times and became a starting point for further legislation. Its defects began to be felt soon after it came into force, and it was amended and supplemented piecemeal by "newly decreed articles." These were its direct continuation: for instance, articles "Concerning Theft, Brigandage, and Murder" added in 1669, "Concerning Hereditary and Service Estates" added in 1677–78, etc. This detailed, often meticulous revision of separate parts of the Ulozhenie showed much hesitancy and now canceled, now reinstated this or that article of the 1649 code. It is of great interest as a reflection of the historical moment when the rulers of the Muscovite state began to doubt the efficacy of the legal norms and methods of administration in which they once had such faith, and somewhat embarrassedly came to recognize the need for something new, not "home grown"—something "European."

Chapter
VIII

Local Government and
the Class Structure

 The Ulozhenie of 1649 brought to completion a number of processes that had begun at the Time of Troubles and under its influence. It gave legal sanction to the state order that had grown out of those processes by the middle of the seventeenth century. We have seen that under the new dynasty new ideas emerged in people's minds, new men took part in administration, a new conception of the supreme power gained ground, and the Zemsky Sobor was organized in a new way. All these innovations followed directly or indirectly from the same calamitous source—the profound upheaval produced by the Time of Troubles, which had undermined the country's resources and shaken the external position of the state. The new dynasty's government was faced with the task of finding a way out of the difficulties that surrounded it.

We have been studying the chief record of Russian legislation in the seventeenth century in order to see by what measures the government sought to remedy the situation and what direction its activity was taking. We have observed that it strove to concentrate in its hands all the available national resources, and to this end abolished privileged exemptions from jurisdiction and prohibited any further increase in various forms of bondage that gave relief from taxation. Indeed, it was trying to get hold of everything that had been left after the devastation and might become useful—the money it needed, people who had run away, taxpayers, soldiers, the country's delegates for consultation, and even laws!

In its struggle with the besetting difficulties, the Muscovite government wanted in the first place to muster its own forces, for it felt the need to act with more energy and greater unity of purpose. With this aim in view, it began after the Troubles to centralize the administration and gather into its own hands the work of local and even of central administrative organs. It must be noted, however, that in those days the Muscovite government understood centralization in its own way. It did not mean subordination of local administrative organs to the appropriate department at the center, but simply meant that one person or one institution dealt with heterogeneous matters that were interrelated in practice. Thus in a village shop various goods that are locally in demand are displayed together and not distributed in special departments. The people themselves wholly agreed with the government on that point and preferred to deal with one institution, whatever their need might be. Sometimes they complained that the separate government departments to which they had to apply about different matters were too much of a nuisance, and that it would be much better if one department dealt with everything, so that people "should be treated fairly and saved ruinous expense." It was precisely these considerations of practical utility that guided the work of reconstructing local administration in Tsar Michael's reign.

The old dynasty had left provincial government in a state of complete disruption. Ivan IV's reforms broke up each district into several departments and a multitude of local corporate communities, urban and rural, some consisting of servicemen and others of taxpayers. Each such community acted separately and had its own elective administrator. These different communities were in no way unified locally except on the rare occasions when men of every rank in the district assembled to elect magistrates. Each community was, through its elected administrators, in direct contact with the central institutions, the governmental departments. Only in frontier towns, where a strong military force was required, were voevodas introduced as early as the sixteenth century. They ruled the whole district and dealt with all matters except those relating to the church.

An elective regional administration that had no organic unity could function only in peaceful times. And it took many years for those times to return after the old dynasty had come to its end. During the Troubles all parts of the country were in danger of enemy attack and therefore voevodas began to appear even in central districts. A document drawn up in 1628 or thereabouts has come down to us. It is a register of thirty-two towns that had no voevodas in the old days, but where they appeared in the reign of the Pretender, in 1605. These were chiefly central towns "beyond Moscow," as they were described—Vladimir, Pereiaslavl, Rostov, Belozersk, and others. Instead of voevodas, they used to have rural magistrates and town bailiffs—elected officials. The register shows that under Tsar Michael voevodas were appointed everywhere. A voevoda had authority over the whole district, over all classes of society and in all matters. His power extended over the district town and all the rural communities in the district in regard to finance, law, police, and military matters.

To an external observer the introduction of voevodas might seem an improvement in local administration. The disconnected local class communities were united under the same authority. The district became a self-contained administrative unit. But this meant that local administration was headed now by a representative of the central power of the state, an official appointed by the government and not elected by the local population. From this point of view the introduction of voevodas was a decisive step toward a bureaucratic system of administration, contrary to the elective principle on which Tsar Ivan's local administration was based. Nor was it a return to the old regional office of *namestnik*. A voevoda was appointed to rule over a district not for his own benefit, but for the sovereign's, as a true servant of the crown. It was therefore not proper for him to receive dues and tolls, which used to be assigned by a special charter to a namestnik.

The introduction of voevodas was certainly to the advantage of the central departments in Moscow. It was more convenient to deal with one general ruler of a district, and their own nominee to boot, than with many elected district authorities. For the local population, however, this meant merely a return to the rule of the namestniks, and a change for the worse. The voevodas of the seventeenth century were sons or grandsons of the sixteenth-century namestniks. In the course of one or two generations there might be a change in institutions, but not in ethics and customs. A voevoda did not collect tolls and contributions in quantities specified in a charter, since no charter was given to him, but he was not forbidden to receive voluntary gifts "as an honor." No formal limits were set, and he took as much as his hand could grab. Applicants for the post of voevoda openly asked in their petitions to be sent to such-and-such a town "to gather sustenance." Contrary to the idea of what his office should be, a voevoda became in practice no better—indeed, worse—than a namestnik. The post of namestnik was supposed to be given as a perquisite of military service, but in fact the service was administrative rather than military, for a namestnik had to govern and act as judge. The post of voevoda was supposed to be unpaid, but in fact it carried with it nonassessed gratuities for administrative service.

The extent of a voevoda's power was not clearly defined, and this encouraged abuse. He received detailed and hampering directions from the department that appointed him, but they contained a final injunction to act "as was suitable, according to the nature of the case, as God enlightened him"—thus giving him complete liberty to do as he pleased. We can understand why provincial people in the seventeenth century came to look back nostalgically to the times when there were no voevodas. Strict regulations combined with encouraging arbitrary decisions inevitably blurred the distinction between rights and duties, and inclined men in authority to abuse their rights and neglect their duties. Voevodas either exceeded their powers or did nothing at all.

Side by side with the voevoda was another administrative agent of the central power, the magistrate (some districts had two or even more). He was the chief judicial and police authority in the district. This post was established in the sixteenth century and was of a composite character. The magistrate was elected by the local assembly of all the ranks in the district, but he dealt with important criminal cases infringing on the general laws of the state, and not with merely local affairs. In the seventeenth century the scope of his jurisdiction was extended, and in addition to brigandage and theft included homicide, arson, enticement from Orthodoxy, offenses against parental authority, and so on. Under the influence of the general domestic policy of the state, the governmental aspect of the magistrate's office decidedly superseded the elective, so that there was little to distinguish it from the voevoda's. This result was not a part of any definite plan, but merely reflected the government's general tendency. Hence we find endless fluctuations in the relative positions of the two offices. The post of the magistrate was sometimes abolished and then reestablished. In some places his work was entrusted to the voevoda, and in others the reverse was the case. At the inhabitants' request a magistrate might rule a town instead of a voevoda, and if he displeased the population, a voevoda was appointed once more and commissioned to take on the magistrate's work in addition to his own. In some cases a magistrate acted independently of the voevoda, and sometimes he was subordinated to him.

But what became of rural self-government, which represented the different ranks and dealt with the taxpaying population? It did not disappear when voevodas were introduced everywhere, but was subordinated to them, and the scope of its activity was restricted. Since judicial power was transferred to the voevoda, local collegiate tribunals of elected elders and assessors were disbanded. Only taxpaying peasant communities on crown lands and in northern districts (the present-day provinces of Arkhan-

gelsk, Olonets, Viatka, and Perm) retained elected local tribunals. The elected administration had now only matters of
finance (collection of state dues) and local economic affairs
left to it. Indirect taxes—customs and excise duties, etc.—were
collected as formerly by trustworthy elders with their assessors.
The collection of direct taxes and the management of the local
urban and rural communities' economy remained in the hands
of the district supervisor and his assessors. They had to collect
funds for communal needs, to manage communal land, to elect
various officials in charge of local administration, and to elect
the parish priest and his assistants. The district supervisor carried
on his work in the local municipal or district office. It was always situated in the township, outside the citadel, which contained the voevoda's and the magistrate's offices. The district
supervisor's activities were supervised by the councilors elected
by the urban or rural population of the district.

When voevodas were introduced, the elected local government had a new and heavy duty laid upon it—to "sustain" the
voevoda and his staff of officials. This expense was perhaps the
greatest drain on district funds. The supervisor kept an account
book to be checked by the councilors, in which he entered
every item bought with public money. Each day he wrote down
all that he had spent on the voevoda and his staff. He took to
the voevoda's house everything that was needed in the household and office—meat, fish, pies, candles, paper, ink, and so on.
On holy days and name days he went to congratulate the voevoda
and took presents—fancy bread or money "wrapped up in
paper"—to him, his wife and children, his official underlings,
his servants, his hangers-on, and even the "crazy saint" living
in the voevoda's house. These account books explain best of
all the part played by local self-government under a voevoda.
The district supervisor and his assessors were merely obedient
instruments of the central government's officials. They had to
do all the rough administrative work with which the voevoda
and his clerks and secretaries did not wish to soil their hands.
The elected local government acted under the voevoda's supervision and at his direction. The district supervisor was per-

petually running errands for him. He seldom ventured to intercede for the community and go to the voevoda's courtyard
to protest against his orders—"revile him," as the local malcontents put it. Such a relationship between the communal and
the crown administration led to grave abuses. "Sustaining" a voevoda often resulted in the financial ruin of the local community.

The government took no radical measures, but tried as far
as possible to abolish or diminish the evil by various methods.
It appointed officials suggested by the community, or let the
community itself appoint them; it handed over to the elected
magistrate matters belonging to the voevoda's jurisdiction, and
both in its decrees and in the Ulozhenie threatened severe penalties for unfair trial, and allowed the litigants to express distrust
of the voevoda, giving them the right to submit their case to
the voevoda of the neighboring district. Under Tsar Alexei it
was forbidden to appoint members of the gentry as voevodas in
towns where they had hereditary or service estates. More than
once in the reigns of Tsar Michael and his successor, voevodas
were forbidden to demand "sustenance" either in kind or in
money, under the threat of having to restore twice the amount
that had been exacted.

The centralization of provincial government lowered the
status of communal elective institutions, distorted their original
character, and deprived them of independence, without dimin-
ishing their duties and responsibilities. That, too, was one of the
sacrifices made by the community for the sake of the state.

Local administration was centralized not only within the
district. A further step in the same direction was taken in
Tsar Michael's reign. During the war with Poland and Sweden
the districts on the western, southern, and southeastern frontiers
of Muscovy were grouped by the government for defense purposes into large regions called *razriadas*, in which the district
voevodas were subordinated to the chief regional ones. These
were the highest local rulers, both civil and military, and leaders
of servicemen forming the regional military corps. Thus at the
beginning of Michael's reign we find references to the Riazan
and Ukraine razriadas, which included Tula, Mtsensk, and

Novosil. Under Tsar Alexei there appear Novgorod, Seversk, Belgorod, Tambov, and Kazan razriadas. Under Tsar Feodor it was proposed to group the home districts into similar military regions—Moscow, Vladimir, and Smolensk razriadas. These razriadas formed the basis of the division into provinces introduced by Peter the Great.

Central administrative organs were also consolidated to a certain extent, less so than the provincial though they needed it even more. In speaking of the Moscow governmental departments in the sixteenth century, I had occasion to observe that in the seventeenth century, too, they were organized on the same pattern. As the needs and functions of the state increased in complexity, the number of departments mounted to about fifty. It is hard to discover any system in them. Rather they were a mass of big and small institutions, ministries, offices, and temporary commissions, as we would call them now. The great number of departments and the haphazard assignment of the kind of affairs they dealt with made it difficult to control and direct their work. At times the government itself did not know to which of them some unusual case should be referred, and without further deliberation created a new department for the purpose. Hence there arose a need to coordinate the disjointed machinery of the central administration. Two methods were adopted: several departments dealing with kindred matters were either subordinated to a single chief or amalgamated into a single institution. In the first case, a group of departments was put under one head, and in the second, several departments received the same organization.

Tsar Alexei's father-in-law, I. D. Miloslavsky, was chief of the Treasury Department—a branch of the Department of Finance—and also of several departments in charge of the new military forces introduced in the sixteenth and seventeenth centuries—the Musketeers, Cavalry, and Foreign Mercenaries, as well as of the nonmilitary Apothecary Department, since it included doctors who were foreigners. The Department of Foreign Affairs superintended nine other departments—Smolensk, Ukrainian, Lithuanian, and others—that looked after the newly acquired provinces, and also the Captives' Department, which dealt with the ransom of prisoners. The nine departments were probably housed next to Foreign Affairs in the long row of offices extending from Arkhangelsky Cathedral along the Kremlin wall as far as the Spassky Gates. By means of such concentration a multitude of small administrative institutions were welded into several large departments, precursors of Peter the Great's Colleges. Under Tsar Alexei two new departments were created for purposes of supervision.

Financial control was entrusted to the Department of Accounts. It calculated the state income and expenditure as recorded in the account books of all the central departments and of provincial offices; collected any surplus left over from current expenses; questioned other departments as to disbursements made by them to government officials, envoys, and military commanders; and summoned from the provinces local assessors with their account books for audit. It was the center of state bookkeeping, and was in existence as early as 1621.

The Department of Secret Affairs was less sinister than its name suggests. It was not the secret police, but merely the department dealing with the Tsar's sports or "amusements," to use the term current at the time. Tsar Alexei was passionately fond of falconry. The Department of Secret Affairs had charge of 200 falconers, over 3,000 falcons, gyrfalcons, and hawks, and some 100,000 pigeons' nests for feeding and training the birds. To these pigeons and hawks the good-natured and thrifty Tsar added a number of various items relating not only to his personal affairs, but to matters of state. Through the Department of Secret Affairs he carried on his personal correspondence, especially on diplomatic and military matters, and watched over the management of some of his estates, including the salt and fishing industries. The department looked after the affairs of his favorite monastery, St. Savva Storozhevsky, his almsgiving, etc. Through it, too, the Tsar issued orders about all kinds of administrative matters when he thought his direct intervention desirable, or when he took the initiative in some new enterprise that had not yet become a part of administrative routine. Thus the Department of Secret Affairs dealt with mining ore and with ordnance works. In short, it was the Tsar's private office.

It also served the purpose of keeping watch over the country's administration, apart from the general control exercised by the Boyars' Council. Kotoshikhin describes one of the methods of this supervision. The Secret Affairs staff consisted only of a secretary and about a dozen clerks. Members of the Council had no access to it. The Tsar attached those clerks to embassies going abroad and to voevodas going on campaigns, to take note of their words and actions. "And those clerks," writes Kotoshikhin, "spy on the envoys and the voevodas and report to the Tsar after coming home." Of course, the highborn envoys and voevodas understood for what purpose those humble supernumeraries were included in their retinues and showered favors upon them "beyond their measure," in Kotoshikhin's words.

As an organ of secret administrative supervision, anticipating Peter the Great's Fiscal Institute, the Department of Secret Affairs could hardly be called a success. Besides, the very idea of it showed a lack of tact. Kotoshikhin says that Tsar Alexei founded it so that "his ideas and plans should be carried out and everything done in accordance with his wishes, without the members of the Boyars' Council knowing anything about it." Thus the Tsar was acting in secret from the men who were carrying out his will, whom he himself had entrusted with power and with whom he apparently lived in such "concord." He was conspiring against his own government! It was as though an atavistic instinct of Oprichnina, dating back to the appanage period, suddenly revived in a tsar whose ancestors had never been appanage princes.

Centralization of government was accompanied by an even more rapid process of consolidating the community. As a result of the old dynasty's constructive activities, the community proved to be as disjointed as its administration. It was broken up into a number of ranks, which might be reduced to four main classes, not counting the clergy: (1) servicemen, (2) urban taxpayers, (3) rural taxpayers, (4) bondsmen. The differences between these classes were determined by the kind of duties they owed to the state in accordance with their property qualifications (and, in the service class, with a man's origin as well). Differences within the classes depended upon the *amount* of the same kind of duties demanded by the state from this or that group. Thus it was the hereditary duty of the service-class landowners to serve in the army and, in connection with this, at the tsar's court or in the administration. The importance and responsibility of such service was proportionate to the landowner's wealth and lineage, and accordingly the service class was subdivided into ranks. There were councilmen, Muscovite servicemen, and provincial servicemen. Townspeople engaged in trade or industry were taxed on "their possessions and trades"; that is, on their turnover and occupations. According to the amount of their profits and stock in trade, and to the burden of municipal dues connected therewith, they were divided into "best men," "intermediates," and "juniors." The class of rural inhabitants or peasants, who were taxed on the amount of land they had under cultivation, was similarly subdivided. Bondsmen, who could have no property guaranteed by law, did no military service and paid no taxes. They were indentured servants of private masters, but there were several kinds of bondage.

None of these classes or ranks was fixed or stable or compulsory. People could pass from one class or rank to another; freemen could do so of their own will or at the tsar's bidding, bondsmen at their masters' will or by law. They could change their occupation or combine it with another. A serviceman could trade in town, a peasant could become a bondsman or take up some urban occupation. In consequence of such mobility, several intermediate transitional social layers were formed between the main classes. For instance, between the classes of servicemen (the gentry) and bondsmen there was a shifting layer of poor or completely landless "boyars' sons," minor gentry, who sometimes did military service on account of their own or their fathers' holdings, and sometimes left home and became bondsmen to the boyars or to higher gentry, thus forming a special social group of boyar servicemen.

Between the gentry and the urban population there was a

layer of servicemen of "smaller ranks" whose service was not hereditary. They were hired by the government to work as blacksmiths, carpenters, gatekeepers, gunners, and bombardiers attached to fortresses and fortress artillery. They formed part of the serviceman class, for they served as military artisans, but were closely allied to the urban population, from which they were generally recruited, and could ply their trades in towns without paying townsmen's taxes.

The shifting class of zakladchiks, of whom I have already spoken and will do so again, were also of town origin. They found shelter with privileged landowners, lay and clerical.

Finally, between bondsmen and the free classes there hovered a numerous mixed population of free or vagrant men, comprising nontaxed relatives of the taxpaying householders—sons who lived with their parents, brothers, nephews, and hangers-on who had no homes of their own but worked for others, sons of the clergy who had no parishes, boyars' sons who had gone astray, given up military service, and not joined anyone's household, peasants who had abandoned their land and had no settled occupation, and bondsmen who had gained their freedom and not yet sold themselves again. All such people, if they lived in the country, had no land apportioned to them and paid no land tax; if they lived in a town they engaged in some trade or industry but paid no urban taxes.

The shifting intermediate social strata and the division into innumerable ranks gave the community the appearance of a motley and disorderly mass. The mobility and variety of the country's social components helped to preserve freedom of labor and movement. But this freedom greatly hampered the central government and went counter to its purpose, subsequently expressed in the Ulozhenie, to draw everyone into working for the state and strictly to regulate the people's labor in the interests of the Treasury. The status of zakladchiks and free vagrant men presented a special difficulty, for it might eventually lead to a decrease in military forces and cut off the main sources of state revenue. Servicemen and taxpayers who did not wish either to serve or to pay taxes could escape these duties by taking advantage of their right to renounce personal liberty and the state obligations connected with it.

To avoid these dangers and difficulties, Tsar Michael's government began from the first to tighten the social structure of the community as it tightened its administrative organization. It united into large closed classes various small ranks whose state dues were similar, leaving them freedom of movement within the class in which they were included; the intermediate social strata were thrust into the class that best corresponded with the men's occupations. This process of social reconstruction was carried on by two methods: by binding the people hereditarily to the status they had at the time, and by depriving free persons of the right to renounce their freedom. In this way the composition of the community was made simpler and more permanent. Military service and payment of taxes, depending on a man's fluctuating financial position or on his changeable occupation, were made into unalterable hereditary duties. Each class became more closely knit in itself and more isolated from others. These self-contained units bound by obligations to the state acquired a hereditary class character for the first time in the history of Russian social organization. The process by which they were built up may be called one of fixation or hardening of social positions. Since this process was carried on at the expense of the people's freedom of labor, the result achieved by it must be reckoned among the sacrifices made by the community for the benefit of the state.

The process began apparently with the class of servicemen, whom the state needed most as a fighting force. In the Sudebnik of 1550 it had already been laid down that only retired members of the minor gentry might be accepted as bondsmen. It was forbidden to accept either those who were still in service or their sons who had not yet begun to serve. Many boyars' sons (this was the name of the lowest and poorest rank of servicemen) were eager to become bondsmen in a boyar household. The decree of 1558 explained that only those of them who had reached the military age of fifteen but had not yet been enlisted had the right to become bondsmen, while minors and those

who were already enlisted could not sell themselves into bondage. Poverty and the hardships of military service prompted men
to disregard these restrictions. Under Tsar Michael, servicemen
of the lower ranks complained that their sons, brothers, and
nephews absconded in droves to become bondsmen. By the decree of March 9, 1642, it was commanded that bondsmen of
gentle birth who had holdings or patrimony and were registered
for military service should be taken away from boyar households and put into the army, and it was forbidden to accept into
bondage anyone belonging to the gentry. This prohibition was
entered in the Ulozhenie. Thus military service became a hereditary and unavoidable class duty of servicemen.

Their special rights as landowners were defined at the same
time. Hitherto boyars' sons and lay brothers in monasteries—
their equals in social status—had the right to own land, and there
were among them servicemen who had both service and hereditary estates. The decree of 1642 brought boyars' sons back to
serving the state, and the Ulozhenie deprived both them and lay
brothers of the right to acquire estates. Personal landownership
became the privilege of the service class, just as military service
was its special class duty. Thus servicemen of various ranks were
united into one corporation and segregated from other classes.

Townspeople were subjected to the same kind of segregation.
We have already seen how the growth of service-class landownership in the sixteenth century hindered urban development.
The Time of Troubles ruined the town population and scattered
it. The difficulties that arose under the new dynasty threatened
to ruin once more the towns that were beginning to revive. To
fulfill their obligations as taxpayers, urban communities bound
by corporate responsibility for the payment of taxes had to have
a sufficient and permanent number of members and a secure
market for their labor and merchandise. The burden of taxation
made the weak members leave the towns, selling or mortgaging
their homesteads to nontaxed ("white") people. At the same
time numbers of men of different ranks settled in the towns:
streltsy, peasants from suburban villages, church servants, priests'
sons. They engaged in trade and industry, bought and sold,

undercutting the urban taxpayers and not sharing their burden of taxation. Even priests and deacons, contrary to church rules, acted as shopkeepers.

Flight from the towns was greatly encouraged by the rich and the powerful. It is noteworthy that in Russia as soon as the supreme power weakened, the ruling classes took advantage of the moment and hastened to make large investments in the people's free labor. Thus under Tsar Feodor, son of Ivan IV, contemporaries complained of the great increase in the number of bondsmen by indenture. The regent, Boris Godunov, and his relatives took an active part in this development.

Under Tsar Michael the same thing happened with regard to the zakladchiks. I have already spoken of this variety of personal dependence, which differed from bondage in that it was not permanent and could be ended at the zakladchik's will. It was chiefly townspeople, traders and artisans, who pledged themselves, usually to "the strong"—the boyars, the patriarch, bishops, and monasteries. This was a great calamity for the taxpaying townspeople. Large townships were surrounded by government settlements of servicemen—streltsy, gunners, postal drivers. These state-employed men competed in trade and industries with the townsmen without sharing their tax burden. The zakladchiks were even more formidable rivals. Rich and influential people accepted them in large numbers and made great settlements of them either in towns or in the suburbs, not only on their own private lands, but on those belonging to the town as well. In 1648 there were living on the Patriarch's lands in the municipality of Nizhni Novgorod more than six hundred newcomers, traders and artisans from other towns, who had settled there "for their own convenience and to carry on their trade," as the townspeople's delegates complained at the Ulozhenie Sobor.

That was a new kind of "self-pledging," and an illegal one. The simple form of self-pledging in the proper sense consisted in obtaining a loan on the security of work that the borrower bound himself to do in the creditor's household or on his land. But now urban taxpayers bound themselves without any loan (or with a fictitious one), usually to privileged landowners, lay or clerical, and instead of working for them, settled on their tax-free lands, either separately or as a whole village. Taking advantage of the owners' exemption from the land tax, they escaped from urban taxation and engaged in all kinds of trade and industry. They were capitalists and not poor household bondsmen working off their loans.

Their behavior was an infringement of the law. As early as 1550 it had been laid down in the sudebnik that urban tradesmen were not to live on untaxed church lands of the township and enjoy its privileges. Under Tsar Michael the law strictly differentiated the taxed, or "black," municipal lands from the untaxed, or "white." People who paid no taxes were forbidden to include in this privilege any taxed landed property they might acquire in the town, and likewise taxpayers who settled on tax-free land were forbidden to "whiten" themselves—to throw off the burden of taxation. Self-pledging was an obvious abuse. It was not permanent bondage, which carried with it exemption from taxation, but it combined the advantages of serfdom with those of the taxed urban trades. Not paying any taxes, zakladchiks enjoyed tradespeople's rights but escaped their duties.

Complaints against this abuse were made in Tsar Michael's reign. The new dynasty's government, true to its habit of taking no preventive measures and of yielding only to threats or to force, satisfied individual complaints but passed no general law on the subject. Thus in 1643 the townspeople of Tobolsk complained of the increase in the number of zakladchiks on monastery lands, who "harassed and worsted them in every trade." The plaintiffs pointed out that they had no men left to do state service or pay taxes. The Tsar commanded that the zakladchiks be included in the urban community and pay taxes like other townspeople.

Insistent complaints of the same nature both before and during the Sobor of 1648, the lingering impressions of the June rebellion in Moscow, the government's apprehensions about state revenue, and the wish to acquire many thousands of new taxpayers—all this led to a thorough overhaul of the urban population. Various measures adopted at the time were codified in

Chapter XIX of the Ulozhenie ("Concerning Townspeople"). All suburban village settlements belonging to private owners and built on municipal land, whether bought or seized, reverted to the crown and were joined to the towns, having to pay the same urban taxes. No compensation was given to the owners, since it was an offense to build on the sovereign's land or to buy municipal land. Contracts made between the zakladchiks and those to whom they had pledged themselves were canceled. Suburban estates and holdings that bordered on the town, so that the houses stood back to back, were included in the township, and in exchange the owners received villages belonging to the crown in other parts of the country. Self-pledging was henceforth forbidden under heavy penalty, and urban taxpayers were attached to their towns so strictly that by the decree of February 8, 1658, they were threatened with the death penalty for moving from one township to another and even for marrying outside their own township. Payment of taxes on their trade and industries thus became a corporate duty of the urban population and the right to trade and engage in industry in the town its corporate privilege. Peasants could sell "all kinds of goods" in the market straight from their carts, but they could not keep shops in the town.

Chapter

IX

The Coming of Serfdom

At the same time that servicemen and townspeople were set apart as two distinct classes, the position of the rural agricultural population was also finally settled. The change affected the greater part of that population, the peasants living on private landowners' estates. It separated them not only from other classes, but also from other groups of the rural population—that is, from the "black" or state peasants and from those living on court lands. I am referring to the introduction of peasant-servitude to private owners. We have seen that at the beginning of the seventeenth century, state and court peasants were already attached to the soil or to village communities. The position of peasants living on private owners' land was still undefined because it involved several conflicting interests. By the beginning of the seventeenth century all the economic conditions attaching peasants to private landowners were fully operative, and it only remained to find a legal formula that would convert their *de facto* servitude into bondage sanctioned by law.

In the sixteenth century the position of manorial peasantry as a social class contained three distinct elements: the payment of land tax, the right to leave, and the need for a loan from the master—that is, elements of political, juridical, and economic significance. Each of them was opposed to the other two, and the changing course of the struggle between them accounted for the hesitancy of legislation in defining the peasants' status. The struggle was due to the economic factor. From the middle of the sixteenth century onward, for various reasons that we have partly considered, the number of peasants needing loans for starting and carrying on their farming began to increase. The need for loans compelled the peasants to remain in bondage and forfeit their right of free movement until they repaid their debts. This right was not abolished by law, but became a legal fiction. The argument against peasant bondage was that as freemen they paid a land tax, from which bondsmen were exempt; and so at the beginning of the seventeenth century legislation tried to prevent peasants from becoming bondsmen, and a law was passed establishing "peasant perpetuity," which made it impossible for a peasant to escape the status of taxpayer. These aspects of the peasants' position, combined with the conditions of personal bondage as it existed in ancient Russia, provided the legal framework for the enslavement of the manorial peasantry.

In ancient Russian law the word "bond" denoted a symbolic or written deed entitling a person to the possession of a certain thing. The power conferred by such a deed gave the owner a bonded right to that thing. In ancient Russia human beings could be objects of possession. Bondage existed in ancient Russia for centuries before the introduction of peasant serfdom, and until the end of the fifteenth century there was only one form of it— "complete" bondage, as it came to be called later. It was brought about in various ways: (1) by captivity, (2) by a free person's selling himself into servitude voluntarily or at his parents' will, (3) as a penalty for certain crimes, (4) by being born of a bondsman, (5) as a penalty for insolvency due to the trader's own fault, (6) by a free person's engaging himself as a servant to another without a contract guaranteeing his personal liberty, (7) by marrying a bondswoman without such a contract. Not only did a "complete" bondsman depend on his owner and the owner's heirs; he handed on this dependence to his children. The right of ownership and the bondage were both hereditary. The main feature distinguishing complete bondage from other kinds of dependence in the eyes of the law was that it could not be terminated at the bondsman's will; he could become free only at the will of his owner.

In Muscovite Russia several varieties of mitigated, conditional servitude developed out of complete bondage. Personal service in the capacity of a bailiff, steward, or overseer on the owner's estate gave rise, at the end of the fifteenth or the beginning of the sixteenth century, to "referable" bondage, so called because the title deed for such bondage had to be referred to the regional governor for confirmation. It differed from complete bondage in that the master's right of ownership was limited. Sometimes it ended with his death, sometimes it was passed on to his children, but no further. I have already spoken of self-pledging, which sprang up at different times and under different conditions. In its original and simplest form it meant making a loan under pledge of working for the creditor while living in his household. Self-pledgers, whether in the eleventh century or in the appanage period or in the seventeenth century, were not bondsmen, because they could end their servitude at will. The loan was redeemed either by direct repayment or by fulfilling the labor contract. We read in a fifteenth-century enactment concerning such debtor servants: "When they have served their appointed time, let them go; if they have redeemed a ruble, but not served as long as they had contracted, let them return all the money they have borrowed."

Sometimes a self-pledger undertook to pay with his labor not his actual debt, but merely the interest on it—"to serve for usury," as it was called—and at the appointed time return the capital he had borrowed. In ancient Russia a promissory note was called *kabala* (a word borrowed from the Hebrew). Personal dependence arising from the obligation "to serve for usury" was confirmed by a deed called "service kabala," in contradistinction to the "loan kabala," pledging the debtor to work off his debt. From the end of the fifteenth century the phrase "kabala people" occurs in official documents, but for almost a century there was no sign of their being bondsmen. A loan kabala accompanied by personal pledging gave the pledger a right to earn the sum that had been given him in advance, and thus to retire the debt, on which no interest was charged. But a service kabala meant that by working in the creditor's home the debtor merely payed the interest, and would have to return the borrowed capital at the appointed time. This is evident from documents of the first half of the sixteenth century and from the sudebnik of 1550, which fixed fifteen rubles (seven or eight hundred rubles in our currency) as the highest limit of a loan advanced on personal pledging. According to a law of 1560, men under service kabala could be sued for the repayment of the debt, which shows that they had not yet become bondsmen, but were still self-pledgers, having a right to ransom their freedom when they could. We also learn from this law that some such men, unable to pay their kabala loans, asked to be accepted by their creditors into bondage, either complete or referable. This was forbidden, and it was decreed that insolvent debtors should be "surrendered" into their creditors' power until they had paid or worked off their debts. The prohibition, the pledgers' readiness to become bondsmen, and the testimony of the English ambassador Fletcher, who was told in Moscow in 1588 that the law allowed a creditor to sell for a time or forever the wife and children of an insolvent debtor "surrendered" to him—all show that the kabala men were drawn by their own and their masters' habits to familiar complete bondage, while the law sought to preserve their status as temporary bondsmen.

In the course of this struggle, pledging oneself to work for a creditor by way of paying interest on a loan did, after all, become a kind of bondage, but it was not complete bondage. "Surrender until repayment" meant in practice that the pledgers, who as a rule were impecunious, had to work for their creditors for an unspecified number of years to redeem the debt. This implied that the kabala "service for usury" included repayment of the actual debt as well as payment of interest on it, and thus the pledger's position was equivalent to that of a hired workman who received his wages in advance. This combination of "service for usury" with the redemption of debt and the personal character of the contract between the creditor and the debtor lay at the basis of service kabala as a form of bondage terminable at a specified date. Being a private contract between two persons, service kabala was nullified by the death of one of them. In the seventeenth century we find in some places contracts binding the pledger to serve in his master's home for the rest of his life. Should the master die first, the pledger was to serve his widow and children.

But there were two other kinds of servants whose obligations ended with their masters' death. As early as 1556 a law was passed that a prisoner condemned to servitude should remain in bondage only while his master lived, and sometimes freemen entered private service on the same condition, without making either a loan or a contract about wages. In a service kabala of 1596 a freeman promised to serve, not for usury and without a loan, until his master's death, after which he was to be released with his wife and children and "any possessions he may have acquired while serving, and neither he nor his children are to be given as an inheritance to the master's children." We find here three conditions of service kabala: the master has lifelong possession of the servant; such possession is not transferable; the servant has a right to property acquired during his service. These conditions were laid down by agreement. At any rate, there is no evidence that prior to 1597 they were compulsory for freemen (as distinct from prisoners) taking up kabala service.

When this service was made lifelong, it became a species of bondage; the servant voluntarily, by contract, renounced the right to redeem himself, and his bondage ended only with the master's death or at his will. In the decree of 1555 service kabala is already ranked as bondage alongside complete and referable bondage, and in a will dated 1571 we find the term "kabala bondsmen" instead of the usual "kabala people." At the same time there was established a form of kabala contract that remained unchanged for a whole century: a freeman, single or with wife and children, borrowed from someone (generally from a serviceman) a few rubles for exactly a year, from such-

and-such a date to a corresponding date in the following year, promising to serve for usury in the master's household throughout this period, and should he fail to repay the money at the appointed time, to go on serving him for usury as before. The stereotyped formula was evidently drawn up after the pattern of a terminable mortgage deed, pledging a person instead of an object and anticipating arrears in payment. Such mortgages were not infrequent and resembled service kabala agreements both in substance and in wording. In 1636 a father gave his son to his creditor in service for a year, promising, if the debt were not paid in time, to let the son stay with the creditor.

Such was the position of kabala bondsmen when the decree of April 25, 1579, came into force. Its object was to regulate bondage as an institution and put in on a firmly established basis. It changed nothing in the legal status of kabala bondsmen, but merely confirmed and defined relations that had already been formed. It was laid down that service kabala agreements were legal only if they had been registered in the Bondsmens' Court in Moscow and in government offices in provincial towns. The pledger, with his wife and children mentioned by name in the agreement, was to remain in bondage till his master's death, just as in the case of referable kabala. If the kabala bondsman offered to pay ransom, the master could refuse to accept it. The law court was not to listen to the bondsman's complaints on this score, but was to surrender him to his master to serve him as long as the master lived. A bondsman's children mentioned in his kabala agreement or born during his bondage also remained in the master's possession as long as he lived.

The decree of 1597 contains, however, some new enactments that reveal the underhanded policy of the ruling classes with regard to free labor. In addition to bondsmen, there existed in those days free servants who served for wages without any kabala agreement. In documents they are called "voluntary bondsmen." Some of them served for ten years or more, refusing to sign a kabala agreement and reserving the right, recognized in the decree of 1555, to leave their masters at will. The law of

April 25, 1597, fixed a term to such voluntary service—less than six months. A person who had served for half a year or more was compelled to sign a kabala binding him to serve his master, who had "fed, clothed, and shod him." Karamzin quite rightly described this enactment as a law unworthy of that name because of its obvious injustice, and said that it was issued solely to please the higher gentry. The legislature, however, was somewhat hesitant about this restriction of voluntary service, and Tsar Vasili Shuisky reverted for a time to the law of 1555, but the Boyars' Council reinstated the six-month limit, and in the Ulozhenie this short period was further reduced to three months.

The decree of 1597 contains another clause showing whose interests were paramount in the reign of the weak Tsar Feodor. As I have said earlier, the law of 1560, aimed at preventing the growth of complete bondage, forbade insolvent kabala servants to sell themselves into either complete or referable bondage to their creditors, but the law of 1597 allowed runaway kabala servants, if caught by their masters, voluntarily to accept bondage to them under stricter conditions than formerly. The decree of April 1597 made the bondsman's position worse rather than better. Avraami Palitsyn, steward of the Troitsky Monastery, an observant man, helps to explain this tendency in legislation. He says that the magnates, especially relatives or supporters of the all-powerful ruler Godunov, and the leading gentry as well, had a passion to enslave everyone they could. They used all kinds of means—favors, gifts, violence, and torture—to entice people into signing away their freedom in service kabala agreements. A man would be invited to come in "just to have a drink," and, having drunk three or four glasses, an incautious guest would find himself a bondsman. Then Tsar Feodor died, and in the reign of Boris Godunov, who succeeded him, there came three terrible years of famine. The masters took stock of the situation, saw that they could not feed their retinue of bonded servants, and freed some of them. Others they drove away without legally freeing them, and some ran away on their own. All this living wealth so sinfully acquired changed to dust in their hands and was scattered in the wind. During the Time of Troubles many of the bondsmen thus abandoned by their masters paid them back cruelly.

I have said enough about the development of kabala bondage to explain its effect upon the position of peasants living on private owners' land. At first sight it seems difficult to find points of contact between two such different social positions as those of a bondsman and a peasant. The first paid no taxes and worked in the master's household; the second paid taxes and worked on the master's land. But the point of contact was provided by the master. The legal and economic positions of bondsmen and peasants alike depended upon him, and he ruled over both.

We have seen that when the new dynasty was enthroned, the peasants' relation to the land and to the landowners was still undefined. Tsar Vasili's law of 1607, attaching peasants to the land in accordance with the registry records, went out of use during the Time of Troubles. Rural life was regulated by customs established at the beginning of the seventeenth century. Peasant contracts were concluded as before on the basis of voluntary agreements. It was stated in them that the peasants undertook to work for the master "as stipulated, and as both sides had settled by mutual consent and recorded in writing." When an estate changed hands, the peasants who were not "old inhabitants" and were not in debt to the former landowner could go where they liked; the new owner had no claim on them or on their possessions. "Let them go altogether" was the phrase used in official documents. "Old established" peasants, born on the estate or in their master's lifetime, and "old inhabitants," who had worked for him for more than ten years, remained where they were, while the newly settled who had been provided with loans were taken by the former owner to some other estate of his. As before, the peasants paid the interest on the loans by working for the master, and it was this that made the status of peasantry similar to that of kabala bondsmen. The peasant's work was his personal obligation to the master just as the kabala bondsman's was, with the only difference that the latter worked in the master's household while the former worked for the benefit of that household.

The similarity in their economic positions increased the similarity of their legal status. As soon as a kabala agreement came in the eyes of the law to mean that the creditor had a claim not only to the work of the debtor but also on his person, this idea found its way into the landowners' minds and affected their attitude toward the peasants. The gradual identification of peasants with bondsmen was also helped by a movement in the opposite direction—by bondsmen's tending toward peasant status. Next to the peasant tiller of the soil working for the benefit of the master's household, there appeared the household bondsman working on the land. The Time of Troubles, sweeping over the country like a hurricane, drove masses of the peasantry out of the central provinces. This created an acute labor shortage, and landowners had to have recourse to the old and well-tried method of finding new supplies of agricultural laborers from among their domestic servants. They began settling their household bondsmen on the land, giving them loans and providing them with homesteads, farming equipment, and plots of land. A special contract was made with the bondsmen, which, like the peasant contract, was called a loan agreement.

In this way there was formed among the bondsmen a special class called *zadvornyi*[1] people, because they were settled in separate huts beyond the master's house. This class appeared as early as the second half of the sixteenth century. In documents of 1570–80 we find references to "outside hamlets," "outside homesteads," beyond the master's large homestead. This class increased in numbers throughout the seventeenth century. It is not often mentioned in the land registers of the first half of the century, but in the second its members usually form a considerable part of the rural population. According to the register of 1630 in the Belev district, bondsmen with homesteads of their own, many of whom were not of the zadvornyi class, formed a

---

[1] The word *zadvornyi* is derived from *za* (beyond) and *dvor* (homestead). [Translator's note.]

little less than 9 percent of the agricultural population living on the estates of service landowners. According to the census of 1678, the zadvornyis alone accounted for 12 percent of it.

In the course of time, some of the gentry's domestic servants were also put on the land. These were entered in the records as living in the landowners' households, but their economic and legal status was exactly the same as that of the zadvornyis. The latter were recruited from all species of bondsmen, mostly from those bound by kabala contracts. The status of a zadvornyi as a bondsman-householder carried with it certain legal implications. According to the law of 1624, a zadvornyi himself, and not his master, answered with his own property for a crime committed by him. That means that his property was regarded as belonging to him, though not entirely so. A zadvornyi entered into bondage by special agreement and signed a loan contract whether he was a freeman settling on his master's land outside the manor house or a servant in the house moving to a place outside the master's home. Thus there came into being a special kind of bondage midway between domestic service and peasant labor.

In a document of 1628 a landowner wrote that he populated an uncultivated piece of land with his kabala bondsmen and house serfs born on his estate, setting them up in the new place as peasants and providing them with loans. This does not mean that he made his bondsmen real peasants, for such a change of status would have meant transforming them from untaxed menials into taxpaying farmers. This would not be in the landowners' interest. Bondsmen had often been resettled by their masters to work on the land. It was the landowners' usual device for carrying on their farming. But it was not called "settling bondsmen as peasants." This phrase was not borrowed from the law code, but expressed the new relations between landowners and tenants, and it shows how close the position of a peasant indebted to the master was to that of a bondsman.

About the same time, a condition tantamount to bondage began to appear in peasant contracts with landowners. In a loan contract of 1628 a freeman promised to live as a peasant of his master for the rest of his life, without ever leaving the place.

The condition of not leaving the place was formulated in various ways. Formerly, a peasant contracting for a plot of land and a loan wrote in his promissory note that if he left without fulfilling his obligations, the landowner was to take his possessions as payment of the loan and as compensation for damages—that is, for the detriment to the work of the farm and for legal expenses—and that was all. But now another condition was added to the peasant's obligation to pay damages for leaving: the landowner, his master, "was free to take him back from wherever he might be," and "in the future I, So-and-So, am to live as a peasant on the same plot and pay taxes or live as a peasant now and in the future"; or "for that loan I am to live as a peasant under my master for the rest of my life and not run away anywhere," and so on. All these statements meant the same thing: a peasant renounced of his own will the right to leave, and converted the payment of compensation for breach of contract into a fine for attempting to escape. Payment of the fine did not annul the contract or restore his right to leave the master. Soon the loss of this right became the general and final condition of obtaining a loan. Promissory notes thus proved to be the basis of peasant serfdom, or "peasant perpetuity," as it was called in the seventeenth century. This condition converted the peasant's loan contract into a contract of bondage, establishing personal dependence of the debtor and denying him the right to end it at will.

It was not accidental that peasant bondage synchronized with the settling of bondsmen as peasants in the third decade of the seventeenth century. Both facts were closely connected with the great change that took place at that time in state and private land ownership. The Time of Troubles shifted masses of the taxpaying population about and disorganized the old communities, both urban and rural, which were jointly responsible for the taxes paid by their individual members. One of the first tasks of the new dynasty's government was to reestablish these communities. At the Zemsky Sobor of 1619 it was decided to re-register and sort out the taxpayers, to return the fugitives to their old dwelling places, and to compel the self-pledgers to pay taxes. The task remained undone for some years, however, because there proved to be no administrators, clerks, and investigating officers able to carry it out. This failure, as well as the big Moscow fire, which destroyed land records kept in various departments, caused the government to make a new census in 1627–28, wider in scope and better organized than previous ones.

The census records were intended to bring to light and assign to appropriate localities the taxpaying resources of the Treasury. These records were used in dealing with the peasantry, both before and after the law code of 1649, to verify the actual relations between the peasants and the landowners, and to settle conflicts and claims. The census introduced nothing new into those relations and did not establish any where they did not already exist; that was a matter to be decided by voluntary agreement between the parties. Nevertheless, a census record showing where a person lived provided a general basis for such agreements, regulated them, and indirectly brought them about. A wandering free laborer caught by the census on a landowner's estate where he had found a temporary refuge was registered there and willy-nilly settled as that landowner's peasant by "voluntary agreement." He was thus attached to the master both by the census record and by his own promissory note.

Many of these agreements were distinctly of the kabala type. In some cases, men contracting as a master's peasants had worked for him "voluntarily" for some years, without a promissory note. Others, making contracts without loans, stated that they promised "to remain their masters' peasants as long as their masters lived. But as soon as their masters, at God's will, departed this life, they, the peasants, were free to go wherever they liked." This was the basic condition of the service kabala. Still others again, as in the above-mentioned contract of 1628, promised to remain their master's peasants all their lives, without ever leaving. The kabala bondsmen sometimes made the same kind of contract. As a rule, however, free peasants pledged themselves to a master on receiving a loan, which they sometimes promised to repay fully by a certain date or to pay by installments, but

generally the subject was not mentioned at all, and the loan was
to be repaid only if the peasant failed to carry out his work on
the land or ran away.

However varied, vague, and complicated the peasants' contracts of the period were, one can trace in them the main conditions that helped to create serfdom: registration of domicile,
monetary indebtedness, effects of kabala bondage, and voluntary
agreement. The first two were the basic sources of serfdom, giving the landowner an opportunity to enslave the peasants; the
second two were of subsidiary importance as means to his actually doing so. The study of peasant contracts makes it possible
to detect almost the very moment of transition from freedom to
serfdom and to see its connection with the general census of
1627. The earliest contract for serfdom known to us dates back
to that year. A landowner's "old" peasants made a new contract
with him, binding themselves "not to leave or run away, but
to remain bound to him as peasants." As "old" peasants they
had certain definite, settled relations with the landowner, and
perhaps, being old inhabitants, they were already permanent occupiers of their plots, unable to pay off the loans they had once
received from him. In other contracts peasants directly promised to be bound to their old master "as formerly." Obviously,
the new contracts were merely a legal confirmation of an already existing position.

Official registration of a man's status and taxability according
to his domicile raised the question of binding the peasant to the
landowner on whose land he happened to be living. There was
no ready-made legal form for doing this, and so the contracts
drawn up in similar circumstances were taken for a pattern—the
service kabala contracts or loan contracts made by the zadvornyis. By voluntary agreement the peasants' duties as taxpayers
were combined in various ways with those of service to the
master.

Such a combination of different legal relations was encouraged by the change in the landowners' economic position
brought about by the Time of Troubles. In the old days a contract between the landowner and the peasant tenant was pri-

marily concerned with the land, for which the peasant was to give either a certain amount of the produce or its equivalent in money. The loan from the landowner had also to be taken into consideration. The peasant's personal labor for the master was part of the payment for it, and so was the peasant's inventory acquired with the help of the loan. After the Time of Troubles the conditions of bargaining for the land were somewhat changed. The land that had been laid waste decreased in value, but the value of peasant labor and of the loans from the landowners had increased. Peasants needed loans more than plots of land, and the landowners needed labor more than tenants. This mutual need may provide the explanation for a certain contract made in 1647, when peasant bondage was well established and had become hereditary. In that contract it was not the peasant who promised not to leave the landowner, but the landowner who bonded himself not to drive the peasant away from his home, and if he did, the peasant was free "to leave and go wherever he liked."

As a consequence of the 1627 census, this mutual need changed the character of peasant contracts. Agreements were no longer concerned with the use of the owner's land, but with compulsory work for the landowner's benefit; the right to the peasant's labor provided the basis of the master's power over him as a person. Indeed, the census itself was due to the Treasury's need to tax the tiller and not the area of land under cultivation. Under the new economic conditions the old social groups tended to change places. Bondsmen became peasants, house servants took to plowing, peasant farmers did domestic work—and the result of this confusion was serfdom.

The state and the landowner apparently supported each other in their pursuit of the peasant. But this concord between them was more apparent than real. Each was pulling its own way. The state needed a settled taxpayer who could always be found as registered at a particular place and was not hindered by private obligations from paying his taxes regularly. The landowner sought a peasant bondsman who could efficiently work for him "on the land, on the threshing ground, and in the master's household," as well as pay him dues in cash or in kind, and who could besides on occasion be sold or mortgaged or given in dowry without his plot of land.

The first tsar of the new dynasty was elected with the support of the church hierarchs and the rank and file of the gentry, but was bound by obligations to the boyars. In dealing with the peasantry he had to reckon both with big landowners, lay and clerical, and the poorer gentry. Taking advantage of the difficult position of the taxpaying population after the Time of Troubles, big landowners—boyars, bishops, monasteries—deprived the Treasury of innumerable taxpayers, including peasants, by beguiling them into becoming privileged "pledgers" under their powerful protection. The Zemsky Sobor of July 1619 decreed that those pledgers should revert to their former conditions, be returned to their old domiciles, and pay taxes as before. But for thirty years in a row the powerful nobility, both lay and clerical, disobeyed this decree of the Zemsky Sobor, and only in the Ulozhenie of 1649 did the delegates of the gentry and of the urban population succeed in passing a final enactment confiscating the boyars' and clergy's settlements populated by pledgers.

The government had to settle many questions with regard to peasants, but it was in no hurry about it. Tsar Michael was by no means a thinking man, nor were any of his councilors. The government followed the flow of events without attempting to forestall them, and let the course of life make knots that the succeeding generations were unable to unravel. As soon as bondage was made a condition in peasants' contracts with the landowners, the government ought to have drawn a clear line between private and state interests. The census register fixed a peasant's status and his obligations as taxpayer according to his domicile. The loan contract attached him to the landowner by personal agreement. This double aspect of the peasants' position found reflection in the fact that there was no set formula for the bondage contract. Most often the peasant vaguely stated that in accordance with "this writing" he would remain bound in the future to serve his master as peasant. Not infrequently a peasant would bind himself to his landlord personally as a tenant without having any special plot assigned to him. He promised to live in bondage to his master in such-and-such a village or "wherever the master might appoint," or contracted for any plot of land "which the master would assign to him according to his strength and ability." Less frequently a peasant bound himself to serve his master "on the plot on which he [the peasant] paid his tax and in accordance with this writing," thus combining personal bondage with land tenure and promising to remain on his plot permanently and "not move from it anywhere." Still rarer, at the end of the seventeenth century we find peasants attached to a particular place, and not to the owner personally. Thus a loan contract of 1688, in addition to the usual bondage agreement to live in such-and-such a village as the master's peasant, contains the condition that "the said peasant shall go on living in that village to whomsoever it may belong in the future."

Just as there was no set formula for bondage contracts, so there was no limit fixed by law to the duration of the bondage and no legal definition of the duties it involved. All this was left to voluntary agreement. Loan contracts, as we have seen, were made on the same indefinite conditions as those of the service kabala. In some localities the amount of work to be done for the master was clearly defined (see the registers of the Zalesky section of the Novgorod domains for 1641–52). Poor peasants (bobyls) had to work for him one day a week (on foot), peasant householders two days a week (with a horse) or one day one week and two days the week following. But this was just a local custom and had nothing to do with official regulations on the subject. The stereotyped general norm was the peasant's unparticularized promise "to do all kinds of work for the master and to pay him dues such as he thinks fit, according to the land I hold, and the same as my neighbors," or "to obey the master in all things, plow his land and do all manner of work in his household," and so on. Thus a question of the utmost social and political importance—the limits of a landowner's right to his peasants' labor—was left to be settled through a chaotic struggle between private interests. This was either an oversight on the part of a negligent legislature or a cowardly concession to the interests of the gentry, which, being the stronger party, hastened to take advantage of its position.

Another concession made to the gentry by the government was the abolition of the time limit for bringing suit against runaway peasants. Throughout the sixteenth century the time limit was five years, but the law of 1607 changed it to fifteen years. After the Time of Troubles, however, the original five-year limit was restored. Within such a short period a runaway could easily evade his owner's efforts to trace him and bring suit against him. In 1641 the gentry asked the Tsar to abolish the time limit, but it was merely increased to ten years for runaway peasants and to fifteen for the "abducted." In 1645 the gentry repeated its request, but in answer the government confirmed the decree of 1641. At last, in 1646, when undertaking a new general census, it complied with the gentry's persistent request and promised in a rescript of the same year that as soon as the peasants and their homesteads were registered, "the peasants and their children, brothers, and nephews would be bonded in accordance with this registration without any time limit." This promise was carried out by the government in the Ulozhenie of 1649, which made it a law that runaway peasants must be returned to their owners in accordance with the registers of 1620 and census registers of 1646–47 "without time limit."

Abolition of the time limit for retrieving the runaways did not in itself change anything in the legal character of peasant serfdom as a civil contract, for the infringement of which the defaulter could be prosecuted at the plaintiff's request; it merely added one more point of similarity between peasants and bondsmen, who could be claimed back by their masters without any time limit.

In abolishing the time limit with regard to peasants, the new rescript was concerned not with individual people, but with entire households, complex family groups. The census registration according to domicile included peasant householders with descendant and lateral branches of the family, binding them to the master, who thus obtained the right to retrieve them as his bondsmen at any time if they ran away. It also changed peasant personal servitude into a hereditary one. There is reason to believe, however, that this extension of serfdom merely confirmed a situation that had actually existed for some time. Among the mass of peasantry, a son who inherited his father's homestead and property normally made no fresh agreement with the landowner. Only if the property was inherited by an unmarried daughter did the landowner conclude a special agreement with her betrothed, who "entered into her father's house and all his belongings." The decree of 1646 had an effect on the nature of peasant agreements. From that time onward there is a marked increase in the number of contracts in which the obligations undertaken by an individual peasant include his whole family. In one case a free and unmarried peasant, in making a contract with St. Cyril's Monastery for a loan and a plot of land, included in his commitments his future wife and children "whom God would grant him after marriage."

The hereditary character of peasant serfdom raised the question of the state's attitude toward serf owners. As early as the sixteenth century the government, in the interests of the Treasury, attached crown peasants to their domiciles or to the plots of land on which they were to pay taxes, and restricted the movements of private owners' peasants. Early in the seventeenth century other social groups were similarly attached to their particular classes. There was a general reshuffling of the community in accordance with the requirements of the state. In the case of privately owned peasants, this reshuffling was complicated by the fact that between the peasantry and the state, in the interests of which it was undertaken, there stood the landowners, who had interests of their own. The law did not interfere with private contracts between people so long as the interests of the Treasury did not suffer from them. That was why obligations of serfdom were allowed to form parts of loan contracts. Those were private agreements with individual peasant householders. But now the landowners gained perpetual possession of the whole peasant population of their estates, including all the members of peasant families sharing the same homestead. Personal peasant serfdom *by agreement*, by loan contract, became hereditary serfdom *by law* in accordance with the registers or the census book. The peasants' private civil obligations led to a new duty imposed upon them by the state. Hitherto legislation had provided for registering and regulating relations that sprang from the peasants' contracts with the landowners. But the decree of 1646 introduced a new norm that was to give rise to new relations, both juridical and economic. The Ulozhenie of 1649 was to foresee and regulate them.

The Ulozhenie, as usual, dealt with the question of peasant serfdom superficially and indeed unfairly. Paragraph 3 of Chapter XI says that "up to the present there has been no tsar's decree to the effect that no one may accept peasants into ownership" (runaway peasants are meant), but the decree of 1641 clearly states: "Do not accept other people's peasants and bobyls." Almost the whole of Chapter XI of the Ulozhenie is concerned with peasant escapes, without explaining the nature of serfdom or defining the limits of the owners' power. It was compiled from old enactments with a few additions, without making full use of its sources.

By systematizing the nature of peasant serfdom on the basis of case law quoted in the Ulozhenie, we are able to fill in the omissions of the unsatisfactory law code. The decree of 1641 distinguishes three elements in peasant serfdom: *peasanthood, peasant inventory,* and *peasant possession.* Peasant possession means the owner's claim on the serf's labor, and peasant inventory means the serf's agricultural and domestic stock, "the plowing and household implements"; hence peasanthood can only mean the state of belonging to the master as his serf—that is, the owner's claim on the peasant's person, apart from his economic position and from his labor. This claim was confirmed in the first place by the registers and census books, and also by other documents that assigned the peasant or his father to the owner.

Distinctions between these three constituent elements of peasant bondage would have been harmless had the law defined the conditions of serfdom precisely. According to the Ulozhenie, a serf was hereditarily bound to the person, real or fictitious, to whom he was assigned in the census book or in a similar record.

He was bound to that person on account of the land—that is, the plot on the owner's estate where he happened to be living when the census was taken. Finally, he was bound to his status of peasant taxpayer, being assessed on the size of his plot. Not one of these three points was consistently worked out in the Ulozhenie. It forbade the transfer of peasants from service estates to hereditary estates, because the former were state property and must not be depopulated. It forbade the owners to make service kabala contracts with their peasants, or to emancipate peasants living on service estates, because in both cases the peasants would cease to be taxpayers, thus causing loss to the Treasury. But at the same time the law allowed the emancipation of peasants on hereditary estates (Chapter XI, paragraph 30; Chapter XX, paragraph 113; Chapter XV, paragraph 3). Besides, the Ulozhenie tacitly admitted or openly confirmed transactions between landowners in which peasants were parted from the land. It allowed the transfer of peasants without the land and even without inventory, and actually laid it down that peasants might be handed over from one owner to another, even though they had given no occasion for it, and it was the owners who were at fault. Thus, if after the census a landowner sold his estate, including serfs who had run away, he was to replace the fugitives by "the same kind of peasants" from some other estate of his, although those peasants had nothing to do with the case. If a landowner inadvertently killed someone else's serf, he would be sentenced to give "one of his best peasants with family" to the victim's owner (Chapter XI, paragraph 7; Chapter XXI, paragraph 71).

The law safeguarded solely the interests of the Treasury or of the landowner. The latter's power was restricted by law only when it conflicted with the interests of the Treasury. A peasant's personal rights were not taken into account. His personality vanished in the petty casuistry of the landowners' relations with one another. The law threw him onto its scales as a mere counterweight to rectify the balance of the gentry's interests. Peasant families were torn asunder in the process. A runaway woman serf who married a peasant widower belonging to another master would be returned to her former owner together with her husband, but his children by his first wife remained with his former owner. The law allowed such unchristian breakup of the family in the case of both peasants and bondsmen (Chapter XI, paragraph 13).

One of the worst omissions in the Ulozhenie was the absence of a clear and exact definition of the meaning of peasant inventory. Neither the legislators nor the Sobor delegates (among whom there were no serfs) thought it necessary to determine what share of a peasant's stock belonged to him and what to his owner. A freeman who inadvertently killed someone else's serf paid the victim's kabala debts, confirmed by his promissory notes. This seems to suggest that a peasant was entitled to make contracts in respect to his property. But a peasant who married a runaway bondswoman was surrendered to her former owner without any of his possessions, which remained in the hands of his former master (Chapter XI, paragraph 12). It appears, therefore, that a peasant's stock was merely his economic appurtenance as a peasant, and not his legal property; it did not belong to him as to a person possessed of rights. He lost it if he married a runaway bondswoman, even if the marriage took place with his master's knowledge or at his express command.

Examination of individual cases brings to light the ambiguities of the law and gives us some idea of the nature of peasant inventory and, to some extent, of its legal significance. Peasant inventory included agricultural implements, money, livestock, grain sown and threshed, "clothing of all descriptions and every kind of domestic stores." We know from the registers that a peasant's inventory passed from him to his son, his wife, or his daughter as a legacy, or to his son-in-law as his daughter's dowry, but in all cases at the owner's will or with his consent. Not infrequently a free and penniless bachelor would, in marrying a peasant serf's daughter, contract to live in his father-in-law's household for a specified number of years, say eight or ten, reserving the right to set up on his own at the end of that time, and take from his father-in-law or his heir a half or a third not only of the inventory, but of "house accommodation, land, plowed fields, and kitchen gardens" as well. The same conditions were observed when a newcomer married a fatherless girl or a widow, settling in her house and taking possession of the goods left her by her father or former husband. But it was from the owner that the suitor received his betrothed and her possessions, contracting to become his peasant—that is, his serf. The reason the same property belonged to two owners, the peasant and the landlord, was that peasant inventory usually had a twofold origin: the peasant's labor and the landowner's loan.

We have seen that according to the Ulozhenie, the husband of a runaway bondswoman lost his inventory when he was handed over to his wife's owner. In the registers of the 1630's we find still more striking cases. Runaway peasants were returned by the law courts to their owners together with the serf women they had meanwhile married, but the wives' property, which they had inherited from fathers or former husbands, was retained by the masters who had allowed them to marry. The landowners even considered themselves entitled to take away their peasants' property in favor of a third party. In 1640 a freeman, marrying a serf's foster daughter, engaged himself by a kabala contract to be a peasant of that serf's owner on condition that, after serving the specified number of years in his father-in-law's household, he could take from him or from his son a half of their inventory and go off wherever he liked together with his wife—to the obvious detriment of the peasant household and the peasant community.

Obviously, peasant inventory meant property with regard to which a distinction was drawn between actual possession and right of ownership. The first was the peasant serf's, the second belonged to the landowner. It was somewhat similar to the slaves' *peculium* in the Roman law, or to the *otaritsa* of the ancient Russian code. A serf at the time of the Ulozhenie reverted to the economic status of his social ancestor, the *zakup* of the *Russkaia Pravda*. Bondsmen could also possess property on similar conditions, and make business transactions even with their own masters. In a service kabala of 1596 a bondsman promised to serve his master "all his life," on condition that should the master die first, the bondsman was to be set free and keep all the property he might have acquired while in service. By law a bondsman had no property rights, and in putting such a condition to his master he could only trust in the master's moral rectitude. The Ulozhenie, too, evidently regarded the peasant serf's property in the same light as the bondsman's; otherwise, it could not have decreed that the debts of insolvent gentry should be collected from their serfs and bondsmen (Chapter X, paragraph 262). The Ulozhenie mentions the serfs' kabala debts, and this shows that a peasant serf could enter into contracts on the strength of his property and consequently claims could be made against that property, just as in the case of the zadvornyi bondsmen.

It should be noted that peasant inventory came to be regarded in the same way as the bondsmen's at a time when the pledge of serfdom was only just beginning to appear in the loan contracts. In 1627–28 we find landowners complaining that their peasants had run away, taking with them their inventory (horses, etc.), worth such-and-such a sum. Serfdom had not yet been established as a state institution, but the owners were already clamoring for the return of peasant inventory, as though it were their own property stolen by the runaways. From the very beginning of serfdom, the peasants found themselves simply bondsmen paying taxes to the state. The fact that a peasant's inventory was regarded as his master's property, and that the law did not clearly define what claim the peasant himself had upon it, was not a consequence of peasant bondage, but one of its main sources. Serfdom was the form the peasant's perpetual financial indebtedness to the landowners finally assumed.

The three slipknots in the noose of serfdom were: (1) attachment by registration and a loan contract as a legal means to hereditary peasant servitude; (2) a loan as the economic basis of the owner's right to the peasant's inventory; (3) work for the landowner in payment for a plot of land as the source of the master's right to use peasant labor at his discretion. In tightening the noose, the lawmakers were guided not by a sense of justice and not even by the idea of the common good, but by what was possible at the moment. It was not framing a law, but making a temporary arrangement. This view of the matter was held as late as Peter the Great's reign, and was forcibly expressed by the peasant Pososhkov in his book *On Poverty and Wealth*. He writes that peasants belong to the landowners temporarily, but to the tsar permanently. Peasant serfs were regarded in much the same way as state lands given out on service tenure; that is, as state property lent for a time to private persons and institutions.

But how could the government even temporarily entrust to private interest the labor of the bulk of the population, which provided food for the country? In its shortsightedness it reckoned only with the actual state of affairs, created partly by legislation and partly by the *de facto* old established relations. From ancient times, many landowners were given the right to act as judges of their peasants in all things except important crimes—murder, robbery, and proven theft. As early as the sixteenth century the landowner acted as a mediator between his peasants and the Treasury in matters of payments to the state, and sometimes paid their taxes for them. In the seventeenth century certain local customs became usual throughout the country. After the census of 1620 the landowners, in addition to their judicial power, had to exercise police supervision over the peasants registered as belonging to them. On the other hand, the life of the serfs became so intertwined with the landowner's, through loans, privileges, work, and taxes, that both parties had difficulty in drawing a line between their respective interests. In the serfs' conflicts with outsiders, especially in disputes about land, the landlord naturally took his peasants' side, being the owner of the object in dispute. The Ulozhenie (Chapter XIII, paragraph 7) merely notes as a generally recognized and long-established custom that the gentry of all ranks were responsible for and defended the interests of their peasants in all matters except burglary, robbery, manslaughter, and murder; that is to say, the landowner represented his serfs in litigation against outsiders in cases lying within his competence to judge his own serfs.

By acting as a judge, exercising police supervision, and carrying on litigations on behalf of his peasants, a landowner fulfilled judicial and administrative functions and replaced a government official. These were duties rather than rights. By carrying out these three functions, he made up for the shortage of government servants. Now a fourth was added, designed in the interests of the Treasury. Serfdom as an institution was countenanced on condition that on becoming a serf, a taxpaying peasant should not cease to be a taxpayer, capable of discharging his duties to the state. A peasant paid a tax on his plot of land for the privilege of tilling it. As soon as his labor was given to the landowner, it became the landowner's duty to sustain the peasant's ability to pay taxes and to be responsible for his solvency. This made the landowner an unpaid inspector of peasant labor and a tax collector responsible for his peasants' taxes. For the peasant the government tax became one of his dues to the master, just as his homestead and plot of land, on which the tax was levied, formed part of the master's property. A runaway serf's taxes were paid by his owner until a new census was made. The Ulozhenie regards it as an established rule that all moneys payable by the peasants to the state should be collected from their landlords. For keeping runaway serfs the receiver had to pay one general fine, covering both the amount of taxes due by them to the state and the profits their owners would have gained through the serfs' labor (Chapter XI, paragraphs 6 and 21).

Legal recognition of the owner's responsibility for his peasants' taxes put a final touch to the juridical structure of peasant serfdom. It reconciled the conflicting claims of the Treasury and the landowners. Private landlordship throughout the country became a police and fiscal agency of the Treasury. From being its rival, it was transformed into a colleague. This reconciliation could have been achieved only at the expense of the peasants' interests. In its early form, as defined by the Ulozhenie of 1649, serfdom was not yet identified with bondage, which had served as a pattern for it. In law and in practice certain differences, however slight, were still observed between the two: (1) a serf remained a taxpayer to the state, thus preserving some semblance of citizenship; (2) on the strength of this, the landowner had to give him a plot of land and an agricultural inventory; (3)

he could not be deprived of his land through being taken as a servant into the master's household (in the case of service estates), not even through being emancipated; (4) his inventory, though in the last resort not his own but his master's, could not be taken away from him "by force," as Kotoshikhin puts it; (5) he could complain of his master's excessive claims and by court order regain what had been taken from him by force.

But badly formulated laws helped to obliterate these points of difference and gradually drove the peasants toward bondage. We shall see this when we come to deal with the economic consequences of serfdom. Hitherto we have been studying its nature and origin. At present I shall only observe that when serfdom became established, the Russian state started on a path that, though apparently paved with external order and even success, led to a waste of national resources, a general decline in the national life, and occasionally profound upheavals.

Chapter
X

The Zemsky Sobor

The segregation of the different classes resulted, among other things, in a new political sacrifice, a new loss for the Russian state order: the Zemsky Sobor was convoked no more.

The most corrosive element in the mutual alienation of the classes was serfdom, which grew out of the bondsmen's and the peasants' servitude. The moral effect of serfdom was wider than the juridical. It greatly lowered the level of civic morality, which had never been high anyway. To a greater or lesser extent all classes directly or indirectly shared in the sin of serfdom. Men of the privileged nontaxpaying ranks, both lay and clerical, made loan contracts with peasants and service kabala and other contracts with bondsmen. Common people and even boyars' bondsmen made contracts of servitude for a specified number of years. Serfdom had a particularly deleterious effect on the social position and political development of the landowning classes. Allowed by the law and supported by police action, serfdom made the masters themselves slaves of state authorities, who encouraged such support, and enemies of any government that favored a different course. At the same time petty litigation between masters and serfs and between masters on account of the serfs became the strongest and most vital interest of the land-owning class. Gradually degenerating into profound social discord, this strife greatly delayed the normal development of the nation, and because of it the landowning gentry as a leading class warped and distorted the whole of Russian culture.

This effect of serfdom was clearly noticeable as early as the seventeenth century. The Department of Bondsmen was deluged with the gentry's complaints about peasants who had run away and carried off their masters' goods, "inciting others, and boasting of blackmail, slander, arson, murder, and all kinds of evil deeds." It was essential to lodge the complaint so as not to be answerable for a runaway in case he took to thieving and robbery. Escapes were a common occurrence among all grades of serfs—ordinary peasants, overseers who had looked after them and their masters' goods for twenty-five years or more, domestic secretaries "who sat writing upstairs in the master's house." The runaways carried off their own possessions—clothes, livestock—as well as their masters' personal property, sometimes to the current value of two or three thousand rubles. They were particularly keen on stealing the masters' strongboxes, containing serf indentures, so as to conceal evidence against themselves and change their names after running away. But the masters, too, were resourceful. When they started in pursuit of the fugitives, they took their pack of hounds with them. When the dogs saw their old acquaintances on the road, they gave them a friendly greeting, as though they were saying, "We know you," and so betrayed them.

People escaped either singly or in groups, five or six families together. An attorney of Suzdal had a serf who ran away, taking his family with him and his master's goods as well, after attempting to set fire to the house with the mistress and her children in it. The attorney, who was in Moscow on business at the time, "ran in pursuit" of the fugitives, and meanwhile another serf whom he had left behind in Moscow ran away also, "taking with him the rest of his master's goods." All this happened within eight days.

Social positions and relations that in themselves had nothing to do with serfdom became distorted and entangled in it. In 1628 a government official's bonded servant, Vaska, escaped with his wife, and eight years later returned to the place as Father Vasili, a priest ordained by the Bishop of Kazan and Sviiazhsk. In later years the Ulozhenie decreed that at their masters' request, such former bondsmen in holy orders should be sent to church authorities to be dealt with "in accordance with the rules laid down by holy apostles and church fathers" (Chapter XX, paragraph 67). The priest Vasili's former owner received him, on what terms we do not know, and that same year "his bondsman, the priest Vasili, and wife ran away from him, taking twenty-eight rubles of his money."

The work of popular education, even in its most elementary form, was affected by the conditions created by serfdom. To be taught reading and writing, a boy would be indentured to a teacher for a specified number of years, the teacher having the right "to subdue" the pupil for disobedience "by every means." In 1624 a Moscow inmate of an almshouse gave his son to the priest of a Moscow convent to be taught reading and writing, and, together with the boy's grandmother, a nun in that convent, stood surety for his good behavior and for his doing "all kinds of housework" while living with his teacher. Father Khariton taught his pupil to read and write within four years, but the indenture was for twenty years. The mother and grandmother, seeing that Father Khariton "had made a man of the boy and taught him reading and writing" but was going to keep him in bondage for sixteen more years, decided, "having plotted with suitable persons, to steal the boy from the priest and then to sue the priest for damages." We do not know how the matter ended.

The fugitives' manner of life, as described in the legal documents, makes one forget that we have to do with a Christian society, provided with all kinds of authorities, lay and clerical. A house serf ran away, abandoning his wife and children, and wandered from one estate to another under a false name, pretending to be a free person and unmarried. On one estate he was made to marry a serf girl and sign a service kabala. The new wife ceased to please him and, "having bethought himself of his sin," he returned to his former master "to steal his first

wife and his daughter," but there he was caught. Such is the
story we read in a legal document of 1627. Adventures of this
kind were so usual among serfs that the Ulozhenie makes special reference to them (Chapter XX, paragraph 84).

The enslavement of the peasantry did harm to popular representation both politically and morally. The Zemsky Sobor had
scarcely begun to be organized as an elected national representative assembly when almost the whole of the rural agricultural population dropped out of it. It lost its broad popular basis
and represented only the service gentry and the urban taxpayers
with their narrow class interests. Putting before the Tsar the
ideas of only a few classes, it could neither attract sufficient attention from above nor inspire enough confidence from below.
The petty details of life under serfdom that I have quoted from
legal documents show the low level and narrow scope of the
everyday interests and relations that characterized serf owners as
members of the Zemsky Sobor. The ruling landowning class,
alienated from the rest of the community by their privileged
position, absorbed by squalid disputes over serf ownership, and
demoralized by unpaid labor, was losing interest in the country's
affairs and growing less and less public spirited. The manor
house, tyrannizing over the village and keeping aloof from the
urban population, could not stand up to Muscovite officialdom
and make the Zemsky Sobor an independent channel of expression of the people's thought and will.

The Zemsky Sobor, "the Council of the Land," the general
assembly of the Muscovite state in the seventeenth century, was
composed of "men of all ranks," or of various ranks of people
from all the towns of the Muscovite state, according to the official documents. As in the sixteenth century, there were two unequal sections in it, the elected and nonelected official members.
The latter consisted of two supreme government institutions,
which appeared at the Sobor in full strength, with the addition
of co-opted persons: (1) the Boyars' Council with secretaries
from the various departments and (2) the Holy Synod of the
Patriarch, Metropolitan, and diocesan bishops, with the addition of co-opted archimandrites, abbots, and senior priests.

The formation of the elected section of the Sobor was somewhat complex, because of the variety and heterogeneity of the electoral units. Such units included the higher service ranks of the capital—stewards, lawyers, Muscovite gentry, and provincial gentry doing military service in Moscow—and the higher ranks of commercial people—merchants belonging to different guilds. Each of these ranks sent its special delegates to the Sobor. Then there were the provincial gentry. Their electoral unit was the district class corporation, consisting of three ranks: the "best," the gentry, and the boyars' sons. All provinces except Novgorod and Riazan formed electoral units. Novgorod was divided into five electoral units and Riazan into eight. Servicemen who did not belong to the gentry by birth and foreigners serving the government also sent delegates to the Sobor. Those living in the capital elected representatives of their military units (the streltsy, for example, sent delegates from their various regiments), and those in the provinces sent representatives of the settlements in which they were stationed (streltsy, Cossack, artillery, etc.).

Representation of the taxpaying population was organized more simply. The electoral unit was territorial—the local community, and not a class corporation scattered throughout the province. The trading population of Moscow was divided into "black hundreds" and "settlements." In the first half of the eighteenth century there were thirty-three of them. At the Sobor we find representatives of the black hundreds of Dimitrov, Pokrov, and Sretenka, and of the Ogorodny, Sadovy, Ordynsky, and Kuznetsky settlements. These names, still attached to Moscow streets, indicate either their locality or their business significance. Provincial towns formed complete electoral units.

Thus, Sobor delegates elected by the higher Muscovite gentry and merchant ·guilds represented ranks; those elected by provincial gentry represented class corporations; delegates elected by the Moscow *priborny* [1] servicemen represented military sections; priborny men in the provinces, as well as the taxpaying population of Moscow and other towns, represented their com-

---

[1] Servicemen who did not belong to the hereditary gentry, but were hired by the state to work for the army. [Translator's note.]

munities. At the 1613 Zemsky Sobor we also find delegates of the provincial towns' clergy and of "district people"—that is, the rural population.

It is hard to say how the elections were conducted. One of the signatures to the proclamation of the election of Tsar Michael is that of the senior priest of the town of Zaraisk, who signed for himself and other priests of the town and district who had been chosen as delegates. It is not clear how these elected priests, headed by the senior priest of the cathedral, had received their electoral rights. It may have been at a general conference of the Zaraisk clergy, which constituted a clerical electoral unit for the district. It is still more difficult to understand how representation of the rural population was organized. In the country, especially in the south and southeast, bordering on the steppes, there were some large settlements of servicemen not of gentry origin—the Cossacks. They were reckoned among the urban representatives and not "district people," and their delegates signed themselves on the manifesto of 1613 as Cossacks. The words "district people" can therefore only refer to peasants. Probably this is why their signatures always come next to those of the townspeople, who were also nonservice taxpayers. But we find them in such districts as Kolomna and Tula, in which, to judge by the registers, there were no crown peasants left by the end of the sixteenth century. So the "district people" who signed the electoral assembly's manifesto must have been landowners' peasants. Therefore in 1613 they were still regarded as free subjects of the state. In the northern provinces bordering on the White Sea, where there were hardly any landed gentry, peasants combined with the townspeople in managing local economic affairs and paying state dues. They formed a rural district community, sending their elected representatives to the municipal offices "for counsel" and common deliberation. They did the same when electing delegates to the Zemsky Sobor, so there may well have been peasants among the delegates. Whether the same procedure was adopted in the southern towns, or whether the peasants formed a special electoral unit, distinct from the urban, I cannot say. But at subsequent assemblies elected delegates from the clergy and the "district people" disappear, and the Zemsky Sobor ceases to represent men of all ranks.

The number of delegates from each electoral unit differed and was of no significance. At the Sobor of 1619 it was decided to call a new assembly in Moscow, electing in every town one delegate from the clergy, two from the gentry, and two from the townspeople. To the Sobor of 1642 they summoned from five to twenty delegates from big electoral units, and two or three from small ones. To the Sobor of 1648 two delegates had to be sent from each unit of Moscow service ranks and from large corporations of provincial gentry, and only one delegate from smaller corporations. Townspeople and Moscow black hundreds and settlements also sent only one per unit. Higher grade hundreds sent two delegates, and rich merchants three. Full representation and uniformity of method either were not sought or could not be achieved. At the Sobor of 1642 there were 192 elected members, and of these 44 were delegates from Moscow service ranks; but at the Sobor of 1648, one of the most numerous and representative, comprising not less than 290 elected delegates, Moscow service ranks were represented by only 8 members. Many gentry corporations and townships sent no delegates at all to some of the sobors because few people attended the local gentry meetings and there was "no one to choose from"; and as for tradesmen, "there are few or none in the town, and such as there are"—so writes a voevoda—"are doing your work, Sire, at pothouses and in the Customs Office."

Altogether, the composition of the sobors was extremely variable and had no stable and definite organization. It is hard to find two sobors that were similarly organized, and probably not at a single one of them were there delegates from all the ranks and districts and from all electoral units. At the Sobor of 1648 there were delegates from the gentry and from townspeople of 117 district towns, but at the Sobor of 1642 only the gentry and forty-two towns were represented. When a sobor was summoned in a hurry, it was considered sufficient to have delegates from only such provincial servicemen as were at the moment on duty in Moscow, and at some sobors only delegates from the

Moscow service ranks were present. On January 28, 1634, the Tsar summoned a sobor to discuss a new tax for military needs, and it met the very next day. Together with delegates from Moscow ranks, it was attended by "provincial gentry who happened to be in Moscow."

The delegates to the Zemsky Sobor were elected at local meetings and conferences, in provincial towns at the invitation and under the supervision of the town voevodas. The decrees prescribed the election of "the best people, good, steadfast, and intelligent." This meant that men of means, sensible and reliable, were required. They were sought, therefore, among the highest ranks. Literacy was not a necessary qualification for election. At the Sobor of 1648, 292 delegates were present. Of 18 of these, it is not known whether or not they could read and write; of the remaining 274, more than half (141) were illiterate.

The protocol of the elections, signed by the electors, was passed on to the voevoda as a guarantee that the chosen men were fit "to transact the Tsar's and the country's business." The voevoda sent the delegates with his own report to the department for his district in Moscow, where the validity of the elections was verified. One voevoda wrote to Moscow that he had carried out the Tsar's decree and sent to the Sobor of 1651 two of the "best" members of the gentry. But as for tradespeople, no "best" two could be found, for there were only three traders in his town and they were a poor lot, wandering from place to place and unfit for such a job, and so he sent as representatives of the urban population one boyar's son and one bombardier. The secretary of the department for the district, safeguarding the freedom of elections, made a stern comment on the voevoda's report: a letter was to be sent to him with a reprimand, saying that "the gentry have been bidden to choose good men from among themselves, and it is not for him, the voevoda, to do the choosing, and he must be severely censured. The voevoda did a foolish thing in neglecting the townspeople and sending instead of them a serviceman of low rank and a bombardier."

It does not appear that the delegates brought with them to the Sobor any written instructions from their electors. Only in

1613 the temporary Muscovite government, in its messages to the towns about electing delegates for the purpose of choosing a tsar, requested that the delegates come to a clear understanding with their electors and take mandates from them about the tsar's election. That was a case of exceptional importance, requiring national unanimity and the direct voice of the people; that was why Prince Pozharsky and Minin, going to the rescue of Moscow and summoning the Zemsky Sobor, wrote that the towns must give their delegates instructions, written and signed by the electors, as to how they, the leaders of the national forces, were to fight the common enemy and choose a tsar. Records of other sobors do not mention written instructions, and the delegates do not refer to them.

The delegates had a certain freedom of action, and at the Sobor of 1648 a delegate of the Kursk gentry actually sent a report to the Tsar denouncing his fellow townsmen, "saying all manner of evil things" against the Kursk citizens and accusing them of spending church festivals in an unseemly fashion. Such zeal for good behavior exceeded the delegate's rights and called forth angry protests from the people of Kursk, who threatened the denouncer with "every kind of harm." The electors empowered their representative, without giving him any formal instructions, to act in concord with them and to intercede for "his brethren's needs," which were declared to him at his election. From the case of the Kursk delegate it is evident that the electors considered themselves entitled to take their representative to task for not putting before the Tsar all the requests they had mentioned in their petition.

That was how the government itself regarded the delegate's duties. In 1619 it summoned representatives of the clergy, the gentry, and the townspeople "who could tell of their grievances, molestations, and plunder," so that the Tsar might know about "their needs and hardships and all their deficiencies," and having read their petitions "might try to arrange everything for the best." At the sobors of the seventeenth century the people's elected spokesmen replaced the government officials of the sixteenth century. Popular representation took the form of submitting communal petitions to the Tsar and provided direct contact between the supreme power and the people. We already know how this helped to complete and amend the original unsatisfactory official draft of the Ulozhenie of 1649.

In this position in relation to the government, the people's representatives could not impose their will upon it or legally compel it to do anything. Questions raised at the Sobor could be settled only by an exchange of views between the two sides, and by their psychological approach to each other. This was reflected in the very method of procedure. The elective Sobor of 1613 was an exception and cannot, of course, be regarded as typical. Its function was constitutive. Generally each sobor was convoked by the Tsar's special decree. Only once did the Holy Synod officially take the initiative in the matter. When Tsar Michael's father returned from Polish captivity and was made patriarch in 1619, he came to the Tsar with other hierarchs of the church and they discussed together various disorders in the Muscovite state. The Tsar and his father, with the whole of the Holy Synod, the boyars, and "all the people of Muscovy, having arranged a sobor," spoke of how to put things right and set the land in order. This is explained by the fact that the Patriarch was not only the president of the Holy Synod, but also a cosovereign.

As a rule the Tsar gave orders for a sobor to be summoned to deal with some particular subject and opened it with a speech, which he either delivered himself or had the Council secretary, at his command and in his presence, "read to all the people," explaining the subject the delegates were to consider. Thus at the Sobor of 1634 it was announced that for continuing the war against Poland it was necessary to impose a new special tax, without which the Treasury "could not carry on." The Tsar's proposal ended with the assurance that he would always remember the people's coming to his aid and show favor to them in the future in every possible way. All the ranks represented at the Sobor, among whom there do not seem to have been any townspeople, said in reply that "they would give money according to their means, as much as they could spare." That was all.

Apparently the matter was settled in one day, then and there, at one general meeting. Six days later the Tsar appointed a committee consisting of two noblemen, two secretaries, and the archimandrite of the Chudov Monastery to collect the new tax "from all sorts of men."

But to judge from the records of the Sobor of 1642, a similar question involved a complicated procedure that may have been adopted at other sobors as well, though it has not been preserved in the summary records. In 1637 the Don Cossacks took Azov from the Turks, repulsed Turkish attacks, and offered the conquered fortress to the Tsar. At the Sobor, in the presence of the Tsar, the Synod, and the Boyars' Council, the secretary of the Council read out the Tsar's decree summoning the Sobor and then read a letter in which the Tsar put two questions to the delegates: "Are we to go to war with the Turks over Azov? And if we do, where is the money to come from? And a great deal of money would be needed." The letter requested the delegates to think hard about the matter and to tell the sovereign in writing what they thought, so that he might be fully informed. After being read aloud, the Tsar's letter was given out "for firsthand information" to the delegates in the boyars' presence, and sent to the church authorities so they could talk it over among themselves and tell the Tsar in writing what they thought. The secretary of the Council was ordered to speak to the delegates about the Sobor's business and to ask their opinion.

At other sobors, too, the ranks were questioned "separately" and gave their answers in writing. This "questioning of the ranks separately" was one of the ways of taking the delegates' vote. Another form of voting was used at the Sobor of 1621, when the Tsar's and the Patriarch's proposal to go to war with Poland was answered by a petition to fight. So far as one can tell from the records, the difference between petitions and written answers to questions was that answers stated merely the ranks' ideas on the subject, leaving the decision to the Tsar, while a petition gave a more decisive answer to the measure proposed by him and could complicate the issue by some proposal made by the delegates; such proposals, however, were allowed in the written answers to the questions as well.

At the Sobor of 1642 the serviceman delegates were divided into three groups: (1) stolniks; (2) *zhiltsi*,[2] Muscovite gentry, and commanders of the streltsy; and (3) provincial gentry. A special secretary was attached to each group, probably for guidance and chiefly for editing their written opinions. Commercial people of Moscow were not given a secretary, and tradesmen from the provinces were not represented at the Sobor at all. But opinions were not collected according to this division into groups. Altogether eleven written "speeches" or "statements" were presented: from the clergy, from the stolniks, from the Muscovite gentry, from two members of it who broke away from their group and expressed a minority opinion, from the Moscow streltsy, from the gentry of the city of Vladimir, from the gentry of three other central towns, from sixteen central and western towns, from twenty-three other towns, chiefly southern, from merchants and city hundreds, and finally from the Moscow black hundreds and settlements. In the Sobor's records the statements are placed in this order, immediately following the list of names of the 192 delegates. The statements show that there were gentry delegates from forty-three district towns instead of the forty-two mentioned in the register. The difference was due to the fact that delegates from eight towns mentioned in the register presented no statements, but delegates from nine towns not mentioned in the register did.

It is hard to say how this could have happened. Apparently not only the elected representatives of the provincial gentry took part in making the statements, but also fellow citizens who happened to be in Moscow at the moment on service business. Thus a statement from three towns includes signatures of citizens of Luga who were "here in Moscow," while officially the town of Luga had only one representative. Besides, provincial gentry delegates mentioned in the Sobor register do not seem

---

[2] Members of the provincial gentry who lived temporarily with the tsar on military service. [Editor's note.]

to have been summoned to Moscow from their hometowns, but to have been elected in Moscow from among those who were doing military service there. The decree summoning the Sobor was issued on January 3, but the collecting of statements from the delegates began as early as January 8. This haste explains why there were no delegates from provincial urban populations at the Sobor.

There is a certain interconnection found in the delegates' statements. The same ideas, phrases, and entire passages occur in many of them. This shows how the Sobor consultations were conducted. The delegates gathered somewhere in various groups, consulted together, exchanged ideas, and expanded or altered their written statements accordingly. Thus the statement of the twenty-three towns closely resembles that of the sixteen, and the report of the black hundreds and settlements follows the pattern of the merchants' and the two upper hundreds' statement, modified to make it applicable to their own class. There is no trace of general consultations of members of the Sobor, and no general decision was passed. The question was settled by the Tsar and the boyars, and settled negatively, probably under the influence of the dejected tone of the delegates' statements. It was decided not to accept Azov and not to go to war with the Turks and the Crimean Tatars because there was no money and no means of obtaining it.

Not all the sobors resembled the one of 1642, but a detailed protocol of it helps us to understand the political significance of the seventeenth-century sobors in general. As in the sixteenth century, they were called on important occasions to discuss the gravest questions of state organization and foreign policy, chiefly of war and the burdens it involved. It was not the competence of the Sobor that had changed, but its composition and character. The government now had to deal not with its own official agents, but with the people's delegates pleading for their electors' needs and grievances. The political significance of the Sobor consultations depended on the participation in it of the Boyars' Council, presided over by the Tsar. There were two

modes of procedure: the Council worked either together with
the delegates or separately from them. In the latter case the
boyars and the Tsar were present only while the government's
proposals were being read to the Sobor. After that they with-
drew and took no further part in the delegates' work. That
work was confined to group consultations and to expressing
private opinions. There was no final general meeting and no
decision was taken by the Sobor as a whole. Its role was merely
advisory or informative. The Tsar and the Boyars' Council
took cognizance of the opinions expressed by the delegates, but
reserved for themselves the right of decision.

That was what happened at the Sobor of 1642 and also at
the Sobor of 1648. The draft of the Ulozhenie was read simultaneously to the Tsar and the Council in one hall and to the
delegates in another. They had "sitting with them" a specially
appointed boyar with two companions, colleagues as it were,
presiding over them. In spite of this division of work, the
Council and the Sobor did not in the least resemble the upper
and lower houses of Parliament, as is sometimes said. The
Boyars' Council, headed by the Tsar, was not simply one of the
legislative organs. It was the supreme government, possessing
full legislative power. As it listened to the articles of the
Ulozhenie, it amended or confirmed them, creating laws. The
assembly of elected delegates was not on the same level as the
Council, but was attached to its codifying committee. Thus,
after listening to the articles of the Ulozhenie, the delegates
would petition the Tsar to amplify or cancel them, and those
petitions would be passed on by the committee to the Tsar
and the boyars, who, in consideration of the plea of "men of
all ranks," would issue new laws in accordance with the people's
wishes.

On other occasions the delegates took a more direct part in
legislation. This happened when the Boyars' Council, headed by
the Tsar, actually formed part of the Sobor, forming so to speak
one legislative body with it. Then the boyars gave their opinion
in the same way as the elected delegates, and the Sobor's

general verdict was pronounced, having the force of law. The Council then became an administrative agency to see that the Sobor's decision was carried out.

This mode of procedure was observed by a whole series of sobors under Tsar Michael—those of 1618, 1619. 1621, 1632, and 1634. It was particularly noticeable at the Sobor of 1621. Turkey, the Crimea, and Sweden invited Muscovy to join a coalition against Poland. It was a tempting opportunity to pay back the Poles for all they had done at the Time of Troubles. At the Sobor summoned to deal with the matter, the church hierarchs promised to pray for victory against all the enemies; the boyars and servicemen of all ranks promised to fight against the Poles, "not sparing their lives"; and commercial people promised to give as much money as they could, according to their means. A general decision of men of all ranks was made at the Sobor to fight against the Polish king, in alliance with the Turkish sultan and the Crimean khan and the Swedish king. The gentry, including its lowest ranks, petitioned the Tsar to distribute them among different towns, so that everyone could serve the Tsar according to his ability, with no absentees. But it was only the two sovereigns— Michael and his father—who, "having spoken to the boyars" without any participation of the Sobor, issued the decree to enroll the gentry, announce the Sobor's decision to the towns, and order servicemen to prepare for war—"feed their horses and save up supplies for the march."

The Zemsky Sobor retained its legislative character until the last years of Michael's reign—until 1642. It also functioned as a legislative body later, when in 1653 it was called to consider the question of the Ukraine. Boyars voted together with the delegates, who were "questioned," each rank separately, as in 1642. The decision to accept Bohdan Khmeltnitsky as a subject was taken by the Tsar on consultation with the Sobor as a whole, and not with the boyars only. Even the purely advisory activity of the 1648 Sobor occasionally became legislative. Thus the Sobor decided to forbid church institutions to acquire the gentry's hereditary estates, or to accept mortgages on them (Ulozhenie, Chapter XVII, paragraph 42). But the very fact that the Sobor's role was sometimes advisory and sometimes legislative showed the political instability of popular representation. Legislative authority descended on the Sobor so to speak as a reflected light. It was not secured to it in any way and did not mean that the will of the people was recognized as a political power. It was merely a temporary gracious extension of the sovereign's power to the subjects, which did not detract from the fullness of his power, but diminished his responsibility for possible failure. It was a favor and not a concession.

Hence the obvious incongruities of the sobors. There were elections, electors and elected delegates, questions put by the government and answers given by the people's representatives; there were consultations, expressions of opinion, verdicts; in short, there was all the parliamentary procedure, but there was nothing politically definite about it. The order in which the work was to be done was not established, the times when the Sobor was to be called were not fixed, there was no uniformity about its composition or its competence or its relation to the highest government institutions. The forms did not follow any pattern, the powers did not carry with them any rights or guarantees; and yet there existed conditions and motives that usually establish rights and guarantees. But the conditions remained without consequences and the motives led to no action.

We know what a powerful source of the people's rights in western Europe was their governments' need of money. It compelled them to summon representatives of the different ranks in the state and ask their help. But the people did not help their treasuries gratuitously. They obtained various concessions, and in exchange for subsidies gained rights and guarantees. In the seventeenth century the Russians too had no lack of such motives and opportunities. Only three of that century's sobors, not counting the elective one, had no apparent connection with finance: the Sobor of 1618, called on account of Prince Ladislas' march on Moscow; the Sobor of 1648, dealing with the Ulozhenie; and the Sobor of 1650, convoked because of the Pskov mutiny, when the government wanted to use the Sobor's moral influence upon the mutineers.

The empty Treasury was the most frequent and impressive reminder of the need to call a sobor. Until the balance between the usual expenses and revenues was restored after the devastation, the government had constantly to have recourse to emergency taxes and loans or requisitions from the capitalists called "aids," without which the Treasury "could not do." Such requisitions could be justified only if the whole country demanded them. In 1616 the wealthy Stroganov family was required to pay, in addition to their annual tax of 16,000 rubles, another 40,000 in advance on their future payments to the crown. This huge demand (more than 600,000 in our currency) was supported by the verdict of the Sobor—of "the authorities and elected men from all the towns"—which it was difficult to disobey.

For the untaxed section of the population the Sobor's demands took the form of a voluntary subscription to meet the urgent needs of the state. In 1632, at the beginning of the Polish war, the Sobor decided to collect from the people who paid no taxes "as much as they could afford" toward payment of the soldiers' salaries. The clergy declared at the Sobor how much they were giving out of their private and public funds. The boyars and servicemen promised to bring a bit of what each one could contribute. The Sobor's verdict made voluntary gifts appear as a compulsory self-imposed tax.

Thus the Zemsky Sobor opened to the Treasury new sources of revenue without which it could not manage, and which without the Sobor it could not collect. In this respect the Treasury was entirely dependent on the Sobor. The delegates complained, but they gave the money without demanding or even requesting any rights. They were content with the kindly but wholly noncommittal promise that "the Tsar would always remember the people's coming to his assistance and would show favors to them in the future in every possible way."

Obviously the idea of a regularized representation and of political guarantees had not yet occurred either to the government or to the community. The Zemsky Sobor was regarded as an instrument of the government. To give advice when asked was not the people's political right, but the same kind of duty as paying taxes demanded of them by the Treasury. Hence people were indifferent to representing their country. Delegates from the towns went to the Sobor to discharge a duty, just as they would go to do military service, and their electors reluctantly—often only after a second reminder from the voevoda—went to their respective towns for the electoral meetings. Having no political ideas to support, the Zemsky Sobor found no support either in the system of administration that was being built up or among its own members.

When after the Time of Troubles the country was faced with difficult problems, they had to be solved not by one particular person, not by some political party or by a narrow circle of high officials; the collective reasoning of the whole country was called on to deal with them. Conclusions arrived at by individual minds, whether in the government or among the common people, were gathered together in one communal thought and expressed in the Sobor's verdict or in the people's petition.

It might be expected that since the Sobor had such significance for the central government, the principle of communal representation would be preserved or even strengthened in the provincial administration. Representation of the people as a whole is unthinkable without local self-government. An independent delegate and a dependent elector are a contradiction in terms. But as it happened, the period when the sobors were most active coincided with the decline of local self-government and its subjection to bureaucracy. Legislative activity under the new dynasty followed two opposite courses; the government was destroying with one hand what it was creating with the other. At the time when the country's delegates were summoned from the provinces to settle questions of vital administrative importance together with the boyars and the Moscow gentry, their electors were being put in the power of those boyars and gentry. A government clerk managed district affairs, and his office was supposed to be the seat of local self-government.

There proved to be the same kind of inconsistency with regard to another matter. Soon after the council of "men of all ranks" that created the new dynasty began its work, almost the whole rural population (85 or 95 percent, counting the crown peasants) was excluded from the community of free citizens, and their representatives ceased to appear at the Zemsky Sobor, which thus lost all semblance of being truly representative of the country.

Finally, the segregation of the classes changed their attitude toward one another and strained their mutual relations. The Sobor of 1642 showed that there was utter discord among the members' opinions and interests.

The Holy Synod gave the conventional answer to the question of going to war: it was a military matter, for His Majesty the Tsar and his boyars to decide, and it was not customary for them, the clergy, whose duty it was to pray for the Tsar, to deal with it. In case of war, however, they promised to give what they could to the men at arms.

The upper ranks of the Moscow gentry sent in a short answer leaving it to the sovereign to decide the question of war, to find the men and the money to wage it, and meanwhile to order the Cossacks to keep Azov and send volunteers to their assistance.

Two members of the gentry, Zheliabuzhsky and Beklemishev, had scruples about signing their fellows' answer, and sent in a well-reasoned statement of their own. They were strongly in favor of accepting Azov and of equitably distributing the burden of the impending war among all the classes, including the monasteries.

The most outspoken expressions of opinion came from the lower ranks represented at the Sobor. Two statements presented by the provincial gentry of thirty-nine southern and western districts were real political pamphlets, sharply criticizing the existing order of things and presenting a full program of reforms. They bitterly complained of pillage, of unfair distribution of service duties, and of the privileged position of the Moscow gentry, especially of those attached to the court. Provincial servicemen felt very angry about the Moscow government classes, who had grown rich "through bribery and corruption" and built themselves splendid mansions such as in the old days even men of noble lineage had not dwelt in. They asked that the landowners' service duties be apportioned not according to land area, but according to the number of peasant homesteads; it should be carefully ascertained how many peasants a landowner had on his estates; the amount of land possessed by the clergy should be checked; the reserve "domestic funds" of the Patriarch, bishops, and monasteries should be used for the needs of the state. The gentry were wholeheartedly prepared to work against the enemy ·and "lay down their heads," but asked that men under arms should be collected from all ranks, with the exception of their bondsmen and peasants. They ended their complaints and proposals for reforms with a sharp criticism of the administration as a whole: "We are despoiled worse than by the infidel Turks and Crimeans by Moscow lawyers, unjust courts of law, and all the wrongs they inflict on us."

The Moscow merchants of the upper rank and the black hundreds and suburban tradespeople, like the provincial gentry, were in favor of accepting Azov, were not afraid of war, and were ready for financial sacrifices, but they spoke more modestly, in a minor key, made fewer suggestions, but complained just as bitterly of being ruined by taxation, by state impositions, and by the voevodas. They begged the sovereign "to consider their poverty" and sadly referred to the abolition of local self-government.

The general tone of the Sobor statements of 1642 is certainly expressive. To the Tsar's question "What are we to do?" some ranks answer dryly, "Do what you like." Others with good-natured loyalty say, "You, Sire, are free to take men and money where you think best, and that is the business of your boyars, our perpetual guardians and providers," but at the same time they let the Tsar understand that his government is as bad as it can be, that the ways introduced by him are no good whatever, that the taxes and services demanded by him are more than the people can give, that the administrators appointed by him—all those voevodas, judges, and especially government clerks—have brought the people to utter penury by their extortions and oppression, and have ransacked the country worse than the Tatars, while the clerical authorities, who pray for the Tsar, are merely piling up their reserve funds—"such is our, your servants', thought and statement."

Discontent with the administration was made more acute by social discord. The different classes were not unanimous; they were dissatisfied with their positions and complained of the inequality of their burdens. The upper ranks tried to pass every new burden on to the lower ranks, commercial people taunted servicemen with having many hereditary and service estates, and servicemen taunted commercial people with making big profits. The Moscow gentry reproached the provincial for having an easy time, and the provincial gentry blamed the Moscow gentry for their lucrative jobs and the great profits they made; and neither lost an opportunity of mentioning the church wealth, which was of no benefit to the state, and of saying that their own peasants and bondsmen should not be interfered with. Reading the statements presented at the Sobor by the delegates of the different classes makes one feel that those delegates had nothing to hold them together, no common cause to work for— there was nothing but a conflict of interests. Each class thought by itself, apart from the others, knowing only its own immediate needs and other people's unfair advantages. Evidently the political segregation of the different classes resulted in their mutual moral estrangement, which was bound to prevent their working together at the Zemsky Sobor.

The idea of the Zemsky Sobor was fading out among the ruling and privileged classes, but it persisted for a time among small groups of the taxpaying population, which remained under the protection of the law after the enslavement of the peasantry to private owners. The statements of the upper ranks of Moscow merchants, of Moscow black hundreds and settlements, which carried on the rough work of administration, contain a scarcely perceptible touch that lifts them above the powerful "white ranks." While expressing their readiness to lay down their lives for the sovereign, commercial and black-hundred delegates declared that the question of accepting Azov was not a class question, but "concerns the whole of the sovereign's land, all Orthodox Christians," and that the whole land without any exceptions must bear the burden of the war, with no defaulters. Nothing of the kind was heard from the service gentry. They merely wrangled with one another, jealously watched other people's mouths, indignant if an extra morsel found its way there, and tried to transfer new state burdens from their own shoulders to other people's.

Commercial and industrial delegates knew for what purpose they had come to the Sobor, and understood the interests of the country as a whole and the true meaning of popular representation. In these black-hundred tradesmen of the seventeenth century the feeling of civic duty was still aglow while it was dying down in the upper ranks that towered above them. When, some time later, it was almost completely extinguished, the idea of consulting the country as a whole was expressed even more directly and forcibly by those same lower classes.

After the unsuccessful credit operation with the copper coinage issued in 1656 there was a great rise in prices, causing much discontent. The crisis affected everyone and could be averted only by the concerted efforts of all social classes acting together with the government, but the government tried to avoid its difficulties by consulting only the Moscow tradespeople. The task of asking them how to help matters was entrusted in 1662 to several men, headed by Ilia Miloslavsky, the Tsar's father-in-law, an utterly unscrupulous man whose abuses were largely responsible for the trouble.

As at the Sobor of 1642, merchants of the upper ranks and members of the black hundreds and suburban settlements presented written statements in which they made many sensible remarks and gave a detailed account of economic relations in the country and their lack of cohesion. They pointed out the class antagonism between the rural and the urban population and between the landowners and commercial interests, and told many bitter truths to the government about its failure to understand what was happening in the country, its inability to maintain law and order, and its indifference to the voice of the people.

By law the right to trade and carry on industries in towns involved payment of special commercial taxes and duties, which helped to fill the Tsar's Treasury, but now, the tradesmen complained, "in spite of the sovereign's ruling, all the best kinds of commerce and industry have been taken over by clerical, military, and legal ranks; bishops, monasteries, priests, servicemen, and government officials carry on trade by special license tax free, which causes much waste to the state, and great losses in taxes and customs and excise to the Treasury." In addition the tradesmen complained that, being obliged to raise the price of their goods because copper money had lost its nominal value, they incurred the hatred of all the ranks, who "could not see reason" and understand their position. After saying what they thought on the subject, the Moscow tradesmen unanimously added that they had nothing more to suggest because it was "a great matter for the whole state, for the whole land, for all towns and all ranks," and they begged that the Tsar would of his favor call together the best men of all ranks both in Moscow and in other towns, because "without people from the towns we alone cannot settle the matter."

This request from well-informed commercial people to summon a sobor was a disguised protest against the government's tendency to replace the Zemsky Sobor by consultations with competent representatives of a particular class. This seemed unreasonable to the trade delegates. They were complaining of the same administrative and social disorganization that they had so fervently denounced twenty years before, at the Zemsky Sobor of 1642. On that occasion they used the Sobor to protest against this disorganization, and now they regarded the Sobor as a means for putting an end to it. But the Sobor of 1642 consisted of men who were responsible for the disorganization—that is, of representatives of the classes that had created it by their mutual antagonism. The Moscow tradesmen evidently thought that a new sobor was the only means of harmonizing the discordant social forces and interests.

A new task was thus set to popular representation. This representation originated during the Time of Troubles for the purpose of reestablishing order and authority. Now it had to create order, which the reestablished authority proved unable to do. It had to organize the community as it had organized the government. But was the Sobor capable of carrying out this task when the government itself was an active factor in social disorganization? Was agreement possible when the ruling circles and the privileged service classes did not need it? They were responsible for the disorganization, which was profitable to them, and they did not care about social discord so long as their bondsmen and peasants were left undisturbed. As for the Moscow "humble tradesmen and merchants," as they styled themselves, they carried too little weight to balance the relations within the community. The clergy had little civic courage and hardly any political significance, and since the introduction of serfdom, the only people who voiced, however feebly, the needs and interests of the taxed population at the sobors were the Moscow and provincial commercial townspeople. Weighed down by their class burdens, these men faced at the sobors an overwhelming majority of the gentry and a government made up of boyars and department officials, also belonging to the serviceman class. The sobor demanded by the tradespeople in 1662 was not summoned, and the government had to deal with another mutiny, raised and suppressed with the usual Muscovite senselessness.

The ambiguous political character of the sobors, their political disarray, centralization and serfdom, class discord, and, finally, the sobors' inability to carry out the new task with which they were faced—such were the most obvious causes of their instability, and they show why the Zemsky Sobor ceased to work and popular representation gradually disappeared. I do not even mention the low level of political ideas, customs, and needs—of the political temperature, so to speak—a level so low as to freeze any governmental institution designed by its very nature to rouse the spirit of liberty. This lay at the root of the matter and accounted for all the unsuccessful or harmful innovations introduced by the new dynasty at the beginning of its activity.

The effect of the conditions enumerated above showed itself in the gradual change in the composition of the Zemsky Sobor.

The change began very early. At sobors following that of 1613 there were no longer any delegates from the clergy and the rural population. Thus the Sobor ceased to represent the land, the whole people, and included only representatives of servicemen and urban taxpayers.

But even this simplified representation, severed from its broad national basis, was sometimes further truncated. In case of need or at its own discretion, the government, without troubling provincial townspeople, called for consultation delegates from Moscow ranks only, and from such provincial gentry as happened to be in Moscow at the time on service duty. At the Sobor of 1654, which imposed a special general tax to be levied "from men of all ranks" (including "the fifth money," which was gathered chiefly from the urban population), there were no representatives of provincial townspeople. Thus the Zemsky Sobor was disrupted from below. Its basic territorial components —representatives of local district communities, of the clergy, of the taxpaying population, both urban and rural, and even of provincial servicemen—were dropping away from it. Losing its representative character, the Sobor was reverting to the old sixteenth-century type of an official gathering of the Moscow ranks, military and commercial, which served the state as well as paid a tax. At the Sobor of 1650 there also were no delegates from provincial townspeople, and the Moscow taxpaying tradesmen were represented by their officials—foremen and bailiffs—as at the sixteenth-century sobors.

The size of territory represented at sobors decreased at the same time that the character of the representation deteriorated. Instead of consulting the assembled representatives of all the people, the government adopted a form of consultation opposed to the very idea of such an assembly. A question of national importance would be treated as though it were only of departmental or class significance, and to discuss it the government summoned, either by choice or by virtue of their office, representatives of the particular class that in its opinion was chiefly concerned in the matter. Thus in 1617 the English government asked permission for English merchants to sail down the Volga to Persia, and have certain trading privileges and concessions. The Boyars' Council answered that it was impossible to decide a single point in such a matter without consulting the country as a whole; but in fact consultation was limited to the merchants and tradespeople of Moscow. Even at a full sobor some questions were decided by only a part of it. The decision about service estates to which we referred earlier, for instance, was accepted by the sovereign and the Council after consultation with the clergy and servicemen, apart from the other classes' representatives.

No sobor was called between 1654 and Tsar Feodor's death in April 1682. State affairs of exceptional importance were decided by the Tsar with the Boyars' Council and the Holy Synod, without the country's representatives. This was done in 1672, when Russia was threatened with a terrible Turkish invasion and special taxes had to be levied. But in 1642, on a similar though less important occasion, a sobor had been convoked.

The government adopted more and more often the practice of consulting members of some particular class. This was the only way in which the community took part in state affairs. Between 1660 and 1682 there were at least seven such consultations with class delegates. In 1681 delegates from service ranks, under the chairmanship of Prince V. V. Golitsyn, were summoned for consultation about military reforms; when financial questions had to be discussed, only delegates from taxpayers were consulted. Thus the government was itself destroying the Zemsky Sobor and replacing it by, or more exactly substituting for it, special wholly noncommittal consultations with interested persons, and treating matters of importance to the state as a whole as though they concerned only a particular class.

The history of the Zemsky Sobor in the seventeenth century is the history of its decline. The reason for this is that the Sobor came into being through the temporary need of a country without a sovereign, as a means of escaping anarchy and disorder, and was afterward kept in being by the new government's temporary need to establish itself in the country. The new dynasty and the classes that upheld it—the clergy and the gentry—

needed the Sobor while the country was still recovering from the shaking that the pretenders had given it. As things calmed down, the need for the Sobor decreased.

The traces of its activity, however, proved to be more lasting than the Sobor itself. Appearing in 1613 as a constitutive gathering of all the ranks of the community, it created a new dynasty, reestablished the shattered order, for over two years acted as a government and was on the point of becoming a permanent institution. Later on it occasionally acquired legislative significance, though this was in no way guaranteed to it. It was convoked not less than ten times under Tsar Michael, sometimes in consecutive years, but only five times under Tsar Alexei in the first years of his reign. It was gradually becoming warped, losing one of its organs after another. Instead of representing all classes, it came to represent only two or even one—the gentry. At last it disintegrated into class consultations of interested men. It was not convoked at all under Tsar Feodor, was convoked hurriedly and with all sorts of accidental members in 1682 in order to place Feodor's two younger brothers together on the throne, and was convoked for the last time by Peter in 1698 to try his sister Sofia for conspiracy.

Though it was not a political force but only a governmental aid, the Sobor more than once helped the government out of its difficulties and left a faint legislative trace in some of the articles in the Ulozhenie. It subsisted for a time in the political consciousness of Moscow tradespeople but was soon forgotten. Only the tenacious historical memory of the maritime north preserved a dim recollection of it in a ballad about Tsar Alexei Mikhailovich —the one who jokingly said that "the community's voice is always heeded," but who in fact brought the Sobor to its end. He is supposed to be telling his people from the rostrum in Moscow:

> Help your sovereign to think his thoughts.
> He has to think hard and take counsel.

The Zemsky Sobor, the assembly of the chosen representatives of the land, appeared in the life of the Muscovite state accidentally because of the jolt produced by the extinction of the old dynasty and afterward functioned irregularly, from time to time. The people, "the land," mounted to the governmental platform for the first time when there was no government to occupy it. They also appeared on it later when the reestablished government needed the people's help. The calamities of the Time of Troubles brought together the last resources of the Russian community for the restoration of order in the state. The representative assembly was created by this enforced social unanimity and helped to sustain it. Popular representation in Russia came into being not in order to limit authority, but to find and strengthen it, and therein lay its difference from representation in western Europe. But in supporting the authority it had created, the Sobor naturally participated in it for a time, and it might have become its permanent partner through force of habit. This did not happen because the methods used by the government to satisfy the needs of the reestablished state destroyed social unanimity born of the country's miseries and broke up the community into segregated classes, while giving most of the peasantry into serfdom to landowners. This deprived the Sobor of its popular character, making it representative of the upper classes only, and at the same time disunited those classes both politically, by the inequality of their rights and duties, and morally, by creating antagonism between their class interests.

At the same time, the trials of the Time of Troubles and the lively activity of the sobors under Tsar Michael did not develop the people's political consciousness sufficiently to make them feel a vital need for popular representation and for converting the Sobor from a governmental auxiliary into a permanent organ for expressing the country's interests and requirements. No influential class with a need for popular representation had arisen in the community. With the introduction of serfdom, the gentry, which gradually absorbed the higher nobility, became in fact the ruling class, and, bypassing the Sobor, found a more convenient way of furthering its class interests—specifically, by direct collective appeals to the supreme power. Aristocratic circles that hereditarily surrounded the throne of weak tsars made this method all the easier. The Moscow merchants, who adopted the idea of popular representation, were not strong enough to defend it, and their delegates in 1662 complained that very few of their suggestions were carried out.

Thus, two processes prevented the Zemsky Sobor from becoming a permanent institution in the seventeenth century. It was at first a support to the new dynasty and its auxiliary organ of administration, but as the dynasty became established and acquired greater administrative means and more departments of officials, its need for the Sobor grew less and less. And the community, broken up into separate classes with different corporate obligations, had a poorly developed sense of civic equity and was incapable of the concerted activity that could have converted the Sobor into a permanent legislative institution, secured by political guarantees and organically connected with state order. Popular representation came to an end because of the increased centralization of the government and the compulsory segregation of the classes.

Chapter

XI

Finances

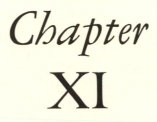The Zemsky Sobor came to an end later than local self-government. The disappearance of the one and the deterioration of the other were parallel though not simultaneous consequences of the two basic changes in the state order to which I referred at the end of the preceding chapter. Increasing centralization crushed local self-governing institutions. Their decay and the disunion between the classes segregated by the state destroyed the Sobor, which had been the chief means of enabling provincial corporate communities to take part in legislation. Both these basic changes sprang from the same source—the financial needs of the state. These needs were the hidden mainspring that directed the government's administrative and social measures, inspired its organizing activities, and compelled it to make so many sacrifices at the expense of good social order and public welfare.

Finance was probably the sorest spot in the Muscovite state order. Under the new dynasty the needs created by the frequent, costly, and seldom successful wars definitely outweighed the means at the government's disposal, and it was at a loss to discover how to restore the balance. The army was ruining the Treasury. In 1634 the Tsar, asking the Sobor's help for con-

tinuing the war with Poland, declared that the funds he had
accumulated during the years of peace from sources other than
direct taxation had all been spent on preparation for the war,
and that it was impossible to provide for the upkeep of the
auxiliary forces without levying special taxes. Defeats inflicted
on the Russians by the Polish and Swedish troops made the
government anxious to improve its armed forces in conformity
with the foreign pattern.

Two documents give an idea of the transformation under-
gone by the serviceman militia in the course of fifty years and
of the growing expenses this involved. The estimate for 1631
enumerates armed forces kept at government expense and receiving salaries in money or in kind or given land on tenure.
They numbered some 70,000 men. These included the Moscow
and provincial gentry, bombardiers, streltsy, Cossacks, and foreign military men. In the former khanate of Kazan and in Siberia there were registered another 15,000 or so belonging to
various Eastern tribes and service gentry—Tatar, pagan Chuvash,
Cheremis, Mordva, and Bashkir—but they received no service
salary and were called up only in exceptional cases, when "the
whole land had to do full service"—that is, when there was
general mobilization. As late as 1670 Reitenfels admired the
Tsar's review of 60,000 militiamen on parade. Obviously these
included not only the Moscow ranks, but also the upper layers
of provincial gentry, outfitted for distant campaigns and accompanied by their armed household serfs. The foreigner was
dazzled by the brilliance of the smart-looking riders' armor and
accouterments. But they produced a stronger impression near
Moscow—especially on the aesthetically impressionable Tsar—
than on the battlefields of Lithuania and the Ukraine, although
a tremendous amount of the people's labor went to their upkeep.
The military fitness of all this motley mass of gentry, Cossacks,
Tatars, and so on, which defended the state and was disbanded
after each campaign, can be gauged by Kotoshikhin's words:
"They are not trained to fight and are not used to military
discipline." Only the streltsy, who formed permanent regiments,
presented a more orderly appearance.

This war material was rearranged as follows: Urban gentry, boyars' sons with little or no land, volunteers and recruits from other classes, even peasants and bondsmen were organized into companies and regiments under foreign (mostly German) commanders imported into Russia by the hundred. There were companies and regiments of cavalry, infantry, and mounted infantry. Entire villages on the southern boundary of Muscovy were turned into military settlements. In 1647 a village of about four hundred peasant homesteads belonging to a monastery in the district of Lebedian was taken over for dragoon service. By the Instruction of 1678, all "gentry of scanty means" fit for military service were to be enlisted as soldiers on a monthly salary. In 1680 it was decreed that all the gentry in the Seversk, Belgorod, and Tambov military districts fit for service should be enrolled as soldiers. These were exceptional measures. For the normal filling up of regiments formed on the foreign pattern, a new and twofold method was introduced: recruits were collected either according to the number of peasant homesteads (a hundred homesteads had to provide one cavalryman and one soldier), or according to the number of men in the family (if two or three sons were living with their father, one would be enrolled; if there were four sons or four brothers living together, two would be taken). This meant levies of conscripts, in addition to the old method of calling up the requisite number of men. It has been calculated that in the course of twenty-five years (1654–79) at least 70,000 men were taken from the working population of the country.

Regiments of the new type were given firearms and military training. The list of men at arms of 1681 shows the results of this slow reorganization of the armed forces. All men learning arms were distributed among nine military districts. Only the Moscow corps, consisting of 2,624 men of various ranks with their campaigning bonded retainers and "given" men and 5,000 streltsy, preserved their old organization. In the other eight districts there were 16 regiments of streltsy and 63 regiments of foreign pattern (25 cavalry and 38 infantry), under the command of foreign colonels. Only three regiments had Russian commanders with the rank of general. According to the 1631 list, the serviceman militia numbered some 40,000. By 1681, only 13,000 remained under the old organization. The rest formed part of the 63 reorganized regiments, comprising 90,000 men.

It could not as yet be called a standing army, because it was not permanent. At the end of a campaign the regiments were disbanded and only officers remained. The list of 1681 gives the number of men under arms as 164,000 plus 50,000 Ukrainian Cossacks. Comparing, as far as possible, the records given in the lists of 1631 and 1681 of the identical sections of the army, and leaving out the Mongol tribesmen, not included in the list of 1681, we find that since 1631 the armed forces supported by the government had increased by two and one-half times. The pay of the numerous foreign colonels and captains—their "monthly sustenance"—was very high, and if they remained in Muscovite service it became a monthly salary, half of which was paid as a pension to their widows and children after their deaths. Cavalry, infantry, and dragoons, recruited mostly from the poorer classes, received good monthly salaries, free military equipment, and free keep on campaign. The upkeep of the army rose from the equivalent of three million rubles of our currency in 1631 to ten million in 1680. This means that while its numbers were increased by about two and one half times, the cost was trebled. Wars grew proportionately more expensive. Under Tsar Michael the unsuccessful Smolensk campaign, lasting eighteen months, cost at least seven or eight million rubles. Under Tsar Alexei the first two campaigns against Poland, ending with the conquest not only of the Smolensk region, but of White Russia and Lithuania as well, cost about eighteen to twenty million, which almost equaled the whole revenue received by the central fiscal institutions in 1680.

The revenues called for by the budget had to be increased to meet the rising cost of the army. To understand how the government attempted to balance its financial resources with the ever increasing state expenditure, it is essential to have some idea of the financial system that had been in force up to that time. The usual revenue of the state consisted of "assessed" and "nonassessed" income. "Assessed" income meant money paid in taxes, the necessary amount of which was fixed in the budget beforehand. There were direct and indirect taxes. Direct taxes in the Muscovite state were payable either by entire communities or by individuals. The total sum payable by a community, each member of which paid his share, was called a *tiaglo*, and the people subject to such payments were called *tiaglie*. It was chiefly lands and homesteads that were assessed, and these too were called tiaglie. The assessment was based upon the division of taxable lands and homesteads into *sokhas*. A sokha was a taxable unit containing a certain number of taxpaying urban homesteads or a certain area of taxpaying peasant tillage. It was reckoned to contain 400 desiatinas of good land on the gentry's estates, 300 desiatinas of monastery land, or 250 desiatinas of taxable crown land. The proportion of middling or poor-quality land in each of these sokhas varied accordingly, the quality of land being determined by the profit it brought and not by the nature of the soil. The composition of an urban sokha differed greatly according to district. In Zaraisk, for instance, at the end of the sixteenth century a sokha included 80 homesteads of the "best," most prosperous citizens, or 100 homesteads of the "intermediates," or 120 of the poor or "junior" ones, but in Viazma in the first half of the seventeenth century a sokha comprised 40 best homesteads, 80 intermediate, and 100 juniors.

The chief indirect taxes were customs dues and imposts on taverns. These were the most abundant sources that fed the Treasury in the seventeenth century. Customs duties were of many kinds, and were paid both on the transit and on the sale of goods. Tavern imposts were levied on the sale of liquor, which was a government monopoly. The government usually assessed these two sources of revenue and either farmed them out or assigned their collection to "sworn-in," trusted overseers and barmen, whom the local taxpayers had to elect from among themselves. Any deficit had to be made good by the elected men, or by their electors if the latter had overlooked the collectors' dishonesty or negligence, or had not reported it in time. Overseers and barmen detected by outsiders in thieving or embezzlement were threatened by the law of 1637 with the "death penalty without any mercy." This meant, in effect, that they were put to death for the negligence or inefficiency of the government, which shirked its obvious duty of controlling its officials' work and laid on the local population the task both of choosing and of supervising them. In the middle of the seventeenth century all the indirect taxes were combined into one. In 1653, instead of the multifarious customs dues there was introduced the so-called ruble duty: ten dengas [1] on the ruble, five from the vendor and five from the purchaser.

The basic direct taxes were "tribute money" (*dan* and *obrok*). "Tribute money" was the name given to various direct taxes paid by the urban commercial and industrial people and the rural agricultural population. These were levied according to the number of sokhas in the different towns and village communities as specified in the register books. "Obrok" had a twofold meaning. Sometimes it meant the payment made to the government for allowing a private person to use crown land or to engage in some industry. Obrok in this sense meant revenue from state-owned fisheries, hayfields, and hunting zones, and also from urban shops, inns, bathhouses, and other commercial and industrial enterprises. In other cases obrok meant a general tax imposed on all the inhabitants of a certain district in place of various other taxes and dues. For instance, when the local government office of namestnik was abolished in the reign of Ivan IV, the dues and sustenance paid to the namestniks were replaced by an obrok. Obroks of that kind formed part of a tiaglo, and were imposed in accordance with the sokha registers. Tribute money and obrok in the sense of a general tax were always paid at fixed rates, while the amounts of other state dues were variable and determined by special devices.

In addition to these regular sources of revenue, there were also special taxes to meet particular needs of the state: money for postal expenses, for the ransoming of prisoners, and for the

---

[1] A denga was a small, irregular silver coin valued at half a kopeck in the mid-seventeenth century. There are 100 kopecks to the ruble. [Editor's note.]

streltsy. Postal money was collected for the upkeep of transport service for ambassadors, government messengers, officials, and military men. Posting stations were established on the highroads. This tax was levied from townspeople and peasants in accordance with sokha registers, and went to a special central institution, the Department of Posts, which had charge of the drivers. They received a salary, were paid mileage, and had to keep a certain number of horses at the posting stations. Prisoners' money was a tax levied on each household for ransoming prisoners from the Turks and the Tatars. In Tsar Michael's reign it was collected from time to time at special government order. Later on it became permanent, and according to the Ulozhenie of 1649 was levied annually "from all conditions of men," from those who paid taxes and those who did not, but not in equal amounts. Townspeople and peasants on church lands paid eight dengas per household, taxpaying peasants on crown lands and those belonging to private landowners paid four dengas, and streltsy, Cossacks, and other servicemen of lower ranks paid only two. According to Kotoshikhin, prisoners' money annually collected at that period amounted to about 150,00 rubles (about two million in our currency). The tax was collected by the Department of Foreign Affairs, which carried on the ransoming of prisoners. The streltsy money was levied for the maintenance of the streltsy, the permanent infantry established in the sixteenth century under Grand Prince Vasili. At first it was a small tax paid in grain. In the seventeenth century the tax was collected both in grain and in money, and as the size of the streltsy organization increased, it became at last the most important of the direct taxes. Kotoshikhin says that in Tsar Alexei's reign there were in Moscow, even in peacetime, more than twenty regiments of streltsy, with 800 to 1,000 men in each (22,452 altogether in 1681), and about as many provincial ones.

All the taxes enumerated above, with the exception of the prisoners' money, were levied in accordance with the division into sokhas. The government imposed a certain amount of tax upon each sokha, letting the taxpayers divide it among themselves according to the paying powers of each, "to apportion it according to their possessions, industries, plowed land, and other sources of income." The sokha assessment was based upon clerks' registers. From time to time the government made a register of taxable immovable properties, sending clerks to all the districts to write down the particulars of such properties, garnered from the statements and documents of the local inhabitants and verified by comparisons with former registers and by personal inspection. They described a given town and district, their population, lands, amenities, commercial and industrial establishments, and the dues payable on them. In doing so, they recorded meticulously the number of taxable homesteads in every town, settlement, suburb, and village, the number of people living there—householders with their children and relatives—the area of arable and uncultivated land, the hayfields and woods. Clerks' registers divided taxable urban homesteads and rural arable land into sokhas, and calculated the amount of tax payable by each settlement according to the acreage of land owned by its taxable inhabitants and to its industries.

In the Moscow archives of the Ministry of Justice there are preserved many hundreds of the sixteenth- and seventeenth-century clerks' registers, which provide the basic material for the study of the financial organization and economic conditions in the Muscovite state. Such registers had been compiled from ancient times, but only a few of them, relating to Novgorod at the end of the fifteenth century, have reached us. Their importance as cadastral surveys and financial records made them useful for the drawing up of various civil enactments. With their help disputes about land were settled, rights to immovable property were confirmed, recruits for the army were called up. In 1619, when Filaret, Tsar Michael's father, returned from Poland, both the sovereigns convoked a Zemsky Sobor at which it was decided to send clerks and inspectors to draw up registers of all the towns, sort out the inhabitants, and refer them to the places where they had lived and paid taxes previously. On the strength of this decision a general census of the taxpaying population was made in the twenties in order to ascertain and organize the country's taxable resources. It was these registers of the late

1620's that the Ulozhenie accepted as the basic document, superseding all others, for establishing the owners' rights to their serfs. Lawsuits about runaway peasants were settled by reference to those registers. As we have seen, it was the census of 1627 that introduced the conditions of permanent bondage into the peasants' loan contracts.

Another category of state revenues—nonassessed dues—consisted chiefly of payments by private persons for having their needs satisfied by government institutions: for instance, duties on various private transactions, on petitions addressed by private individuals to administrative offices and courts of law, on documents received from them, on copies of legal decisions, and so on.

On the basis of this financial system, the Treasury in the seventeenth century went in for two kinds of enterprise—it either made experiments that disturbed the established order or tried to reorganize it by means of innovations. To begin with, the Treasury began collecting its vanished taxpayers. The Time of Troubles caused masses of them to give up their share in the communal financial burden. When order was restored they resumed their former trades but paid no taxes. A long administrative and legislative struggle was waged against these absentees. Beginning with the Zemsky Sobor of 1619, the government sought to suppress the "pledgers," and barely succeeded in this with the help of the 1643–49 Sobor. It was then laid down in the Ulozhenie that people who traded in a town but did not belong to it had either to give up their trade or pay urban taxes.

In order to secure to the Treasury a permanent supply of persons working for it directly or indirectly, the legislature, as we have seen, herded the community into closed corporate classes, each having its special duties. It forbade people to leave a township at will and transformed the peasants' lifelong bondage by contract with private landowners into hereditary serfdom. But however carefully the authorities registered and fixed to their domiciles the people capable of paying taxes, there remained many defaulters who managed to escape state dues. The government wanted to catch with one general measure, as with a big fishing net, all the people, common and privileged, men and women, adults and children, to make them work for the Treasury.

At the time when western European adherents of the mercantile theory advocated replacing direct taxes by indirect, and taxing consumption instead of capital and labor, Muscovy attempted to take the same course quite independently, not on the strength of any imported theory, but out of bad home-bred practice. In Muscovite financial policy, indirect taxes were generally preferred to direct. In the seventeenth century the government was particularly zealous in exploiting this source of revenue, in the belief that a man would more readily give a higher price for goods than pay a direct tax, for then he would at least get in exchange for the surcharge something he could use, while by paying a tax he got nothing except an official receipt.

It was probably this consideration that led to a plan suggested, it was said, by a certain Nazari Chistoy, a former merchant and subsequently a government secretary: it was proposed to replace the chief direct taxes by a higher duty on salt. Everyone needed salt, and consequently everyone would contribute to the Treasury; there would be no defaulters. Up to 1646 the duty on salt was five kopecks (about sixty kopecks in our currency) per *pood*.[2] In that year it was increased to twenty kopecks—that is, up to half a kopeck per pound. Half a kopeck in those times was equivalent to six kopecks now, so that the state duty alone exceeded by six times the present-day market price of a pound of salt. This measure was justified in the decree by a number of naïvely crude considerations. The streltsy and postal money— the heaviest and most unequally distributed of the direct taxes— would be abolished, everyone would be paying the same duty, there would be no defaulters. All would pay in the natural course of events, without cruel requisitions and penalties. Foreigners living in Muscovy and paying nothing to the Treasury would pay like everybody else.

But the subtle calculations proved mistaken. Thousands of pounds of cheap fish, on which common people fed during

---

[2] Forty Russian pounds, or 36.11 avoirdupois pounds.

Lent and on other fast days, were left to rot on the banks of the Volga because fishmongers were unable to salt it. Considerably less salt than usual was sold, and the Treasury suffered severe losses. In 1648, therefore, it was decided to abolish the new tax, which had greatly increased the people's irritation at the authorities and caused a rebellion in the summer of that year. The rebels put Nazari Chistoy to death, saying, "That's for the salt, you traitor!"

Financial need compelled the pious government to go against the people's and the church's feelings and make the sale of tobacco, "the herb that is an abomination unto the Lord," a state monopoly, although by the decree of 1634 its use and sale were punishable by death. The Treasury sold tobacco for almost its weight in gold—fifty or sixty kopecks per *zolotnik*.[3] After the rebellion of 1648 the tobacco monopoly was also rescinded and the law of 1634 came into force again. The government, at a loss what to do, issued positively foolish decrees.

Another financial undertaking ended still more lamentably. The need for money made Muscovite financiers of the seventeenth century highly enterprising. Having arrived at the idea of replacing direct taxes by indirect, they thought out unaided the idea of national credit. In 1656, when the victorious first war with Poland was coming to an end and a rupture with Sweden was imminent, the Muscovite Treasury was short of silver currency to pay the army. It was suggested—by the Tsar's friend F. M. Rtishchev, people said—that copper money should be coined of the same nominal value as the silver.

The Moscow market was accustomed to monetary tokens of nominal value. Devaluation of the currency was an auxiliary source of state revenue, used by the Treasury in case of need. No Russian gold or silver coins of large value were in ordinary use. The ruble and half a ruble were monetary units of calculation. The coins in common circulation were small kopecks, half kopecks, and quarter kopecks. In the marketplace the buyers kept these small, badly made, and irregularly shaped oval coins tucked away in their mouths, for fear of pickpockets. The

[3] A measure of weight equivalent to 2.4 drams. [Translator's note.]

Muscovite Treasury minted no silver of its own, but minted silver money from the imported German *Joachimthaler,* called in Russian *efimok.* The interests of the state were not neglected in the process. The efimok was worth 40 to 42 kopecks in the Moscow market, but it was reminted to represent 64 kopecks, so that the Treasury gained 52 to 60 percent on the operation. Sometimes the reminting consisted merely in stamping the efimok with the Tsar's seal, thus converting it from a 40-kopeck piece into one of 64 kopecks. Only at the beginning of the first Polish war did they begin minting silver rubles and quarter rubles at the nominal value of the stamped efimok.

And so in 1656 small copper coins of the same shape and weight as the silver were minted. At first these metal "credit notes" were completely trusted and were at par with silver money. But the attractive financial transaction fell into the hands of men open to temptation. Workers at the mint—men of humble means—suddenly grew rich and began squandering money right and left, built themselves splendid houses, decked out their wives like fine ladies, and bought goods in the shops without haggling about the price. Rich merchants, even those of the upper ranks, appointed as sworn supervisors of the issue of copper, bought copper for themselves, took it to the mint together with the state copper, had it made into credit currency, and took it home. The market was flooded with "thieves' money," copper coins stolen from the state credit. Copper money began to fall in value more and more rapidly. At first the difference between silver and copper currency was only four kopecks, but by the end of 1660 two copper rubles were given for one silver ruble, and in 1663 it was as much as twelve, and later fifteen. Prices increased accordingly, and the situation was particularly difficult for men under arms, who received their salaries in copper coinage at its nominal value. Inquiry showed that the mintmasters' and merchants' frauds were screened by heavily bribed government officials, who behaved with their usual unscrupulousness. They were headed by the Tsar's father-in-law, Ilia Miloslavsky, and by a member of the Boyars' Council, Matiushkin, husband of the Tsar's maternal aunt. Both were in

charge of the copper business. Miloslavsky was said to have
taken part in the actual stealing. Minor officials, merchants, and
workers at the mint were punished by having hands and feet
cut off and then being sent into exile. The Tsar's father-in-law
incurred the sovereign's displeasure for a time, and the Tsar's
uncle was dismissed from his post.

Seeing that the men in power got off so easily, others who
were implicated in the fraud decided to take advantage of the
general outcry against high prices and stir up trouble, so as to
give a shaking to the nobility, as in 1648. Proclamations posted
in Moscow accused Ilia Miloslavsky and others of treason. In
July 1662, when the Tsar was staying at his suburban estate,
Kolomenskoe, a mutinous crowd of about five thousand accosted
him with the demand that he commit the traitors to trial. The
rebels held the Tsar by the buttons of his coat and made him
promise on oath, and shake hands upon it with one of them,
that he would himself investigate the case. But when, next day,
another crowd from Moscow joined them and began rudely demanding the traitors, threatening that if he did not surrender
them of his own accord they would be taken by force, Alexei
called to the streltsy and to his courtiers, and then a wholesale
massacre of the unarmed rebels began. It was followed by tor-
tures and executions. Numbers of people were thrown into the
river, and whole families were sent into perpetual exile in Siberia.
The Tsaritsa was ill for a whole year after the shock of that July.
People of many classes had taken part in false coining and in the
mutiny—priests and sextons, monks, rich merchants, tradesmen
and artisans, peasants and bondsmen; even soldiers and a few
officers joined the mutineers. Contemporaries reckoned that over
7,000 people were executed and more than 15,000 had hands
and feet cut off, more were sent into exile, or had their property
confiscated. But it was said that real thieves and mutineers numbered not more than 200. The rest of the crowd that went to
the Tsar consisted of idle spectators.

The operation with copper money greatly disorganized commerce and industry, and in trying to find a way out of the difficulty the Treasury merely made things worse. In 1662, at con-

sultations with that same Ilia Miloslavsky and Streshnev about
the causes of the rise in prices, Moscow tradesmen gave a very
clear account of their position. In order to replenish the exhausted supply of imported foreign silver currency, the Treasury
compelled Russian merchants to sell to the government for
copper money Russian export goods such as furs, hemp, potash,
and lard, and then sold these to foreigners in exchange for their
efimoks. At the same time Russian merchants had to pay in silver
for goods imported from abroad, because foreigners would not
accept copper money, and to resell them to their own customers
for copper. So the silver they spent did not return to them, and
further purchases of foreign goods became impossible. They
were left without silver and without merchandise, and could
not carry on their trades.

The complete failure of the scheme made the government
liquidate it. The issue of copper credit tokens as a state debt
bearing no interest presupposed the possibility of changing the
tokens into real money. The decree of 1663 reestablished silver
currency and forbade the hoarding or use of copper coins.
These were either to be melted and made into various articles or
brought to the Treasury, which, according to Kotoshikhin, paid
ten silver dengas for a copper ruble; but according to the decree
of June 26, 1633, it was only two dengas. The Treasury acted
like a real bankrupt, paying its creditors five kopecks or even
one kopeck on the ruble. In order to buy export goods from
Russian merchants, the government collected in all its ministries
together almost a million and a half in copper money (about 19
million in our currency) at its nominal value. This was no doubt
only a part of the copper currency that had been minted. The
rumor was that the total amount minted in the course of five
years reached the incredibly high figure of 20 million (about
280 million in our currency).

Innovations introduced by the government in the administration of finance were far more important. They were three in
number: change in the assessment unit of direct taxation in accordance with the new land census, distribution of direct taxes
among the various classes, and the delegation of local financial
administration to the rural communities.

Direct taxes were now levied not on sokhas, but on every homestead. The transition from the sokha to the homestead as a unit of taxation was not immediate, but went through an intermediate stage, "the living *chetvert*." The first to observe and study this stage was A. S. Lappo-Danilevsky, in his monograph on direct taxation in the Muscovite state in the seventeenth century.

Clerks' registers help us to understand the origin of this unit of assessment. The rural sokha was not a stable taxable unit. The system of cultivation constantly required that some of the land should lie fallow, and this interfered with the assessment. In the second half of the sixteenth century the sokha as a taxable unit was broken up in the central provinces by the peasants' drift to the borderlands and the consequent decrease of the tilled area. The number of abandoned plots kept increasing at the expense of the "living"—that is, the taxpaying cultivated area. Wasteland was not reclaimed; the reverse was the case. The Time of Troubles had almost completely stopped agricultural work in the country. According to a contemporary's testimony, plowing was given up nearly everywhere and people somehow subsisted on their old stocks of grain. When peace was restored to some extent, the peasants who had remained where they were or returned from flight found numerous empty homesteads and sites with plots of arable land that were not as yet overgrown with scrub. Returning to farming after the upheaval, they plowed tiny portions of their own taxable plots and saved up their labor for the "newly found" arable land—the abandoned and no longer taxed fields of their farmer neighbors who had been killed or captured or had disappeared without a trace. We see from the clerks' registers that in places where the peasants tilled 4,350 desiatinas at the end of the sixteenth century, in 1616 there were left only 130 desiatinas of "living"—that is, tilled and taxable—land, and 650 of the untaxed reclaimed land. In a certain estate in the district of Riazan in 1595 there were 1,275 desiatinas of tilled peasant land, but in 1616 nine peasant homesteads had only three taxable desiatinas among them and plowed 45 untaxed desiatinas belonging to the neighboring empty homesteads. In other places we sometimes find six or seven peasant homesteads to one living chetvert—that is, to 1.5 desiatinas of tilled taxable land in three fields—and 40 to 60 of the untaxed tillage.

The practice of cultivating abandoned plots that had dropped out of taxation, involving in some places a sharp decrease in the area of taxable land, meant a loss to the Treasury, which sought to regulate the situation. When undertaking a general land census in the 1620's, the government issued several decrees determining for each district the maximum number of homesteads bound to pay tax on the living chetvert. It hesitated, reconsidered its decisions, and changed its proposals. For instance, at first the tax payable on the living chetvert on the estates of Moscow servicemen was distributed among a good many homesteads: twelve peasant and eight bobyl homesteads, or sixteen peasant homesteads (counting one normal peasant homestead as equivalent to two poor ones). Later the assessment was raised by more than five times, with only three peasant homesteads paying the tax on each chetvert. Then things were easier again and the number of homesteads was raised to five. A homestead's share of the tax payable on the living chetvert depended on the number of homesteads assigned to it. If there were eight of them, and a peasant tilled an eighth of the living chetvert, he paid tax on every *chetverik* [4] of the plowed land.

As the area of tilled taxable land increased, the living chetvert gradually lost its significance as a fraction of the sokha and became merely a conventional unit for calculating assessment. If there were eight homesteads apportioned to one living chetvert, each was taxed on a chetverik of the plowed land, even if its tillage included two or three taxable desiatinas. Of course, as the area of taxable cultivated land increased, the assessment of the living chetvert, as a section of the sokha, increased also, but the tax on the group of homesteads apportioned to it was distributed among them according to their numerical share in it. If the chetvert was assessed at two rubles, a homestead taxed on every quarter of a desiatina (chetverik) would pay twenty-five kopecks, however much land it might have under the plow. This, however, was only an officially calculated and not a real

---

[4] A measure of area equivalent to one quarter of a desiatina. [Translator's note.]

payment. In fact a homestead that tilled four desiatinas paid less tax than one that tilled eight, although both were assessed on a chetverik of plowed land—that is, on three-sixteenths of a desiatina in three fields. To distribute the tax proportionately to the area of the plowed land was the business of the peasant community or of the landowner, and not of the assessment clerk.

Financial needs suggested the idea of taking into account for purposes of taxation not only the area of actually tilled land, but also the available labor and the local agricultural conditions. The government wanted to tax not only the land under plow, but the plowman as well, so as to make him plow more. This consideration accounted for the variations and changes in the number of homesteads apportioned to the living chetvert in the different districts. It will be easily seen, however, that a system of taxation built upon two different bases—on the assessment of land and of labor—was bound to be confusing both to the taxpayer and to the assessor, and increased the technical difficulties of the division into sokhas. It was difficult to measure the arable areas and combine them into sokhas, excluding fallow land and the untaxed abandoned fields, either tilled by peasants to whom it did not belong or overgrown with scrub. To calculate the subdivisions of the sokha was a complicated business, since ancient Russian arithmetic recognized only the number 1 as numerator, and only numbers divisible by 2 or 3 as denominators; and it was not easy to classify the soil as good, medium, or poor. It was difficult to verify the local people's testimony and to discover mistakes made by the clerk—to say nothing of the subterfuges to avoid paying the tax or to reduce its amount. All this provided plenty of opportunities for arbitrary decisions, underhanded deals, and misunderstandings. Taxation of homesteads was simpler and could be made more equitable. At the Zemsky Sobor of 1642 the provincial gentry urgently petitioned the government to collect money and stores for men under arms according to the number of peasant homesteads, and not according to clerks' registers. Small landowners saw better than anyone else that since the introduction of serfdom, the agricultural force to be exploited was labor with its equipment, and not land as such.

In 1646 there was a general census of homesteads, which en-

slaved every peasant to the landowner without a time limit and
at the same time introduced taxation per homestead instead of
per sokha. A census of homesteads was made again in 1678–79.
Assessment registers called census books were compiled. These
differed from the former clerks' registers. They described labor
forces—homesteads with their inhabitants who paid taxes—instead of describing economic resources—fields, woods, local industries, etc., on which the population was assessed. These census
books served as a basis for taxation per homestead. But with this
new unit of assessment the method of calculating and distributing
direct taxes remained the same as before. The government fixed
for every taxable district the average amount of tax per homestead and calculated the general amount payable by the district
as a whole. The taxpayers apportioned that sum to individual
homesteads in the community according to the means and industries of each, just as they had done when the sokha was the
unit of taxation.

When assessment per homestead was introduced, it became
essential to unify direct taxes, which in the course of years had
greatly increased in number. It was difficult to apportion them
to such small assessment units as homesteads. Besides, the unification of indirect taxes in 1653 served as a pattern for unifying
the direct as well. There was one important difference, however:
an indirect tax is concerned with the consumer regardless of his
economic position, but a direct tax is bound to reckon with that
position. Serfdom broke up the taxpaying population into two
sections: free urban and rural inhabitants paid on their capital
and labor to the state only, but serfs divided their labor between
the Treasury and the landowner's countinghouse. A unified direct tax had to be distributed between the two classes of payers
proportionately to their unequal capacity to pay. The government preferred another solution, dictated by its financial needs.
None of the direct taxes, which in the seventeenth century became permanent, increased as rapidly as the streltsy money, the
tax for the upkeep of the constantly growing streltsy corps.
From 1630 to 1663 it increased almost ninefold.

The consequence of raising the tax beyond the people's power to pay was arrears. After the census of homesteads in 1678, several other direct taxes were added to the streltsy tax. By the device of September 5, 1679, it was divided according to the number of homesteads at various rates of assessment. The arrears increased. Canceling them, the government in 1681 summoned delegates, two from every town, and asked whether they were able to pay the present amount of the streltsy tax, and if not, why not? The delegates answered this artless and ignorant question by saying that they could not pay because they were ruined by various dues and levies. After this, a committee of Moscow's leading merchants was charged to work out an easier assessment, and they lowered the tax by 31 percent.

The Muscovite government was not ashamed of its inefficiency and ignorance of the state of affairs, and indeed readily pointed out these defects as its lawful and natural shortcomings, which it was the subjects' duty to correct, just as it was their duty to make good its financial deficits. Both were the people's obligations. By the same device of 1679 the prisoners' money and the postal tax were combined into one and distributed between the two categories of taxpayers. The taxpaying urban population in all the towns and the peasants on crown land in the northern and northeast provinces had to pay, instead of all former direct taxes, only the streltsy tax, at ten different rates of assessment varying from two rubles to eighty kopecks per homestead, according to the particular district's capacity to pay. In other districts landowners' peasants, burdened as they were with their masters' dues, had to pay only the combined prisoners' money and postal tax at the rate of ten kopecks per homestead from peasants in church lands, and five kopecks from those belonging to the crown and to secular landowners—eight or sixteen times less than the lowest assessment of the streltsy tax. We can see from this what a tremendous source of revenue the Treasury relinquished to the irresponsible use of the serf owners. Financial policy thus followed the general pattern of tax discrimination, which determined the social order of Muscovy in the seventeenth century.

Unsuccessful attempts to invent new sources of income made

the government careful with those at its disposal. The striving to centralize all revenues in the state treasury led to curtailing local expenditure and abolishing local salaried posts, which were now pronounced superfluous—the posts of town engineers, secret police agents, postal overseers, grain inspectors, even district magistrates. All the business connected with these offices was entrusted to the voevodas, so that taxpayers would be relieved of providing sustenance for the officials, and would find it easier to pay state taxes. Levies for the upkeep of the voevodas and their staff of clerks and secretaries were also abolished. In order to make local taxgathering cheaper, the voevodas were relieved of the duty of collecting the new streltsy tax and of taking part in the collection of customs and excise dues. These tasks were entrusted to the taxpayers themselves—to the urban and rural population—through their elected elders, trusted overseers, and sworn tavernkeepers, for whom the electors were held responsible. This was a return to the rural institutions of the sixteenth century, but it did not mean a renewal of local self-government; it only meant transferring government business from mercenary crown officials to the local unpaid and responsible workers.

The transition to taxation based on the household unit is important in two other ways for the study of the social structure of the Muscovite state in the seventeenth century: it widened the limits of taxation or, more exactly, brought within them new sections of the population; at the same time it provided us with data that show how the people's labor was distributed among the ruling powers of the state. Assessment per homestead helped the Treasury to find a large class of new taxpayers. We have already seen that the zadvornyis, whose legal status was that of bondsmen, were in much the same economic position as the peasants, and even their contracts with the landowners were similar. They lived in separate homesteads, had plots of land allotted to them, and did peasant work for the landowners. When homesteads replaced tillage as units of assessment, the zadvornyis were registered for taxation just like the peasants. Such registration began after the census of 1678, as can be seen from the evidence discovered by P. N. Miliukov in the records of payment. It was the beginning of the juridical fusion of bondsmen and land-owners' peasants into a single class of serfs. This process was completed under Peter the Great by his first census.

Census books of 1678 contained a record of the total number of taxable homesteads throughout the country, and even under Peter the Great the government made use of them in assessing taxes. This record enables us to form a fairly clear idea of the social structure of the Muscovite state in the last quarter of the seventeenth century, on the eve of Peter's reforms. The figures of the total are given differently in the different documents, but the highest are the most reliable. The lower totals may have been based upon incomplete data or upon the desire to diminish the number of taxable homesteads, but there was no incentive to exaggerate it. The highest figure given in the 1678 census books is 888,000 taxable homesteads, urban and rural. Kotoshikhin and the decrees of 1686 and 1687 give the numbers of homesteads belonging to townspeople and to free peasants, to the church, the court, and the boyars. Subtracting the number of homesteads of all these ranks from the general total given in the census book of 1678, we arrive at the number of peasant homesteads belonging to servicemen, both in the capital and in the provinces—to the gentry in the strict sense. The whole mass of the taxpaying population was distributed among the different sections of land-owners as follows (in round figures):

Classes of Landowners	Numbers of Peasant Homesteads	Percentage
Urban dwellers and free peasants	92,000	10.4
The church, bishops, and monasteries	118,000	13.3
The crown	83,000	9.3
Boyars	88,000	10.0
Gentry	507,000	57.0
TOTAL	888,000	100.0

This distribution of the people's labor suggests several interesting reflections. To begin with, only a little more than one tenth of the whole taxpaying mass, urban and rural, retained freedom as it was understood in those days—that is, stood in a direct relation to the state. More than half were given to service-men in exchange for their obligation to defend the state against external enemies; one tenth were allotted to the ruling class for its work of ruling the country; less than one tenth belonged to the Tsar's court; considerably more than one tenth belonged to the church. Almost twenty thousand (one sixth of the church peasantry) was obliged to work for the church hierarchs—that is, for monks who had renounced the world in order to rule it spiritually—and almost five sixths (not counting peasants at-tached to cathedrals and parish churches) worked for monasteries —that is, for monks who had renounced the world in order to pray at its expense for its sins. Thus, almost nine tenths of the taxed population were serfs of the military servicemen, the church, and the crown. It would be unfair to expect a state organism constituted in this way to follow a desirable course in its political, economic, civic, and moral development.

However much the government increased taxation, it gen-erally was unable to balance its budget, for it could not make an accurate estimate of the expenses it had to face, and it no-ticed too late the mistakes in its preliminary calculations. It then had recourse to exceptional measures. At the most difficult time, in the early years of Michael's reign, the government, together with the Zemsky Sobor, made compulsory loans from big capital-ists like the Stroganovs or the Troitsky Monastery. These, how-ever, were rare occasions. The usual sources of the exceptional revenues were appeals and percentage taxes; the first source pro-vided "appeal money," and the second "percentage money"— fifth, tenth, fifteenth, or twentieth denga, as it was called. Both sources had a class significance.

Appeal money meant a voluntary subscription for which the government, at the Sobor's decision, asked the privileged classes —the landowners, the clergy, and the servicemen—so as to meet exceptional military expenses. We have already seen that in 1632, at the beginning of the war with Poland, clerical and serviceman delegates, in answer to the two sovereigns' and the Sobor's request, either declared then and there or promised to submit the amount they would give. In the same way "voluntary contributions" were demanded from the Zemsky Sobor in 1634. Appeal money was levied from free peasants too; not in the form of a voluntary subscription, but as a definite tax, ranging from one ruble to twenty-five kopecks per homestead (from fourteen to three rubles in our currency).

Percentage tax was a financial invention of the elective Sobor of 1613, and was payable by tradespeople as "fifth denga." In 1614, a year after Michael's election, that same sobor decreed that a collection for men under arms should be made "from net income according to assessment. If a man can gather from his possessions and industry a net income of a hundred rubles, he shall pay a fifth part of it—twenty rubles—and he who can gather more or less shall be charged at the same rate." The decree thus gives simultaneously at least three incompatible bases of assessment: property; industry—that is, circulating capital, combined with labor; and net income as reckoned by the assessment committee. In addition, there was the possibility of giving more or less—that is, a conscientious declaration of one's financial position.

The Sobor's decree, sent out as a circular, was edited by government clerks in accordance with the usual official method of all ages, in such a way that it could be interpreted in no less than three different senses. The Sobor's idea was fairly simple. Why did they choose the fifth denga, and not the fourth or sixth denga? In those days the usual and the highest lawful rate of interest on commercial loans was 20 percent. A man could borrow money at such high interest only if he had a chance to gain far more than 20 percent on his loan. That interest, therefore, represented the lowest net income from the borrowed capital, and under normal conditions doubled it in the course of five years. The Sobor's decree, requesting commercial people to pay a fifth denga, meant that they should yield to the Treasury the profits made by their circulating capital during one year, and wait six years, instead of five, to double it. That was the idea of the decree. It did not demand the fifth part of a man's property or his whole income from it, but asked for the smallest net annual income from his circulating capital or from profit-bearing immovable property—shop, factory, etc. But the clerks' version of the decree was so badly worded that it gave rise to many misunderstandings and even riots.

In some places the fifth denga was understood as a tax on property, and the assessors began to make an inventory of people's possessions, which the taxpayers resisted. In other places it was levied at the same rate as some ordinary tax like the streltsy money. The nearest approach to the meaning of the tax was made by the assessors who interpreted it as a tax on commercial turnover and, having calculated from the customs registers "how many rubles' worth of goods a trader had bought and sold," charged him a fifth of that sum. Conflicts and misunderstandings occurred at subsequent percentage collections as well, because of the vagueness of the stereotyped expression "from property and industry."

In fact, however, these collections were taxes on income, as was plainly stated by Reitenfels, a foreigner who was in Moscow in 1670. They were payable by men of all ranks engaged in commerce and industry (except the clergy and "white" servicemen)—by the streltsy, artillerymen, peasants, and bobyls, and even by bondsmen "to whomsoever they belonged if they did any trading."

The fifth denga collection of 1614 was repeated in 1615, and during the Polish war under Tsar Michael in 1633 and 1634. In 1637–38, for purposes of defense against the Crimean Tatars, the government, having doubled the streltsy tax, obtained the Zemsky Sobor's consent to recruit additional men for the army from among peasants belonging to private owners and to the palace, and to make an increased levy of twenty rubles (in our currency) per homestead on commercial people, and of ten rubles on crown peasants. In 1639 a special levy of money was repeated. Receipts from these levies came in with tremendous arrears—a sign that the taxpayers' resources were exhausted. Indeed, the people complained of being "sorely overburdened." If we add to all this that the Treasury compelled tradespeople to sell to it at a fixed price the most profitable merchandise (flax, for example, in Pskov), we shall understand the bitter complaint of a local chronicler: "The price is compulsory and the purchase unfriendly, great sorrow everywhere and unutterable enmity, and throughout the country no one dares to buy or to sell freely." Money levies were particularly heavy and frequent under tsars Alexei and Feodor, when the long and ruinous wars with Poland, Sweden, the Crimea, and Turkey demanded heavy sacrifices of money and of men. In the course of twenty-seven years (1654–80) there were levies on income, one of 5 percent, one of 6.66 percent, five levies of 10 percent, and two of 20 percent, apart from the annually repeated collections of a fixed amount per homestead. Thus all these supernumerary taxes acquired the character of being temporarily permanent. Special taxes formed a particular nonassessed item of state revenue.

What financial success, then, had the government achieved in the seventeenth century with its burdensome, changeable, and badly organized system of taxation? Referring to the 1660's, Kotoshikhin says that annually there comes from the whole country into the Tsar's Treasury, counting all the Muscovite departments, 1,311,000 rubles, in addition to the revenue from Siberian furs, the exact amount of which he does not know but presumes to be over 600,000. More than twenty years later a French agent, Neuville, who came to Moscow in 1689 in the employ of the Polish government, heard there that the state revenue did not exceed seven or eight million French livres a year. In the seventeenth century a French livre was equivalent to one sixth of a ruble, so that the sum mentioned by Neuville closely approximates that given by Kotoshikhin. Neuville, too, finds it difficult to define receipts from the sale of goods belonging to the state. A record of state income and expenditure for 1680 has been preserved. It was discovered by Miliukov, who analyzed it in his monograph on Russian state economy in connection with Peter the Great's reforms. In the record, state revenue is estimated to be almost 1.5 million rubles (about 20 million in our currency). The biggest item in the money revenue, 49 percent of it, was indirect taxes, chiefly customs and excise duties. Direct taxes provided 44 percent, and the chief of them were special taxes, which accounted for 16 percent of the total. Almost half of the money revenue was spent on military needs (about 700,000 rubles). The Tsar's palace absorbed about 15 percent of it, and less than 5 percent was allowed for social welfare, public building, and postal expenses—that is, public transport.

The record of 1680, however, gives only an approximate idea of the state economy of the period. Not all the receipts reached the central departments. A great deal of money was received and spent locally. The record shows a considerable credit account, but its real significance must be gauged by the fact that the annual estimates of revenue from taxes greatly exceeded actual receipts. Arrears that had accumulated up to 1670 amounted to more than a million rubles and had to be canceled in 1681. The people's taxpaying powers were evidently almost exhausted.

Chapter
XII

Social Critics

In reestablishing state order after the Time of Troubles, the Muscovite government did not intend to change it radically. It wanted to preserve the old foundations. It introduced only partial, technical changes, which it regarded as corrections and improvements. Its attempts to reform the system of administration, to segregate social classes, to increase economic productivity were timid and inconsistent. They did not follow any broadly conceived and practically worked-out general plan, but were apparently inspired by accidental suggestions of the moment. These suggestions, however, were all on the same lines, because they issued directly or indirectly from one common source—the government's financial difficulties. Reformatory measures inevitably tended, as compulsively as a physiological need, to remove these difficulties, and all came to the same sad end—all were failures. The administrative system, more tightly pulled together and strictly centralized, was not made cheaper or more efficient, and did not relieve the taxpaying communities of their heavy state dues. The more strictly differentiated class structure merely increased the discord between social attitudes and interests. Financial innovations led to the exhaustion of the people's resources, to bankruptcy and perpetual accumulation of arrears. All this created a general feeling that things were not as they should be. The court, the representatives of the reigning dynasty, and their foreign policy increased that feeling to the point of profound popular discontent with the state of affairs in the country.

Under the first three tsars of the new dynasty the Moscow government gives the impression of having acquired power accidentally and undertaken a job beyond its competence. With three or four exceptions its members were men of high personal ambition but without talents to justify it, even without the governmental training that might have replaced talent, and—worst of all—utterly devoid of civic sense. An apparently accidental circumstance was partly responsible for the fact that men of such a type managed state affairs. It was as though the new dynasty were pursued by fate, which was determined not to let its representatives grow to manhood before coming to the throne. Three of the first five tsars—Michael, Alexei, and Ivan—were enthroned while mere adolescents, one at the age of sixteen and two still earlier: Feodor was fourteen and Peter was ten.

The Romanov dynasty had another hereditary peculiarity. The daughters were strong and vigorous, sometimes manly and energetic, like Tsarevna Sofia, but the sons took after their progenitor and proved to be physically weak and short-lived. Even Tsar Alexei, in spite of his lively, blooming appearance, had a frail constitution and died at the age of only forty-six. No one can tell what Alexei's younger brother Dimitri, who resembled in character his great-grandfather Ivan the Terrible, would have been like. If we are to believe Kotoshikhin, the ill-natured boy was poisoned by his father's, Tsar Michael's, courtiers so cleverly that everyone thought it was a natural death. Peter, too, must be left out of account. He was an exception in every way. A new tsar acquired a governmental environment before he was old enough to understand or wish to understand the character of the men around him, and his first associates gave color and direction to the whole of his reign.

This disadvantage was particularly noticeable in foreign affairs. Foreign policy, more than anything else, created financial difficulties for the government, and at the same time it was the field in which, after the territorial losses of the Time of Troubles, the new dynasty had to justify its election by the whole country. Tsar Michael's diplomacy, especially after the badly planned and inefficiently conducted Smolensk campaign, still exhibited the usual cautiousness of the defeated, but under Tsar Alexei the knocks received by his father began to fade from memory. After long deliberation Moscow was drawn against its will into war for the annexation of the Ukraine, but the brilliant campaign of 1654–55 inspired it with confidence. Not only the Smolensk region, but the whole of White Russia and Lithuania were won almost overnight. The Muscovite politicians' imagination ran far ahead of good sense. They did not reflect that the credit for such successes was due not to them, but to the Swedes, who at that time attacked the Poles from the west and drew upon themselves the best Polish forces. Moscow conducted its policy in the grand manner, sparing neither men nor money in order to demolish Poland and put the Russian tsar on the Polish throne, drive the Swedes out of Poland, expel the Tatars and the Turks from the Ukraine, and seize not only both banks of the Dnieper in its lower reaches, but also Galicia, where Sheremetev's army was dispatched in 1660. All these intertwined designs were so bewildering and drained the country's powers so thoroughly that after twenty-one years of exhausting struggle on three fronts, Moscow had to give up Lithuania and White Russia and the Ukraine west of the Dnieper, contenting itself with the Smolensk and Seversk regions and the Ukraine east of the Dnieper with Kiev west of it. Even the Crimean Tatars could not be induced to give Moscow a convenient steppe boundary or to abolish the shameful tribute annually imposed by the Khan or to recognize Moscow's sovereignty over the Zaporozhye.

Discontent with the conduct of affairs increased together with the feeling that the heavy sacrifices made by the country had resulted in nothing but defeat. The general sense of unrest left by the Time of Troubles had prepared the soil in which that feeling developed, gradually engulfing the whole community, though manifesting itself differently in its upper and lower strata.

Among the masses it found expression in a whole series of rebellions, which gave a troubled character to the seventeenth century. It was an epoch of popular uprisings. Far more than the occasional riots flaring up here and there under Tsar Michael, the mutinies in Tsar Alexei's reign show the intensity of the people's discontent. In 1648 there were riots in Moscow, Ustiug, Kozlov, Solvychegodsk, Tomsk, and other towns; in 1649 a fresh mutiny of the self-pledgers began in Moscow, but it was stopped in time; in 1650 there were risings in Pskov and Novgorod; in 1662 there was another mutiny in Moscow on account of the copper coinage; and finally in 1670–71 came Razin's great rebellion in the southeast along the Volga. It arose among the Don Cossacks but spread to the common people in general, who rose against the upper classes. In 1668–1676 there was a rising in the Solovetsky Monastery against the use of the newly revised church books. These mutineers sharply revealed the common people's attitude to the authorities, which was carefully disguised by official ceremony and by clerical preaching. There was no trace of politeness, let alone reverence, toward the government, not even toward the actual bearer of the supreme power.

In the upper classes discontent took a somewhat different form. Among the masses it stirred the emotions, but among the top layers of society it awakened thought and led to an intensive criticism of the dynasty. The motive power in the lower strata was malice against the upper. The dominant note in the upper classes' protests was that of complaint against the people's backwardness and helplessness. Almost for the first time we find Russian thought on the hard and slippery path of public welfare, taking up a critical attitude to the social environment. Statements that bear witness to this were made as early as 1642 at the Zemsky Sobor and in 1662 at the conference between the government and Moscow tradespeople about the high cost of living. True to their political discipline and preserving a respectful tone, without indulging in loud denunciations, the delegates spoke with great feeling of the disorganized administration, of privileged persons breaking the law with impunity, of the contempt for public opinion shown by the government, which at the sovereign's request questioned the tradespeople and asked them to write down what they thought and then did next to nothing about it. There were cautious collective statements of class needs and opinions. Personal judgments of individual observers were expressed more vigorously. I shall confine myself to a few examples to show how the country's life was reflected in these early attempts at political criticism.

The first such attempt dates back to the beginning of the seventeenth century, to the Time of Troubles, and was no doubt inspired by it. As a young man, Prince I. A. Khvorostinin occupied a prominent position at the court of the first pretender, made friends with Poles, learned Latin, began reading Latin books, came under Roman Catholic influence, and venerated Roman icons equally with the Orthodox. As a punishment he was sent in Tsar Vasili's reign to St. Joseph's Monastery for correction, and returned from there a thoroughly embittered and reckless man. He became a freethinker, rejected prayer and belief in the resurrection of the dead, "wavered in his faith, reviled the Orthodox doctrine, and uttered impious words about God's holy saints." At the same time he retained his interest in Slavonic church literature, was well versed in ecclesiastical history, showed irrepressible defiance in literary discussions, had a very high opinion of himself as a scholar, and "considered no one his equal in intelligence." He knew how to wield his pen, too; in Michael's reign he wrote a fairly good account of the times, though he talks more of his ideas than of people and events.

This mixture of heterogeneous tastes and opinions was scarcely welded into a firm and coherent whole, but it was distinctly opposed to the Byzantine Orthodox traditions and ideas and made Prince Khvorostinin hostile to everything Russian. He regarded the rites of the church with defiant contempt, "did not keep fasts and Christian customs," and forbade his house serfs to go to church. In 1622 he drank throughout Holy Week, and on Easter morning, while it was still dark, he got drunk before breaking the fast with Easter food. He did not go to the palace to exchange Easter greetings with the Tsar and had not been to the midnight service. Such conduct and way of thinking completely cut him off from society. He wanted to ask permission to go to Lithuania or to Rome or to escape there without permission, and was already selling his Moscow house and family estates. The Tsar's decree, enumerating Prince Khvorostinin's misdemeanors, blames him with special bitterness for his sins against his compatriots. When his house was searched, all his manuscripts in prose and in verse, written in Polish syllabic meter, were confiscated. In these books as well as in his conversations he expressed his boredom, his longing for foreign countries, and his contempt for home-bred ways. He said many bitter things about Muscovites, denounced them for senselessly worshiping icons, and complained that in Moscow there were no people worth knowing, they were all stupid, there was no one to live with, and he could have nothing to do with them. By saying all this, the decree points out, "he dishonored all Muscovite people including his own parents of whom he was born, reviled them and accused them of foolishness, and would not even write the sovereign's title properly, but called him 'Russian despot' and not 'Tsar and autocrat.' " The Prince was sent away once more "for correction," this time to St. Cyril's Monastery. He repented there, was allowed to return to Moscow, was reinstated in his rank, and was admitted to the Tsar's court. He died in 1625.

Prince Khvorostinin was a curious type that appeared early in the history of Russia's spiritual development and much later became fairly common. He was not one of the Russian sixteenth-century heretics with Protestant tendencies whose minds were preoccupied with ritualistic and dogmatic doubts and interpretations—a distant echo of the Reformation storm in the West. His was a peculiar type of Russian freethinker on a Roman Catholic basis, full of profound antipathy to the arid Byzantine ritualism and to Russian life, which was saturated with it—a distant spiritual ancestor of Chaadaev.

It is rather surprising to find among the denouncers of domestic political disorder the supreme guardian of the home-bred moral and religious order, the Patriarch of all Russia. But he was not merely a patriarch—he was Patriarch Nikon. A simple peasant by birth, he rose to occupy the Patriarch's throne. He had tremendous influence on Tsar Alexei, who called him his "special friend." But later on the friends quarreled, and in consequence Nikon left his see in 1658 of his own will, hoping that the Tsar would humbly beg him to return, but the Tsar did not do so. In a passion of anger at the wound to his vanity, Nikon wrote a letter to the Tsar about the state of things in his realm. One cannot expect the Patriarch's judgment to be fair, of course, but the colors in which he chooses to paint the gloomy picture of the country's position are rather significant. They all emphasize the financial difficulties of the government and the people's economic distress. Nikon was particularly bitter about the Department of Monasteries, established in 1649, which supervised large estates belonging to the church and tried the clergy for secular offenses. The staff consisted of a nobleman and government clerks, and did not include a single representative of the clergy.

In 1661 Nikon wrote another letter to the Tsar, a letter full of denunciations. Hinting at the department he hated, he said: "Secular judges dispense justice and violate it, and through this you have gathered against yourself a great assembly on the Day of Judgment, crying aloud at your wrongdoings. You preach to everyone that they should fast, but there is scarcely anyone left now who is not fasting, because bread is scarce; in many places they fast to death because there is nothing to eat. No one is spared: the destitute, the blind, widows, monks, and nuns are burdened with heavy taxes. Everywhere there is weeping and misery. No one makes merry nowadays."

Nikon paints the financial position of the state in equally dark colors in a letter to the Eastern patriarchs that was intercepted by Moscow agents in 1665. Complaining that the Tsar has seized church property, he writes: "Men are taken for military service, bread and money are taken mercilessly. The Tsar has doubled and trebled the tribute laid on the Christian people—and all in vain."

Under the same Tsar another Russian attempted in rather

exceptional circumstances to describe the Muscovite social order
and its shortcomings. Grigori Kotoshikhin was a junior clerk
in the Department of Foreign Affairs, did unimportant diplomatic jobs, was unjustly treated, and in 1660 was beaten with
sticks for having made a mistake in the sovereign's title. During
the second Polish war, while attached to Prince Iuri Dolgoruky's
army, he refused to carry out an unlawful order of the commander in chief and, to escape his wrath, ran away to Poland.
Later on he went to Germany and eventually to Stockholm.
In his wanderings he was struck by the difference between the
foreign and the Russian ways of life, and it occurred to him to
describe the conditions in the state of Muscovy. The Swedish
chancellor, Count Magnus de la Gardie, appreciated Selitsky's
(so Kotoshikhin called himself abroad) intelligence and experience and encouraged him to go on with his work. It was so well
done that it became one of the most important historical records
of seventeenth-century Russia. But Kotoshikhin came to a bad
end. He lived in Stockholm for about eighteen months, became
a Protestant, and formed too close a friendship with his landlord's
wife. The husband grew suspicious and they had a quarrel in
which Kotoshikhin killed him. He was beheaded in consequence.
The Swedish translator of Kotoshikhin's work says that he was
a man of outstanding intelligence. A Russian professor found it
in Uppsala in the last century, and it was published in 1841.

In the thirteen chapters into which the book is divided the
author describes the customs of the Moscow court, the courtiers
as a class, the daily life of Moscow, diplomatic relations with
foreign states, the organization of central administrative offices,
the army, the urban and rural population, and finally the manner
of life of the Muscovite upper classes. Kotoshikhin does not
indulge in reflections, but for the most part describes in simple,
clear, and businesslike language his native country's way of life.
All through, however, the reader is conscious of his contemptuous attitude to the fatherland he had abandoned, and this attitude provides a somber background against which Kotoshikhin
paints an apparently dispassionate picture of Russian life. Sometimes he makes direct statements, always unfavorable, denounc-

ing many serious defects in the Muscovite people's customs and morals. Kotoshikhin blames them for their "irreverent nature," foolish pride, deceitfulness, and most of all for their ignorance. Russian people, he writes, "pride themselves on their descent and are not trained in any work, for in their country they are not taught anything good and learn nothing but arrogance, shamelessness, hatred, and wrongdoing. They do not send their children to foreign countries to study and acquire good manners, for fear that having come to know those countries' faiths and customs and blessed *liberty*, they would forsake their own faith and take up some other, and not care or even think of returning home to their relatives."

Kotoshikhin caricatures the sittings of the Boyars' Council, at which the boyars, "thrusting out their beards," answer nothing to the Tsar's questions and cannot give him any good advice, "since the Tsar confers the boyar rank on many not according to their intelligence but according to their ancient lineage, and many of them are illiterate and have had no schooling."

Kotoshikhin gives an equally gloomy picture of Russian family life. The last chapter of his book, "Of the Manners of Life of the Boyars and Men of Other Ranks," is a stumbling block to those who believe that ancient Russia, in spite of all its political and social defects, had succeeded, with the help of church rules and instructions, in building up the family, which was closely knit both morally and legally. He dispassionately describes the tyranny of the parents over their children, the cynical way in which marriages were arranged, the unseemly wedding rites, the crude deceptions practiced by parents anxious to get rid of unattractive daughters, the lawsuits to which this led, the unloved wives who were beaten or forced to enter convents, the husbands who were poisoned by their wives and wives by their husbands, and the heartless, purely formal interference of the ecclesiastical authorities in family quarrels. The somber picture he had painted frightened the author himself, and he ended his simple and objective narrative with a lively exclamation: "Sensible reader! Be not surprised. It is perfectly true that in the whole world there is not so much deception about maidens as in the Muscovite state;

they have not the custom there, as in other countries, for a man to see his affianced and to speak to her."

It is interesting to compare the judgment of a Russian who had abandoned his native land with the impressions of an outside observer who came to Russia in the hope of finding there his second fatherland. Iuri Krizhanich, a Croat and a Roman Catholic priest, was a man of fairly wide education, something of a philosopher, a theologian and economist, a great philologist, and above all a patriot, or rather an ardent Pan-Slavist. His true fatherland was not any historically known state, but united Slavdom—a political dream hovering somewhere outside history. He was born a subject of the Sultan of Turkey and as a poor orphan was taken to Italy. He was educated in the theological seminaries of Zagreb, Vienna, and Bologna, and at last entered the Roman College of St. Athanasius, in which the Roman Congregation for the Propagation of the Faith trained special missionaries to the schismatics of the Orthodox East. Krizhanich, as a Slav, was destined for Moscow.

He was attracted by that distant country. He collected information about it and submitted to the congregation complicated plans for its conversion. But he had his own secret plan. Missionary enthusiasm served the poor Slav student as a means for securing material help from the congregation. He regarded the people of Muscovy not as willful heretics or schismatics, but as Christians who erred through simple ignorance. Early in life he began to think and deeply to grieve about the calamitous position of the Slavs, enslaved and disunited, and it does credit to his political good sense that he rightly guessed the way to their unification. To make friends people must, first of all, understand one another, and the Slavs were hindered in this by having no language in common. And so Krizhanich, while still in the Latin school, tried not to forget his native Slav tongue. He diligently studied it so that he could speak it eloquently and did his best to free it from foreign idioms and local deterioration. He wanted to refashion it so that it would be understandable to all Slavs, and for this purpose he wrote grammars, composed philological treatises, compiled dictionaries.

He had a glimpse of another idea, even bolder than the first. Unification of the scattered Slav peoples had to be conducted from some political center, but at the time no such center existed. It had not yet become a historical reality; it was not even an object of political hopes for some and a bugbear for others, as happened later. Krizhanich solved the riddle as to where it was to be sought. He, a Croat and a Roman Catholic, sought this future Slav center not in Vienna or Prague or Warsaw, but in Orthodox Russia, which was regarded in Europe as a Tatar country. One might have laughed at his idea in the seventeenth century, and perhaps one may smile at it even now, but there were moments between that period and the present when it was difficult not to value it. It is because Krizhanich thought of Russia as the future center of Slavism that he called it his second fatherland, though he had not had a first one, except his Turkish birthplace.

It is hard to say whether it was the intuition of an enthusiastic patriot or political thought that inspired his guess. At any rate, he did not stay in Rome, where the congregation set him the task of carrying on polemics against the Greek schism; in 1659 he went off to Moscow without its sanction. There, of course, the idea of Roman Catholic propaganda was abandoned, and he had to conceal that he was a Roman priest, or he would not have been admitted to Moscow. He was received there simply as a Serbian immigrant, Iuri Ivanovich, who came to take up service under the Tsar like other foreigners.

To obtain a secure position in state service he suggested several things to the Tsar. He offered to be the Muscovite and Pan-Slavic publicist to the Tsar's librarian, to write a "truthful" history of Muscovy and of all Slav people as the Tsar's "historian and chronicler," but in the end he was given a salary of one and a half and then of three rubles per day (in our currency) for doing his favorite work on the Slavonic grammar and dictionary. After all, he had gone to Moscow with the purpose of working there for the linguistic and literary unification of the Slavs. He himself admitted that he had nowhere to go with his idea of a Pan-Slavic language except Moscow, "because from childhood he had devoted himself wholeheartedly to a single cause," to the correction of "our distorted, or rather of our ruined, language, and to the improvement of my own and all the people's minds."

In one of his works he says: "They call me a wanderer, a tramp; this is not true. I have come to the sovereign of my race, I have come to my people, to my fatherland, to the only country where my labors may find application and be of use, where my goods may have value and find a market—I mean dictionaries, grammars, translations."

But after a little more than a year he was for some unknown reason banished to Tobolsk, where he spent fifteen years. Exile, however, did nothing but help his literary activities. He received sufficient money for his keep and had complete leisure, which he found positively irksome, complaining that he was not given any work, but was well fed, like cattle fattened for the slaughter. In Siberia he wrote a great deal, and there he finished his Slavonic grammar, over which he had taken so much trouble and, as he says, had thought and worked for twenty-two years.

At last Tsar Feodor let him return to Moscow, and there he obtained permission to return to his own land, no longer concealing that he was a Roman Catholic priest. In 1677 he left his adopted fatherland.

The above account of Krizhanich's life has a certain interest, for it throws light on the circumstances under which his judgments about Russia were formed. He expressed them in the longest of his works, also written in Siberia, *Political Thoughts, or Conversations about Politics*. It consists of three parts: in the first the author discusses the economic resources of a state, in the second he discusses its military resources, and in the third he speaks about wisdom—that is, about spiritual resources, including most diverse subjects, chiefly of political character. This voluminous work is a political and economic treatise showing the author's wide and varied knowledge of ancient and modern literature and even some acquaintance with Russian writings. What is of chief importance for us is that the author constantly compares conditions in the western European states with those in

Muscovy. Russia is here for the first time put face to face with western Europe. I shall summarize Krizhanich's main ideas.

The treatise has the appearance of rough sketches written now in Latin, now in some peculiar Slavic language of his own devising, with corrections, additions, and disconnected notes. Krizhanich firmly believed in the future of Russia and all the Slavic people. They stood next in the order of succession in the world process of cultivating wisdom and handing down arts and sciences from one nation to another in turn. A similar idea about the rotation of learning was expressed later by Leibnitz and Peter the Great.

Having described cultural achievements of other nations, Krizhanich writes: "Let no one say that we Slavs are debarred by some heavenly decree from acquiring knowledge. I think it is precisely now that the time has come for our race to begin studying. Now God has raised in Russia a Slav empire more powerful and glorious than our race has ever had, and such empires usually foster enlightenment. Accordingly, we too must study, so that under the honorable rule of the Tsar Alexei Mikhailovich we may rub off the mildew of our inveterate uncouthness, acquire learning, begin to improve our communal life, and attain a happier condition." (This is written in the Pan-Slavic language with which Krizhanich was so much concerned.) "Two afflictions from which all Slavs suffer stand in our way: an insane passion for everything foreign, and as a consequence, the burden of a foreign yoke."

A vindictive note sounds in Krizhanich's words whenever he touches on this subject. His imagination provides him with a lavish supply of repulsive colors and images to depict the hated tyrants, especially the Germans. "Not a single nation under the sun has ever been so injured and humiliated by foreigners as we Slavs by the Germans. We have been flooded with aliens. They fool us, lead us by the nose, sit on our backs, and drive us like cattle, call us dogs and swine, regard themselves almost as gods and us as fools. All that is wrung by oppressive taxation and harsh treatment out of the tears, sweat, and enforced fasting of the Russian people is devoured by foreigners, Greek merchants, German colonels and merchants, and Crimean brigands. It is all due to our insane worship of everything foreign: we marvel at it, praise it, extol it to the skies, and despise our own way of life."

Krizhanich devotes a whole chapter to the enumeration of the wrongs and humiliations inflicted by the foreigners upon the Slavs. Russia is destined to save the Slavic peoples from the evils with which it is itself beset. Krizhanich addresses Tsar Alexei with the following words: "It has fallen to your lot, most honorable Tsar, to take care of all the Slavs. You alone, Tsar, have been given us by God to help the people beyond the Danube, the Czechs and the Poles, so that they should understand the shame of foreign oppression and begin to throw off the German yoke."

But when in Russia Krizhanich became familiar with the life of the Slavs' saviors, he was struck by the many defects and vices from which they suffered. He attacks most of all the Russians' conceit, their excessive attachment to their own customs, and especially their ignorance; that was the chief cause of the people's bad economic condition. Russia was a poor country by comparison with western European states because it was incomparably less civilized. In the West, Krizhanich writes, people are quick and keen.

There are many books about agriculture and other industries, there are harbors, a flourishing maritime trade, farming, various crafts. There is nothing of this in Russia. It is closed on all sides for trade by inconvenient seas, by deserts, or by savage tribes. It has few commercial cities, no valuable and necessary merchandise. The people's minds are slow and dull, they are not skilled in either commerce or agriculture or domestic management. They will not invent anything of themselves, but must be shown how to do things. They are lazy, unenterprising, do not want to do what is good for them unless they are forced to it. They have no books either about agriculture or about other industries. Merchants do not even learn arithmetic and foreigners always mercilessly cheat them. We do not know history, do not know our own part in it, and cannot carry on any conversation about politics, and foreigners despise us for it. The same mental sloth is responsible for the unattractive style of clothes, our general appearance, our housekeeping, and our whole manner of life. Unkempt hair and beards make a Russian repulsive, ridiculous, a kind of forest goblin. Foreigners blame us for our dirty habits. We hide money in our mouths, do not wash dishes; a peasant will hand to a guest a full tankard of drink, dipping both thumbs in it. It has been said in foreign newspapers that if Russian merchants enter a shop, no one can come in for an hour afterward because of the stench. Our dwellings are uncomfortable. The windows are low. Peasant huts have no chimneys and no ventilation, so that people go blind with the smoke.

Krizhanich also notes many moral failings in Russian society: drunkenness, lack of spirit, of noble pride, of enthusiasm, of the feeling of personal and national dignity.

In war Turks and Tatars may run away, but they will not be slaughtered unresisting; they will defend themselves to their last breath. But if our "warriors" start running away, they never so much as look back. Hit them and they will fall like ninepins. Our great national failing is lack of moderation. We cannot preserve a sense of proportion or follow a middle course, but always tend to wander off and walk on the edge of a precipice. In some of our countries the government is utterly lax, arbitrary, and disorderly, and in others too firm, strict, and cruel. In the whole world there is no state so disorderly and anarchic as the Polish, and none so stern and oppressive as the great Russian state.

Krizhanich was so grieved by all these defects that he was ready to prefer Turks and Tatars to the Russians, whom he advised to learn from them sobriety, justice, courage, and even modesty. He obviously did not shut his eyes to the Russian people's faults and perhaps actually exaggerated them. Evidently Krizhanich too, being a Slav, could not observe a sense of proportion and look at things simply and fairly. But he did not merely complain; he also reflected and suggested means of healing the ills he bewailed. He worked out a whole system of reforms, which is of greater importance to us than the mere leisurely reflections of a Slav visitor to Muscovy in the seventeenth century. He suggested four means of improving the Russians' position:

(1) Enlightenment, learning, books—inanimate but wise and truthful advisers.

(2) Government regulation, action issuing from those in authority. Krizhanich believed in autocracy. In Russia, he says, the Tsar has complete autocratic power, and by his order everything can be set right and everything useful introduced, while in other countries this would be impossible. He writes to Tsar Alexei: "You, Tsar, hold in your hands the miraculous rod of Moses by which you can work wonderful miracles in the administration; you have unlimited power." Krizhanich puts great faith in this means, though he suggests rather peculiar ways of using it. For instance, if a tradesman does not know any arithmetic, his shop should be closed by a special decree until he learns it.

(3) Political freedom. Under an autocratic regime there must be no administrative cruelties, no imposition of crippling taxes and levies, no "fleecing" of the people. To ensure this, certain liberties, political rights, corporate self-government, are essential. Tradespeople must be given the right to choose their elders and have their own law courts; artisans should be united in guilds; all industrial workers should be given a right to put their needs before the government and ask for its defense against the local rulers; the peasants must have freedom of labor secured to them. Krizhanich regards moderate liberties as a rein restraining the rulers from "evil lusts," as the only shield to protect the people from the officials' malpractice and safeguard justice in the state. In the absence of liberties, no prohibition, no penalties will prevent rulers from pursuing their greedy designs.

(4) Spread of technical education. For this purpose the state must authoritatively control the national economy. It must establish technical schools in all the towns and open girls' schools of needlework and housekeeping. A bridegroom should have to ask his bride elect for a certificate stating what she had been taught. Bondsmen who had learned crafts involving special technical knowledge should obtain their freedom. German books on com-

merce and industry should be translated into Russian, and German master craftsmen and capitalists should be invited to teach Russians handicrafts and commerce. All these measures ought to be directed toward intensive compulsory exploitation of the country's natural resources and a wide increase in new industries, especially in metallurgy.

Such was Iuri Krizhanich's program. It was quite complicated, as we can see, and not altogether coherent. A good deal in it was inconsistent or at any rate obscure. It is difficult to understand how he reconciled the various means he suggested for reforming the faults of Russian society. For instance, where did he draw the line between the autocratic government's directives and the activity of communal self-government, and how did he hope to save Slavs from Germans "astride their necks" by translating German technical books and importing German craftsmen, and how did he combine his xenophobia with the conviction that Russia could not manage without skilled foreigners? But reading Krizhanich's program, one cannot help exclaiming, "Why, this is Peter the Great's program!" It has the same defects and inconsistencies, shows the same naïve faith in the creative power of government decrees, in the possibility of spreading education and commerce by means of appropriate German textbooks in Russian translations or by temporarily closing the shop of a tradesman who has not learned arithmetic. It is precisely these similarities and contradictions that make Krizhanich's judgments especially interesting.

Of all the outside observers of Russian life, he is unique, quite unlike the numerous foreigners who came to Moscow accidentally and wrote their impressions of it. They regarded the characteristic features of Russian life as curious peculiarities of an uncivilized people, amusing to an idle observer—that was all. Krizhanich was in Russia both an alien and a native: alien by origin and education and a Russian in his racial sympathies and political hopes. He came to Moscow not simply to observe but to preach, to proclaim the idea of Pan-Slavism and to fight for it. This purpose is clearly expressed in the Latin epigraph to *Conversations:* "In defense of the people I want to push out all the foreigners. I call to battle all the peoples along the Dnieper, Poles, Lithuanians, Serbs, all Slavs of warlike spirit who will fight together with me!"

It was necessary to count the forces on both sides, to make good one's own deficiencies after the pattern offered by the opposite side, to study it and borrow everything in which it was superior. This accounts for Krizhanich's favorite method of exposition. He constantly makes comparisons, contrasting the same kinds of facts among the Slavs and in the hostile West, and proposing to preserve some things unchanged and to remodel others in the Western way. Hence his apparent inconsistencies. They were inherent in the life he was observing and were not due to the observer's mistakes. We had to borrow from foreigners, to learn from our enemies. Krizhanich sought and willingly recorded everything in which Russian life was superior to other countries, he defended it against the foreigners' slanders and mistaken imputations, but he did not want to delude either himself or others. He expected miracles from autocracy, but in his *Conversations* he described more forcibly than any prejudiced foreigner the destructive effects of the harsh Muscovite rule on the people's morals, welfare, and relations with other countries. He was not an admirer of power as such, and thought that if the question were put to all the monarchs, many of them could not explain for what purpose they served. He valued authority as an idea, as a means for introducing culture, and he had a mystical faith in Muscovy's "rod of Moses," although he had probably heard of the Terrible Tsar's terrible staff, as well as of Tsar Michael's invalid's crutch.

The final result of Krizhanich's comparisons was by no means favorable to his compatriots. He admitted that foreigners were decidedly superior to them in intelligence, knowledge, morals, orderliness, and all their ways of life. He asked what place, then, did we Russians and Slavs occupy among other nations, and what historical part was assigned to us on the world's stage? Our people stood midway between civilized nations and Eastern savages, and therefore should become an intermediary between the two.

Krizhanich's thought ascends from trivial observations and detailed programs to bold generalizations. The Slavo-Russian East and multiracial West represent for him two sharply differing cultural types. In one of the conversations introduced into his treatise he rather wittily compares the distinctive characteristics of the Slavic, chiefly Russian, people and of the western Europeans. The latter are of handsome appearance and therefore proud and daring, for beauty breeds daring and pride; we are neither good- nor bad-looking, but of middling appearance. We are not eloquent and do not know how to express our thoughts, but they have ready tongues, are bold in their speech and quick at making caustic, wounding, abusive remarks. We are simple-hearted and slow-witted; they are full of wiles. We are not thrifty, but inclined to be prodigal, we keep no accounts of income and expenditure and are wasteful with our goods; they are stingy, grasping, and night and day think only of stuffing their moneybags more tightly. We are lazy about work and study; they are industrious and will not waste in sleep a single profitable hour. We are dwellers in a poor country; they are natives of rich, luxurious lands, and entice us with the alluring produce of their countries as a hunter baiting his trap for prey. We think and speak simply and we act simply, quarrel and make peace again; they are reserved, dissembling, unforgiving. They will not forget an insult to their dying day. Having once quarreled, they will never be sincerely reconciled, but after making peace will always seek an opportunity for revenge.

Krizhanich's works deserve a special and prominent place among our historical sources. For more than a hundred years we find nothing in our literature to equal his observations and judgments. His observations provide the student with new material for picturing Russian life in the seventeenth century, and his judgments serve to verify the impressions given us by its study.

Neither Nikon's letters nor Kotoshikhin's and Krizhanich's works were widely known at the time. Kotoshikhin's book had not been read by anyone in Russia till the forties of the last century, when it was found by a Russian professor in the library of Uppsala University. Krizhanich's book was in the palace, in

Tsar Alexei's and Tsar Feodor's possession. Influential supporters of Tsarevna Sofia, Medvedev and Prince V. V. Golitsyn, had copies of it. Apparently there was a proposal to publish it under Tsar Feodor. Krizhanich's thoughts and observations might have increased the supply of reformatory ideas swarming in Muscovite statesmen's minds at that time. But in any case the opinions of these three men are of great importance to students of the seventeenth century, since they reflect the mood of the Russian society of that period. The sharpest feature of that mood was discontent with the general situation. Krizhanich's testimony is particularly valuable in this respect, for he describes with obvious regret unpleasant facts it grieves him to find in a country that from a distance seemed to him a mighty support for the whole Slavic race. This discontent was an extremely important turning point in the life of seventeenth-century Russia. It was followed by innumerable consequences, which form the main content of Russia's subsequent history. The most immediate of these consequences was that Russia began to feel the influence of western Europe. I want to draw your attention to the origins and first manifestations of that influence.

Chapter
XIII

Russia and the West

Before starting to discuss the beginnings of Western influence in Russia, it is essential to define the exact meaning of "influence." In the fifteenth and sixteenth centuries Russia already knew something about western Europe, did a certain amount of business with it, diplomatic and commercial, borrowed the fruits of its enlightenment, extended invitations to its artists, craftsmen, physicians, and military men. That was intercourse and not influence. Influence begins when a society comes to recognize the superiority of the culture that influences it, the necessity of learning from it, of morally submitting to it, and of borrowing not merely its practical achievements, but the actual principles of social order, views, ideas, customs, public relations. This sort of thing began to appear in Russia only in the seventeenth century. It is in this sense that I speak of the beginnings of Western influence at that period.

At this point we turn to the origins of the different trends in our history that continue to this day. Why did not this influence, this moral and spiritual subordination, begin in the sixteenth century? Its source lay in discontent with one's life, one's situation, and this discontent sprang from the difficulty in which the Muscovite government found itself under the new dynasty, and which affected more or less painfully every class of the community. The difficulty lay in the fact that it was impossible to satisfy the essential needs of the country by means of domestic resources available under the prevailing regime. It was recognized that the regime had to be reorganized to provide the resources the state lacked. There was nothing new about the situation. The difficulty had occurred before. The need for reform was not being felt for the first time by the Muscovite society. But it had never before led to such consequences as now. From the middle of the fifteenth century onward the Muscovite government was more and more aware that it was impossible to rely upon the resources of the appanage period in dealing with the new tasks created by the unification of Great Russia. It began to build a new state order and gradually to demolish the old. It was building the new order without outside help, according to its own lights, out of material provided by the national life, and under the guidance of former experiences and lessons of the past. It still believed that the spiritual heritage of its native land could provide a firm basis for the new order. Accordingly, the reconstruction merely increased the prestige of the past, confirmed the builders' faith in the country's powers, and nourished national self-confidence. In the sixteenth century Russians actually came to regard Moscow, the unifier of the Russian land, as the center and mainstay of all the Orthodox East.

But now things were different. The obvious defects of the existing social order and the unsuccessful attempts to improve it suggested that its very foundations were rotten and made many people think that the people's creative powers and native good sense were exhausted, that the past held no useful lessons for the present, that nothing more could be learned from it, and that therefore there was no reason to cling to it. It was then that a profound change began in the Muscovite people's minds. Among the ruling circles and in society at large there appeared men oppressed by doubt as to whether the past had bequeathed to the country sufficient resources to ensure it a prosperous future. They lost their former national complacency and began to look around, to seek instruction and direction from strangers, from western Europe, in the growing conviction of its superiority and of their own backwardness. The vanishing faith in the traditions of the past and in national strength gave way to dejection and distrust of one's own powers, and this opened the door wide to foreign influence.

It is hard to say what caused this difference in the course of events in the sixteenth and seventeenth centuries, and why we had not noticed our backwardness sooner and renewed our forefathers' creative attempts at reform. Was it that the Russian people of the seventeenth century had less staying power and were spiritually weaker than their sixteenth-century ancestors? Did the moral and religious complacency of the fathers undermine the children's spiritual energies? Most likely the difference was due to the change in attitude toward the Western world. In the sixteenth and seventeenth centuries great centralized states were built there on the ruins of the feudal system. At the same time the people's labor broke away from the narrow sphere of the feudal agricultural economy to which it had been forcibly confined. Thanks to geographical discoveries and technical inventions, a wide field of activity was opened to it. Intensive work began in new areas and with new capital, which successfully competed with the feudal, landowning capital. Both these facts—political centralization and urban bourgeois industrialism—resulted in considerable achievements: developments in administrative, fiscal, and military techniques, the organization of standing armies, new systems of taxation, new theories of communal and state economy. Economic technique was developed, merchant fleets were created, trade and commercial credit were organized.

Russia had no part in all these achievements. It was spending its powers and resources on external defense and on the upkeep of the court, the government, and the privileged classes including the clergy, while they did nothing and were incapable of doing anything for the people's economic and spiritual development. That was why in the seventeenth century Russia proved to be more backward in comparison with the West than at the beginning of the sixteenth. The Western influence gained ground as we recognized our material and spiritual poverty, brought out more and more clearly by wars, diplomatic relations, and commercial transactions with other countries. Comparison with the resources of the western European states made us aware of our own backwardness.

As the Western influence penetrated into Russia, it met with another influence—Eastern, Greek, or Byzantine—which had so far been predominant in it. There was a great difference between the two, and I shall compare them in order to show what one of them had left in Russia and what the other was bringing in.

The Greek influence was introduced and propagated by the church and was directed toward moral and religious ends. The Western influence was initially introduced by the state to meet its material needs, but it did not remain within set boundaries, as did the Greek. The Byzantine influence by no means extended to the whole sphere of Russian life. It was only a religious and moral guide to the people. It supported and embellished the supreme power of the state, but gave little guidance in state administration. It introduced certain norms into civil law, specifically those concerning family relations. It was faintly reflected in everyday life and still more faintly in the national economy. It regulated the way people spent their leisure and behaved on holy days, at any rate till the end of the liturgy, but it did little to increase the amount of positive knowledge and left no perceptible trace on people's everyday customs and ideas, leaving all this entirely to their creative imagination and primeval ignorance. But without dominating the whole of a man's life or depriving him of his national characteristics and individual peculiarities, within its own sphere it affected the whole community from top to bottom, penetrating with equal force into every class. It was this that made ancient Russian society a spiritually integrated whole.

Western influence, on the contrary, gradually came to dominate every aspect of life. It changed ideas and relations and affected both the state regime and public and private everyday life. It gave rise to new political ideas, civic demands, and social relations. It opened up new fields of knowledge, changed the Russian people's manners, customs, and attire, altering their outer appearance and remodeling their mentality. But though it gained possession of the whole man as a person and a citizen, it failed to gain possession—up to that time, at any rate—of the whole community. It powerfully affected only the thin, ever shifting, and restless top layer of our society.

And so the Greek influence came from the church, and the Western from the state. The Greek extended to the whole community but did not affect man's whole personality; the Western affected the whole of it, but did not extend to the community as a whole.

The encounter and struggle between these two influences gave rise to two tendencies in Russian society's intellectual life, two ways of looking at our national culture. Growing increasingly complex, changing their coloring, names, and forms of expression, these two tendencies run through our history like parallel streams. Disappearing at times and coming to the surface again like rivulets in a sandy desert, they enlivened the sluggish public life directed by the obscurantist, oppressive, and vapid governmental activity—a life that, with a few bright intervals, dragged on till the middle of the nineteenth century. Both tendencies first found expression in the second half of the seventeenth century, in the dispute about the exact moment of the transubstantiation of the Holy Gifts and, in connection with this, about the comparative value of studying Greek and Latin. The opponents might be called respectively Hellenists and Latinists. In the second half of the eighteenth century the apple of discord was thrown by the literature of the French Enlightenment, in connection with disputes about the significance of Peter's reforms and independent national development. The nationalists called themselves Russophiles, and nicknamed their opponents "Russian semi-Frenchmen," Gallomaniacs, freethinkers, and most often Voltairians. Some seventy years ago the adherents of the two camps were respectively called Slavophiles and Westerners. At this last stage the substance of both parties' views might be expressed as follows.

The Westerners said: Our culture is basically European, but historically we are younger than our brothers of western Europe, and we must follow in their footsteps, assimilating the fruits of their civilization.

Yes, the Slavophiles replied, we are Europeans, but eastern ones. We have our own original life principles, which we must work out by our own efforts, not in the West's leading strings. Russia is not a pupil or a companion or even a rival of Europe— it is its successor. Russia and Europe are two contiguous historical realities, two successive stages in the cultural evolution of mankind, and western Europe, scattered with monuments—if I may slightly parody the Slavophiles' somewhat grandiloquent tone—is a large and spacious graveyard in which the great dead men of the past sleep under ornate marble monuments. Russia, with its steppes and forests, is a dirty rustic cradle in which the world's future uneasily tosses about and cries helplessly. Europe is coming to the end of its life, Russia is just beginning to live; and since it has to survive Europe, it must learn to live without it, by its own resources, by its own principles, which are to replace the moribund principles of European life and bring new light into the world. And so our historical youth lays upon us the duty not to imitate, not to borrow the fruits of other nations' cultural efforts, but to work out independently the basic principles of our own historical life, which are hidden in the depths of our national spirit and have not yet been worn threadbare by mankind.

Thus the two theories do not merely express different conceptions of the historical position of Russia and Europe, but suggest different paths for future development. This is not the moment to pass judgment on these theories, to discuss Russia's historical fate and ask whether it is destined to be the light of the East or to remain merely a shadow of the West, but we can cursorily remark on the attractive features of both. The Westerners were noted for their clear thinking, love of exact knowledge, and respect for scholarship. The Slavophiles displayed a fascinating breadth of ideas, lively faith in the nation's

potentialities, and a streak of lyrical dialectic that pleasantly con-
cealed slips in logic and gaps in erudition.

I have set out both views in their final forms, complicated by
various local and extraneous admixtures in the course of the
two preceding centuries. My task is to determine the moment
when they first appeared in their original unadorned condition.
It is a mistake to date them from Peter's reforms. They were
conceived in the minds of the seventeenth-century people who
had lived through the Time of Troubles. Perhaps the first appearance of· those tendencies was noted by Ivan Timofeev, a
government clerk who at the beginning of Michael's reign wrote
an account of the times, beginning with the reign of Ivan the
Terrible. He was a very intelligent observer with definite ideas
and principles. In politics he was a conservative. He attributed
all the miseries of his time to the people's forsaking the old customs and breaking the ancient rules; that was why Russians began
to spin round and round like the spokes of a wheel. He bitterly
complains of the lack of manly fortitude among them, of their
inability to prevent arbitrary or unlawful innovations by concerted effort. Russians do not believe one another. They turn
their backs on each other; some look to the East, others to the
West.

I cannot say whether this was an accidental remark or a subtle
observation. In any case, in the twenties of the seventeenth century, when Timofeev was writing, "Westernism" was a foible
of individual eccentrics like Prince Khvorostinin rather than a
responsible social movement. In every society there always are
to be found sensitive people who, without knowing why, think
and do earlier than others what all will think and do later on,
just as there are abnormally sensitive people who feel a coming
change in the weather, and normal ones who often fail to notice
it after it has come.

Let us now consider the first manifestations of the Western
influence. In so far as it was felt and encouraged by the government, it developed step by step, gradually increasing in scope.
The process was slow because the government wanted, or rather

was obliged, to compromise between the country's needs, which urged it to learn from the West, and the people's psychology and its own inertia, which resisted foreign influence. To begin with, it turned to foreigners for help in its chief material needs —armaments and national defense. In this respect the country's backwardness led to particularly painful consequences. The government took from abroad military and later other technical achievements, but it did this reluctantly, without looking far ahead to the possible results of its endeavors, without inquiring by what efforts the Western mind had attained such technical success and what view of the world and of the purpose of life had inspired those efforts. Russia needed cannons, guns, machines, ships, various industries. It was decided in Moscow that all these things presented no danger to the salvation of the soul, and that even the study of these cunning devices was in itself a harmless and morally neutral occupation. Even the rules of the church allowed, in case of need, departure from canonical directions on the details of daily routine. But in the sacrosanct domain of feelings, beliefs, and ideas, where the higher guiding principles of life reigned supreme, not an inch of ground was to be surrendered to foreign influence.

Thanks to this cautious concession, important innovations were introduced into the Russian army and Russian industry enjoyed its first successes. More than once bitter experience had shown that our mounted militia of servicemen could not stand up to trained Western infantry provided with firearms. At the end of the sixteenth century the Muscovite government already began to add foreign military units to its army. At first it was proposed to make direct use of Western military technique by hiring foreign mercenaries and importing armaments. From the first years of Michael's reign the government sent detachments of mercenaries on campaigns with its own army. One of them was commanded by an Englishman, Lord Aston. Later it dawned on the government that it would be cheaper to learn military art from foreigners than to hire them, and Russian servicemen were sent to be trained by foreign officers so that we could have properly organized and disciplined regiments of our own.

This difficult transformation of the Russian militia into a regular army was begun about 1630, before the second war with Poland. Long and elaborate preparation for that war was conducted with the caution of those who had suffered defeat. There were plenty of volunteers in western Europe for Muscovite service. In countries directly or indirectly affected by the Thirty Years' War, many military men were wandering about, seeking employment for their swords. It was known that the Deulino armistice between Russia and Poland was coming to an end and that there would be war. In 1631 a mercenary, Colonel Leslie, contracted to collect an infantry detachment of five thousand volunteers in Sweden, buy arms for them, and engage German technicians for the new artillery factory founded in Moscow by a Dutchman named Coet. At the same time another contractor, Colonel Fandam [Van Dam?], undertook to hire in other countries a regiment of 1,760 "good and trained soldiers," and also to bring German bombardiers and experienced instructors to teach Russian servicemen the art of war.

Foreign military technique was a considerable expense to Moscow. Recruiting, arming, and providing a year's keep for Fandam's regiment cost 1.5 million rubles in our currency. The commander of the infantry regiment hired by Leslie was to receive by contract a yearly salary of 22,000 rubles in our currency.

At last in 1632 an army of 32,000 men with 158 guns was sent to Smolensk. This army included six foreign-trained infantry regiments commanded by hired colonels. In these regiments there were 1,500 hired Germans and up to 13,000 Russian soldiers trained in the foreign fashion. A contemporary Russian chronicler remarked with surprise that there had never been in a Russian army so much infantry with firearms—Russian infantry trained in soldiering. The failure at Smolensk, in spite of all these preparations, did not stop the reorganization of the army; we already know its further development. Instructions for teaching foreign military arts to servicemen were drawn up under Tsar Michael and printed under Tsar Alexei in 1647.

The establishment of a semiregular army naturally raised the question of providing arms for it. Military equipment was imported from abroad. Before the war of 1632, Colonel Leslie was ordered to purchase in Sweden 10,000 muskets with ammunition and 5,000 swords. During the war tons and tons of gunpowder and iron cannonballs were imported from Holland, and heavy duty had to be paid on them. This was expensive and troublesome, and the idea gained ground that we might make our own weapons. The need to do so drew attention to the country's mineral wealth. We used to obtain iron from local ore in the neighborhood of Tula and Ustiug. The metal was made into nails and other household articles in domestic furnaces, and in Tula they actually made firearms. But all this did not satisfy the needs of the War Department, and iron was imported by the ton from Sweden. To do metallurgic work on a broad scale the help of foreign skill and capital was needed. Intensive search for ore of every kind was begun, and mining engineers and craftsmen were called in from abroad. In 1626 free entry into Russia was allowed to an English engineer, Bullmer, who "through his training and knowledge could find ore of gold, silver, copper, and precious stones, and knew where such places were." With the help of foreign experts expeditions were organized to discover and mine silver and other kinds of ore at Solikamsk, on the northern Dvina, Mezen, Kanin Nos, Iugorsky Shar, beyond the Pechora, on the river Kosva, and even at Eniseisk. In 1634 a commission was sent to Saxony and Brunswick to hire coppersmiths with the promise that there would be plenty of work for them in Muscovy. Evidently abundant supplies of copper ore had been discovered.

Foreign capitalists to run the industry were also found. In 1632, just before the Polish war, a Dutch merchant named Andrew Vinius and his partners obtained a concession for establishing metalworks near Tula on condition that they provide the state with cannon, cannonballs, gun barrels, and steel articles of every kind at low rates. That was the origin of the Tula armament factories, which were eventually taken over by the state. To secure a supply of workers for them, a whole volost belonging to the crown was attached to them. This was how the class of factory peasants was created. In 1644 another foreign company, with a Hamburg merchant named Marselis at its head, obtained a twenty-year concession for founding iron-smelting works on the rivers Vaga, Kostroma, and Sheksna and in other places on the same conditions. Under Tsar Michael there was in Moscow itself, by the river Neglinny, a foundry in which foreign workers made a large number of cannon and bells. The Russians too learned the craft fairly well. The owners had strict injunctions to teach their Russian apprentices everything, and not to conceal from them any useful craft.

Workshops for making glass, potash, and so on were established at the same time as metal foundries. Following the mining engineers, all kinds of craftsmen began coming to Moscow at the government's invitation—weavers of velvet, goldsmiths, watchmakers, hydraulic engineers, masons, painters, and so on—always on condition that they teach Russians their crafts.

Even European scholars were in demand. In 1639 Adam Olearius, a master of arts of Leipzig University, who had been to Moscow several times as secretary of the Holstein legation and had written a remarkable description of the Muscovite state, received an invitation to enter the Tsar's service. The invitation was worded as follows: "We, the Great Tsar, have been informed that you are highly learned and familiar with astrology and geography and the courses of heavenly bodies and geometry and with many other useful arts and sciences, and such a scholar would suit us." Hostile rumors spread through Moscow that a wizard who could foretell the future by the stars would soon be coming, and Olearius declined the invitation.

In western Europe, countries and individuals grew rich through lively maritime trade carried on by numerous fleets of merchant ships. As early as the middle of the seventeenth century the Muscovite government began thinking about a navy, harbors, and maritime trade. There was an idea of hiring Dutch shipwrights and men who could navigate seagoing ships. Vinius, the merchant whom we have mentioned before, offered to build a fleet of galleys for the Caspian Sea. In 1669 a ship named *Orel* was built on the river Oka for the Caspian by shipwrights

imported from Holland. The ship and a few small vessels cost
9,000 rubles (about 125,000 in our currency) and reached Astrakhan, but in 1670 this firstborn of the Russian fleet was burned
by Razin. Muscovy had harbors on the White Sea at Arkhangelsk
and at the mouth of the river Kola at Murmansk, but these were
too far from Moscow and from western European markets and
were cut off from the Baltic by the Swedes. The government had
the peculiar idea of leasing foreign harbors for the future Muscovite fleet. In 1662 the Moscow ambassador, on his way to England, had lengthy discussions with the chancellor of Kurland as
to whether Muscovite ships could somehow be stationed in Kurland harbors. The chancellor's answer was that it would be more
fitting for the Tsar to build ships near his own town of
Arkhangelsk.

Amidst all this concern about mines and factories, the Muscovite government seems at last to have become dimly conscious
of an idea it had found particularly hard to grasp. Its financial
policy always had as its sole object profit for the Treasury, and
completely ignored the question of the national economy. When
the government was faced with a new expense that could not
be met out of current revenue, it had recourse to its usual financial arithmetic: it counted the number of registered taxpayers,
calculated the total amount to be collected from them, and
commanded that the payment be made under threat of penalties,
either as a special levy or as a regular tax, leaving it to the taxpayers to settle among them what each was to pay and to find
the money as best they could. Arrears and persistent complaints
of inability to pay were the only restraints on such a casual financial policy. While increasing taxes, the government did
nothing to increase the people's capacity to pay them. But
observation of the foreigners' industrial skill and commercial
resources, as well as insistent reminders from its own tradespeople who had also observed the foreign ways, gradually introduced Moscow financiers to a hitherto unknown range of polit-
ico-economic ideas and relations, and widened their field of
vision against their will. Thoughts that the rulers found hard to
assimilate were forced upon them. They saw that an increase in

taxation should be preceded by an increase in the productivity of labor, which must be directed to new and profitable industries, to the discovery and exploitation of the country's latent wealth, and that this required experts, training, knowledge, proper organization. Such thoughts were aroused in the Muscovite government by the Western influence, and they found an echo among the people as well.

The government's new concerns, the search for ore, for ships' timber, for suitable sites for saltworks, the building of sawmills, inquiries addressed to the local inhabitants about the natural wealth of their districts—all this created hopes of new earnings and of reward from the Tsar for giving useful information. Men who pointed out a profitable place for mining ore were promised a reward of 500 rubles, or 1,000 or more rubles in our currency. If a report reached Moscow that there was a large alabaster mountain on the northern Dvina, an expedition headed by a German would be dispatched from Moscow to investigate and describe the mountain, to settle with the tradespeople at what price a pood of alabaster could be sold abroad, and to hire workmen to break up the stone. Rumors spread that the Tsar rewarded all who made useful discoveries or inventions.

When a striving is engendered in people in response to some essential need, it gains possession of the community as does a fashion or an epidemic. It excites the imagination and in the more impressionable types gives rise to morbid fancies or risky enterprises. The organization of Muscovy's external defenses and the discoveries and inventions serving to improve them acquired vital importance after the defeats and humiliations inflicted upon the country by foreigners at the Time of Troubles. In 1629 a certain priest named Nestor in the city of Tver submitted a petition to the Tsar, telling him of "a great work that God had not yet revealed to any man either in our land or in other states, except to him, the priest Nestor, to the glory of the Tsar and the deliverance of our distressed country, and to the dismay and amazement of its enemies." The priest Nestor promised the Tsar to build for him at low cost a small movable redoubt in which men at arms could defend themselves as in a real immovable fortress. In vain did the boyars beg the inventor to make a model or a draft of his movable fortification so they could show it to the sovereign. The priest declared that unless he could see the Tsar in person he would not do anything, for he distrusted the boyars. He was banished to a Kazan monastery and kept in chains for three years because "he boasted of a great work, but would not say what it was, and apparently did it just to make trouble, as though not in his right mind."

And so the Muscovite government and the community at large came to feel the vital need of western European military and industrial technical knowledge, and were actually prepared to try to acquire it. Perhaps such technical knowledge was all that the state really needed at the time. But once a social movement is set going by some particular impetus, its course usually comes to be influenced by other forces that draw it far beyond the limit originally fixed for it.

Increased demand attracted to Muscovy a multitude of foreign technicians, officers, soldiers, physicians, craftsmen, merchants, factory owners. As early as the sixteenth century, under Ivan the Terrible, western Europeans working in Russia formed a "German Settlement" on the outskirts of Moscow, on the river Iauza. The storms of the Time of Troubles destroyed this foreign nest. When Michael came to the throne, more foreigners arrived at the capital and settled wherever they liked, buying houses from local inhabitants. They opened taverns and built their chapels in the city. Close contacts between the aliens and the natives, resulting conflicts and annoyances, complaints of the Moscow clergy about the chapels' being next door to the Russian churches perturbed the city authorities, and under Tsar Michael a decree was issued forbidding foreigners to buy houses from the townspeople and to build chapels in Moscow.

Olearius describes one of the incidents that made the government take steps to separate Muscovites from foreigners. Many of the German officers were married to daughters of foreign merchants living in Moscow. These ladies looked down on ordinary tradesmen's wives and wanted to sit in front of them in chapel, but the latter would not give in, and one day their altercation with the officers' wives degenerated into an open fight. The noise could be heard in the street and attracted the attention of the Patriarch, who by ill luck was driving past the chapel. Having learned what was happening, the Patriarch, as guardian of church order irrespective of denomination, commanded that the chapel be demolished, and it was razed to the ground that very day. This must have happened in 1643, when it was decreed that all old chapels in Moscow be demolished and sites for new chapels were given beyond the Zemlianoi Val [Earthen Ramparts].

In 1652 the foreigners scattered throughout Moscow were moved beyond the Pokrovka to the river Iauza, to the place where the Germans had lived in the old days. There they were given plots of land in accordance with their rank and occupation. That was how the new German or Foreign Settlement was founded. It soon became a well-ordered little town, with straight and wide streets and pretty wooden houses. Olearius reckoned that in the first years of its existence the settlement had a thousand inhabitants. Another foreigner, Meyerberg, who visited Moscow in 1660, speaks of a great number of foreigners living in the settlement. There were four Protestant chapels in it, and a German school. The thriving population, distinct in language, race, and rank, lived in cheerful contentment, free from all interference with its customs and ideas. It was a corner of western Europe sheltering in an eastern suburb of Moscow.

It was this German Settlement that helped to transmit European culture to such spheres of Muscovite life as had nothing to do with the essential material needs of the state. Craftsmen, capitalists, and officers imported by the government for the external defense of the country and for its internal economic needs brought to Moscow, together with their military and industrial skill, European ideas of comfort, domestic amenities, and amusements. It is interesting to see how eagerly the Moscow upper classes seized upon foreign luxuries and attractions imported from the West, forsaking their old prejudices, tastes, and habits. External political relations undoubtedly encouraged this predilection for foreign comforts and amusements. Embassies frequently coming to Moscow from abroad made the Russians wish to be seen at their best by foreign observers and to show that in Moscow too people knew the proper way to live. Besides, Tsar Alexei was for a time considered as a candidate to the throne of Poland, and he tried to organize his court life on the Polish pattern.

When Russian envoys were sent abroad, they were bidden to observe carefully all the appointments of foreign courts and their amusements. One can see from diplomatic dispatches what importance these envoys attached to court balls and especially to theatrical performances. A certain Likhachov, sent on a diplomatic mission to the Duke of Tuscany in 1659, was invited by the Duke to a ball and a play, and in his dispatch he described this play in great detail; evidently Moscow took an interest in such matters. The envoys were anxious not to miss a single scene.

A hall was shown, and after a time it sank down, and this happened six times; and in the same hall there appeared a sea with moving waves, and in the sea there were fishes and men riding on fishes, and above the hall there was the sky and people sitting in clouds. . . . And there came down from the sky a gray-haired man in a carriage, and from the opposite side a beautiful maiden, also in a carriage, and the horses pulling the carriages were as good as real horses and moved their legs. And the Duke said it was the sun and the moon. . . . And in another scene about fifty men in armor appeared and began fighting with sabers and swords and shooting with pistols, and it looked as though they had killed three or four men, and many marvelous young men and maidens dressed in gold came out from behind the curtain and danced and did many wonderful things.

In describing the life of the Muscovite upper classes, Kotoshikhin says that "the people of Muscovy live in poorly arranged houses, without particular comfort and adornment." A drawing by Meyerberg, whom we have already mentioned, shows a bishop driving in a clumsy sledge, and the Tsaritsa's windowless closed carriage. Now, following other countries' example, the Tsar and the Moscow boyars took to driving in ornate German carriages upholstered in velvet, painted and fitted with glass windowpanes. The boyars and rich merchants began building brick houses instead of humble wooden ones, and furnishing them in the foreign fashion. The walls were covered with "gilded leather" of Belgian workmanship, the rooms adorned with pictures and clocks. Tsar Michael, who could not take exercise because of his bad legs and did not know what to do with his time, developed such a liking for clocks that he lined a whole room with them. Music was introduced at festive meals. In Tsar Alexei's palace at supper "a German played the organ, trumpets blew, and cymbals clanged."

Foreign arts were called in to adorn native crudeness. Tsar Alexei presented Boris Ivanovich Morozov, his friend, former tutor, and subsequently a relative by marriage, with a wedding coach covered with gold brocade, lined with expensive sable fur, and plated with silver instead of iron. Even the heavy bindings on the wheels were of silver. (In the rebellion of 1648 the mob pulled this coach to pieces.) At the supper party with German music to which we have just referred, that same Tsar regaled his guests, including his father confessor, till they were all drunk. The party went on till the small hours of the morning.

Muscovite envoys were instructed to try while abroad to engage for the Tsar's service the best and most skilled trumpeters "who could play dance music on the highest register." The court and the nobility developed a passion for theatrical performances. They had some religious scruples about indulging in this amusement, which strict guardians of true piety regarded as "the devil's game and a spiritual abomination." Tsar Alexei consulted his confessor on the subject, and the confessor allowed him to attend theatrical performances, following the example of Byzantine emperors. The plays were acted at the palace by a dramatic company hastily recruited from among the children of foreign soldiers and merchants and trained to some extent by the pastor of the Lutheran church in the German Settlement, Master Johann Gottfried Gregory. In 1672 the Tsar, overjoyed at the birth of Tsarevich Peter, commanded a play to be produced. For this purpose a theater was built in the suburban village of Preobrazhenskoe, in later years Peter's favorite playground. There at the end of 1672 the Tsar watched a play about Esther, staged by the pastor, and liked it so much that he presented the producer with sable furs worth 1,500 rubles in our currency. In addition to *Esther*, Pastor Gregory staged *Judith*, a gay comedy about Joseph, a "pitiful" play about Adam and Eve—that is, about the Fall and Redemption—and other plays.

In spite of the biblical subjects, these were not medieval mystery plays with a moral, but plays of a new type, translated from the German, impressing the spectators with terrible scenes of executions, battles, and cannonades, and at the same time introducing (except in the tragedy of Adam and Eve) a comic element represented by the buffoon—an inevitable appendage to the cast—with his crude and often indecent sallies. Russian actors were also being hastily trained. In 1673 Gregory was already training for the stage twenty-six young men recruited in the Novomeshchansky suburb of Moscow. While there was as yet no elementary school to teach reading and writing, a theatrical school was founded. Plays on biblical subjects soon gave way to the ballet. At Preobrazhenskoe in 1674 the Tsar with his family and the boyars watched a play about Artaxerxes and his orders for the hanging of Aman, and after that, Germans and the servants of Matveev, the Foreign Affairs minister, who were also being trained by Gregory in theater arts, "played viols, organs, and other instruments and danced."

All these novelties and amusements, I repeat, were luxuries for Moscow high society, but they developed in it new and more refined aims and requirements unknown to the Russian people of former generations. Would it rest content with simply enjoying the things it had so eagerly borrowed?

In western Europe the amenities of daily life and elegant amusements had their source not only in the fortunate economic position of the well-to-do leisured classes and in the capricious fancies of sophisticated taste; centuries of spiritual effort on the part of individuals and whole communities helped to create them. External adornments of life went hand in hand with the development of thought and feeling. Man strives to build up for himself an environment that corresponds to his tastes and to his view of life, but to achieve this correspondence he must seriously think about his tastes and about life in general. In borrowing another people's environment we unconsciously and involuntarily assimilate the tastes and ideas that created it. Otherwise the environment will seem to us tasteless and incomprehensible.

Our seventeenth-century ancestors thought differently. They imagined that in borrowing European achievements, they would not have to acquire other nations' learning and ideas and renounce their own. That was their simplehearted mistake—a mistake made by all overcautious and belated imitators. In seventeenth-century Muscovy, the people, while eagerly seizing upon foreign attractions, gradually became dimly aware of the spiritual efforts and interests that had created them. They came to love those interests without first ascertaining how they tallied with home-grown ideas and tastes—to love them, to begin with, as another fresh amusement, as a pleasant and novel exercise for minds that had pored too long over prayer books.

While borrowing foreign "artifices" and inventions for entertainment, the upper strata of Moscow society apparently began to develop intellectual curiosity, interest in learning, a desire to reflect upon subjects that in the old days lay beyond the Russians' field of vision and were unnecessary for their daily life. A circle of influential men, admirers of European culture, was formed at the court. It included Tsar Alexei's uncle, the gay and kind Nikita Ivanovich Romanov, the richest man in Russia next to the Tsar and the most popular of the boyars, a patron and admirer of the Germans, a great lover of their music and fashions, and a bit of a freethinker; Boris Ivanovich Morozov, the Tsar's former tutor and his relative by marriage (he had allowed his foster child to wear German clothes and in his old age bitterly complained of having received no education in his youth); Feodor Mikhailovich Rtishchev, a zealous champion of learning and education; Afanasi Lavrentievich Ordin-Nash-chokin, head of the Department of Foreign Affairs, a well-educated diplomat; and his successor, Artamon Sergeevich Matveev, also a favorite of the Tsar, a government clerk's son who had had boyar rank bestowed on him. Matveev's home was furnished in Western style, and he was the first man in Moscow to hold receptions to which guests came not to drink, but to talk, to exchange thoughts and news, with the hostess taking part in the conversation. It was he who organized the court theater.

Thus Russian society's attitude to western Europe was imperceptibly changing. At first Europe was regarded merely as a workshop of military and other articles, which could be bought without asking how they were made; now it was beginning to be looked upon as a school, in which one could learn not only crafts, but the arts of living and thinking.

The old Russia, however, still preserved its habitual caution; it did not venture to bring Western learning straight from its native land, from its masters and workers, but sought intermediaries who could pass on this learning to Muscovy in an expurgated form. Where could they be found? Between the old Muscovite Russia and western Europe lay a Slavic but Roman Catholic country—Poland. Ecclesiastical kinship and geographical proximity connected it with Romano-German Europe. The early and unrestrained development of serfdom and the political liberty of the upper classes made the Polish gentry ready receptacles for Western culture, but the peculiarities of the country and of the national character imparted to that borrowed culture a distinctly local coloration. Confined to the class that dominated the state, it gave rise to a gay and lively mental outlook that was at the same time both narrow and irresponsible. Poland was the channel through which the spiritual influence of the West first penetrated into Russia. In the seventeenth century Western civilization came to us in Polish guise. To begin with, however, it was not purebred Poles who brought it.

A considerable part of Orthodox Russia was forcibly united to the Polish Rzecz Pospolita by political bonds. The religious and national struggle of the Orthodox population against the Roman Catholic Church and the Polish state compelled the Russian champions to take up the weapons their opponents wielded so successfully—schools, literature, the Latin language. In this respect western Russia was far ahead of eastern Russia by the middle of the seventeenth century, and it was an Orthodox monk trained in a Latin or Russo-Latin school who was the first representative of European learning to be invited to Moscow.

The invitation was issued by the Muscovite government itself. In Moscow the Western influence met with a movement coming from the opposite direction. When we come to study the origin of the Russian church schism, we shall see that this movement was called forth by church needs and was partly directed against Western influence, but the opponents were united by one common interest, enlightenment, and temporarily joined hands. In ancient Russian literature there was no complete and fully adequate version of the Bible. Church hierarchs, who raised a dogmatic storm of almost ecumenical proportions about such matters as the sequestration of monastery estates and the number of times "alleluia" should be sung, had for centuries managed unperturbed to do without a full and exact text of the Holy Writ. In the middle of the seventeenth century (1649–50) the Muscovite government commissioned three learned monks from the Kiev Academy and the Pechersky Monastery—Epiphani Slavinetsky, Arseni Satanovsky, and Damaskin Ptitsky—to translate the Bible from the Greek into Slavonic. The Kiev scholars were paid at a lower rate than the hired German officers. Slavinetsky and Satanovsky each received a yearly salary of about 600 rubles in our currency, free board and lodging at the Chudov Monastery, plus two glasses of wine and four mugs of mead or beer sent daily from the palace. Later their salary was doubled.

In addition to the main task entrusted to them, the Kiev scholars had to satisfy other needs of the Muscovite government and society. At the wish of the Tsar or the Patriarch they compiled and translated educational books, manuals, lexicons, encyclopedias, treatises on cosmography, geography, and so on. There was a great demand for such books among the Moscow reading public, especially at the court and the Department of Foreign Affairs. The same kind of works were obtained through Russian envoys from abroad, chiefly from Poland. Slavinetsky translated a book on geography, a book titled *Medical Anatomy*, and another titled *Citizenship and Training of Children*, dealing with politics and education. Satanovsky translated a book titled *The Royal City*, a collection of extracts from Greek and Latin writers, pagan and Christian, embracing the whole sphere of contemporary popular knowledge on all sorts of subjects, from theology and philosophy down to zoology, mineralogy, and medicine.

Use was made of all literary resources that came to hand. Germans were invited to work together with the Kiev scholars. A certain Von Delden, who worked as an official interpreter, translated several French and Latin books into Russian. Dorn, a former Austrian ambassador to Moscow, translated a manual of cosmography. Mentioning this, Olearius adds that such books were much in demand by men of an inquiring mind among the aristocracy.

Practical as well as theoretical interests furthered the spread of this kind of literature. Translations of medical *vade mecum* books became popular at that period. In the archives of the Department of Foreign Affairs we find a curious piece of information: in 1663 a Dutchman in the Russian service, Van der Heen by name, submitted to the Department an article about "alchemical science and other matters," and in 1626 a note about "the highest philosophic alchemy." Evidently Muscovy was greatly interested in collecting information about the mysterious and enticing science by means of which it was hoped to learn the art of making gold. But the content of books translated or compiled by Slavinetsky and Satanovsky shows that a genuine interest in science as such was awakened in Muscovite minds in so far as science was accessible to them.

It was in this way that Moscow society came to feel the need of book learning and scientific training, and to develop schooling as a necessary means to them. The need was kept alive by the more and more frequent contacts with western European states, the conditions and mutual relations of which the Moscow diplomats had to study. Both the government and private persons attempted to establish schools in Moscow. Greek hierarchs had more than once pointed out to the tsars of Muscovy that a Greek school and printing press ought to be established in Moscow. Moscow asked for teachers for that school, the Greeks offered to send them, but somehow nothing came of it. Under Tsar Michael the school was almost organized. In 1632 a monk called Joseph was sent by the Patriarch of Alexandria and was prevailed upon to stay in Moscow. He was commissioned to translate Greek polemical books against Latin heresies into Slavonic, and also "to teach small children the Greek language and reading in the schoolhouse." But Joseph's early death put an end to the work.

The idea of founding in Moscow a school that would serve as a fountainhead of learning for the whole of the Orthodox East was not abandoned, however, either by the Russians or by the Greeks. Close to the Patriarch's court at Chudov Monastery a Greco-Latin school was established under the leadership of a Greek, a certain Arseni. He came to Moscow in 1649 but was soon banished to the Solovetsky Monastery on suspicion of heresy. Both Epiphani Slavinetsky and Arseni Satanovsky had been invited to Moscow to teach rhetoric, among other things, but it is not known whether any pupils were found for them. In 1665 three assistant clerks from the Palace Department and the Department of Secret Affairs were commanded to learn Latin from a Kiev scholar, Simeon Polotsky. For this purpose a special building was added to the Spassky Monastery in Moscow and named "School of Grammatical Learning." You must not think that these were regular, properly organized schools with a definite curriculum, a syllabus, a permanent teaching staff, and so on. All it meant was that temporary and accidental commissions were given to this or that visiting scholar to teach Greek or Latin to young men who were sent to him by the government or came of their own accord.

Such was the original form of state schools in Russia in the seventeenth century. It was a direct continuation of the ancient Russian method of teaching, whereby members of the clergy or special teachers took children as pupils for a specified payment. In some places private persons or perhaps communities erected special buildings for the purpose, so that something like a permanent public school was established. In 1685 in the town of Borovsk, close to the marketplace and next door to the municipal almshouse, there was a "school for teaching children" built by a local priest. Textbooks, which began to appear about the middle of the seventeenth century, were probably intended to serve the needs of either home or school education. Thus in 1648 a Slavonic grammar by Meleti Smotritsky, a scholar from western Russia, was published in Moscow, and in 1649 a short catechism by Peter Mohila, rector of the Kiev Academy and subsequently metropolitan of Kiev, was reprinted from the Kiev edition.

Private persons competed with the government in promoting education. Most of them belonged to the governing class themselves. The most zealous of these champions of learning was Tsar Alexei's trusted adviser Feodor Mikhailovich Rtishchev. He built the Andreevsky Monastery on the outskirts of Moscow and in 1649 installed there at his own expense as many as thirty learned monks from the Pechersky Monastery in Kiev and other Ukrainian monasteries, who were to translate foreign books into Russian and to teach Greek, Latin, Slavonic grammar, rhetoric, philosophy, and other literary subjects. Rtishchev himself became a student in this free school. He sat up night after night talking to the masters, learned Greek from them, and persuaded Epiphani Slavinetsky to compile a Greek and Slavonic lexicon for the school. The Ukrainian scholars were joined by some of the Moscow learned monks and priests. Thus there was formed a fraternity of scholars, a kind of free academy of learning. Taking advantage of his position at the court, Rtishchev made some of the young men in government service go to the Kiev scholars at the Andreevsky Monastery to learn Greek and Latin.

In 1667 the parishioners of the Moscow church of St. John the Divine (in Kitay Gorod) decided to found a school in connection with it. It was not to be an elementary parish school, but one for general education in which "grammatical art, Slavonic, Greek, and Latin languages, and other free subjects" would be taught. They sent a petition about it to the Tsar and another to a certain "pious and honorable person," asking him to intercede for them with the Tsar. They asked the Patriarch of Moscow and the Eastern patriarchs who happened to be in the city in connection with Nikon's trial to give them their blessing. At last the Moscow Patriarch, chiefly out of respect for the persistent entreaties of "the pious and honorable person" who inspired the idea of the school (probably it was Rtishchev again), gave his blessing "so that industrious students might rejoice in the freedom of research and the wisdom of liberal studies and gather together in the gymnasium to sharpen their wits with the help of skillful masters." It is not known whether the school was actually opened.

Members of the upper class did their best to provide home education for their children and engaged monks from western Russia and even Poles as resident tutors. Tsar Alexei himself set the example. He was not content with the elementary schooling that his elder sons, Alexei and Feodor, received from the official Moscow teacher, but had them taught Latin and Polish, and to complete their education he summoned Simeon Sitianovich Polotsky, a learned monk who had studied at the Kiev Academy and had experience of Polish schools as well. Simeon was a pleasant teacher who presented his subject matter in an attractive form. His verses give a short summary of his lessons. He touched on political subjects too, trying to develop in his royal pupils a responsible attitude toward politics.

> It is fitting that rulers should know
> How public welfare can be made to grow.

He taught his pupils that the ideal relation of a tsar to his subjects was that of a good shepherd to his sheep.

> This should be the object of a ruler's care:
> His subjects' burdens he should manfully bear.
> He should not despise them or treat them like dogs,
> But love them as a father his children loves.

The study of the Polish language, taught by private tutors, awakened an interest in Polish literature in translation and even in the original, and penetrated into the Tsar's palace and the boyars' houses. As I have just said, Tsar Alexei's elder sons were taught Polish and Latin. Tsarevich Feodor also learned the art of versification and collaborated with Simeon Polotsky in putting the Psalter into verse. He made a rhymed version of two psalms. It was said of him that he loved the sciences, especially mathematics. One of the Tsar's daughters, Sofia, was also taught Polish and read Polish books. According to Lazar Baranovich, archbishop of Chernigov, in his time the Tsar's family and friends "did not despise the Polish language but enjoyed reading Polish books and stories."

Some members of Moscow society sought to acquire Western learning at first hand, the more so because it came to be considered necessary for success in state service. Artamon Sergeevich Matveev taught his son Latin and Greek. His predecessor at the Department of Foreign Affairs, Ordin-Nashchokin, surrounded his son with Polish prisoners of war, and these inspired the young man with such love for western Europe that he emigrated to Poland. The first Russian ambassador to Poland, Tiapkin, had his son educated at a Polish school. In 1675, sending him to Moscow on a diplomatic mission, the father presented him in Lvov to King Jan Sobieski. The young man addressed the King with a speech in which he thanked him "for bread and salt and schooling." The speech was delivered in the scholastic jargon of the day, half Latin and half Polish, and Tiapkin reported that his son spoke so clearly and expressively that he did not stumble over a single word. The King presented the young man with a hundred zlotys and fifteen *arshins* [1] of red velvet.

And so the people of Muscovy came to want foreign art and amenities of life and later on to want education. They began with foreign officers and German cannons and ended with German ballet and Latin grammar. The Western influence, called forth by the essential material needs of the state, brought with it things that were not required by those needs and could have waited.

[1] A unit of measurement equivalent to thirty-two inches.

Chapter
XIV

The Cultural
Pattern

The need for Western knowledge ran counter to the inveterate antipathy of the Muscovites to everything that was brought in from the Roman Catholic and Protestant West. No sooner had Moscow society tasted the fruits of the new learning than it began to feel painful doubts as to whether it was safe or would harm the purity of faith and morals. These doubts marked the second stage in the intellectual mood of seventeenth-century Russia, after the initial period of discontent with the state of things at home. This stage, too, led to consequences of great importance.

There has come down to us a fragment of a judicial inquiry dating back to 1650, which clearly shows how these doubts began and what inspired them. The inquiry was concerned with young Moscow students: Lukian Timofeevich (Luchka) Golosov (subsequently a member of the Council of State), Stepan Alabev, Ivan (Ivashka) Zasetsky, and Constantine (Kosta) Ivanov (a sacristan of Blagoveshchensky Cathedral). It was a circle of intimate friends sharing the same ideas. "Rtishchev is learning Greek from the Kiev people," they said, "but there is heresy in those Greek writings." Alabev said at the inquiry that when the Greek elder Arseni lived in Moscow, he, Alabev, began learning Latin from him, but when that elder was banished to Solovki, he stopped learning and tore up the textbook, because his relatives and Luchka Golosov and Ivashka Zasetsky began saying to him, "Stop learning Latin, it's a bad thing to do," but "in what way it was bad they did not say." Golosov himself, at Rtishchev's insistence, had to learn Latin from the Kiev monks at the Andreevsky Monastery, but he was against their teaching and considered it dangerous for the faith. He said to Ivanov the sacristan: "Tell your senior priest [Stefan Vonifatiev, the Tsar's confessor] that I don't want to take lessons from the Kiev monks. They are not good monks. I haven't found anything good in them or in their teaching. Up till now I have been trying to please Rtishchev out of fear, but in the future I will not receive instruction from them at any price." Luchka added to this: "All who have learned Latin have gone astray."

About the same time two other young men from Moscow, Ozerov and Zerkalnikov, set off with Rtishchev's help for Kiev to complete their education at the academy there. The sacristan Kosta Ivanov and his friends disapproved of this, fearing that when these young men had finished their studies in Kiev and returned to Moscow, they would cause a lot of trouble. They thought, therefore, that it would be a good thing to call them back before they had reached Kiev, for "even now they found fault with everyone and criticized pious Moscow priests, saying that they talked a lot of nonsense and were not worth listening to, and did themselves no credit teaching things beyond their own understanding."

The same zealots whispered that Boris Ivanovich Morozov kept a father confessor in his house merely for the sake of appearances, and his showing favor to the Kiev monks clearly proved that he erred in the same way and shared their heresies.

We see that one faction of the young students blamed the other for self-confidence engendered by the new learning and for arrogant criticism of home-grown authorities acknowledged

by everyone. This was not senile conservative grumbling against
everything new, but an expression of an attitude deeply rooted in
pious Russian minds. Art and science were valued in ancient
Russia through their connection with the church, as a means to
the understanding of God's word and to the salvation of the
soul. An interest in knowledge and artistic embellishments of
life having no such connection were regarded as the idle curiosity of superficial minds or as mere amusements, on the same
level as ballad singing, fairy tales, and masquerades. The church
silently tolerated them as children's games and frolics, though at
times a stern preacher would denounce them as dangerous dis-
tractions that might easily become the devil's wiles. In any case,
no educational value was ascribed to secular art and science and
they had no place in the training of the young. They were rele-
gated to the lower levels of life and considered as weaknesses of
fallible human nature, if not exactly as vices.

Art and science imported from the West appeared in a
more imposing guise and were ranged with life's higher interests.
They were not concessions to human weakness, but legitimate
requirements of man's heart and mind, and necessary conditions
of a well-ordered and dignified social life. They were justified
in themselves and not through serving the needs of the church.
A Western artist or scholar appeared in Russia not in the capacity of a jester or a wizard, but as a respectable "master of
theatrical arts" or as a geographer whom the government itself
acknowledged to be "highly expert in many crafts and branches
of knowledge useful to us."

Thus Western learning—or, to put it more generally, Western
culture—came to Russia not as an obedient servant of the church,
not as a sinner censured though tolerated by it, but rather as its
rival or at best as its helper in the task of fostering human welfare. Ancient Russian thought, fettered by tradition, naturally
drew back in alarm from such a helper, let alone rival. It can
be easily understood why acquaintance with this new learning at
once raised in Russian minds the anxious question whether it
was safe for the true faith and good morals, for the centuries-old
foundations of the country's life. The question had been raised

at a time when the new learning was being introduced through our own Orthodox scholars from western Russia. It became much more acute when the teaching was entrusted to foreigners who were Catholics or Protestants. Doubts as to whether western European influence and the new learning were morally and religiously harmless led to a painful rift in Russian church life—to the schism. The close connection between this event and the various trends of thought in contemporary Muscovite society compels me to draw your attention to the origin of the schism.

The Russian church schism separated a considerable part of the Russian Orthodox community from the established church. It began in the reign of Tsar Alexei because of the ecclesiastical innovations introduced by Patriarch Nikon, and it continues to this day. The schismatics consider themselves Orthodox Christians just as we do. "Old Believers" in the strict sense of the words do not differ from us in a single dogma of faith, in a single fundamental doctrine of religion, but they severed themselves from our church and ceased to recognize our ecclesiastical authorities in the name of "the Old Belief," which they think those authorities have renounced. Accordingly, we regard them not as heretics, but merely as schismatics, and they call us "church people" or Nikonians and themselves "Old Believers," preserving pre-Nikonian rites and pious customs. But if they do not differ from us with regard to dogma and the essentials of faith, the question is how did the schism arise, and why did a considerable part of the Orthodox community find itself outside the pale of the established church? Here is a brief account of the origin of the schism.

Before the time of Patriarch Nikon the Russian ecclesiastical community was one single flock with one chief shepherd at its head. At different periods and from different sources it acquired certain local traditions, customs, and rites distinct from those of the Greek church, which had brought Christianity to Russia: Russians made the sign of the cross with two fingers instead of three, spelled the name Jesus differently (Esus), used seven instead of five offertory loaves in celebrating the liturgy; in church processions they followed the course of the sun instead of walking eastward; they worded two sentences of the Creed differently ("His kingdom *has* no end" instead of "shall have," and "the Holy Ghost, *true* and giver of life" instead of "Lord and giver of life"), and sang double instead of triple alleluias. Some of these peculiarities were recognized by Russian hierarchs at the church council of 1551 and thus received legal sanction. In the second half of the sixteenth century, when printing was introduced in Moscow, these divergences found their way from manuscripts into printed service books that were used throughout the country. Thus the printing press gave new importance to local peculiarities and made them more widespread.

Correctors of church books printed under Patriarch Joseph from 1642 to 1652 perpetuated some of the discrepancies. Since the text of Russian liturgical books was far from perfect, Patriarch Joseph's successor, Nikon, zealously set about the work of revision as soon as he was appointed to the patriarchate. At the church council of 1654 he passed a resolution to issue a new edition of liturgical books after revising them in accordance with the correct texts, ancient Greek books and Slavonic parchments. Piles of ancient Greek and Slavonic books in manuscript were brought to Moscow from the Orthodox East and from remote corners of Russia. New editions, duly amended after comparison with them, were sent out to all Russian churches with the order to confiscate and destroy the defective old books, whether printed or handwritten. Orthodox Russian people were horrified when they looked into these amended books and found that the name Jesus was spelled in an unfamiliar way, and that nothing was said about using only two fingers to make the sign of the cross, or other time-honored customs. The new editions seemed to them to contain a new faith, different from the one by which the holy fathers had gained salvation in olden days. They cursed the new books as heretical and continued using the old. The Moscow church council of 1666–67, at which two Eastern patriarchs were present, anathematized the dissidents for opposing ecclesiastical authorities and excommunicated them from the Orthodox Church; and the dissidents ceased to recognize as a lawful ecclesiastical authority the hierarchy that excommunicated them. The Russian church community was thus broken, and the schism continues to this day.

What, then, was the cause of the schism? Old Believers think it was due to Nikon's arbitrarily abolishing rites and customs that form part of the patristic Orthodox tradition essential to salvation, and then excommunicating from his corrupted church men who remained faithful to that tradition and defended it. But this explanation does not make everything clear. How had the Old Believers come to think that crossing oneself with two fingers and walking westward were part of the sacred patristic tradition essential for salvation? How could a mere ecclesiastical custom, a liturgical rite or text, have acquired the importance of dogma and become sacrosanct?

The explanation given by the Orthodox goes deeper. They say that the schism was due to the dissidents' ignorance, to their narrow interpretation of the Christian religion, to their inability to distinguish the essential from the external, the content from the form. But this answer, too, is insufficient. Certain rites sanctified by ancient local tradition may have wrongly acquired the significance of dogma, but then the authority of the church hierarchy was also sanctified by ancient tradition, not merely local but churchwide, and recognition of it was as necessary for salvation as the observance of those rites. How could Old Believers have ventured to reject one ecclesiastical commandment in favor of another, and to seek salvation without the guidance of the legitimate hierarchy they repudiated?

In explaining the origin of the schism, people often and somewhat contemptuously lay special emphasis on the Old Believers' blind attachment to ritual, to the letter of the scriptures—as though this were of any importance to religion. I do not share this contemptuous attitude to religious rites and texts. I am not a theologian, and it is not my business to expound their theological significance. But religious as well as all other rites and texts that affect practical everyday life have a general psychological import in addition to their specific meanings, and in that respect may be the subject of historical investigation. It is only from this nationally psychological point of view that I touch upon the origin of the schism.

Religious texts and rites express the essential content of the doctrine. A religious doctrine is composed of two kinds of belief: some are "truths," which determine the believer's conception of the world and solve for him the fundamental problems of existence; others are imperatives, which direct his moral actions and point out to him the tasks he has to fulfill in life. These truths and imperatives transcend the cognitive capacities of rational thought and the natural impulses of human will, and are therefore regarded as revealed from above. Conceptual—that is, intelligible—formulations of religious truths are dogmas; conceptual formulations of religious imperatives are commandments. How can either dogmas or commandments be comprehended if they are inaccessible either to logical thought or to natural will? They are grasped through religious experience or cognition and religious education.

Do not take exception to these terms. Religious thinking or cognition, though distinct from the logical or rational, is as much an avenue to knowledge as artistic perception is, but it is directed upon loftier objects. Man grasps by no means everything through logical reflection, and indeed it probably reveals to him the smallest fraction of knowable reality. Through learning dogmas and commandments a believer acquires certain religious ideas and moral impulses, which, just like artistic ones, elude logical analysis. Can the burden of a musical phrase that is clear to you be subsumed under a logical scheme? Religious ideas and impulses are *beliefs*. Certain liturgical rites that, taken together, constitute divine service are an aid to acquiring them. Dogmas and commandments are expressed in sacred texts and embodied in church ritual. All this is only an outer covering of the doctrine and not its essence. But religious as well as aesthetic comprehension differs from the logical and mathematical in that the idea, or the musical phrase, is inseparable from the form in which it is expressed. We can understand a logically deduced conception or a mathematically demonstrated theorem in whatever style, symbols, or language known to us they may be formulated. The case is different with religious and aesthetic perception. Here, by the law of psychological association, the idea and the motif are organically interconnected with the text, the rite, the image, the rhythm, the sound. If you forget the picture or the musical combination of sounds that has invoked a certain mood in you, you will not be able to reproduce that mood. The most magnificent poem rewritten in prose will lose all its charm.

Sacred texts and liturgical rites were created in the course of history and are not unchangeable or inviolable. One might invent better, more perfect texts and images than those that have developed our religious feeling, but they will not replace for us the old, inferior ones. When an Orthodox Russian priest intones at the altar, "Lift up your hearts," Orthodox believers experience a familiar feeling of exaltation that helps them "to lay aside all earthly care." But let the same priest say in Latin, "*Sursum corda*," which stylistically is even more impressive, and the believers, however well they may understand the words, will have no sense of exaltation simply because they are not used to them. The religious beliefs and feelings of every community are inextricably interwoven with the rituals and formulas that have helped to form them.

But perhaps such a close connection between church rites and the essence of religious doctrine is merely a defect of religious education. Perhaps a believing spirit can do without this heavy ritualistic overlay, and should be helped to do so. Yes, perhaps someday in the course of time the overlay will become superfluous, and the human spirit, through further evolution, will free its religious feeling from the influence of external impressions and from the very need of them, and will pray "in spirit and in truth." Then our religious psychology will be different, quite unlike the one developed by the practice of all religions known up to now. But so far as human memory extends, for thousands and thousands of years and down to the present day, men have not been able to manage without forms in either religion or social and moral relations.

A sharp distinction must be drawn between the way in which

intellect and will assimilate truth. For the intellect a certain effort of thought and of memory is sufficient in order to understand and remember it. But this is by no means sufficient to make truth the guide of will, the ruler of a community's life. To achieve that end, truth must be embodied in forms, in ritual, in a whole organization, which by providing a continuous stream of the right impressions will shape our thoughts, moods, and feelings, pound and soften our rough will, and through constant exercise transform the moral imperative into a spontaneous requirement of our own nature. How many beautiful truths that enlightened the human spirit and might have given light and warmth to communal life have vanished without a trace simply because they had not at the time been embodied in an organization with the help of which men could have assimilated them! This happens not only with religion, but with everything else as well. The most wonderful melody will fail to give us proper artistic impressions in the schematic form in which it is conceived by the composer. To do so it must be elaborated, instrumented, arranged for orchestra, repeated in many tones and variations, and played before an audience. One listener's enthusiasm will infect the people next to him, and these limited individual experiences of delight will create an overwhelming general impression, which every listener will take home with him, so that for many days he will find refuge in it from the troubles and vulgarities of everyday life.

The people who heard Christ's Sermon on the Mount died long ago and carried away with them the impressions they had experienced. But to some extent we share in their experience because the text of that sermon forms part of our liturgical services. A rite or a text is something like a recorder, preserving for us a dormant shape of a moral reality that once inspired men's good feelings and actions. Those men have long been gone, and the moment when they had a glimpse of that reality never occurred again. But with the help of the rite or the text that has saved it from oblivion we can bring it back and experience its effect according to the degree of our moral receptivity. Rites, customs, and conventions, reflecting thoughts and feelings that improved human life and provided an ideal for it, are the means whereby a social community is gradually built up amid dissensions, hesitations, struggle, and bloodshed. I do not know what mankind will be like in a thousand years' time, but if you deprive the man of today of all this acquired and inherited accumulation of rites, customs, and every kind of convention, he will forget and unlearn all he has ever known and will have to begin everything afresh.

But if the psychology of all religious communities is such that they cannot manage without texts and rites, why has there been in no other country so much quarreling and schism about these things as in seventeenth-century Russia? To answer this question we must recall certain aspects of our church life at that period.

Until the fifteenth century the Russian church was an obedient daughter of Byzantium. It received from there its bishops and metropolitans, its canon law and the whole organization of ecclesiastical life. For many centuries the authority of Greek Orthodoxy was unassailable. But in the fifteenth century it was undermined. Russian grand princes became aware of their national importance and promptly made it felt in interchurch relations. They did not want to depend even in ecclesiastical matters on any external power, whether that of the Emperor or of the Patriarch of Constantinople. They established the custom of appointing and consecrating metropolitans of all Russia at home, in Moscow, selecting the candidates from the Russian clergy only.

It was all the easier for them to introduce this change because Greek hierarchs were not too highly thought of in Russia. Ancient Russia greatly esteemed the ecclesiastical authority and sanctity of the East, but the words "a Greek" and "a rogue" were always synonymous among us. A chronicle of the twelfth century says of a certain bishop that "he was deceitful because he was a Greek." Such a view was formed quite early and quite naturally. As a rule, by no means the best of the Greek hierarchs were sent to spread Christianity in a distant and barbarous diocese of the Constantinople patriarchate. Cut off from their flock

by the difference of language and of mental outlook as well as
by official ceremonial, they could not acquire a pastoral influence. They confined themselves to organizing the beautiful external settings of church services, were well content with the
pious princes' zeal, and conscientiously sent Russian money to
their native land. A much respected Russian bishop in the
twelfth century thought fit to hint at this in a pastoral address to
his diocesan clergy. In the wake of the Greek hierarchs, many of
their lay compatriots came to Russia to make profit out of the
new converts.

In the fifteenth century the Greek church lowered itself
disastrously in Russian eyes by accepting the Florentine union
of 1439—that is, by agreeing to an alliance between the Orthodox and the Roman Catholic Churches, concluded at the Council of Florence. In its struggle against the Latins Russia had
placed complete trust in the Byzantine hierarchy, and now that
hierarchy had surrendered itself to the Pope of Rome and betrayed Eastern Orthodoxy, established by the apostles and confirmed by the holy fathers and the seven ecumenical councils.
Had not the Grand Prince of Moscow, Vasili Vasilievich, denounced the crafty enemy and "Satan's son" Metropolitan Isi-
dore, a Greek, who brought the union to Moscow? That man
would have Latinized the Russian church and corrupted the
ancient holy faith implanted in our country by St. Vladimir.

Several years later Byzantium was conquered by the Turks.
The Russians had for some time been inclined to look down
on the Greeks and regard them with suspicion. When Constantinople fell into the hands of the infidels, it was taken as a sign
of the final downfall of Greek Orthodoxy. See how confidently
the Russian metropolitan Philip interprets the connection of
world events. In 1471 he writes to the people of Novgorod,
who had risen against Moscow: "Think also of this, children:
Tsargrad [1] stood impregnable so long as piety shone in it like the
sun, but as soon as it abandoned truth and joined the Latins, it
fell into the hands of the pagans."

[1] Old Russian name for Constantinople. [Translator's note.]

In Russian eyes the light of the Orthodox East was darkened. Just as the first, ancient Rome had fallen through pride and heresies, so the second Rome, Tsargrad, through inconstancy fell prey to the godless. The impression produced by these events on Russia was profound, but it was not one of unrelieved gloom. The old lights of the church had faded. Greek piety was plunged into darkness. Orthodox Russia felt utterly alone in the world. Political events inevitably made it compare its own position with that of Byzantium. Moscow was throwing off the yoke of the infidels almost at the same time as it was being imposed upon Byzantium. Other empires fell because they betrayed Orthodoxy, but Moscow would stand fast and remain true to it. Moscow was the third and last Rome, the last and only refuge of the true faith in the world.

These ideas broadened the Russian sixteenth-century thinkers' political outlook and raised it to a higher level, making them anxious about Russia's historical destiny. "Fatherland" acquired a new and lofty significance for them. A Russian monk, Filofei (Philotheus), wrote as follows to Grand Prince Vasili, father of Ivan the Terrible: "Give heed to this, devout Tsar! Two Romes have fallen; the third—Moscow—stands, and a fourth there will never be. Our Apostolic Church alone shines with the light of holiness in your mighty realm and throughout the world, brighter than the sun in heaven." Our sixteenth-century scribes wrote that "the Orthodox faith in Tsargrad was defiled by the Mahometan lure of godless Hagarites, while with us in Russia it shone all the brighter thanks to the teachings of the holy fathers."

This view became a tenet of faith among the educated society of old Russia, penetrated to the masses, and called forth a number of legends about the flight of saints and of holy objects from both of the fallen Romes to the third Rome, Moscow. In the fifteenth and sixteenth centuries there arose legends about St. Anthony the Roman arriving with holy relics at Novgorod after a sea voyage on a rock, about the miraculous transportation of the wonder-working icon of Our Lady of Tikhvin from

the Byzantine East to Russia, and so on. The people who came
to Russia from the devastated Orthodox East to ask for alms
or shelter helped to confirm this national conviction.

In Feodor Ivanovich's reign the Patriarch of Constantinople,
Jeremiah, came to Moscow to ask for alms and in 1589 consecrated the Moscow Metropolitan Job as Patriarch of All Russia,
thus finally giving formal recognition to the long-standing *de
facto* separation of the Russian church from the Constantinople
patriarchate. The words he addressed to the Tsar on this occasion are so close to those of Filofei that one might imagine the
visiting prelate had read the Russian people's cherished thoughts:
"In truth the Holy Spirit abides in thee, and this idea has been
inspired by God. The ancient Rome fell because of heresies; the
second Rome, Constantinople, has been seized by the Hagarites,
the godless Turks; but thy great Russian realm, the third Rome,
has surpassed all in piety. Thou alone in all the world art called
a Christian tsar."

All these events and impressions produced a peculiar kind of
mood in Russian church people. By the beginning of the seventeenth century they were full of religious self-confidence, bred
not by any religious achievements of Orthodox Russia, but by
its political success and by the political disasters of the Orthodox
East. Russia appeared to them as the sole possessor and guardian
of Christian truth, of pure Orthodoxy. Through a slight transpo-
sition of ideas, national self-confidence deduced from this that the
Christianity professed in Russia, with all the local features and
interpretations given to it by aboriginal minds, was the only
true Christianity, and that there never had been and never
would be any true Orthodoxy except the Russian.

According to Orthodox teaching, the guardian of Christian
truth is not any local church, but the universal church, which
includes both those who are living at a particular time and
place and all true believers of all times, wherever they may
have lived. As soon as Russian believers came to regard themselves as sole guardians of the true faith, they made their own
religious ideas the criterion of Christian truth; that is, the conception of the universal church was restricted to the narrow

geographical boundaries of a particular local denomination. The universal Christian consciousness was identified with the limited outlook of men belonging to a certain time and place.

I have said that Christian doctrine is embodied in particular forms. It is expressed in certain rites for direct comprehension, is formulated in certain texts to be studied, and finds practical realization in church rules. The understanding of the texts and the practice of church rules increase in depth and perfection with the development of religious consciousness and of its moving force—reason armed with faith. With the help of rites, texts, and rules, religious thought penetrates deeper into the mysteries of the Christian doctrine, gradually making them clearer to itself and being guided by them. I repeat, these rites, texts, and rules do not constitute the essence of the doctrine, but through religious upbringing and experience they become an integral part of it and determine the community's religious attitude and general view of the world. They are forms not easily separated from their content. If, however, in some particular society they become distorted or deviate from the original doctrine, there is a remedy. The interpretation of Christian truth by a particular religious community can be checked and corrected by the religious sense of the universal church, whose authority rectifies local ecclesiastical deviations. But as soon as Orthodox Russia proclaimed that it alone was in possession of Christian truth, such a means of verification ceased to exist for it. Having taken itself for the universal church, the Russian ecclesiastical community could not allow anyone from outside to call in question its beliefs and liturgical rites.

Once Russian Orthodox minds adopted this point of view, they grew firmly convinced that their local church had all the spiritual fullness of the universal church, and that they had already acquired everything necessary for salvation. They had nothing more to learn, nothing to borrow, and no one to borrow from in matters of faith. All they had to do was carefully to preserve their precious heritage. Not the judgment of the universal church, but the national local tradition became the criterion of Christian truth. It was a recognized rule that we must

believe and pray as our fathers and forefathers had believed and
prayed, and that nothing was left for the grandchildren to do
but preserve the ancestral tradition without further reflection.
But that tradition was a static, crystallized expression of truth.
To accept it as the criterion of truth meant to reject all movement in religious thought, all possibility of correcting its mistakes
and imperfections. Once this standpoint was accepted, the efforts
of Russian religious minds were bound to be directed solely to
preserving their present stock of ideas, rites, and customs, with
all their limitations and local peculiarities, and protecting them
from change or deleterious outside influences, instead of going
deeper and deeper into the mysteries of Christian doctrine and
striving to assimilate as completely as possible the living thought
and experience of the universal church.

This attitude gave rise to two important consequences closely
connected with the origins of the schism: (1) church rites as
determined by local tradition came to be regarded as sacrosanct;
(2) the Russians adopted a suspicious and contemptuous attitude
toward the introduction of intellectual thought and knowledge
into questions of faith. All Russian people argued that the learning
that flourished in other Christian countries had not saved those
countries from heresies, and the light of reason had not prevented their faith from fading out. Vaguely remembering that
the roots of secular learning were to be found in the pagan
Greco-Roman world, the Russians thought with fastidious disdain that this learning was still nourished by the impurities of
that evil soil. Accordingly, our forefathers felt a timorous dis-
gust at the thought of "philosophical and rhetorical Hellenic
wisdom," which was the work of man's sinful intellect left to
its own resources. In an ancient Russian moral treatise we read:
"Everyone who loveth geometry is an abomination unto God.
It is a spiritual sin to learn astronomy and Hellenic books. Following his reason, a believer easily falls into various errors.
You must love simplicity more than wisdom. Do not seek that
which is beyond you, do not try that which is too deep for you,
but hold to the ready-made doctrine that has been given you
by God."

Texts in school copybooks included the following instructions: "Brothers, do not indulge in high-flown reflections! If you are asked, do you know philosophy, answer: I have not run Hellenic races, have not read the rhetoricians' astronomy, have not kept company with wise philosophers, and have not set eyes on philosophy; I am learning the books of gracious law as to how I may cleanse my sinful soul of sins."

Such a view encouraged the complacency of ignorance. "I am unskilled in words but not in reason," an ancient Russian scribe wrote about himself. "I have not been taught dialectics, rhetoric, and philosophy, but I have the mind of Christ." The old Russian ecclesiastical community was thus losing the means of correcting its errors and indeed any incentive to do so.

I have put before you the views firmly held by Muscovite church people in the seventeenth century. In this naïve form they were the common people's views, though a large section of the rank-and-file clergy, both priests and monks, shared them. Among the hierarchs they were expressed less crudely, but formed part of the church's general attitude. While celebrating the divine liturgy with a visiting Greek bishop or even patriarch, and carefully watching his every movement, our ecclesiastical authorities with magnanimous condescension pointed out to him then and there every slight deviation from the ritual adopted in Moscow: "That's not the way we do things, that's not the custom of our true Orthodox Christian Church." These differences in procedure confirmed the Russian hierarchs' sense of superiority to the Greeks in matters of ritual, and, content with this, they did not trouble about the offense that their altercations during the service gave to the congregation.

It was quite natural and indeed psychologically inevitable that the Russians loved the church rites in which they had been brought up, and that their understanding of religion was conditioned by this attachment to ritual. It was a sign of the people's historical age, and not of an organic or chronic disease of their religious feeling. The organic vice of the church people of ancient Russia was to consider themselves the only true believers in the world, and their conception of God the only correct one.

They thought of the Creator of the universe as their own Russian God, belonging solely to them and unknown to anyone else, and ascribed universal character to their local denomination. Having adopted this complacent attitude, they regarded their local church rites and customs as holy and inviolable, and took their own religious ideas to be the norm and criterion of human knowledge of God. When these views came into conflict with the policy of the state, their adherents clung to them all the more fervently.

We have seen that with the enthronement of the new dynasty, several political and economic innovations were introduced in order to organize national defense and the state economy. A need was felt for new technical devices, which had to be borrowed from other countries, and the government called in numbers of foreigners, including Lutherans and Calvinists. True, they were called in to train soldiers, make guns, and build factories, and all this had very little to do with moral ideas, and still less with religious ones. But the people of ancient Russia with their concrete way of thinking were not accustomed to discriminate between practical relations, could not and would not draw fine distinctions between the different aspects of life. If a German was in command of Russian servicemen and taught them his military craft, that meant that one had to dress in German fashion, shave off one's beard, accept the German faith, smoke tobacco, drink milk on Wednesdays and Fridays,[2] and abandon one's old beliefs. A Russian man's conscience hesitated at the choice between the native tradition and the German Settlement.

By the middle of the seventeenth century all this made the Russian community extremely anxious and suspicious, and that mood showed itself plainly on every occasion. In 1648, when the young Tsar Alexei was going to be married, rumors spread through Moscow that the old-time faith would soon come to an end and foreign customs be introduced. In such a mood, the attempt to rectify church rites and revise the text of liturgical books may well have seemed to the perplexed and easily alarmed

---

[2] Wednesdays and Fridays are fast days for the Orthodox. [Translator's note.]

community an attack upon faith itself. It so happened that the work of correction was undertaken by a hierarch whose temperament made him likely to bring the tension to highest pitch. Patriarch Nikon, consecrated to that rank in 1652, deserves as a person to have some attention given to him in this brief account of the schism.

He was born in 1605 into a peasant family. Thanks to being literate, he became a village priest, but circumstances led him to take monastic vows early in life, and he disciplined himself by the stern ordeal of ascetic life in the northern monasteries. He had a great gift for influencing people and thus acquired the unbounded confidence of the Tsar. In 1648 he was appointed Metropolitan of Novgorod, and finally, at the age of forty-seven, he became Patriarch of All Russia.

Among seventeenth-century Russians I know no one of greater stature and more pronounced individuality than Nikon. But he is not easy to understand. His was a complex nature and a difficult temperament. In quiet times and everyday life he was irritable, capricious, hot-tempered, domineering, and, above all, proud and vain. But these qualities could scarcely have been his real, essential characteristics. He could exercise a tremendous moral influence, which people suffering from personal vanity are incapable of doing. He was thought to be hardhearted because he was a fierce fighter, but hostility distressed him, and he readily forgave his enemies if they showed a desire to meet him halfway. To obstinate enemies Nikon was cruel, but he forgot everything at the sight of human suffering and tears. To do good, to help the weak and ailing were to him not so much pastoral duties as the instinctive responses of a kind heart.

His moral and intellectual powers fitted him to be a doer of great deeds, though not of lesser ones. Things that everyone could do he did worse than anyone else; but he could and wanted to do things—whether good or bad—that no one else could tackle. His behavior in Novgorod in 1650, when he took a beating from the rebels in order to bring them to their senses, and again during the Moscow plague of 1654, when in the Tsar's absence he rescued the royal family from the infected city, shows remarkable courage and self-possession, but the merest trifles of everyday life easily threw him off balance and made him lose his temper. A momentary impression often developed into a settled mood. At moments when all his intellectual resources were needed to deal with difficulties of his own making, he occupied himself with matters of no importance and was ready to make a great fuss about nothing. After being condemned and banished to the Ferapontov Monastery, he often received presents from the Tsar. On one occasion the Tsar sent him a quantity of excellent fish. Nikon took offense and reproached the Tsar for not having sent vegetables, grapes in syrup, and apples.

When he was in a good humor, he was resourceful and witty, but when he was aggrieved or annoyed, he became utterly tactless· and took the fancies of his embittered imagination for realities. While in exile Nikon began treating the sick and he could not resist taunting the Tsar with stories of his miraculous healings. He sent the Tsar a list of people he had cured and told the messenger that he had heard a voice from above saying, "The patriarchate has been taken from thee, and the cup of healing given thee instead: heal the sick!"

Nikon was one of those people who calmly endure agonies of pain but are reduced to despair by a pinprick. He had a weakness from which a good many strong but inwardly undisciplined people suffer: quietness bored him; he could not wait in patience. He needed perpetual agitation, the excitement of carrying out a bold idea or a broadly conceived plan, or simply of quarreling with his opponents. He was like a sail, which reveals its true identity only in the wind, but in calm weather flaps about the mast like a useless rag.

Chapter XV

The Church Schism

Nikon became Patriarch of the Russian church when he was in the prime of life and at the height of his powers. He was at once plunged into a turbid whirlpool of conflicting strivings, political plans, ecclesiastical misunderstandings, and court intrigues. The state was preparing to wage war upon Poland, to settle accounts with it overdue since the Time of Troubles and to defend western Russia from the Roman Catholic onslaught conducted under the Polish flag. To succeed in this struggle Russia needed the Protestants' military skill and industrial guidance. This created a twofold care for the Russian church hierarchy. It was necessary to encourage the government in its struggle with the Roman Catholics and to restrain it from being attracted by the Protestants.

Under the pressure of this difficulty the stagnant ecclesiastical mentality began to show signs of life. In preparation for the struggle, the Russian church community grew vigilant. It hastened to set itself to rights, collect its forces, pay more attention to its failings. Stern decrees were issued against superstitions, pagan customs, unseemly ways of spending feast days, boxing matches, lewd shows, and drunkenness, against the clergy's ignorance and irregularities in church services. Haste was made to sweep out the rubbish that through negligence had been accumulating together with church riches for six and a half centuries. The church began to look for allies. The state needed German craftsmen; the church began to feel the need of Greek or Kiev teachers.

Relations with the Greeks had improved. The former suspicious and contemptuous attitudes because of their tarnished faith disappeared, and now they were regarded in Moscow as strictly Orthodox. Communication with the Eastern hierarchs grew more lively. They came to Moscow more and more often with petitions and suggestions, and the Moscow clergy more and more often appealed to the Greek bishops about church needs and perplexities. The independent Russian church regarded Constantinople with due reverence as its former metropolis. The opinion of the Eastern patriarchs was taken to be that of the universal church. No questions of ecclesiastical importance were settled without their consent.

The Greeks responded to Moscow's appeals. While Moscow was seeking light from the Orthodox East, the Greeks urged that it should itself become a source of light, a nursery of spiritual enlightenment for the whole Orthodox world, should open a school for higher theological education and organize a Greek printing press. At the same time the writings of Kiev scholars were in demand and their services were made use of trustfully. But it was easier to collect all these spiritual resources than to unite and organize them for concerted work. The Kiev scholars and learned Greeks came to Moscow as proud guests whose cultural superiority was a standing reproach to their hosts.

Such court champions of Western culture as Morozov and Rtishchev valued Germans as craftsmen and welcomed Greeks and Kievans as church teachers. They helped Nikon's predecessor, Patriarch Joseph, who was also in favor of the new tendencies. Together with the Tsar's confessor, Stefan Vonifatiev, he was busy establishing a school and publishing translations of educational books. In order to spread better morals and ideas among the masses, Stefan called popular preachers to Moscow from different parts of Russia—the priests Ivan Neronov from Nizhni Novgorod, Daniel from Kostroma, Loggin from Murom, Avvakum from Iurievets-Povolzhsky, Lazar from Romanov-Borisoglebsk. Nikon too, for the time being, belonged to this group, silently taking stock of his companions—his future enemies.

But Rtishchev was suspected of heresy because of his love for learning, and the apparently humble and good-natured Vonifatiev, after the first conflict with the Patriarch, called him and the whole of the Holy Synod "wolves and malefactors" and said that in the state of Muscovy there was no Christian church at all. The Patriarch complained to the Tsar, pointing out that according to the Ulozhenie blasphemy against the holy apostolic church was punishable by death. Finally the men whom the Tsar's confessor had selected as helpers ceased to obey him, "spoke cruelly against him," and with fanatical vehemence hurled themselves in the name of the Russian God upon the Patriarch and all innovators with their new books, ideas, systems, and teachers, whether Greek or German or Kievan.

The Tsar's confessor was right in saying that there was no Christian church in Muscovy, if he meant by "church" ecclesiastical discipline and decorum. Utter disorder reigned there. The believers, though pious and well trained, found it tedious to stand through long church services. To please them, the clergy introduced an unauthorized quick method of conducting the services. Different prayers were said or sung at the same time, or the deacon recited the litany while the sacristan was reading and the priest intoned his part. One could not make out a word, but this did not matter so long as nothing was omitted. Such unseemly services had been strictly forbidden by the Stoglav council in 1551, but the clergy did not obey the council's injunction. It would have been sufficient to impose disciplinary measures on the disobedient clergy, but at the Tsar's order the Patriarch convened a new council to deal with the subject. The new council, afraid of displeasing the clergy and the laity, sanctioned the irregularities. The discontent of the people who cared for church decorum made it imperative to call another council in 1651, and this council canceled the previous decision and forbade polyphonous services.

Church hierarchs were afraid of their flock and even of the subordinate clergy, and the flock had a low opinion of its pastors. Swayed by variable influences, they constantly shifted their ground, and in their legislative activity were as much at a loss as the government.

One might have admired the spiritual strength that enabled Nikon, in the midst of these ecclesiastical discussions raging around him like a stream in flood, to work out a clear idea of the universal church—had he given that idea a more profound meaning. When he began governing the Russian church he was firmly determined to reestablish complete agreement between it and the Greek church by abolishing ritualistic peculiarities in which the Russian differed from the Greek. There was no lack of reminders to confirm his conviction that such agreement was essential. Eastern hierarchs, who came to Moscow more and more often in the seventeenth century, reproachfully pointed out to the Russian clergy that these peculiarities were local innovations, and that they could break up the unity between the Orthodox churches. Something that happened shortly before Nikon's accession to the patriarchate pointed to the reality of such a danger. The monks of all the Greek monasteries on Mount Athos declared in council that it was heretical to cross oneself with two fingers, burned the Muscovite liturgical books that prescribed this, and wanted to burn as well the monk in whose possession the books were found.

It may be guessed what personal motives prompted Nikon's efforts to consolidate the close communion between the Russian and the Eastern churches, between the Russian and the ecumenical patriarchs. He understood that the feeble attempts at reform made by Patriarch Joseph and his supporters would not save the Russian church from its unhappy position. He saw with his own eyes that the Patriarch of All Russia might play the part of a pitiable supernumerary on the court stage. He knew from experience how easily a forceful man could turn the young

Tsar in any direction; the former Patriarch, toward the end of his life, had expected to be dismissed any day. Nikon's explosive pride made him indignant at the thought that he too might become a plaything in the hands of a presumptuous royal confessor. Even at the height of his Moscow apostolic throne Nikon must have felt threatened and sought support outside, in the Orthodox East, in close union with his fellow patriarchs. The authority of the universal church, hard as it was for the Russian ecclesiastics to grasp the idea of it, inspired a certain amount of awe in the timorously pious Muscovite conscience.

Nikon was wont to use his imagination in developing every idea, every feeling that possessed him, and accordingly he tried to make himself a Greek, forgetting his native Nizhni Novgorod. At the church council of 1655 he declared that, although he was Russian and the son of a Russian, his faith and convictions were Greek. In that same year, after a solemn service in Uspensky Cathedral, he took off his Russian monastic cap before all the congregation and put on the Greek one. This provoked a great murmur instead of a smile, as a challenge to all who believed that everything in the Russian church had been handed down from the apostles and inspired by the Holy Ghost. Nikon even wanted to have his meals cooked in the Greek way. In 1658 the archimandrite and the steward of the Greek monastery in Nikolsky Street prepared dinner for the Patriarch "in Greek fashion," and each was rewarded by half a ruble (about seven rubles in our currency).

Having found a support outside the range of Moscow's power, Nikon wanted to be not simply Patriarch of Moscow and All Russia, but one of the patriarchs of the universal church, and to act independently. He wanted to impart real force to the title of "great sovereign," which he shared with the Tsar, no matter whether it was a graciously condoned usurpation or the Tsar's incautiously given favor to his "special friend." When Nikon was reproached for papistry he answered without any embarrassment: "Why not revere even the Pope for what is good in him? The chief apostles, Peter and Paul, are there, and he is in their service."

Nikon threw out a challenge to the whole past of the Russian church as well as to his contemporary Russian environment. He did not want to take this into consideration. Everything local and temporary had to give way before the bearer of the eternal and universal idea. His problem was to establish complete concord and unity between the Russian and other local Orthodox churches. Once this was achieved, he, the Patriarch of All Russia, would know how to take a fitting place among the hierarchs of the universal church.

Nikon tackled the business of reestablishing that concord with his usual passionate zeal. Before accepting the patriarchal throne he bound the government and the people by a solemn oath to let him arrange church affairs, and thus obtained, so to speak, ecclesiastical dictatorship. After being consecrated as patriarch he shut himself up in his library for many days to examine and study the old books and debatable texts. He found there, among other things, the charter establishing a patriarchate in Russia, signed in 1593 by Eastern patriarchs. It said that the Patriarch of Moscow, as brother of all other Orthodox patriarchs, must be in complete agreement with them and stamp out all innovations within the pale of his church, for innovations always cause ecclesiastical dissension. Nikon was overwhelmed by fear at the thought that the Russian church might have been guilty of some deviation from the Greek Orthodox law. He began examining the Slavonic texts of the Creed and of the liturgical books and comparing them with the Greek, and he found differences and alterations everywhere.

Feeling it his duty to remain in agreement with the Greek church, he decided to undertake the correction of Russian liturgical books and church rites. Just before Lent, without calling a council, he sent on his own authority an order to all the churches as to how many prostrations were to be made in reading the Lenten prayer of St. Ephraim the Syrian, and also commanding that the sign of the cross be made with three fingers and not with two. After that he turned against Russian icon painters of his time, who had abandoned the Byzantine patterns and adopted the methods of Roman Catholic painters. Next, with the help of monks from southwestern Russia, he replaced the ancient Muscovite unison singing by the new Kievan polyphonic part singing, and he also introduced the unheard-of custom of extemporaneous preaching in church. In ancient Russia such sermons were regarded with suspicion and thought to be a sign of the preacher's self-conceit. The proper thing was to read the sermons of the holy fathers, though as a rule they were not read for fear they would make the service too long. Nikon liked preaching and was very good at it. Following his example, the visiting clergy from Kiev also began preaching in Moscow churches, and sometimes spoke on contemporary subjects.

It is easy to understand the perplexity these innovations must have produced in Orthodox Russian minds already anxious and uneasy. Nikon's commands implied that the Russian Orthodox community had not yet learned how to pray or to paint icons, and that the clergy did not know how to officiate properly. This perplexity was well expressed by one of the first leaders of the schism, the archpriest Avvakum. When the order about the Lenten prostrations was issued, "we gathered together and pondered," he wrote. "We saw that winter was coming; our hearts were chilled within and our legs trembled." The perplexity was bound to increase when Nikon embarked upon the correction of liturgical books, although he did so with the sanction of the church council of 1654, under the presidency of the Tsar himself and in the presence of the Boyars' Council. It was decided that before going into print, new liturgical books should be revised in accordance with the old Slavonic and Greek texts. In ancient Russia liturgical books were regarded almost as Holy Writ, and therefore Nikon's enterprise raised in people's minds the questions: Can the scriptures be wrong too? And if so, what remains right in our church?

The anxiety was further increased by the fact that the Patriarch issued all his orders peremptorily and ostentatiously, without preparing the public for them, and accompanied them with stern measures against the disobedient. Rudely to silence an opponent, to abuse, anathematize, or beat him—these were the usual methods of his despotic rule. He treated even a bishop this way. At the council of 1654, Bishop Paul of Kolomna argued against him, and without a trial by the council he was deprived of his see and condemned to be "cruelly beaten" and exiled. He went out of his mind and died an unknown death.

A contemporary tells of how Nikon combatted the new icon painting. In 1654, when the Tsar was away on a campaign, the Patriarch ordered a house-to-house search in Moscow, and all icons of the new pattern were to be confiscated, even from the houses of the nobility. The eyes of the confiscated holy images were gouged out and the disfigured icons were carried about the city while a decree was read out, threatening with severe penalties all who painted such icons in the future.

Soon after this there was an outbreak of the plague in Moscow, and also an eclipse of the sun. The townspeople were in great agitation. They held public meetings and railed against the Patriarch, saying that the eclipse and the pestilence were a punishment from God for the impiety of Nikon, who desecrated holy icons; they even talked of killing the iconoclast.

On the first Sunday in Lent in 1655 the Patriarch was celebrating a solemn liturgy at Uspensky Cathedral in the presence of the Patriarchs of Serbia and Antioch, who happened to be in Moscow at the time. After the service Nikon read a homily about the veneration of icons, made an impressive speech against the new Russian icon painting, and excommunicated all who painted icons in the new style or kept them in their houses. Meanwhile the confiscated icons were brought to him. Showing each one to the people, he flung it on the floor with such force that it was shattered. At last he commanded that the faulty icons be burned. Tsar Alexei, who had been humbly listening to the Patriarch all this time, went up to him and said quietly, "No, Father, do not have them burned. Better let them be buried in the ground."

The worst of it all was that Nikon's fierce attack upon the familiar church customs and rites was not due to any real belief that they were detrimental to the soul and that the new ones were salutary. Until the question of revising the books was raised, he too crossed himself with two fingers instead of three, and even afterward he allowed the alleluia to be sung in Uspensky Cathedral either three or two times in succession. Toward the end of his patriarchate, in a conversation about the old and the revised liturgical books with his former opponent Ivan Neronov, who had by then submitted to the church, Nikon said, "Both are good. Use whichever you prefer, it makes no difference. . . ." So it was not rites as such that mattered, but disobedience to ecclesiastical authority. Neronov and his companions were anathematized by the council of 1656 not because they made the sign of the cross with two fingers and adhered to the old liturgical books, but because they disobeyed the council. The question of ritual was replaced by that of obedience to ecclesiastical authorities. It was on this account that the council of 1666–67 excommunicated the Old Believers.

The position, then, was this: Church authorities made obligatory some rites unfamiliar to the flock. Those who disobeyed the injunctions were excommunicated, not for observing the old ritual, but for disobedience. If, however, they repented, they were reunited with the church and allowed to keep the old rites. It was something like a simulated attack in a military camp, accustoming the soldiers to be always on the alert. But such tests of ecclesiastical obedience mean playing with the religious conscience of the flock. The archpriest Avvakum and others found that their conscience was not sufficiently flexible for the purpose, and they became leaders of the schism. But there would have been no schism at all had Nikon said to the whole of his flock at the very beginning what he said to Neronov, who had submitted to the church.

Nikon greatly helped the success of the schism by failing to understand the people with whom he had to deal and undervaluing his early opponents, Neronov, Avvakum, and others. They were not only popular preachers, but national agitators. They displayed their didactic gifts in expounding patristic writings, especially St. John Chrysostom's book of homilies called *Margarites*. While Neronov was priest in Nizhni Novgorod he never parted with this book; he read and interpreted it from the pulpit, in the streets and town squares, attracting large crowds. There is no telling whether there was much theological value in these exegetic improvisations, but there certainly was fervor enough and to spare. He was the bane of clowns and jesters, and inveighed against the vices of the laity, against drunkenness among the clergy, and even against the voevodas' abuses—for which he was beaten more than once. When he became vicar of Kazan Cathedral in Moscow, the whole capital gathered to hear him, filling the body of the building and the portico, and clinging to the windows from outside. The Tsar himself came with his family to hear the preacher. Other members of the group centered around the Tsar's confessor resembled Neronov. Popularity and the good will of the court made them inordinately insolent. They were accustomed to treat Nikon as one of themselves before he was made a patriarch, and now they became rude to him, reviled him at the council, denounced him to the Tsar.

The Patriarch retaliated with cruel penalties. The archpriest Loggin of Murom, while visiting the voevoda's house and giving a blessing to his wife, asked her if she had put chalk on her face. The host was offended and said, "You complain about chalk, but even icons can't be painted without it." Other guests echoed his sentiments.

Loggin answered, "If the pigments used in icon painting were put on your ugly faces you wouldn't like it. The Saviour, the Holy Mother of God, and all the saints are more worthy of honor than their icons."

The voevoda immediately reported to Moscow that Loggin reviled the icons of the Saviour, Our Lady, and all the saints. Without investigating the absurd incident, Nikon imposed strict confinement on Loggin, in revenge for his having in the past accused Nikon of pride and self-conceit. By introducing personal hostility into ecclesiastical affairs, Nikon both lowered his pastoral position and bestowed the martyr's crown upon his opponents. Banishing them to various parts of Russia, he supplied remote corners of it with skilled propagandists of the Old Belief.

Thus Nikon failed to justify his dictatorship and to reorganize church affairs; on the contrary, he threw them into worse confusion. Power and court society extinguished the spiritual powers with which nature had generously endowed him. He brought nothing reformative or renovating into his pastoral activity, least of all into his revision of liturgical books and rites. Revision does not mean reform, and if corrections of printers' errors were mistaken by a section of the clergy and the laity for new dogma and caused a church rebellion, Nikon himself, with the whole hierarchy of the Russian church, was first and foremost to blame for it. Why did he undertake such a work, knowing what would come of it? And what had the Russian pastors been doing for centuries if they had not taught their flock to distinguish a dogma from a twice-repeated alleluia? Nikon did not rebuild the church order in a new spirit or new direction, but merely replaced one set of forms by another. The very idea of the universal church, in the name of which he began all this clamorous business, was understood by him in too narrow a sense, in its ritualistic aspect only. He could neither convey a broader interpretation of that idea to the Russian religious community nor give a permanent expression to it through some ecumenical ordinance of a church council—and he ended by calling the Eastern patriarchs who were his judges "slaves of the Sultan, thieves and vagabonds." In his zeal for the unity of the universal church he broke up that of his own national church. Nikon overstrained the basic cord in the Russian ecclesiastical mentality—religious inertia. It snapped with the tension, and on the recoil it gave a sharp cut to him and to the ruling Russian hierarchs who approved of his work.

In addition to his own methods of action, Nikon had two auxiliaries in his struggle against the Old Believers' obduracy, but he used them in such a way that they greatly helped the schismatics' success. To begin with, Nikon's closest collaborators in the introduction of his ecclesiastical innovations were scholars from south Russia, known to have been in intimate contact with Polish Roman Catholicism; also there were Greeks like Arseni, Nikon's trusted literary editor. He was a wanderer, a convert from Catholicism or, some said, from Islam, brought by Nikon

from the Solovetsky Monastery, where he was undergoing reformatory discipline—"an exiled monk tainted with dark Roman
errors," as he was described.

To make matters worse, ecclesiastical innovations were introduced to the accompaniment of sharp rebukes directed at the
Russians by the Ukrainians and the Greeks. The Kiev monks
perpetually piqued the Muscovites and especially the clergy,
maliciously taunting them with ignorance and continually saying that they knew nothing about grammar, rhetoric, and other
scholarly subjects. Simeon Polotsky solemnly declared from
the pulpit of Uspensky Cathedral that in Russia wisdom had nowhere to lay its head, that Russians avoided study and despised
wisdom, which is of God. He spoke of ignoramuses who presumed to call themselves teachers though they had never been
anyone's pupils: "Truly they are not masters, but disasters."

Such phrases were aimed, in the first place, at the Moscow
priesthood. Goaded by these accusations, the guardians of the
ancient Russian faith angrily asked themselves were they really
so ignorant, and was all this imported learning truly necessary
for preserving the treasure entrusted to the Russian church? The
people were already in an anxious and suspicious mood because
of this influx of foreigners, and now on top of it all the national
dignity was being injured, attacked by their own Orthodox
brethren. Finally, at the council of 1666–67, Russian and Eastern
hierarchs anathematized several rites and customs sanctioned by
the Stoglav council of 1551 and solemnly declared that the
teachers of that council had "in their ignorance reasoned
unwisely."

Thus Orthodox hierarchs of the seventeenth century condemned the ancient Russian ecclesiastical tradition, which was
regarded as universal by a considerable portion of the community. One can well understand the confusion that all these
events created in Orthodox Russian minds, nurtured in religious
complacency and now so uneasy. It was this confusion that led
to the schism, as soon as the explanation of the incomprehensible
ecclesiastical innovations was discovered. The part taken in
Nikon's work by Greeks and scholars from western Russia, sus-

pected of connections with the Latins; their insistence on teaching subjects that flourished in the Latin West; the fact that changes in church ritual were a sequel to the mundane Western novelties; the government's foolish predilection for borrowing from the West, whence they called in so many heretics and abundantly fed them—all this made the Russian public surmise that church innovations were due to secret Roman Catholic propaganda and that Nikon and his Greek and Kiev collaborators were agents of the Pope, who was once more planning to Latinize the Russian Orthodox people.

It is sufficient to glance at the early specimens of the Old Believers' literature to see that the first champions of the schism and their disciples were influenced by precisely such fears and impressions. Among those specimens a prominent place must be assigned to two petitions submitted to Tsar Alexei—one in 1662 by a monk named Savvati and the other in 1667 by the brotherhood of the Solovetsky Monastery, who had rebelled against Nikon's innovations. Editors of the newly revised liturgical books taunted the partisans of the old unrevised ones with their ignorance of grammar and rhetoric. In answer to this, the monk Savvati writes to the Tsar: "Yea, Sire, they have lost their bearings and are spoiling the books, and it is only recently that they have gone astray. Their faulty grammar and the Ukrainian newcomers have driven them crazy."

Nikon's innovations were approved by the Greek hierarchs, but the purity of the Greeks' Orthodoxy had long been suspect in Russia, and the Solovetsky monks, commenting on the appeal to the authority of the Greeks, said in their petition that Greek teachers themselves did not know how to make the sign of the cross properly and did not wear crosses around their necks; they ought to learn piety from the Russian people, and not come teaching it to us. Church innovators affirmed that the rites of the Russian church were not correct, but the petition defends the old tradition. Confusing ritual with doctrine, it says: "Now new religious instructors teach us a new, unheard-of faith, as though we were some outlandish tribe knowing nothing about God. Maybe we shall have to be baptized again and throw out of the church the icons of holy saints and miracle workers; as it is, foreigners laugh at us and say that to this day we haven't learned what Christian faith is."

Evidently church innovations touched the believers on a tender spot—their national and ecclesiastical self-complacency. The archpriest Avvakum, one of the first and most fervent champions of the schism, expounded better than anyone else its motives and basic position. His behavior and his writings express the very essence of the old Russian religious views at that period. Avvakum thought the disaster that befell the Russian church was caused by the new Western influences and new books. "Alas, poor Russia!" he exclaims in one of his writings. "What possessed you to seek Latin customs and German practices?" He believed that the Eastern ecclesiastics, called in to teach and guide Russia in its religious perplexities, themselves needed teaching and guiding that only Russia could give them.

In his autobiography he describes a matchless scene that took place at the church council of 1667, which sat in judgment upon him. The Eastern patriarchs said to him: "You are stubborn, archpriest! All our Palestinians and Serbs and Albanians and Romans and Poles—all make the sign of the cross with three fingers. You alone are stubborn and cross yourself with two fingers. That isn't right."

Avvakum retorted: "Ecumenical teachers! Rome fell long ago, and the Poles perished with it, remaining to the end enemies of the Christians. And your Orthodoxy, too, is not pure. The violence of the Turkish Mohammed has made you frail. So in the future come and learn from us. By the grace of God we have autocracy, and until Nikon the apostate appeared, our Orthodoxy was pure and undefiled and the church was at peace." Then Avvakum walked to the doors of the hall and lay on his side on the floor, saying, "You go on sitting, and I'll lie down for a bit."

Some people laughed and said, "The archpriest is being silly. He does not respect the patriarchs."

Avvakum continued: "We are fools for Christ's sake. You are

honorable, but we are despised; we are weak, but you are strong."

Avvakum expressed as follows the main idea that guided the early leaders of the schism: "Although I am a foolish and untutored man, I do know that everything handed down to the church by the holy fathers is pure and holy. I hold it unto death as it was given me. I change nothing in the eternal truth. It was laid down before our time—let it lie so forever and ever."

These features of the ancient Russian faith, to which the events of the seventeenth century gave a morbidly fanatical and one-sided character, found full expression in the schism and formed the basis of the Old Believers' religious attitude.

These, then, are the origins of the schism. Let us recall once more what has been said, so as to form a clear estimate of the facts and of their significance.

External calamities that befell Russia and Byzantium isolated the Russian church and weakened its spiritual intercourse with the churches of the Orthodox East. This obscured in Russian minds the idea of the universal church, and they substituted for it the thought that the Russian church alone was orthodox and took the place of the universal church. The authority of universal Christianity was replaced by the authority of the local ecclesiastical tradition. Russia's isolation encouraged the development of local peculiarities in church practice, and the exaggerated value ascribed to local ecclesiastical tradition made those peculiarities appear sacrosanct.

The new temptations and spiritual dangers brought in by the Western influence roused the attention of the Russian church community. Its leaders felt the need to muster their forces for the impending struggle, to look around and put their house in order, to secure the help of other Orthodox communities, and to that end to enter into closer relations with them. Thus by the middle of the seventeenth century the vanishing idea of the universal church was revived in the best Russian minds. It inspired Patriarch Nikon's impetuous and impatient activity aimed at establishing greater uniformity of ritual between the Russian

and the Eastern Orthodox churches. The idea itself, the circumstances in which it was revived, and especially the methods of
realizing it greatly alarmed Russian church people. The idea of a
universal church disturbed their religious self-satisfaction, their
national and ecclesiastical self-conceit. Fitful and angry attacks
upon the familiar rites wounded national pride and gave be-
wildered minds no time to think things over and break with the
old habits and prejudices. The observation that the striving for
reform first arose under the Latin influence suggested the terrible thought that the destruction of Russia's ancient traditions
was the secret handiwork of insidious Rome.

And so the schism as a religious attitude and as a protest
against Western influence sprang from the conflict between the
reform movement in the church and the state, the psychological
significance of church ritual for the masses, and the people's idea
of the position occupied by the Russian church in the Christian
world. In all these respects the schism was simply a product of
the national psychology, and as such it contained three basic elements: (1) ecclesiastical self-conceit, owing to which Orthodoxy
came to be regarded as a national monopoly (nationalization of
the universal church); (2) inertness and timidity of theological
thought, which failed to assimilate the spirit of new, alien knowledge and feared it as evil Latin wizardry (fear of Rome); (3)
inertness of religious feeling, which was incapable of renouncing
the habitual forms that aroused and expressed it (pagan ritualism). The Old Believers' opposition to the church became open
rebellion when they refused to obey ecclesiastical authorities
whom they supposed to be in sympathy with Rome. Then at
the Moscow council of 1667 Russian hierarchs and two Eastern
patriarchs excommunicated the rebellious Old Believers for their
disobedience to the canonical authority of the church pastors.
From that moment the schism, in addition to being a religious
attitude, gave rise to a distinct ecclesiastical community separate
from the established church.

The effect of the schism upon the spread of education and
of Western influence soon made itself felt. That influence was
directly responsible for the reaction that eventually led to the

schism, and now the schism indirectly helped to further the secular enlightenment it had so fiercely attacked. Both the Greek
and the western Russian scholars insisted that the Russian people's ignorance was the basic cause of the schism, and now the
question of establishing a proper permanent school was raised in
earnest. But of what type and tendency should it be? With regard to this question, the schism helped to clarify the difference
between two views that, through a misunderstanding, had been
merged into one. So long as the people's attention was centered
upon foreign heretics—papists and Lutherans—the government
hospitably invited both Greeks and western Russian scholars to
help in the struggle against them. Epiphani Slavinetsky, who
taught Greek, and Simeon Polotsky, who taught Latin, were both
made welcome. But now there appeared home-grown heretics—
Old Believers, who broke away from the church because of its
Latin innovations, and "bread worshipers," who upheld the
Roman teaching about the exact moment of the transubstantiation of the Holy Gifts, a heresy supposed to have been started
by a "Latinist," Simeon Polotsky.

There arose a heated argument as to the correct attitude
toward the two languages: Which of them should be put at the
basis of Orthodox school education? It was not simply a question
of Greek or Latin grammar and vocabulary, but of different systems of education, mutually hostile cultures, irreconcilable points
of view. Latin stood for "free learning," the "freedom of research" mentioned in the benedictory charter given to the parishioners of the Church of St. John the Divine. It included
studies that satisfied both the higher spiritual needs of man and
his everyday practical needs. Greek represented "sacred philosophy"—grammar, rhetoric, dialectic as auxiliaries to the understanding of God's word.

Of course, the Hellenists won. In Tsar Feodor's reign there
was printed an article in defense of Greek that began by stating
the question and answering it: "Is it more useful for us to learn
grammar, rhetoric, philosophy, theology, and the art of versification and derive therefrom a knowledge of Holy Scriptures, or,
studying these subtleties, merely strive to serve God and to

understand the meaning of Holy Writ by reading it? It is better for Russian people to learn Greek rather than Latin."

The author of the article thinks that Latin studies are decidedly harmful, and threatens us with two great dangers. Hearing that Latin has been taken up in Moscow, the sly Jesuits will creep in with their incomprehensible syllogisms and "soul-corrupting" arguments, and then the same thing will happen to Great Russia as happened to the Ukraine, where "almost all are unionists, and very few Orthodox are left." Besides, if the people, especially "the simple," hear about Latin studies, "I do not know what good will come of it," says the author, "and may God save us from disaster."

In 1681 a school was opened in Nikolsky Street, adjoining the printing house. It had two classes, one for the study of Greek and the other for the study of Slavonic. The school was under the guidance of a regular priest, Timothy, who had long lived in the East, and two Greek masters. At first there were only 30 pupils of various social positions, but in 1686 their number increased to 233. Later on a school for more advanced studies was founded, the Slavonic Greco-Latin Academy, opened in 1686 at the Zaikonospassky Monastery, also on Nikolsky Street. The Likhud brothers, Greeks were called in to superintend it. Senior pupils were transferred to it from the printing-house school, which became a lower section of the academy. In 1635 Polotsky's pupil Sylvester Medvedev submitted to the regent, Tsarevna Sofia, the academy statute, drafted in Tsar Feodor's reign. Certain points in the statute bring out clearly the aims and character of the academy. It was open to all classes of society and gave the pupils a rank in the civil service. Only Russians and Greeks were eligible for the posts of rector and tutors. Ukrainian Orthodox scholars could be appointed to these posts only on the recommendation of pious and trustworthy people.

It was strictly forbidden to keep foreign tutors in one's house and to possess and to read Polish, Latin, German, and other heretical books. The academy was to watch over this, as well as over non-Orthodox propaganda among the Orthodox. It also judged those who were accused of blaspheming against the

Orthodox faith. This offense was punishable by burning. And so, long years of effort to create in Moscow a center of "free studies" for the whole Orthodox East finally produced an ecclesiastical educational institution of a police character, which became the prototype of church schools. Appointed to guard Orthodoxy against all European heretics, the academy, having no preparatory schools, could not exercise its educational influences upon the masses and was of no danger to the schism.

The schism proved distinctly helpful to the Western tendencies that had brought it about. The ecclesiastical storm raised by Nikon did not affect by any means the whole of Russian society. The schism began among the clergy, and at first the struggle went on chiefly between the ruling hierarchy and that section of the community which was incited by agitators among the rank-and-file clergy to oppose Nikon's innovations in ritual. But even some of the bishops were at first against Nikon. The exiled bishop of Kolomna, Paul, while in exile mentioned three other bishops who had also remained true to the "old faith." Unanimity between the hierarchs was restored only when the dispute shifted from matters of ritual to canon law, and dealt with the flock's disobedience to its lawful pastors. Then the ruling prelates understood that it was not a question of an old or a new faith, but of either keeping their sees without the flock or of following the flock and losing the see, like Paul of Kolomna.

Most people, including the Tsar, were of two minds in the matter: they accepted the innovations in obedience to the church but were out of sympathy with the innovator because of his repellent character and methods of action; they were sorry for the victims of his fanaticism but could not approve his frenzied opponents' unseemly attacks upon authorities and institutions traditionally regarded as mainstays of morals and religion. Respectable people were bound to recoil at the scene that took place when the archpriest Loggin was being unfrocked. When his cloak and coat were removed, he spat at Nikon across the sanctuary threshold, shouted abuse, and, tearing off his skirt, hurled it in the Patriarch's face.

Thinking people tried to understand the issues at stake for themselves so as to find a point of support for their consciences, since the pastors failed to provide one. Michael Rtishchev (the father of the promoter of education) said to one of the first martyrs for the Old Belief, Princess Krusov: "What troubles me is that I don't know whether you are suffering in the cause of truth." He might also have asked himself whether they were being tormented in the cause of truth. Even Deacon Feodor, one of the first champions of the schism, fasted while he was in prison in order to discover what was wrong in the "old faith and right in the new." Some of these doubters became dissenters, but the majority found a solution in a compromise with their consciences. While remaining sincerely devoted to the church, they drew a line between it and its hierarchs, concealing complete indifference to the latter under customary outward respect.

The ruling political circles showed more resolution. They preserved a lasting memory of the way the head of the church hierarchy sought to put himself above the Tsar and at the tribunal of 1666, in the presence of Eastern patriarchs, abused the supreme ruler of the Muscovite state. Recognizing that nothing but trouble could be expected from such a hierarchy, the government decided—informally, by tacit consent—to leave it alone but not to let it have a share in ruling the state. This brought to an end the political part played by the clergy in ancient Russia— a part that had always been badly staged, and performed even worse—and one of the main obstacles to the spread of Western influence was thus removed.

The quarrel between the Tsar and the Patriarch was closely, though imperceptibly, connected with the church storm raised by Nikon, and therefore the effect it had on the political significance of the clergy may be regarded as a service that the schism indirectly rendered to the "Westernizers." It rendered them another and more direct service by weakening the effects of another obstacle to Peter's reforms, which were inspired by the Western influence. A suspicious attitude to the West was widespread in Russian society, and even the ruling circles, particularly susceptible to foreign influence, were still under the spell of the old native tradition. This slowed down the reform movement and weakened the innovators' energy. The schismatics lowered the prestige of that tradition by rebelling in its name against the church, and thus indirectly against the state.

The majority of church people now saw what bad feelings and propensities the old tradition could breed, and what dangers lay in a blind attachment to it. Leaders of the reform movement who still hesitated between the old national ways and the West could now with an easy conscience pursue their course more confidently and resolutely. This effect of the schism was particularly strong in the case of the chief reformer himself. In 1682, soon after Peter's election to the throne, the schismatics raised another mutiny in the name of the Old Belief (the dispute in the Granovitaia Hall on July 5). That occasion, as an impression of childhood, was engraved in Peter's memory for the rest of his life, and indissolubly bound together in his consciousness the ideas of ancient Russian tradition, schism, and mutiny. The tradition meant schism; schism meant mutiny; hence, ancient tradition meant mutiny. It is easy to see what attitude to the old Russian customs and ideas such a chain of reasoning created in the reformer's mind.

Chapter
XVI

Tsar Alexei

We have considered the movement toward reform that characterized Russian society in the seventeenth century. It remains to us now to consider the men who stood at the head of it. This is necessary in order to complete the picture. One of the two conflicting currents that agitated Russian society was driving it back to the old order of things, and the other was drawing it forward to dim and alien horizons. These mutually opposed tendencies gave rise to vague feelings and aspirations in the community at large, but in men who were in advance of it, those moods and strivings became clear-cut ideas to be carried out in practice. The study of such representative types will help us to understand more fully the kind of life that had bred them. They focused in themselves, as it were, and vividly exemplified interests and characteristics of their environment that escape notice in everyday life, where they only occasionally come to the surface as accidental individual peculiarities leading nowhere. I shall draw your attention to some of the men who stood in the forefront of the reform movement preparatory to Peter's work. The results achieved by this movement can be plainly seen from the fact that those men's aims and ideas became an integral part of Peter's program of reform, bequeathed to him by his predecessors.

The first place among those predecessors unquestionably belongs to Peter's father. He typifies the first stage of the reform movement, when its leaders had as yet no intention of breaking with the past and shattering the existing order of things. Tsar Alexei Mikhailovich's attitude might be described as that of a man who firmly rested one foot on the native Orthodox ground and lifted the other to cross the boundary—and permanently remained in this uncertain position. He belonged to the generation that was driven by necessity to look with care and anxiety at the heretical West in the hope of finding there means to overcome domestic difficulties without giving up the ideas, customs, and beliefs of his pious ancestors. His was the only generation that thought it possible. Neither the preceding nor the succeeding generations shared this view. In former days people were afraid to borrow even purely material comforts from the West, lest by doing so they impair the ancestral moral tradition cherished as a sacred heritage. Later on, this tradition was readily abandoned by many in order to relish Western comforts all the more.

Tsar Alexei and his contemporaries valued their Orthodox tradition no less than their ancestors had done. But for some time they were convinced that one could "wear a German coat and even watch a foreign entertainment while keeping intact such feelings and ideas as pious fear at the very thought of breaking fast on Christmas Eve before the first star appeared in the sky."

Tsar Alexei was born in 1629. He went through the whole course of ancient Russian education on "literary learning," as it was then called. According to custom, at the age of six he was set to learn the alphabet from a textbook specially compiled for him at the request of his grandfather, Patriarch Filaret, by the Patriarch's secretary, on the familiar pattern of ancient Russian elementary "readers." It contained the alphabet, the usual abbreviations, the Commandments, a short catechism, and so on. The

Tsarevich was taught, as was the custom of the Moscow court, by the secretary of one of the government departments. After a year the elementary reader was replaced by the Book of Hours, which after about five months was replaced by the Psalter. After another three months the study of the Acts of the Apostles was begun; after six more months the boy was taught to write. When he was nine years old the choirmaster of the palace choir began instructing him in the *Oktoikh*, a book of liturgical chants, and some eight months later he taught him the Holy Week chants, particularly difficult musically. At ten the Tsarevich had finished "the whole course of ancient Russian secondary education. He could easily read the hours in church and successfully join in the singing of the hymns and the canons. He had mastered the order of church services to the smallest detail, and could vie in this matter with any specialist from a monastery or even a cathedral.

In former days a tsarevich would probably have stopped at this, but Alexei was being educated at a time when people were becoming aware of a vague but persistent urge to go further, to probe the mysterious realm of Hellenic and Latin wisdom, which pious Russian scholars of an earlier period timidly passed by, protecting themselves by a spell and the sign of the cross. The Germans, having found their way into the ranks of the Russian army with their newfangled devices, wormed themselves into the palace nursery as well. As a child Alexei already had a toy horse of German workmanship, German pictures bought at the vegetable market for about a ruble and a half in our currency, and even a suit of armor made for him by a German craftsman, Peter Schalt. At the age of eleven or twelve the Tsarevich possessed a library of about thirteen volumes, most of them presents from his grandfather, tutors, and instructors. The books were chiefly copies of the scriptures and liturgical texts, but among them was a grammar printed in Lithuania, a book on cosmography, and a lexicon, also printed in Lithuania. The person in charge of Alexei's education was one of the foremost Russian boyars, Boris Ivanovich Morozov, who was greatly attracted by the western European ways. He introduced the method of visual demonstration into the Tsarevich's course of study, and familiarized him with certain subjects by means of German engravings. He brought a still more daring innovation into the Tsar's palace by dressing Tsarevich Alexei and his brother in German fashion.

In his mature years Tsar Alexei combined in a most attractive way the good qualities of an old-time Russian, loyal to ancient traditions, with a liking for useful and pleasant novelties. He was a pattern of piety—of the decorous, orderly, disciplined piety that the religious feeling of ancient Russia had so assiduously cultivated for centuries. He could rival any monk in the arts of praying and fasting. On Sundays, Tuesdays, Thursdays, and Saturdays in Lent and during the fast before Assumption the Tsar had only one meal a day, consisting of cabbage, mushrooms, and berries, without dressing. On Mondays, Wednesdays, and Fridays he did not eat anything during the fasts. In church he sometimes stood for five or six hours on end, made a thousand and sometimes fifteen hundred prostrations a day. He was a truly devout worshiper in the old Russian style, and fully and harmoniously combined spiritual and physical exertion in seeking salvation.

This piety had a powerful influence both on Tsar Alexei's political ideas and on his relations with people. Son and successor of a sovereign whose power was limited, Alexei was an autocrat and firmly held the exalted view of a tsar's authority worked out by the old Muscovite community. The ideas of Ivan the Terrible find an echo in the words of Tsar Alexei: "God has blessed and appointed us tsar, to rule and judge with fairness our people in the east and west and south and north." But the way in which he wielded his autocratic power was softened by his gentle piety and profound humility; he strove to remember his humanity. In Tsar Alexei there was not a trace of proud self-confidence, of the touchy, suspicious, jealous love of power that afflicted Ivan the Terrible. "It is better to perform one's tasks with contrition, zeal, and humility before God than do it forcefully and with haughty conceit," he wrote to one of his provincial governors. Kindliness combined with authority helped him to be on good terms with his boyars, to whom he assigned a large part in the administration. To share his power and act together with them was his customary rule, and not a sacrifice or an annoying concession to circumstances. "And we, the great Tsar," he wrote in 1652 to Prince Nikita Odoevsky, "daily pray to the Lord God and His Most Pure Mother and all the saints that the Creator should accord it to us, the great Tsar, and you, the boyars, to be of one mind and rule the people in fairness and justice to everyone."

There has come down to us a characteristic little note of Tsar Alexei's giving a short summary of matters to be discussed in the Boyars' Council. This document shows that the Tsar prepared himself for the Council sittings. He not merely listed the questions he submitted to the boyars for discussion, but put down what he himself proposed to say and noted how this or that question was to be settled. About some matters he had made inquiries and written down figures, about others he had not yet formed an opinion and did not know what the boyars would say; on some points he held an undecisive opinion, which he was prepared to give up in case of objections. But on certain questions he had firmly made up his mind and would staunchly defend his decision before the Council. These were questions of simple justice and conscientious service. It was rumored that the voevoda of Astrakhan allowed the Kalmuks to keep Orthodox captives they had seized. The Tsar decided to write to him "with threats and mercy," and if the rumor proved to be true to put him to death, or at any rate to cut off his hand and banish him to Siberia. This little note shows better than anything else the Tsar's simple and straightforward attitude to his councilors, as well as the serious attention he paid to his duties as a ruler.

In some cases, however, the morals and customs of the time proved stronger than the Tsar's good qualities and intentions. In ancient Russia a man in authority easily forgot that he was not the only person in the world and failed to recognize that his will had limits beyond which lay other people's rights and the universally binding rules of decorum. Ancient Russian piety had a somewhat restricted field of action. It nurtured religious feeling but did little to control the will. Quick, lively, and impressionable, Alexei was hotheaded, easily lost self-control, and gave too much rein to his hands and tongue. On one occasion the Tsar, whose relations with Patriarch Nikon were already strained, quarreled with him in the cathedral on Good Friday about a church rite, and, angered by the Patriarch's arrogance, swore at him, using a coarse expression common in those days among highly placed Muscovite people, including the Patriarch himself.

On another occasion the Tsar was visiting his favorite monastery, the newly restored St. Savva Storozhevsky, to attend a festive service commemorating the holy founder of the monastery in the presence of the Patriarch of Antioch, Makarios. During the solemn matins the cantor, before beginning to read from the life of the saint, intoned as usual, "Give the blessing, Father." The Tsar leaped up from his chair and shouted, "What are you saying, you clodhopper? A patriarch is present! You should say 'My lord,' not 'Father!' " During the service the Tsar moved about among the monks, telling them what to read and how to sing. If they made mistakes, he rudely corrected them. He acted as if he were a churchwarden, lighted, trimmed, and extinguished candles before the icons, and kept talking to the Patriarch, who stood next to him. He behaved in church as though he were at home with no one looking on. Neither the Tsar's natural kindness nor the thought of his high office and others' efforts to be pious and decorous raised him above the rudest of his subjects. Religious and moral feeling was powerless against undisciplined temperament, and even good impulses found unseemly expression.

The Tsar's explosive temper was chiefly roused by actions that were morally repulsive, especially those that showed conceit and arrogance. Observation of life had taught him that "pride will have a fall." In 1660 Prince Khovansky was defeated in Lithuania and lost almost the whole of his army of 20,000. The Tsar asked the boyars in council what was to be done. I. D. Miloslavsky, the Tsar's father-in-law, who had never taken part in a campaign, suddenly declared that if the Tsar favored him and made him commander in chief, he would soon bring the King of Poland to Moscow as prisoner. "How dare you," the Tsar shouted at him, "you lowborn churl, boast of your military skill! When did you lead a regiment? What victories have you won?" And he leaped up from his seat, slapped the old man's cheek, pulled his beard, and pushed him out of the council chamber, banging the door after him.

The Tsar would flare up at a braggart or a bully, perhaps even use his fists if the culprit was close by, and certainly swear at him to his heart's content. Alexei was past master of the kind of picturesque abuse of which only the wrathful but unresentful Russian good nature is capable. The treasurer of St. Savva's Monastery, Father Nikita, having taken a drop too much, had a fight with the streltsy who lodged at the monastery, gave a beating to their officer, and ordered their clothes and arms thrown out of the place. The Tsar was indignant. He was on the verge of tears and walked about like one dazed, as he put it. He could not resist writing a furious letter to the unruly monk. The very form of address is characteristic: "From the Tsar and Grand Prince Alexei Mikhailovich of All Russia to the enemy and hater of God and betrayer of Christ, destroyer of the holy miracle worker's house and friend of Satan, cursed enemy, futile scoffer, and wicked crafty reprobate, Treasurer Nikita."

But the wave of the Tsar's anger subsided at the thought, which never left him, that no one in the world was sinless before God and that tsars and their subjects were equals before His judgment seat. At the height of passion Alexei tried not to forget that both he and his guilty subject were human. "Let me tell you, you limb of Satan," he wrote in his letter to Nikita, "that only you and your father, the devil, care for and value your worldly honor, but to me, sinner that I am, the honor of this world is like dust, and unless we fear God, you and I and all our heartfelt thoughts are of little value before Him." The autocrat, who could blow Father Nikita off the face of the earth like a speck of dust, says further in his letter that he will tearfully pray to St. Savva graciously to defend him against the ill-natured treasurer: "In the world to come God will judge between you and me, but here I have no other means of defense against you."

The Tsar's good nature and mildness and his respect for a subject's human dignity greatly attracted both his own people and aliens, and earned him the name of "the gentle tsar." Foreigners never stopped marveling at the fact that this tsar who wielded absolute power over his people, who was accustomed to complete servitude, never attempted to deprive anyone of life or property or honor (this was said by the Austrian ambassador Meyerberg). Other people's bad actions affected him painfully, chiefly because they laid on him the distasteful duty of imposing punishment. His anger did not last long and was a momentary flash that never went further than threats and a blow. The Tsar was the first to approach the victim with apologies and seek reconciliation, trying to appease him by special kindness.

One day the Tsar, who suffered from obesity, called in a German doctor to bleed him, which gave him relief. From his habit of sharing every pleasure with other people, he offered his courtiers the same treatment. The only person to refuse was Streshnev, the Tsar's maternal uncle, who said he was too old. The Tsar flared up and gave the old man several blows. "Is your blood more precious than mine? Do you think you are better than anyone else?" But soon the Tsar was doing his utmost to mollify the injured party, and scarcely knew what presents to send him to appease his anger and make him forget the insult.

Alexei liked everyone around him to be content and cheerful. He could not bear to think that someone was annoyed with him, or murmuring against him, or ill at ease with him. He was the first to relax rigid court etiquette that made relations with the sovereign so strained and cumbersome. He condescended to joke with his courtiers, paid informal visits to them, invited them to evening parties, treated them to drinks, took an interest in their home life. One of his best features was his ability to put himself in other people's shoes, to understand and take to heart their

joys and sorrows. Tsar Alexei's warm letters of condolence to
Prince Nikita Odoevsky on the occasion of his son's death and
to Ordin-Nashchokin, whose son escaped to Poland, show how
delicately considerate and morally sensitive his sympathy for
other people's grief made him, in spite of his uncertain temper.

In 1652, when Prince Nikita Odoevsky was serving as voevoda in Kazan, his son died of fever almost before the Tsar's
eyes. The Tsar wrote to the old father to comfort him, and among
other things he said in his letter: "You shouldn't grieve overmuch, our dear prince, but of course one can't help grieving and
shedding tears, and indeed it is right to weep, but within reason,
so as not to offend God." He gave a detailed account of the unexpected death, poured out a flood of comforting words to the
father, and at the end of the letter could not resist adding one
sentence more: "Prince Nikita Ivanovich, do not grieve, but
trust in God, and rely on me."

In 1660 Ordin-Nashchokin's son, a very promising young
man, fled from Russia. Foreign tutors had turned his head with
their stories of western Europe. The father was dreadfully em-
barrassed and overcome with grief. He informed the Tsar of
his misfortune himself, and asked to be dismissed from his post.
The Tsar could understand this kind of situation and wrote a
warm letter to the father defending him against his self-accusa-
tions. He said, among other things: "You ask to be dismissed;
but what could have made you ask that? Excessive sorrow, I
think. Your son has done a silly thing, but there's nothing
extraordinary about it, it was just foolishness on his part. He is
young, he wanted to have a look at God's world and at what
is happening there. Just as a bird flies hither and thither and
having had enough of it flies back to its nest, so your son will
recall his nest and his spiritual attachment, and soon return to
you."

Tsar Alexei Mikhailovich was the kindest of men, a good
Russian soul. I am prepared to say that he was the best representative of ancient Russia—at any rate, I know of no other who
produced a more pleasant impression—but certainly not on the

throne. He was too passive a character. Whether by nature or owing to his upbringing, his chief qualities were those that are most valuable in everyday intercourse and bring so much light and warmth into home life. But with all his moral sensitiveness, Tsar Alexei lacked moral energy. He loved his fellow men and wished them well because he did not want his quiet personal joys disturbed by their distress and complaints. He was, if one may put it so, something of a moral sybarite, one who loves the good because it gives him pleasant sensations. He was little able and little disposed to introduce anything on his own initiative, or stand up for it, or carry on a long struggle. He appointed to important posts both gifted and honest public servants and men of whom he himself had a very poor opinion. Unprejudiced and impartial observers carried away contradictory impressions of him, which went to form the general verdict that the Tsar would have been the kindest and wisest of rulers had he not listened to bad and stupid advisers. There was no trace of the fighter in Tsar Alexei. Least of all was he able or willing to urge people forward, to direct them and drive them on, though he liked sometimes "to discipline"—that is, to give a beating to—"an inefficient or unscrupulous servant."

Contemporaries, even foreigners, recognized his rich natural endowments. Receptivity of mind and love of learning helped him to acquire considerable knowledge, by the standards of his time, both of theological and of secular writings. It was said of him that he was "familiar with many philosophical sciences." The spirit of the needs of the moment provoked thought, posed new problems. This was reflected in Tsar Alexei's literary inclinations. He liked writing and wrote a great deal, perhaps more than any other tsar after Ivan the Terrible. He tried to record his campaigns and actually made attempts at writing verse. A few lines in his handwriting have been preserved, which may have seemed to the author to be poetry.

But most of his literary remains are letters to various people. In these letters there is much simpleheartedness, gaiety, and sometimes genuine sadness. They show subtle understanding of everyday human relations and sensitive appraisal of the trifling details of life and of commonplace people, but there is no trace of the bold, quick flights of thought or of the irony in which Ivan the Terrible's letters abound. Tsar Alexei's writings are pleasant, wordy, sometimes lively and imaginative, but on the whole rather colorless, subdued, mild, and slightly mawkish. The author was evidently a man of an orderly disposition and not one to be carried away by an idea or ready to disturb the existing order for the sake of it. He was willing to follow all that was good, but only to a certain point, so as not to disturb the comfortable equilibrium either in himself or in his surroundings. His moral and intellectual makeup was reflected to perfection in his comfortable-looking, indeed rather portly, figure, his low brow, fair skin, puffy rosy cheeks framed by a well-trimmed beard, light-brown hair, mild features, and gentle eyes.

And it was this tsar who was caught in the whirlpool of internal and foreign events of the gravest importance. It so happened that in his reign social and ecclesiastical questions and many-sided relations, old and new, with Sweden, Poland, the Crimea, Turkey, and western Russia, came to the fore all together, out of their historical turn, forming an inextricable knot and requiring immediate solution. And towering above them all stood the question that was the key to the whole situation: Should Russia remain faithful to her native past, or take lessons from foreigners? Tsar Alexei settled this question in his own fashion. So as not to choose between antiquity and innovations, he did not break with the old and did not reject the new. Habits, family ties, and other relations bound him to the conservative camp. Needs of the state, personal sympathies, and responsiveness to everything that was good drew him to the side of the intelligent and energetic men who wanted to change the old ways in the interests of national welfare. The Tsar did not hinder the reformers, indeed he supported them, but the first forceful objection from the conservatives made him draw back. Under the influence of new ideas the Tsar departed in many respects from the traditional order of life. He drove about in a

German carriage, took his wife hunting with him, took her and his children to see foreign amusements—theatrical performances with music and dancing—and treated his boyars and his father confessor to too many drinks at his evening parties, at which "a German blew trumpets and played organs." He engaged as tutor for his children a learned monk from Kiev whose teaching went far beyond the Book of Hours, the Psalter, and the *Oktoikh*, and included Latin and Polish. But Tsar Alexei could not stand at the head of the new movement, give it a definite direction, find the right men and show them the way and the methods of action. He was not averse to plucking the flowers of foreign culture, but he did not want to soil his hands with the rough work of planting it in Russian soil.

And yet in spite of his passive disposition and his good-naturedly hesitant attitude to the questions of the day, Tsar Alexei greatly helped the success of the reform movement. His striving, often illogical and unsystematic, for something new and his gift for smoothing out differences and settling things amicably accustomed timorous Russian minds to influences coming from alien lands. He provided no leading ideas about improvements to be introduced, but he helped the first reformers to come forward with their own ideas, made it possible for them to feel free to use their powers. He opened a fairly wide field of activity to them, and while giving no plan and indicating no direction for the reforms to follow, he created a favorable atmosphere for the reform movement.

We shall now turn to one of the active participants in that movement, Tsar Alexei's helper and close associate. He seems to have resembled the Tsar in his basic qualities, and yet what a difference there was in the way those qualities were combined and expressed! During almost the whole of his reign, Tsar Alexei had beside him Feodor Mikhailovich Rtishchev, who served in the Court Department. He was first the chief groom of the bedchamber and later chamberlain and tutor of the oldest Tsarevich. Rtishchev, born in 1625, was four years older than the Tsar and died three years earlier, in 1673. He was little noticed by outside observers. It was his lifelong habit not to thrust himself forward, but remain in the shadow. Fortunately, some contemporary left a short biography of Rtishchev, which is more like a eulogy than a biography, but does give some interesting facts about the life and character of this "merciful man," as the biographer calls him.

He was one of those rare and rather peculiar people who are utterly devoid of personal vanity. Contrary to man's natural instincts and inveterate habits, Rtishchev fulfilled only the first half of Christ's commandment to love one's neighbor as oneself. He did not love himself as much as he loved his neighbor. He was completely true to the spirit of the Gospel; smitten on the right cheek, he turned the left quite simply, without vaunt or calculation, as though it were a natural physical reaction and not an act of supreme humility. Vindictiveness and a sense of injury were as incomprehensible to him as the taste for wine is to some people, who wonder how others can drink such unpleasant stuff.

A certain Ivan Ozerov, who had once been greatly helped by Rtishchev and educated at the Kiev Academy, eventually became his enemy. Although Rtishchev was Ozerov's chief, he did not want to make use of his authority, and tried to appease the man's enmity by kindness and invariable humility. He often went to Ozerov's door, knocked quietly, was refused admittance—and came again. Exasperated by such persistent and annoying meekness, the host sometimes let him in and shouted abuse at him. Rtishchev would go away without a word of rebuke and later make another friendly call, as though nothing had happened. Things went on in this way till his obdurate enemy's death. Rtishchev had him buried as if he had been a good friend.

The wealth of moral ideas that Christianity brought to ancient Russia contained one that particularly appealed to our ancestors and was hardest of all to put into practice: humility. It was this virtue that Rtishchev cultivated in himself. Tsar Alexei, who had grown up together with Rtishchev, could not of course fail to become attached to such a man. Rtishchev used his influence as the Tsar's favorite to act as peacemaker at the court, to prevent conflicts and enmity, and to restrain powerful and overbearing or stubborn men like Morozov and Avvakum and Nikon. This task was not too difficult for him because he knew how to tell the truth without giving offense, never flaunted his personal superiority, was completely free from pride of birth or of office, hated wrangling about precedence, and refused the boyar rank offered to him by the Tsar for acting as tutor to the Tsarevich. Thanks to the combination of such qualities, he impressed people with his exceptional sagacity and indomitable moral strength. The Emperor's ambassador Meyerberg said that Rtishchev, while not yet forty years old, was wiser than many old men, and Ordin-Nashchokin considered Rtishchev the most steadfast man at Tsar Alexei's court. Even the Cossacks wanted to have him as the Tsar's representative, "Prince of the Ukraine," because of his uprightness and kindness.

Rtishchev's support greatly furthered the success of the reform movement. Faithful to the noblest principles and traditions of ancient Russia, he understood its needs and defects, and he occupied a prominent place among the reformers; and a cause defended by a man like him could not be either bad or unsuccessful. He was one of the first to raise his voice against disorderly church services, to which we referred earlier. He strove more than anyone else in Tsar Alexei's reign to implant education in Moscow with the help of scholars from Kiev, and indeed it was he who took the initiative in this matter.

Rtishchev enjoyed the Tsar's complete confidence and was constantly with him, but he neither took advantage of this to gain power nor remained a mere spectator of events surging around him. He took part in all kinds of work at his own wish or as commissioned by the Tsar. He administered various government departments and once successfully carried out a diplomatic mission, in 1665. Wherever an attempt was being made to improve the existing state of things, Rtishchev at once came forward with his help, advice, and intercession. He responded to every need for new measures; not infrequently he himself suggested them and then immediately retreated to the background so as not to hinder the workers or stand in anyone's way. Peaceable and full of good will, he could not endure malice and hostility, and was on good terms with all the prominent public men of his time—Ordin-Nashchokin, Nikon, Avvakum, Slavinetsky, Polotsky—in spite of all the differences in their character and ideology. He tried to keep the Old Believers and Nikonians within the domain of theological thought and theoretical argument, and not let them break up the unity of the church. He used to arrange discussions in his house at which Avvakum "wrangled with the apostates," especially with Polotsky, to the point of frenzy and utter exhaustion.

If it is true that the idea of copper currency was suggested by Rtishchev, it means that his administrative influence extended beyond the Court Department, in which he served. But it was not administrative activity in the strict sense that was Rtishchev's real lifework, by which he is remembered. He chose for himself an equally difficult but less prominent and more self-sacrificing field of activity: the service of the poor and the suffering. His biographer gives some touching details about this service. When Rtishchev accompanied the Tsar in the Polish campaign of 1654 he picked up the sick, the destitute, and the disabled on the way and put them into his carriage till at last it was so crowded that he had to get out and travel on horseback, although he had for years suffered from a weakness of the legs. He organized temporary hospitals for these people in the towns and villages along the way and paid for their keep and treatment out of his own money and money given to him for the purpose by the Tsaritsa. In Moscow too he gave orders that sick and drunken people lying about in the street should be taken to a special refuge, where they were kept at his expense till they recovered or grew sober. He founded an almshouse for incurables, old people, and the disabled, and maintained it also out of his own pocket. He spent a great deal of money ransoming Russian captives from the Tatars, helping foreign prisoners of war in Russia, and aiding men imprisoned for debt.

His philanthropy was inspired not only by compassion for the helpless, but also by a sense of social justice. It was a very kind action on his part to give his suburban lands to the town of Arzamas, which badly needed the land but could not afford to buy it, while a private purchaser was offering him 14,000 rubles (in our currency) for it. In 1671 Rtishchev heard that there was famine in Vologda and sent there a train of wagons loaded with grain, ostensibly entrusted to him by certain lovers of Christ to be given to the poor in prayerful remembrance of the donors' souls; later on he sent the stricken city about 14,000 rubles (in our currency), which he raised by selling some of his clothes and furniture.

Apparently Rtishchev understood not only other people's needs, but also the defects of the social system, and he was perhaps the first to express his attitude toward serfdom in practice. His biographer describes what care he took of his house serfs and especially of his peasants. He tried to make their tasks and the dues they paid proportionate to their means, and helped their work of farming by giving them loans. When he had to sell one of his villages, he reduced its price on condition that the purchaser promise on oath not to increase the amount of work and of the dues imposed upon the peasants. Before his death he set all his house serfs free and begged only one thing of his daughter and her husband, who were his heirs: "for the repose of his soul" to treat the peasants whom he bequeathed to them as well as possible, "for they are our brethren."

We do not know what impression Rtishchev's attitude toward his serfs produced on society, but his philanthropic work apparently had some influence on legislation. In the reign of Alexei's successor it was proposed to organize charitable institutions run by the church and the state. At the Tsar's order, the Moscow beggars and disabled persons living on alms were sorted out, and the really helpless ones were put in two almshouses designed for the purpose and maintained by the state; the able-bodied were given various kinds of work. At the church council of 1681 the Tsar proposed that the Patriarch and the bishops establish such shelters and almshouses in every town, and the members of the council accepted the proposition.

Thus private initiative of a kind and influential man formed the basis of a whole system of ecclesiastical charitable institutions, which from the end of the seventeenth century gradually increased in number. The activity of the progressive men of the period was particularly important in so far as their personal ideas and individual efforts set new tasks to legislation and gave rise either to political movements or to state institutions.

Chapter
XVII

A Muscovite Statesman: Ordin-Nashchokin

A Moscow statesman of the seventeenth century! The very phrase seems to involve a misuse of present-day political terminology. To be a statesman means to have a mind well trained in politics, capable of observing, understanding, and directing a social movement and taking an independent view of contemporary problems; to have a well-thought-out program of action and a fairly wide field of political activity —conditions we do not expect to find in the old Muscovite state. And indeed up to the seventeenth century there was no evidence of them in the land of the Moscow autocrats, and it would be difficult to discover any statesmen at their court. The course of public affairs was in those days determined by the established order of things and by the tsar's will. Individual men were merely instruments of that will, personal intelligence was submerged by routine, and both the routine and the sovereign's will were subordinated to the still more powerful influence of custom and tradition. In the seventeenth century, however, Muscovite political life began finding new channels for itself. The established order, the old traditions were undermined. Intelligence and personal resourcefulness came to be greatly in demand, and for the sake of the common good Tsar Alexei readily submitted his will to that of any strong-minded, intelligent, and well-intentioned man.

As I have already said, he created a reformative mood in Russian society. The first place among public men affected by that mood unquestionably belongs to the most brilliant of Tsar Alexei's helpers, Afanasi Lavrentievich Ordin-Nashchokin, who expressed his contemporaries' striving for new ways of life more energetically than anyone else. He is of particular interest to us because he was preparing the ground for Peter the Great's reforms. None of the other Muscovite seventeenth-century politicians had so many ideas and plans for reform eventually carried out by Peter. Second, Ordin-Nashchokin had not only to act in a new way, but to create the environment for his activity. He did not belong by birth to the society in which he had to work. The privileged breeding ground of Muscovite politicians was the upper layer of the nobility, boyar families of ancient lineage who looked down contemptuously on the provincial gentry. Ordin-Nashchokin was, I believe, the first member of that gentry to make his way into the exclusive set of proud aristocrats, and he was followed by a long train of his provincial brethren, who soon disrupted the closed rank of the boyar nobility.

Afanasi Lavrentievich was the son of a very humble landowner in the province of Pskov, where there was quite a family nest of Nashchokins descended from a serviceman prominent at the Muscovite court in the sixteenth century. Since that time the family to which Afanasi Lavrentievich belonged had come down in the world. He had made a name for himself in Tsar Michael's reign and had more than once been appointed to embassy commissions to determine the Russo-Swedish boundary. At the beginning of Alexei's reign Ordin-Nashchokin was considered in Russia to be an able administrator and a devoted servant of the government. This was why the Pskov rebels of 1650 wanted to kill him. While the mutiny was being suppressed by

Muscovite regiments, he showed much tact and energy. From that time on he rose steadily.

In 1654, when the war with Poland began, he was given an extremely difficult task: with a small military force he had to defend the Muscovite frontier against attack from Lithuania and Livonia. He carried it out admirably. In 1656 war with Sweden broke out, and the Tsar himself led the campaign against Riga. When Muscovite troops took a Livonian town on the Dvina, Kokenhausen (the ancient Russian town Kukeinos, which had once belonged to the princes of Polotsk), Nashchokin was appointed voevoda of it and of other newly annexed towns. In this capacity he did very important work, both military and diplomatic. He guarded the frontier, won small Livonian towns, carried on a correspondence with Polish authorities. Not a single diplomatic transaction of importance was made without his help. In 1658 he succeeded in arranging an armistice with Sweden on conditions that surpassed Tsar Alexei's expectations. In 1665 Ordin-Nashchokin was voevoda of his native Pskov. Finally he rendered a most important and difficult service to the Moscow government: after eight wearisome months of negotiation with Polish delegates, in January 1667 he concluded the Andrusovo armistice with Poland, putting an end to a devastating war that had gone on for thirteen years. In these negotiations Nashchokin showed great diplomatic skill and a capacity for establishing friendly contact with foreigners. He managed to gain from the Poles not only the Smolensk and Seversk regions and the eastern Ukraine, but also Kiev and the adjoining district in the western Ukraine.

Through concluding the Andrusovo Treaty, Nashchokin rose to a very high position in the government and gained great renown as a diplomat. Belonging to the provincial gentry by birth, he had the boyar rank bestowed on him after the Andrusovo Treaty and was put at the head of the Department of Foreign Affairs, with the imposing title of "Keeper of the Tsar's Great Seal and of the Chief Ambassadorial Affairs of State"; in other words, he became Chancellor of State.

Such was Nashchokin's career as an official. His native province of Pskov played a certain part in it. Having a common boundary with Livonia, it had for centuries been in close contact with its German and Swedish neighbors. Early acquaintance with foreigners and constant relations with them gave Nashchokin opportunities of carefully observing and getting to know the western European countries nearest to Russia. This was all the easier for him because by a lucky chance he had received a good education in his youth. He was said to know mathematics, Latin, and German. His official duties compelled him to learn Polish as well.

Thus, early in life he thoroughly prepared himself for taking an active part in the relations of the Muscovite state with western Europe. His colleagues in the service said that he knew "German business and German customs." Careful observation of foreign ways and the habit of comparing them with the Russian made Nashchokin a devoted admirer of the West and a sharp critic of his own countrymen's manner of life. He thus got rid of narrow and exclusive nationalism and worked out his own political point of view. He was the first in our country to proclaim that "there is no shame in learning good things from others, from aliens, and even from enemies." He left behind him a number of papers, official notes, memoranda, and reports addressed to the Tsar on various political questions. These documents are very interesting and throw light both on Nashchokin himself and on the reform movement of his day. It is evident that the author was a good talker and a lively writer. Even his enemies admitted that he could write "smoothly."

Another and rarer characteristic of his was his broad, subtle, and tenacious intelligence, quick at grasping a given situation and gathering together the possibilities it offered. He was past master of original and unexpected political schemes. It was difficult to get the better of him in argument. Clear-sighted and resourceful, he sometimes exasperated foreign diplomats with whom he was negotiating, and they complained to him of how difficult he was to deal with. He would at once detect a slip or an inconsistency in diplomatic dialectics, trip up and nonplus an unwary or shortsighted opponent, and poison the good intentions he himself had inspired—as the Polish negotiators once accused him of doing. At the same time he was scrupulously conscientious. It was his habit to point out people's slow-wittedness to them, and he considered it his duty to grumble at them in the interests of truth and sound judgment. Indeed, he found much pleasure in doing this. In his letters and reports to the Tsar there is one predominant note. They are full of unceasing and often virulent complaints of Muscovite people and Muscovite ways. He was always grumbling and finding fault with everything: government institutions, official methods, military organization, social morals and customs.

His sympathies and antipathies, little shared by others, placed him in an awkward and ambiguous position in Muscovite society. His predilection for western European ways and disapproval of his native ones pleased foreigners who made friends with him, and they condescendingly admitted that he was quite an intelligent imitator of their customs. But this created a number of enemies for him among the Russians and gave occasion to his Muscovite ill-wishers to mock at him and call him a foreigner. His position was all the more difficult because of his origin and temperament. Both his countrymen and foreigners recognized that he was a man of sharp intelligence, which would take him far. This piqued his rivals' vanity, especially as he did not follow the course for which his origin predestined him; and his harsh and somewhat provocative manner was not likely to mollify them.

Nashchokin was an outsider in Muscovite bureaucratic circles, and as a novice in the political world he had to fight for his official position, feeling that his every advancement increased the number of his enemies, especially among the boyar aristocracy. This accounted for the peculiar attitude he took up in a society hostile to him. He knew that his only support was the Tsar, who disliked arrogance. Anxious to make sure of his support, Nashchokin sought the Tsar's protection against his enemies by assuming the air of a meek and defenseless man who is being hounded, and feigned humility to the point of self-

abasement. He did not think much of his "poor service," but
the service of his highborn enemies was no better, and he bitterly
complained of them all the time. He wrote to the Tsar: "Of
all men no one is so greatly hated as I am for the work done
on your sovereign behalf." He called himself "a wronged and
hated fellow who has nowhere to lay his sinful head." In every
difficulty or conflict with influential enemies he asked the Tsar
to dismiss him from office as a trying and inefficient servant who
could do nothing but harm to the interests of the state. "Men
hate state business because of me, your bondsman," he wrote
to the Tsar, asking him "to cast away his obnoxious servant."

But Nashchokin knew his own worth, and one may well say
that this feigned modesty was "pride under the cloak of humility"—which did not prevent his believing that he really was
not of this world. "If I were of the world, the world would
love its own," he wrote to the Tsar in a letter complaining of
people's hostility. "Members of the Boyars' Council dislike listening to my reports and my suggestions . . . because they see not
the ways of truth, and their hearts have grown fat with envy."
Bitter irony sounds in his words when he writes to the Tsar
about the vast superiority of the boyar aristocracy to a lowborn man like himself in dealing with government matters.
"None of the Council's members want me, nor do they want
to deal with great affairs of the state. Such affairs should be
the province of boyars, who stand nearest to the Tsar. They
come of illustrious families, have many friends, know how to
live and to show great understanding of everything. I give back
to you, gracious sovereign, my sworn oath, for I am much too
slow-witted to hold my office."

For many years the Tsar steadfastly supported his capricious
and irascible minister, patiently put up with his tedious complaints and reproaches, assured him that he had nothing to fear
and would not be betrayed to anyone, threatened his enemies
with severe displeasure for their hostility to Nashchokin, and
gave him considerable freedom of action. Thanks to this, Nashchokin was able to make good use of his administrative and
diplomatic abilities, and to work out and even partly realize his

political plans. In his letters to the Tsar he mostly finds fault with the present state of things or argues against his opponents, rather than expounding his own program. However, one can find in his writings a number of ideas and projects that, when properly worked out, in practice could and did become the leading principles of Russian foreign and domestic policy for years to come.

First, Nashchokin stubbornly insisted on taking the West as a pattern in all things and following the example of foreign lands. This was the starting point of his plans for reform. But we should not borrow from abroad indiscriminately. "Foreign customs do not concern us," he used to say. "Their clothes do not fit us, and ours do not fit them." He was one of the few Westernizers who thought of what should and should not be borrowed, and who wanted to combine general European culture with the nation's individual peculiarities.

Second, Nashchokin could not reconcile himself to the spirit and habits of Muscovite administrators, whose activity was unduly influenced by personal motives and relations and not by the interests of governmental work entrusted to this or that official. "With us," he writes, "a cause is loved or hated not on its own account, but because of the man who works for it. They dislike me, and so they hold my work in contempt." When the Tsar reproved him for being on bad terms with one or another of his aristocratic ill-wishers, Nashchokin replied that he had no personal hostility against them, but "his heart ached on account of the work of the state and would not let him keep silence when he saw negligence in the conduct of state affairs."

And so it was work and not personal considerations that mattered; this was Nashchokin's second guiding principle. His chief field of activity was diplomacy, and his contemporaries, even foreign ones, admitted that he was a first-class diplomat. At any rate, he was probably the first Russian statesman to inspire foreigners' respect. Tsar Alexei's English physician, Collins, called Nashchokin a great politician, in no way inferior to the best of European ministers. And Nashchokin himself thought highly of his office. He considered diplomacy to be the chief function of state administration, and thought that only men of real moral worth should engage in it. "Affairs of state should be pondered upon by specially chosen men of blameless character, with the object of expanding the state in every direction, and this is the business of the Department of Foreign Affairs alone."

Nashchokin had his own diplomatic plans, his own ideas of the aims that Muscovite foreign policy should pursue. He had to act at a time when the knotty problems that nourished implacable hostility among Russia, Poland, and Sweden—the problems of the Ukraine and the Baltic coast—assumed a critical form. Circumstances plunged Nashchokin into the whirlpool of negotiations and conflicts arising from these problems. But this vortex did not make him dizzy. In the most complicated matters he could discriminate between the important and the merely spectacular, the useful and the pleasant, the attainable and the fanciful. He saw that in its present condition and with the means at its command Muscovy could not completely solve the Ukrainian problem, that is, the question of reuniting the whole of southwestern Russia with Great Russia. This was why he favored peace with Poland and even a close alliance with it. Although he well knew, as he put it, "the highly unstable, soulless, and changeable Polish people," he expected various advantages from the alliance. He hoped, among other things, that Turkish Christians, Moldavians, and Walachians, hearing about the alliance, would break away from the Turks, and then all the children of the Eastern church between the Danube and Great Russia, at that time cut off from us by a hostile Poland, would be merged in one numerous Christian nation under the protection of the Orthodox Tsar of Muscovy. Swedish intrigues, made possible only by the quarrel between Russia and Poland, would then stop of themselves. When in 1667 Polish envoys arrived in Moscow to ratify the Andrusovo Treaty, Nashchokin delivered a spirited address. He spoke of the glory the Slavic nations would win, of the great enterprises they could carry out if all the tribes dwelling in the two states and almost all Slavic-speaking peoples between the Adriatic, the North Sea, and the Arctic Ocean would unite. What glory, he said, awaited both states when, standing at the head of the Slavic peoples, they were joined under one sovereign rule!

In seeking a close alliance with Russia's inveterate enemy, and even dreaming of a dynastic union with Poland under the suzerainty of the Tsar or his son, Nashchokin was making a radical change in Muscovite foreign policy. He had reasons that justified it. The question of the Ukraine seemed to him of secondary importance for the time being. If the Cossacks are disloyal, he wrote, are they worth defending? And in fact the annexation of the eastern Ukraine settled the main point at issue. Poland ceased being dangerous to Muscovy, which was firmly established on the upper and middle reaches of the Dnieper. Besides, it was impossible for Poland to annex the western Ukraine and permanently hold Kiev, which had been temporarily ceded to us, without violating the Andrusovo Treaty and committing an international crime. Nashchokin was one of the rare diplomats who had a professional conscience, a characteristic that even in those days was unwelcome in diplomacy. He refused to do anything unfair. "It would indeed be better to accept an end to my miserable life and be free forever than to act against truth." When Doroshenko, hetman of the western Ukraine, seceded from Poland, swore allegiance to the Sultan of Turkey, and then expressed a wish to put himself under the mighty power of the Tsar of Muscovy, Nashchokin received a query from Moscow as to whether Doroshenko should be accepted. In his answer he strongly protested against such a violation of treaties and expressed indignation at being asked so unseemly a question.

In his opinion, things ought to be managed in such a way that the Poles, after weighing their own and Moscow's interests, would voluntarily hand Kiev over to Muscovy, and the whole of the western Ukraine with it, in order to consolidate the Russo-Polish alliance against infidels and bring peace to the Ukraine. "But to write to Poland bluntly about it is impossible." Even before the Andrusovo armistice, Nashchokin was persuad-

ing Tsar Alexei not to make the conditions of peace with the
King of Poland too exacting, lest the Poles should afterward
seize the first opportunity to retaliate. "Take Polotsk and Vi-
tebsk, but if the Poles prove stubborn, do not claim even those
two towns."

In his report on the necessity of close alliance with Poland,
Nashchokin dropped an incautious hint that for the sake of
consolidating this alliance we might give up the whole of the
Ukraine and not only its western part. But the Tsar vehemently
opposed his friend's faintheartedness and expressed his indignation in very strong terms. "This proposal," wrote the Tsar,
"we have put aside and commanded to be left out because it is
unseemly, and also because we have found in it one mind and
a half: one firmly made up and half of another swayed by
the wind. A dog is unworthy to eat even one slice of Orthodox
bread [it is not right for Poles to own even the western part
of the Ukraine]. This, however, is not willed by us, but is a
punishment for our sins. But if the dog gets both pieces of the
holy bread, oh, what justification can there be for him who
allowed this to happen? He will have for requital the nethermost
hell, scorching flames and merciless torments. Go in peace by
the royal road, man, follow the middle course, end as you have
begun, lean neither to the left nor to the right. The Lord be
with you!"

And the stubborn man yielded to the pious lament of his
sovereign, whom sometimes he simply disobeyed. He clutched
at both pieces of the Orthodox bread, and at Andrusovo ex-
tracted from the Poles, in addition to the eastern Ukraine, Kiev
in the western part.

The idea of uniting all Slavs under the friendly leadership of
Muscovy and Poland was Nashchokin's idyllic dream, but as a
practical politician he was more interested in actual affairs of
the day. He looked around with a diplomatic eye, searching
everywhere for new gains for the Treasury and the people,
or carefully preparing the ground for them. He did his best
to organize trade relations with Persia and central Asia, Khiva
and Bokhara, sent an embassy to India, kept an eye on the Far

East and China, thought of establishing Cossack colonies in the Amur region. But amidst all these plans his mind was first and foremost occupied, of course, with the part of the West that lay nearest—the Baltic Sea. Guided by economics no less than by political considerations, Nashchokin understood how important the Baltic was for Russian trade, commerce, and culture, and therefore he paid particular attention to Sweden, and especially to Livonia, which in his opinion should be acquired at all costs. He expected tremendous advantages for Russian industry and the Tsar's Treasury from this acquisition.

Tsar Alexei, carried away by his minister's ideas, looked in the same direction and strove for the return of former Russian territory and for "maritime shelters"—the harbors of Narva, Ivangorod, Oreshek, and the whole course of the river Neva with the Swedish fortress of Njenschantz, where eventually St. Petersburg was built. But even in this matter Nashchokin took a broader view. He insisted that a trifle must not be allowed to obscure the view of the main object, that Narva, Oreshek, and the rest were unimportant and that the essential thing was to penetrate to the sea and acquire Riga, the port that opened the most direct and nearest route to western Europe. To form a coalition against Sweden in order to rob it of Livonia was a cherished idea that inspired Nashchokin's diplomatic plan. For its sake he strove for peace with the Khan of the Crimea and a close alliance with Poland at the cost of sacrificing the western Ukraine. The plan was not realized, but Peter the Great fully inherited the ideas of his father's minister.

Nashchokin's political horizon was not limited to questions of foreign policy. He had his own views about the internal administration of the Muscovite state. He was dissatisfied both with the system and with the way it worked. He protested against the unnecessary regimentation that prevailed in it. The system was entirely based upon strict supervision by central administrative organs of the subordinate executive institutions, which had blindly to obey the orders given them. Nashchokin demanded a certain amount of freedom for the executors. "They should not always wait for the Tsar's decree," he wrote. "Everywhere a voevoda's consideration is needed"—that is, the person in authority must use his own judgment. He pointed to the example of western Europe, where they put an experienced commander at the head of an army and let him issue orders to his subordinates, without asking for directions from the central government about every trifle. "Where the eye sees and the ear hears, judgment must be passed then and there," he wrote.

But while demanding more independence for executive officers, he laid great responsibility upon them. Their actions should be determined not by decrees or custom and routine, but by consideration of the actual circumstances of the case before them. Nashchokin uses the word "sagacity" to describe activity based upon the agent's use of his intelligence. Brute force is of little avail. "Sagacity is better than any amount of force. What matters is sagacity and not the number of men; there may be many men but if there be no one to think for them, nothing will come of it. Take Sweden, for instance: it is less populous than all its neighboring states, but through sagacity it gets the better of them all. In Sweden no one dares to deprive an intelligent man of freedom of action. It would be more profitable to sell half the army and buy one sagacious leader."

Finally, Nashchokin's administrative activity displayed a feature that particularly tells in his favor. Efficient and exacting as he was, he showed genuine concern for his subordinates' welfare—a thing unheard of in Muscovite officialdom. His attitude toward them was warm and sympathetic. He tried to make their work easier for them, to arrange matters so that they could be of most profit to the state with the least expenditure of energy.

During the Swedish war Russian cavalry and Don Cossacks began plundering and ill-treating the people of the conquered territories along the western Dvina, who had already sworn allegiance to the Tsar of Muscovy. Nashchokin, who was at that time voevoda of Kukeinos, was profoundly indignant at such savage methods of warfare. The complaints of the pillaged population made his heart bleed. He wrote to the Tsar that he had to send military help both against the enemy and against the Russian plunderers. "I would rather see wounds on my own body than have them inflicted on innocent people. I would rather be in perpetual confinement than live here and see the people endure such dreadful calamities." Tsar Alexei was particularly disposed to appreciate this feature of his minister's character. In 1658, in the patent conferring membership in the Boyars' Council on Nashchokin, the Tsar praised him for "feeding the hungry, giving drink to the thirsty, clothing the naked, being kind to men at arms, and not letting thieves go unpunished."

Such were Nashchokin's principles and methods of administration. He made several attempts to apply his ideas in practice. Observation of western European life made him aware of the main defect of the Muscovite state administration—the fact that it was concerned solely with exploiting the people's labor and not with developing the country's natural resources. The people's economic interests were sacrificed to fiscal ends and valued by the government merely as additional sources of state revenue. Nashchokin saw this, and he always insisted on the need to develop trade and industry in Muscovy. He was probably the first to understand that the national economy as such should be one of the chief concerns of state administration. He was one of the earliest political economists in Russia.

But in order for the industrial class to act more productively, it had to be freed from the dead weight of bureaucratic administration. While Nashchokin was voevoda of Pskov he tried to introduce there his project of municipal self-government "after the example of other, foreign countries"—that is, of western Europe. It is a unique instance of its kind in the history of Muscovite local administration in the seventeenth century and somewhat dramatic in character. It throws a vivid light both on Nashchokin himself and on the environment in which he had to act. On arriving in Pskov in 1665, the new voevoda found great unrest in his native town. There was bitter enmity among the townspeople. The "best" merchants—that is, the richest ones —taking advantage of their influence in urban administration, treated the middling and small people unfairly in apportioning taxes and assigning men to work for the state. They conducted

municipal affairs "at their own will," without consulting the
rest of the community. Both rich and poor were being ruined
by lawsuits and officials' malpractice. Goods flowed in and out
of Pskov across the German frontier free of customs duty.
Small traders with no working capital secretly borrowed money
from the Germans, bought Russian goods as cheaply as they
could, and sold them—or rather passed them on—to their creditors, contenting themselves with very small earnings as commission agents. In this way they brought down the prices of Russian
goods to the lowest possible level, did much damage to the Pskov
capitalists' business, got into hopeless debt to foreigners, and
often were completely ruined.

Soon after his arrival Nashchokin proposed to the Pskov urban
community a number of measures to be considered with every
care and attention by the town elders and "best men," gathered
together in the town hall "for general consultation." Seventeen
articles concerning municipal organization—a kind of charter
for the self-government of the town of Pskov and its suburbs—
were drawn up with the voevoda's cooperation. The charter was
approved in Moscow, and the Tsar graciously praised the voevoda for his zealous service and the Pskov elders and townspeople for their good counsel and zeal in all good works.

The most important articles of the charter deal with reforming municipal administration and courts of law and with better
ordering of foreign trade—one of the most important elements
in the economic life of the Pskov region. The townspeople were
to elect fifteen men from among themselves for a period of three
years. Five of them in turn were to conduct the current affairs
of the town for one year. They had charge of the town's
economy, and supervised the sale of liquor, the collection of customs, and commercial transactions between the local people and
foreigners. They also tried their fellow townsmen for commercial and other offenses. Only the most serious crimes, such as
treason, brigandage, and murder, remained within the voevoda's
jurisdiction. The voevoda of Pskov thus voluntarily relinquished
a considerable part of his authority in favor of municipal self-
government. In particularly important affairs the five representa-

tives on duty for the year conferred with the others and even called in for consultation the "best men" of the urban community.

Nashchokin thought that the chief defects of Russian commerce were due to the Russian traders' "being weak in dealing with one another," unreliable, unused to concerted action, and easily inveigled into dependence upon foreigners. The main causes of this were lack of capital, mutual distrust, and absence of satisfactory credit. The articles of the Pskov charter concerning trade with foreigners were intended to remedy these defects. Small traders were distributed "according to their family connections and acquaintanceship" among large capitalists, who were to look after their business. The municipality lent them money for the purchase of Russian export goods out of public funds. Two fairs, each lasting two weeks, were established near Pskov for duty-free trade with foreigners, one beginning on January 1 and the other on May 9. Small traders, supported by the capitalists to whom they had been assigned, bought goods for export with the money they had on loan, registered them in the town hall, and handed them over to their principals in time for the fairs. The principals paid them the purchase value of the goods so that the men could buy new stocks for the ensuing fair, and also gave them an additional sum "for maintenance." After selling those goods to foreigners at officially fixed high prices, the capitalists paid their clients "the full share of profit" due to them.

Such an organization of the merchant class was intended to concentrate foreign trade in the hands of a few rich men, who would be in a position to maintain the price of export goods at an appropriately high level. These special commercial companies presupposed the possibility of friendly relations between the upper layer of the merchant class and the urban rank and file; that is, they presumed the end of the social hostility that Nashchokin found in Pskov. The arrangement would be of advantage to both the patrons and the clients. Big capitalists would secure good profits to small tradesmen, and the latter would not cut down the prices for their patrons. Another important point was that the companies were under the auspices of the municipal council, which became a lending bank to the impecunious members and exercised control over their patrons. The urban community of Pskov, and the suburbs dependent upon it, was able to direct the export trade of the whole province through its administrative center.

But social discord prevented the success of the reform. The needy townsmen accepted the new statute as a favor from the Tsar, but "men of substance," the rich, those who in fact controlled the town affairs, were opposed to it, and they found support in Moscow. We can well imagine with what hostility Nashchokin's proposal was met by the Moscow boyars and government officials. They saw in it nothing but an attempt to limit the ancient rights and customs of voevodas and government secretaries in order to please the taxpaying rabble of the town. It is a wonder that within eight months of his term of office Nashchokin had found time not only to think out the plan of a complicated reform, but to organize the intricate details of its practical application. Nashchokin's successor at Pskov, Prince Khovansky, a conceited champion of boyar pretensions, a "jabberer," as he was nicknamed in Moscow—a braggart and babbler whom "everyone called a fool," as Tsar Alexei remarked—presented Nashchokin's work to the sovereign in such a light that in spite of his opinion of Khovansky, the Tsar countermanded the charter, yielding to his besetting weakness of making decisions on the strength of the latest impression.

Nashchokin did not like surrendering either to enemies or to adverse circumstances. He had such faith in his Pskov reform that in spite of his critical intelligence, so well trained in detecting other people's mistakes, he succumbed to self-illusion. In the Pskov municipal charter he expressed the hope that when these "Pskov civic rights are established and organized among the people, the inhabitants of other towns, seeing this, will hope that they too will be similarly favored." But in Moscow the reverse decision was taken. It was not fitting that Pskov should have a local organization of its own. In 1667, when Nashchokin was put at the head of the Department of Foreign Affairs, he could not resist the pleasure of repeating in his new trade statute the considerations he had urged at Pskov. He insisted again, quite fruitlessly, that impecunious traders should be given loans from the Moscow customs office and local town halls, that tradesmen of humble means should go into partnership with big capitalists so as to keep up the prices of Russian export goods, and so on.

In this statute Nashchokin took another step forward in his plan of organizing Russian commerce and industry. As early as 1665 the townspeople of Pskov petitioned Moscow to centralize all their affairs in one department, so that they would not have to trudge from one government office to another, "suffering affronts and ruination." In the new trade statute Nashchokin proposed a special Department of Commerce to protect tradespeople in frontier towns against other states and to help and defend them in all towns against oppression by the local voevodas. This Department of Commerce was to become the predecessor of the Moscow *Rathaus,* or Burmistersky Hall, founded by Peter the Great to look after the commercial and industrial urban population of the whole country.

Such were Nashchokin's plans and experiments of reform. One can well marvel at the breadth and novelty of his schemes and the diversity of his activities. He had a fertile mind and a direct and simple way of looking at things. To whatever sphere of state administration Nashchokin was called, he sharply criticized the established order and suggested a more or less clear plan of reform. He made several experiments with regard to the army, noticed the defects of its organization, and submitted a plan for reforming it. He thought that the mounted militia of provincial gentry was quite unfit as a fighting force and proposed replacement by a foreign-trained infantry and cavalry consisting of "given men" or recruits. This evidently was a casual suggestion for a regular army to be formed by enlisting recruits from all classes of society.

Whenever something new was planned in Moscow—building a fleet on the Baltic or the Caspian, arranging postal service to other countries, or simply planting beautiful gardens with trees and flowers imported from abroad—Ordin-Nashchokin stood, or was said to stand, at the head of it. At one time it was actually rumored in Moscow that he was revising Russian laws and re-organizing the state as a whole, making it less centralized and weakening the control exercised by the Moscow departments over local administrative organs—a control against which Nash-chokin waged war all his life.

It is possible that he did not succeed in doing all he might have done. His stubborn and peevish disposition brought his political activities to a premature end. Nashchokin was not in full agreement with the Tsar about the aims of our foreign policy. Being a conscientious diplomat, the author of the Andru-sovo Treaty firmly insisted on carrying it out to the letter and, if need be, restoring Kiev to Poland. But the Tsar considered this not merely undesirable, but a downright sinful thing to do. This difference of opinion gradually estranged the sovereign from his favorite. In 1671 Nashchokin was appointed to open new negotiations with Poland in which he would have to destroy his own work and violate the treaty that only a year before he had ratified with his oath. He refused the appointment, and in February 1672 the abbot of the Krypetsky Monastery at Pskov received him into the monastic order under the name of Anthony. Nashchokin wrote down in his memoranda the day of his retirement, December 2, 1671, when the Tsar, in the presence of all the boyars, "graciously let him go and freed him from all worldly vanity." Brother Anthony's last worldly concern was the alms-house he founded in Pskov. He died in 1680.

In many respects Ordin-Nashchokin anticipated Peter the Great, and he was the first to express many ideas that the Re-former Tsar carried out. He was a bold and self-confident bureaucrat who knew his own value, but he was kind and solici-tous for the governed. He had an active and practical mind, and in all he did he was concerned first and foremost with the inter-ests of the state, the common good. He did not rest content with routine, clearly detected the shortcomings of the established order, thought out the best ways to remedy them, and rightly guessed what problems had to be tackled next. He had great practical sense and set himself no far-distant aims or tasks too wide in scope. Knowing how to find his way in various spheres of activity, he did his best to settle each particular case with the means at his command. But though he never ceased finding fault with the established order of things, he did not attack its foundations; he hoped to mend it piecemeal. In his mind the vague reformative aspirations of the period began for the first time to take shape as definite projects, forming part of a coherent plan of reform. But it was not a radical plan, demanding a general breakup. Nashchokin was by no means an irresponsible innovator. His program of reform did not go beyond three basic demands: to improve administrative institutions and service discipline, to choose conscientious and capable administrators, and to increase state revenue through increasing national wealth by the development of trade and industry.

I began this chapter by remarking that in the seventeenth century a Russian statesman was no longer an impossibility. If you think of all the vicissitudes of Ordin-Nashchokin's political activity, of the ideas and feelings of this man of outstanding character and intelligence, and of his struggle against the circumstances in which he had to act, you will understand why such lucky exceptions were rare among us.

In spite of all the differences in their characters and activities, Rtishchev and Ordin-Nashchokin had one common feature that brought them close together: they were new men of the period and did new work—one in politics, the other in the moral sphere. In this they differed from Tsar Alexei, who was rooted in ancient Russian tradition with his whole heart and mind, and merely diverted himself with the new ideas, using them to embellish his surroundings or smooth out foreign relations. Rtishchev and Nashchokin managed to find something new in the old Russian way of life, to discover its still untouched and unexploited resources and make use of them for the good of all. They used scholarship and Western achievements not to undermine Russia's spiritual heritage, but to defend its vital principles against deadening routine, against a harsh and narrow interpretation instilled in the masses by bad political and ecclesiastical leadership.

Nashchokin, a diplomat, argued insistently and angrily that external successes, military and diplomatic, were short-lived unless they were prepared and maintained by a constant improvement in the internal conditions of the country, and that foreign policy must further the development of the nation's productive forces, not deplete them. Rtishchev, a wealthy courtier, expanded his irascible friend's ideas by gently showing, through his own way of acting, that economic successes, too, are of little value if the principal conditions of a well-ordered community life are absent. These conditions include equitable relations between the classes; enlightened religious and moral sense, undistorted by superstitions and spurious rites; and charity that finds expression not only in occasional individual impulses, but also in the organization of public institutions.

Rtishchev and Nashchokin were lonely fighters in the field but not "voices crying in the wilderness." They both still held fast to the old traditional forms and sympathies (one founded a monastery and the other ended by becoming a monk), but their ideas, half understood and half accepted by their contemporaries, penetrated to another age, helping us to understand the perversions of the political, religious, and moral life in ancient Russia.

Chapter
XVIII

V. V. Golitsyn and Plans
for Reform

The youngest of Peter's predecessors was Prince V. V. Golitsyn, and he was much further in advance of the existing state of things than his elders had been. As a young man he already occupied a prominent position in government circles under Tsar Feodor, and he became one of the most influential people under Tsarevna Sofia when she was proclaimed regent at her eldest brother's death. An ambitious and well-educated woman, Sofia could not fail to notice the cultured and intelligent young nobleman, and through personal friendship Prince Golitsyn linked his political career with that of the Tsarevna. He was an ardent admirer of the West, for the sake of which he renounced many time-honored traditions of ancient Russia. Like Nashchokin, he spoke fluent Latin and Polish. In his spacious Moscow house, considered by foreigners to be one of the most magnificent in Europe, everything was arranged in Western fashion. Wall space between the windows was taken up with tall mirrors; the walls were hung with pictures, portraits of Russian and foreign sovereigns, and German maps in gilt frames; the planetary system was painted on the ceilings; a number of clocks and a thermometer of artistic workmanship served as accessories. Golitsyn had a large library of various printed and manuscript books in Russian, Polish, and German. In between Polish and Latin grammars stood *The Kiev Chronicles,* a German book on geometry, the *Koran* in a Polish translation, four manuscripts about the staging of plays, and Krizhanich's manuscript. Golitsyn's house was a meeting place for educated foreigners who happened to visit Moscow, and his hospitality to them went further than that of other Moscow xenophiles, for he received even Jesuits, which was more than the others were prepared to do. Obviously, such a man was bound to be on the side of the reform movement in its Latin, western European form, and not as represented by Likhud.

Golitsyn eventually succeeded Ordin-Nashchokin at the Department of Foreign Affairs and developed his predecessor's ideas. With his help the Moscow Treaty, or perpetual peace with Poland, was concluded in 1686, and in accordance with it the State of Muscovy formed a coalition with Poland, the Holy Roman Empire, and the Venetian Republic against Turkey. It thus formally entered the concert of European powers. In exchange, Poland permanently ceded to Moscow Kiev and other towns that had been temporarily surrendered to it by the terms of the Andrusovo Treaty.

In questions of internal policy Prince Golitsyn also went further than the former statesmen who sympathized with the reform movement. In Tsar Feodor's reign he was appointed chairman of a committee to draw up a plan for reorganizing the Muscovite military forces. The committee proposed to introduce the German system in the Russian army and to abolish the rule of precedence (this was done by the law of January 12, 1682). Golitsyn never ceased urging the boyars to educate their children, obtained permission to send them to Polish schools, and advised the parents to engage Polish tutors for them. There is no doubt that his mind was full of broadly conceived plans of reform. Unfortunately, only fragments of them have come down to us, along with vague accounts written down by a foreigner, the Polish envoy Neuville, who arrived in Moscow in 1689, shortly before the fall of Sofia and Golitsyn. Neuville saw the Prince and talked with him in Latin of contemporary political events, especially of the English revolution. He may have heard from Golitsyn something about the state of affairs in Moscow, and carefully collected information and local rumors about him.

Golitsyn was greatly concerned with the problem of the Russian army, the defects of which he knew very well, having more than once been in command of regiments. According to Neuville, he wanted the gentry to go abroad and study military techniques there, for he thought of recruiting good soldiers to replace the "given" peasant recruits, who were unfit for the job and whose lands remained untilled in wartime. Instead of doing useless military service, the peasants should pay a moderate poll tax. This meant that no more recruits would be taken from among the taxpaying population and bondsmen to fill up the ranks of the serviceman regiments. Contrary to Ordin-Nash-chokin's idea, the army would be a class organization, consisting of regular soldiers belonging to the gentry and commanded by properly trained officers of the same social class.

In Golitsyn's mind military and technical reforms were inseparable from social and economic changes. He proposed to begin the reorganization of the state by freeing the peasants and leaving to them the land they cultivated, for which they would pay a yearly tax. This would profit the Tsar—that is, the Treasury —and increase state revenue, according to Golitsyn's calculation, by more than half. Neuville evidently missed something that Golitsyn said, for he does not explain the conditions of the land transaction. Since the gentry would still have to bear the burden of compulsory and hereditary military service, Golitsyn's idea probably was to raise their salaries at the expense of the land tax payable by the peasants. The increase would compensate the landowners for the lands assigned to their former serfs and for the loss of income from the serf labor. In Golitsyn's plan the landowners would thus receive compensation not in a lump sum covering their losses, but as a regular income in the form of an increased salary for military service paid by the government.

Unrestricted and purely arbitrary exploitation of serf labor by
the landowners would be replaced by a definite land tax payable
by the peasants to the Treasury. Similar ideas for solving the
problem of serfdom reappeared in Russian statesmen's minds
more than a century and a half after Golitsyn's time.

Neuville heard a great deal about these plans, but he did not
write it all down, contenting himself with the following somewhat highly colored report: "If I wished to record all that I
have heard about this prince, I would never finish. It is sufficient
to say that he wanted to populate deserts, to enrich the destitute,
to transform savages into human beings, cowards into men of
courage, shepherds' huts into stone mansions."

Reading Neuville's notes in his *Account of Muscovy*, one may
well marvel at the bold schemes of reform conceived by "the
great Golitsyn," as the author styles him. Those schemes,
though reported by a foreigner as disconnected fragments, show
that they were based on a broad and apparently well-thought-
out plan of reorganizing not only the administrative and economic order of the state, but also the system of dividing the
community into separate classes; they even touched upon public
education. Of course, these were only dreams, subjects of
private conversations with intimate friends, and not legislative
projects. The circumstances of Golitsyn's personal life gave him
no chance even to begin carrying out his ideas in practice. Having bound up his fortunes with Tsarevna Sofia, he fell with her
and took no part in Peter's reformative activity. But he was
Peter's immediate predecessor in that field and could have been
a good helper to him, perhaps the best.

The spirit of his plans found some faint reflection in legislation: conditions of bondage for debt were mitigated; wives who
had murdered their husbands were no longer buried alive; the
death penalty for seditious speech was abolished. As for the
increasingly severe punitive measures against the Old Believers,
Tsarevna Sofia's government was not entirely responsible for it.
Ecclesiastical authorities dealt with the matter, and secular administration usually was merely the punitive instrument. By that
time church persecutions had bred among the Old Believers a

set of fanatics at whose word thousands of their misguided converts burned themselves to save their souls, while pastors of the church, with the same object in view, burned the preachers of self-immolation. Nor could the Tsarevna's government do anything for the serfs. She kept the unruly streltsy in order by threatening them with the gentry, until she had a chance of threatening the gentry with the streltsy and the Cossacks.

Nevertheless, it would be unjust to deny that Golitsyn's ideas played a part in the life of the state. Their influence found expression not in new laws, but in the whole character of Tsarevna Sofia's regency, which lasted seven years. Tsar Peter's brother-in-law and consequently Sofia's enemy, Prince B. I. Kurakin, left in his notes a remarkable comment on her regency: "Tsarevna Sofia Alexeevna began her rule with every care and justice to all, and the people were well content, so that never before had there been in the Russian state such wise government. During the seven years of her regency the whole country blossomed out into great wealth, commerce and all kinds of industries prospered, the learning of Latin and Greek was resumed. . . . And the people rejoiced in their welfare." Kurakin's testimony about the country's "blossoming out into great wealth" is apparently confirmed by Neuville's statement that during Golitsyn's ministry more than three thousand brick houses were built in Moscow, which had about half a million inhabitants living in wooden houses.

It would be rash to think that Sofia herself, by her mode of action, had called forth from an enemy such a commendation of her rule. This plain and stout semispinster, with a thick and short waist, a big clumsy head, and crude features, who looked forty at the age of twenty, had sacrificed her conscience to ambition and her modesty to the demands of her temperament. Having attained power through intrigues, crimes, and bloodshed, she needed to justify her usurpation, and, "as a princess of great intelligence and a great politician," in the words of that same Kurakin, she was ready to take the advice of her chief minister and "gallant," who also was "of great intelligence and was loved by everyone." He surrounded himself with assistants who were devoted to him, capable men of humble birth such as Nepliuev, Kasogov, Zmeev, and Ukraintsev, and with their help achieved the administrative successes noted by Kurakin.

Prince Golitsyn continued Ordin-Nashchokin's work, but as a man of another generation and different upbringing he went further in his plans of reform. He did not have Nashchokin's intellect or his administrative gifts and experience, but he was better educated. He worked less than Nashchokin but reflected more. Golitsyn's thought, less hampered by experience, was bolder; he saw more deeply into the existing order and touched upon the very foundations of it. His mind was at home in general questions about the state and its functions, the structure and the interrelations of social communities. It was not for nothing that his library contained a manuscript "About Civic Life and Rectifying All Matters That Concern the People as a Whole." He did not content himself, like Nashchokin, with administrative and economic reforms, but thought of enlightenment and tolerance and freedom of conscience, of free entry of foreigners into Russia, of improving the social system and raising the moral level of the community. His plans were bolder and broader than Nashchokin's, but less realistic. Representatives of two successive generations, the two men were prototypes of statesmen who came to the fore in Russia in the eighteenth century. All of them were of either the Nashchokin or the Golitsyn type. Nashchokin was the progenitor of the practical administrators of Peter the Great's time, and in Golitsyn we can detect traits of the liberal and rather impractical *grand seigneur* of Catherine's reign.

I have finished my survey of the period preparatory to Peter's reforms. Let me make a summary of what has been said.

We have seen with what fluctuations the preparatory work was carried on. Russian people of the seventeenth century took a step forward and then stopped to think of what they had done and whether they had gone too far. A spasmodic movement forward, then a halt, hesitation, and a timid look backward—that was how they approached culture in the seventeenth century. Thinking over every step they had taken, they covered less distance than they imagined. The idea of reform was forced upon them by the requirements of national defense and the financial needs of the state. To satisfy these needs it was necessary to make extensive changes in state administration, in economic life, and in the organization of labor. The men of the seventeenth century, however, confined themselves to timid attempts and halfhearted borrowings from the West. While borrowing and experimenting they argued and quarreled with one another, and the arguments made them think.

Their military and economic needs came into conflict with their cherished beliefs, deep-rooted habits, and inveterate prejudices. It appeared that they needed more than they could or would or were prepared to accept; that in order to safeguard their political and economic existence they had to change their ideas and feelings, to alter their whole conception of the world and of life. They thus found themselves in the awkward position of people outstripped by their own requirements. They needed technical knowledge, both military and industrial, and not only did they have none, but they had been conditioned to believe that it was unnecessary and even sinful because it did not lead to the salvation of the soul. What, then, had they achieved in this struggle both with their needs and with themselves, with their own prejudices?

To satisfy their material needs they made but few successful changes in state administration. They called several thousand foreign soldiers and craftsmen into Russia, and with their help they managed, after a fashion, to turn a considerable part of Russia's military forces into something like a regular army, though a poor one for lack of necessary equipment. They built several factories and ordnance works. Aided by these factories and the reorganized army, they recovered with great difficulty the Smolensk and Seversk regions and barely succeeded in holding the half of the Ukraine that had voluntarily surrendered to Muscovy. This was all that their material achievements amounted to, after seventy years of effort and sacrifice! They had not improved the state order, but, on the contrary, had made it more burdensome by giving up local self-government, increasing social disunity through segregation of the classes, and sacrificing the freedom of peasant labor. But in their struggle with themselves, with their habits and prejudices, they won several important victories that made this struggle easier for succeeding generations. This was unquestionably a great service rendered by the men of the seventeenth century to the cause of reform. They did not exactly prepare the reform itself, but they made their own minds and consciences ready for it. This is a less noticeable kind of work, but it is equally difficult and necessary. I shall try briefly to recount their gains in the moral and intellectual sphere.

In the first place, they admitted their ignorance of many things that they needed to know. This was the most difficult victory they won over themselves, over their pride and their past. The people of ancient Russia gave a great deal of thought to moral and religious questions, to what they regarded as the salvation of the soul, to disciplining conscience and will and subordinating intellect to faith. But they did not ponder on the conditions of earthly existence, which in their view was the legitimate domain of fate and sin, and therefore with helpless submissiveness they left it at the mercy of rude instinct. They doubted whether it was possible or worthwhile to bring anything good into this earthly world, which, according to the scriptures, lies in wickedness and is therefore doomed to it. They were convinced that the existing order of everyday life was as unchangeable and as little dependent upon human effort as the cosmic order.

It was this faith in the fatal immutability of man's earthly existence that began to waver under the impact of a twofold influence coming both from within and from without. The influence from within can be traced to the calamities experienced by the country in the seventeenth century. The Time of Troubles gave a painful shock to somnolent Russian minds, and made those who were capable of thought open their eyes to their surroundings and look at life directly and clearly. The writings of that period—Avraami Palitsyn's, Ivan Timofeev's, Prince Khvorostinin's—obviously show what may be called historical thought, a striving to account for the conditions of Russian life, to understand the basis of the existing social relations, so as to discover the causes of the disasters that had befallen the country. This striving persisted throughout the seventeenth century because the ever increasing state burdens bred continued discontent, which broke out in a series of rebellions. At the Zemsky Sobor and in special consultations with the government, the delegates, pointing out various wrongs, showed thoughtful understanding of the unsatisfactory state of things and suggested ways of improving it. It was evident that the people's thought was astir and trying to set the stagnant public life in motion, no longer seeing in it any inviolable, divinely appointed order.

At the same time, Western influence brought with it ideas concerned with the conditions and amenities of this earthly life, suggesting that its improvement was in itself an important task for the state and society. But for this purpose knowledge was needed, such as ancient Russia held in contempt and did not possess, especially knowledge of nature and of the ways in which it can serve the needs of man. Hence the growth of interest in Russian seventeenth-century society in works on cosmology and similar subjects. The government itself encouraged this interest. It was beginning to think of exploiting the latent wealth of the country and exploring for various minerals, and to this end, too, knowledge was required. The new tendency affected even such feeble characters as Tsar Feodor, who was rumored to be a great lover of learning, especially of mathematical sciences. According to Sylvester Medvedev's testimony, the Tsar cared not only about theological studies, but also about technical education. He assembled in his palace craftsmen of all sorts, paid them good wages, and took an intelligent interest in their work.

From the end of the seventeenth century onward the idea that scientific knowledge was essential became prevalent among the advanced section of the community. Complaints about its absence in Russia were constantly made in the descriptions of the country's condition. Do not imagine, however, that this conviction and these complaints led to the acquisition of the much-needed knowledge, or that since it became the question of the day, there immediately arose a practical demand for it. Far from it. Preparations for dealing with the question were extremely cautious and protracted. The whole of the eighteenth century and most of the nineteenth were taken up with pondering and discussing which kind of knowledge would be useful and which dangerous. But the awakened intellectual need soon changed the attitude toward the existing state of things. As soon as people's minds assimilated the idea that with the help of knowledge, life could be made better than it actually was, belief in the unchangeability of present conditions was undermined, and there arose a desire to improve them; but it arose while people had not yet discovered how the improvement could be achieved. They came to believe in knowledge before they had acquired it. They began examining every nook and cranny of the established order, and they found everywhere, as in a house long out of repair, neglect, disorder, decay. Aspects of life that had seemed invulnerable ceased to inspire confidence in their stability. Up till then, Russians had considered themselves strong in faith, which could understand the mind of Christ without grammar and rhetoric, and now an Eastern hierarch, Paissi Ligarid, was insisting on the necessity of school education for combating schism, and the Russian patriarch Joachim, agreeing with him, wrote in a work against the schismatics that many pious people had fallen into schism from lack of intelligence and education. Intelligence and education were thus recognized as supports of piety. In 1683 a certain Firsov, an interpreter in the Department of Foreign Affairs, translated the *Book of Psalms,* and even this humble official thought it necessary to amend the state of things in the church with the help of scholarship. "Our Russian people," he wrote, "are rude and unlearned. Not only simple laymen, but even the clergy do not seek true knowledge and understanding of Holy Writ, revile learned men, and call them heretics."

It seems to me that the chief moral success in the work of preparing the ground for Peter's reforms lay precisely in this awakening of simplehearted faith in knowledge and the trustful hope of putting everything right with its help. The Reformer

Tsar himself was guided in his activity by this faith and hope. And the same faith supported us, too, each time that, exhausted by the pursuit of western Europe's achievements, we plunged into fierce self-abasement, succumbing to the suspicion that we were not made for civilization.

But these moral acquisitions were gained by the men of the seventeenth century at the price of a new discord introduced into the community. Up to this time Russian society had lived under native influences, in conditions created by their natural surroundings. When the influence of a foreign culture, rich in knowledge and experience, made itself felt, it came into conflict with the home-grown ideas and customs, disturbing and confusing the Russians, complicating their lives, and causing them to develop at a rapid and uneven rate. Mental ferment produced by the influx of new ideas and interests resulted in a change that brought further difficulties with it. Up to that time Russian society had been remarkably homogeneous in its moral and religious character, forming one integral whole. In spite of all the differences in their social positions, the people of ancient Russia were spiritually very much alike and drew on the same sources to satisfy their spiritual needs. Boyars and bondsmen, the literate and the illiterate, did not stock in their memory the same number of sacred texts, prayers, holy chants, profane secular songs, fairy tales, and legends, did not understand things with the same clearness, did not learn their life catechism with the same accuracy, but the catechism was the same for all. With the same thoughtlessness they sinned at appointed seasons and with the same godly fear went to confession and Holy Communion and then relaxed again. Such uniform and automatic twists of conscience helped the people of ancient Russia to understand one another, to form a homogeneous moral whole, and established a certain spiritual concord between them in spite of social differences. Successive generations were periodic repetitions of the old established type. Just as the Tsar's palace and boyars' mansions disguised with their fanciful carving and gilt ornament the simple architectural plan of a peasant's wooden hut, so the elaborate eloquence of a sixteenth- or seventeenth-century scribe served as a cover for the humble spiritual content inherited from "an untutored villager of simple mind and feeble intelligence."

Western influence destroyed the spiritual wholeness of the ancient Russian society. It did not penetrate far among the masses, but it gradually became predominant in the upper classes, which were more exposed to external influences by their very position. Just as a pane of glass cracks when its different parts are unequally heated, so Russian society, unequally affected by the Western influence, broke apart. The church schism of the seventeenth century was an ecclesiastical reflection of the cleavage that took place in Russian society under the influence of Western culture. Two different conceptions of the world, two hostile orders of ideas and feelings came into sharp conflict with each other. Russian society was divided into two camps: those who revered the native past and the adherents of the new— that is, foreign—Western ways. The leading social classes, which remained within the pale of the Orthodox Church, began to grow indifferent to the native traditions championed by the schismatics, and all the more easily succumbed to foreign influence. Old Believers, thrust beyond the pale, hated imported innovations all the more, regarding them as the cause of decay in ancient Russian piety. Indifference on the one side and hatred on the other became the new components of Russian society, hindering social progress and pulling men apart.

The success of the reform movement was largely due to individual people who took active part in it. They were the last and best representatives of ancient Russia, and gave a coloring of their own to the tendencies they introduced or supported. Tsar Alexei Mikhailovich awakened a vague general taste for novelty and improvement without breaking with the native past. Good-naturedly blessing incipient reforms, he gradually accustomed timid Russian minds to them. His kindly disposition inspired belief that there was no moral harm in foreign novelties, and that we must not lose faith in our own powers.

His minister, Ordin-Nashchokin, was not so good-natured or so piously devoted to native traditions as the Tsar, and his constant grumbling against everything Russian might well have reduced one to hopeless dejection and inertia. But his honest energy was irresistible, and his bright intellect converted vague strivings toward reform into such simple, clear, and convincing plans that their usefulness seemed obvious, and one wanted to believe that they were both reasonable and practical. For the first time in Russian history a coherent system of reforms was being developed from his suggestions, suppositions, and experiments. It was not a wide program, but it was a well-delineated plan for administrative and economic innovations. Other, less prominent public men completed this program, introducing new elements into it or extending its application to other spheres of social and political life, and thus furthering the cause of reform.

Rtishchev endeavored to introduce a moral element into state administration and raised the question of organizing public charity. Prince Golitsyn, by his imaginative conversations about the necessity of many reforms, roused the somnolent thought of the ruling class, which had been completely satisfied with the established order.

With this I conclude my survey of the seventeenth century. The whole of it was an epoch preparatory to the reforms of Peter the Great. We have been studying the activity of several men brought up under the new influences. Those men were the most prominent figures in the reform movement, and behind them stood many others less notable: the boyars B. I. Morozov, N. I. Romanov, A. S. Matveev, a whole series of scholars from Kiev, and, apart from them, the stranger and exile Iuri Krizhanich. Each of these men furthered some new tendency, developed some new thought and sometimes a whole series of thoughts.

One may well marvel at the wealth of progressive ideas that had accumulated in the active minds of that turbulent age. Those ideas were worked out hastily, disconnectedly, without a general plan, but putting them together we can see that they naturally form a fairly harmonious program of reform, in which questions of foreign policy are intertwined with military, financial, economic, social, and educational problems.

Here are the most important points of the program: (1)

peace and even alliance with Poland; (2) struggle against Sweden for the eastern shores of the Baltic and against Turkey and the Crimea for south Russia; (3) final reorganization of the military forces as a regular army; (4) replacement of the old complicated system of direct taxation by two taxes—poll tax and land tax; (5) development of the export trade and of home industries; (6) introduction of municipal self-government with the object of improving the productivity and welfare of the commercial and industrial class; (7) emancipation of the serfs with their land; (8) establishing schools for general and religious education, and technical schools adapted to the requirements of the state.

All this was to be done in conformity with foreign patterns and even with the help of foreign instructors. It will be easily seen that these suggestions taken together are identical with Peter's program of reform, and they were ready before he began his work. It is this that constitutes the significance of the seventeenth-century statesmen's activity. They not only created the spiritual environment in which Peter grew up, but also drew up for him a plan of action—a plan that in some respects went further than the reforms he introduced.

Index